VIZ GRAPHIC NOVEL
MAISON IKKOKU™
INTENSIVE CARE

CONTENTS

PART 1 BODY OF LOVE 4

PART 2 MESSAGE IN THE SNOW 32

PART 3 MENDING A BREAK 55

PART 4 JUST DO YOUR BEST! 75

PART 5 IN HOT WATER 99

PART 6 GOING SHOPPING IN A SUIT 121

PART 7 THE FACE IN THE DARKNESS 145

PART 8 A GRAVE MATTER 165

This volume contains MAISON IKKOKU PART FIVE #5 (second half) through #9 in their entirety.

**STORY AND ART BY
RUMIKO TAKAHASHI**

**ENGLISH ADAPTATION BY
GERARD JONES**

Translation/Mari Morimoto
Touch-Up Art & Lettering/Wayne Truman
Cover Design/Viz Graphics
Editor/Trish Ledoux
Assistant Editors/Annette Roman & Toshifumi Yoshida

Editor-in-Chief/Satoru Fujii
Publisher/Seiji Horibuchi

Printed in Canada

Published by Viz Communications, Inc.
P.O. Box 77010 • San Francisco, CA 94107

10 9 8 7 6 5 4 3 2 1
First printing, May 1997

Vizit our World Wide Web site at http://www.viz.com and
our new Internet magazine, j-pop.com, at http://www.j-pop.com!

From the company that's had its finger on the pulse of Japanese popular culture and art for eleven years comes j-pop.com, Viz Communication's Internet magazine, featuring the latest and greatest news about Japanese anime, manga, video games, music, and pop culture! Get the truth about the most exciting trends before they're trendy, and the scoop on the most explosive pop culture before it's popped!

VIZ GRAPHIC NOVEL

MAISON IKKOKU™ VOLUME SEVEN

INTENSIVE CARE

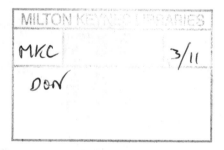
STORY AND ART BY
RUMIKO TAKAHASHI

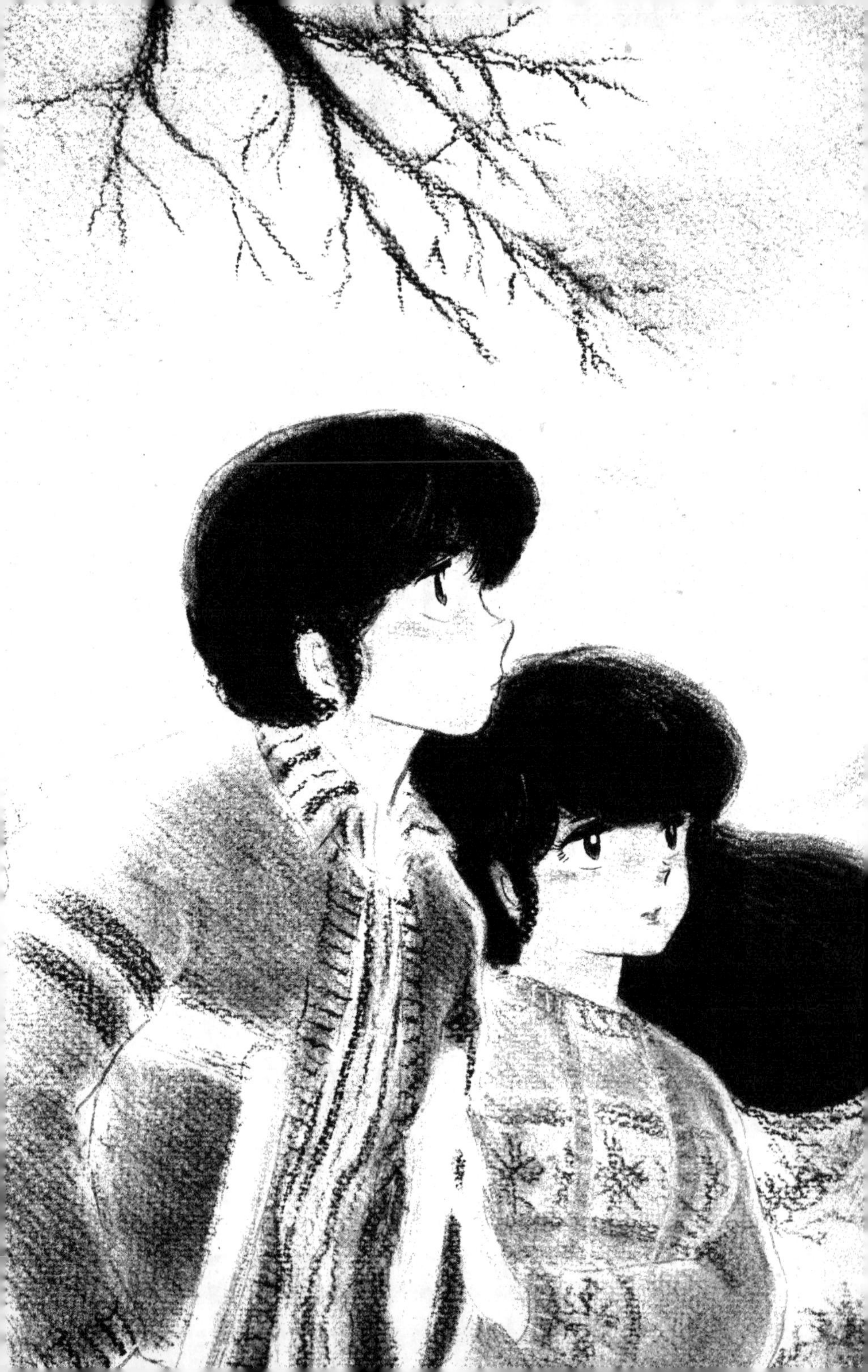

PART 1

BODY OF LOVE

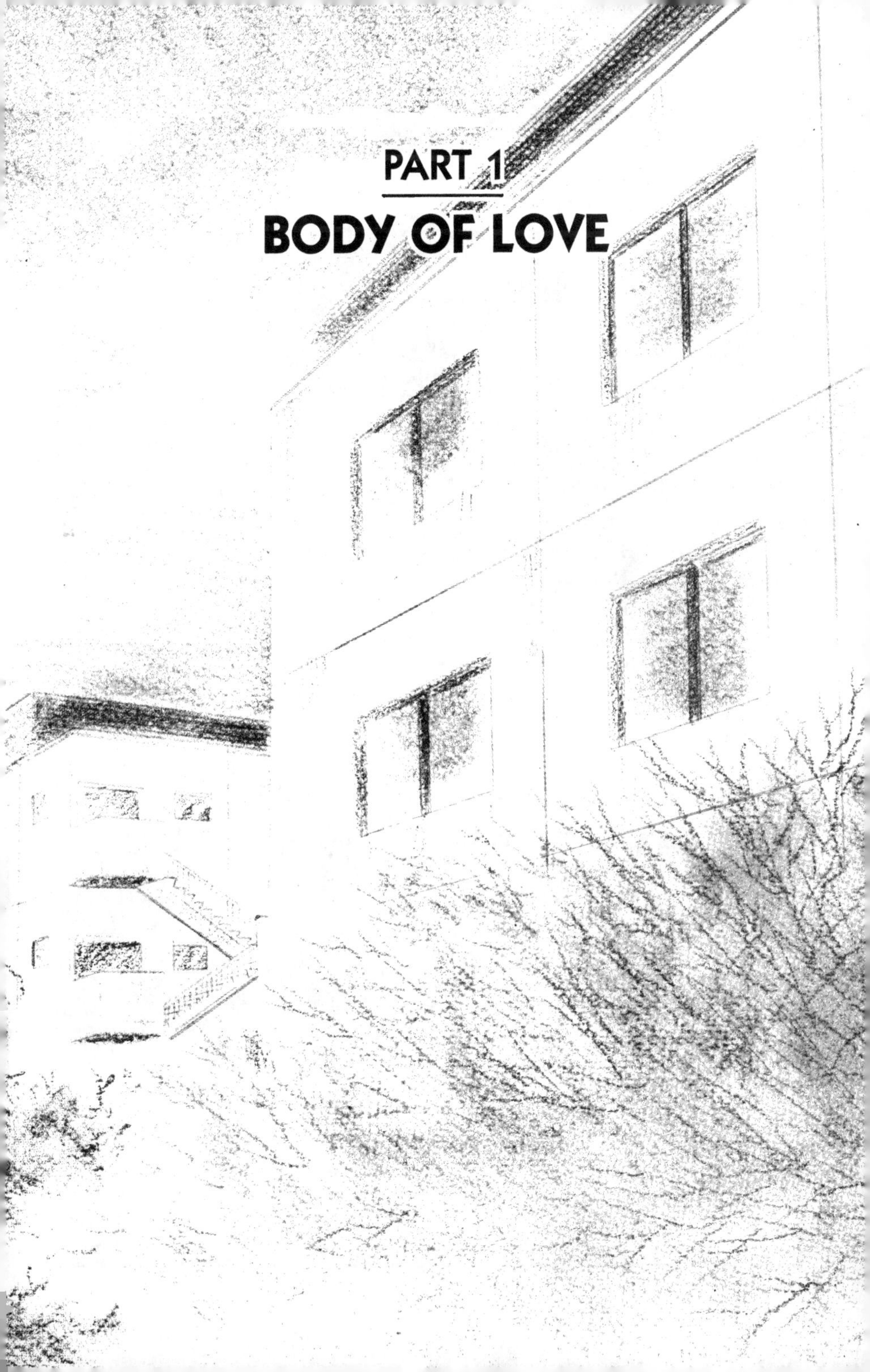

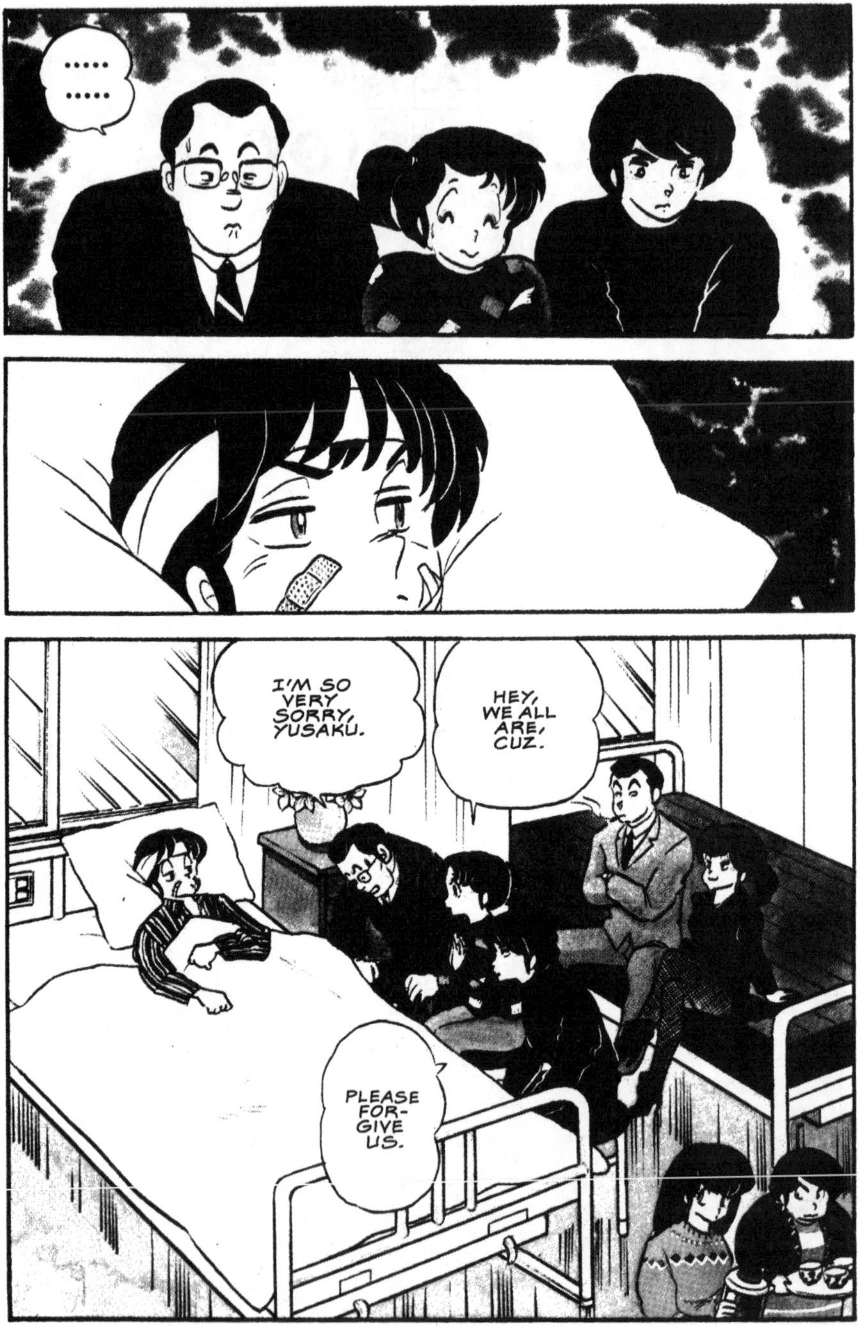

……
……
I'M SO VERY SORRY, YUSAKU.
HEY, WE ALL ARE, CUZ.
PLEASE FOR-GIVE US.

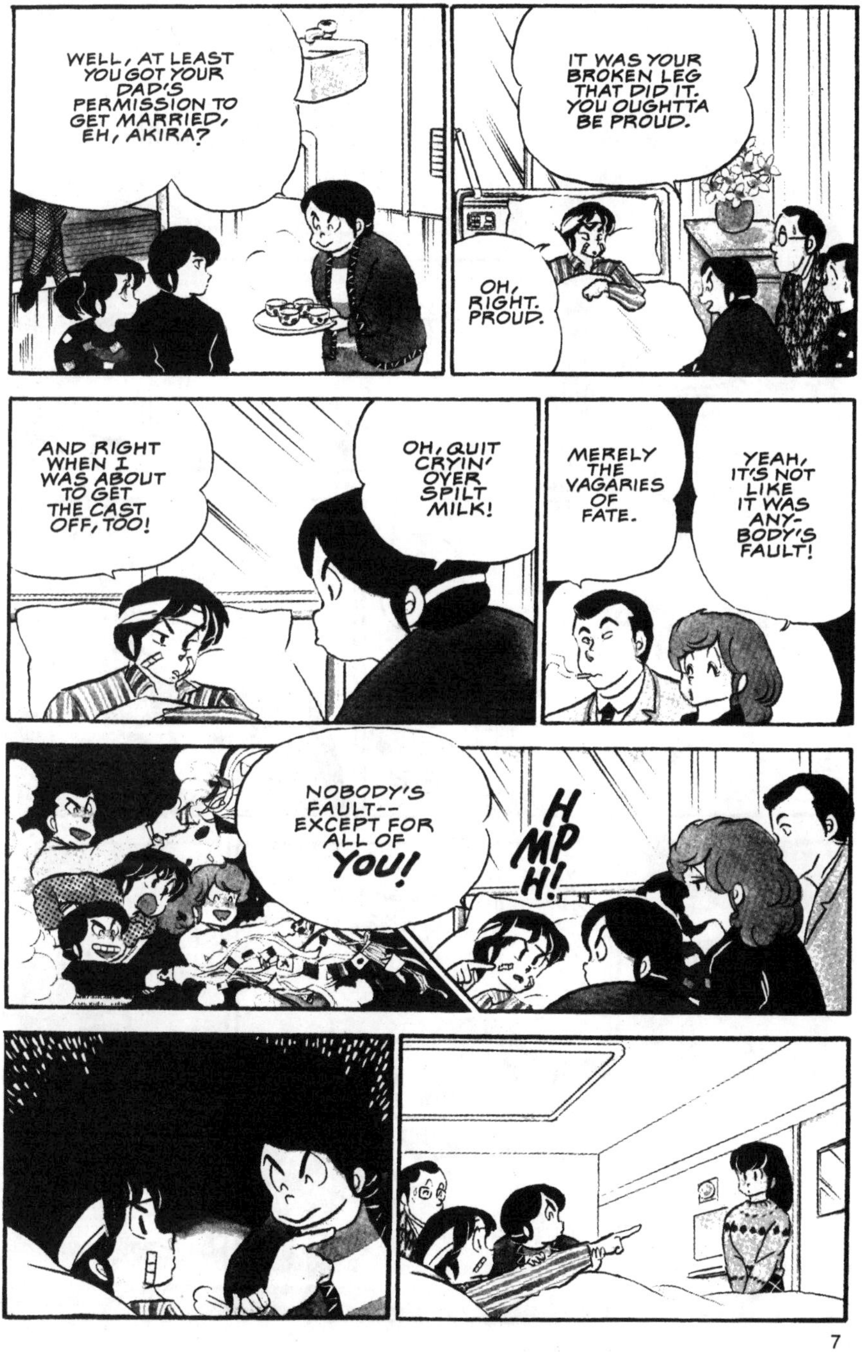
WELL, AT LEAST YOU GOT YOUR DAD'S PERMISSION TO GET MARRIED, EH, AKIRA?
IT WAS YOUR BROKEN LEG THAT DID IT. YOU OUGHTTA BE PROUD.
OH, RIGHT. PROUD.
AND RIGHT WHEN I WAS ABOUT TO GET THE CAST OFF, TOO!
OH, QUIT CRYIN' OVER SPILT MILK!
MERELY THE VAGARIES OF FATE.
YEAH, IT'S NOT LIKE IT WAS ANY-BODY'S FAULT!
NOBODY'S FAULT-- EXCEPT FOR ALL OF YOU!
HMPH!

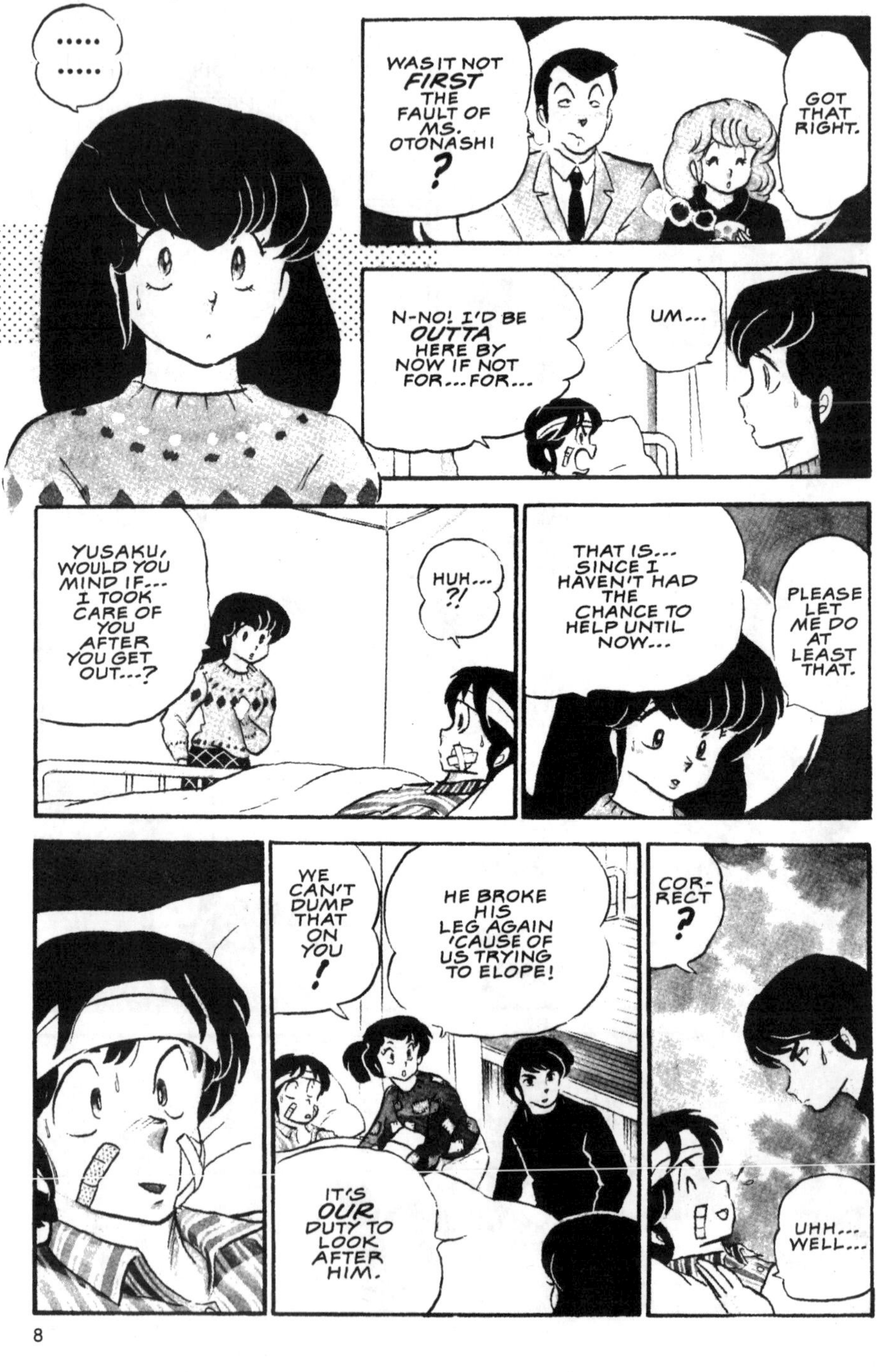
......
......
WAS IT NOT FIRST THE FAULT OF MS. OTONASHI ?
GOT THAT RIGHT.
N-NO! I'D BE OUTTA HERE BY NOW IF NOT FOR...FOR...
UM...
YUSAKU, WOULD YOU MIND IF... I TOOK CARE OF YOU AFTER YOU GET OUT...?
HUH... ?!
THAT IS... SINCE I HAVEN'T HAD THE CHANCE TO HELP UNTIL NOW...
PLEASE LET ME DO AT LEAST THAT.
WE CAN'T DUMP THAT ON YOU !
HE BROKE HIS LEG AGAIN 'CAUSE OF US TRYING TO ELOPE!
IT'S OUR DUTY TO LOOK AFTER HIM.
COR-RECT ?
UHH... WELL...

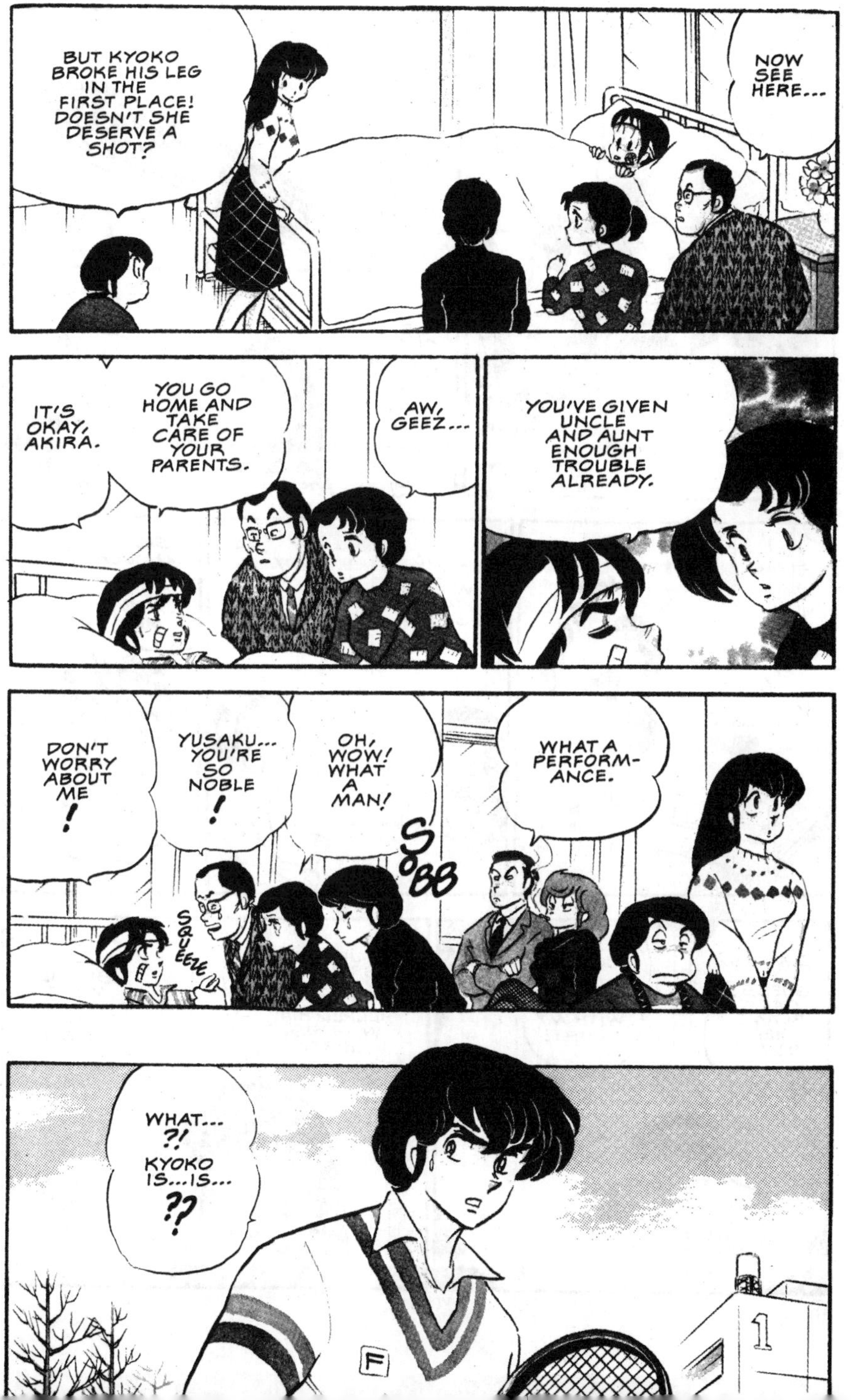
BUT KYOKO BROKE HIS LEG IN THE FIRST PLACE! DOESN'T SHE DESERVE A SHOT?
NOW SEE HERE...
IT'S OKAY, AKIRA.
YOU GO HOME AND TAKE CARE OF YOUR PARENTS.
AW, GEEZ...
YOU'VE GIVEN UNCLE AND AUNT ENOUGH TROUBLE ALREADY.
DON'T WORRY ABOUT ME!
YUSAKU... YOU'RE SO NOBLE!
SQUEEEZE
OH, WOW! WHAT A MAN!
SOBB
WHAT A PERFORM-ANCE.
WHAT...?!
KYOKO IS...IS...??
F
1

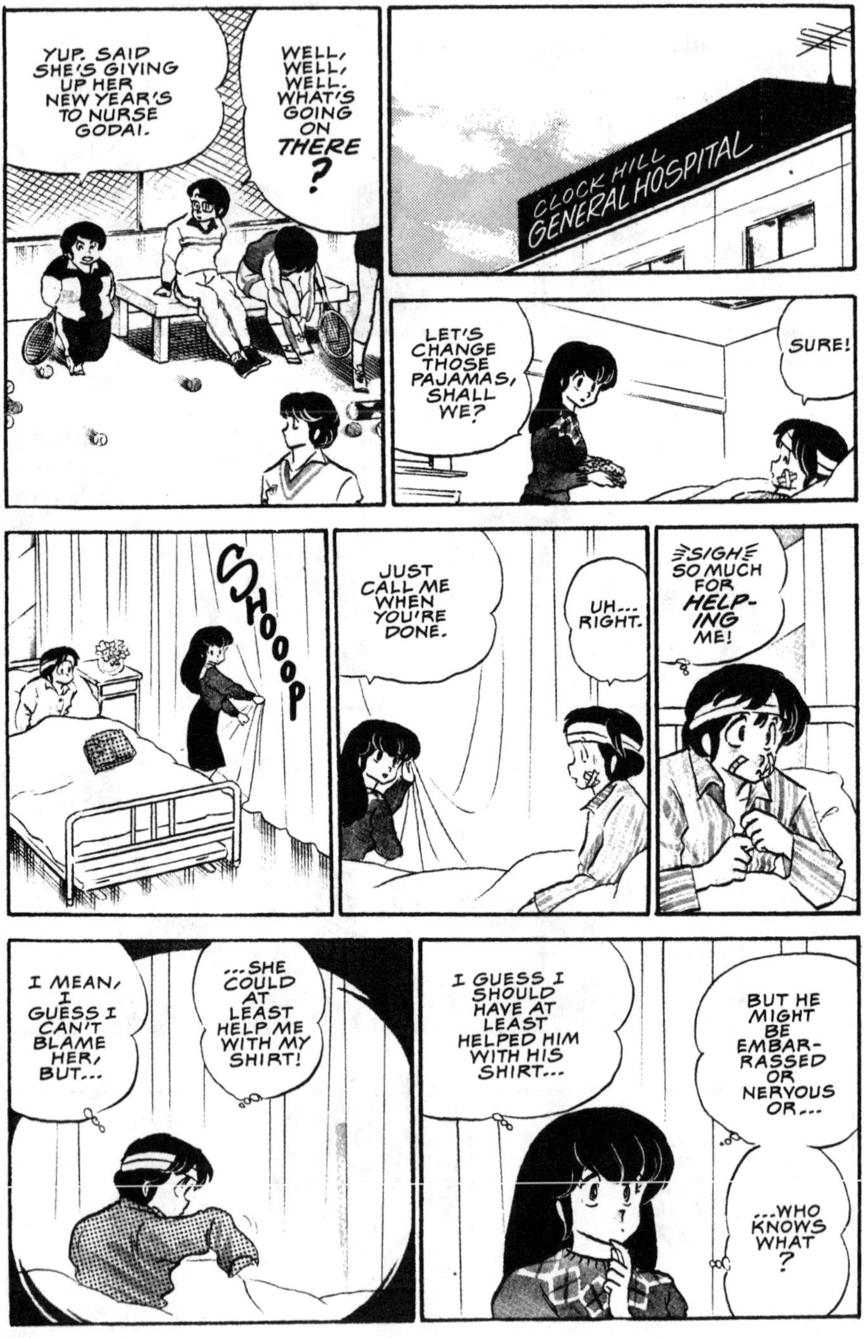
YUP. SAID SHE'S GIVING UP HER NEW YEAR'S TO NURSE GODAI.
WELL, WELL, WELL. WHAT'S GOING ON THERE?
CLOCK HILL GENERAL HOSPITAL
LET'S CHANGE THOSE PAJAMAS, SHALL WE?
SURE!
SHOOOOP
JUST CALL ME WHEN YOU'RE DONE.
UH... RIGHT.
SIGH SO MUCH FOR HELPING ME!
I MEAN, I GUESS I CAN'T BLAME HER, BUT...
...SHE COULD AT LEAST HELP ME WITH MY SHIRT!
I GUESS I SHOULD HAVE AT LEAST HELPED HIM WITH HIS SHIRT...
BUT HE MIGHT BE EMBARRASSED OR NERVOUS OR...
...WHO KNOWS WHAT?

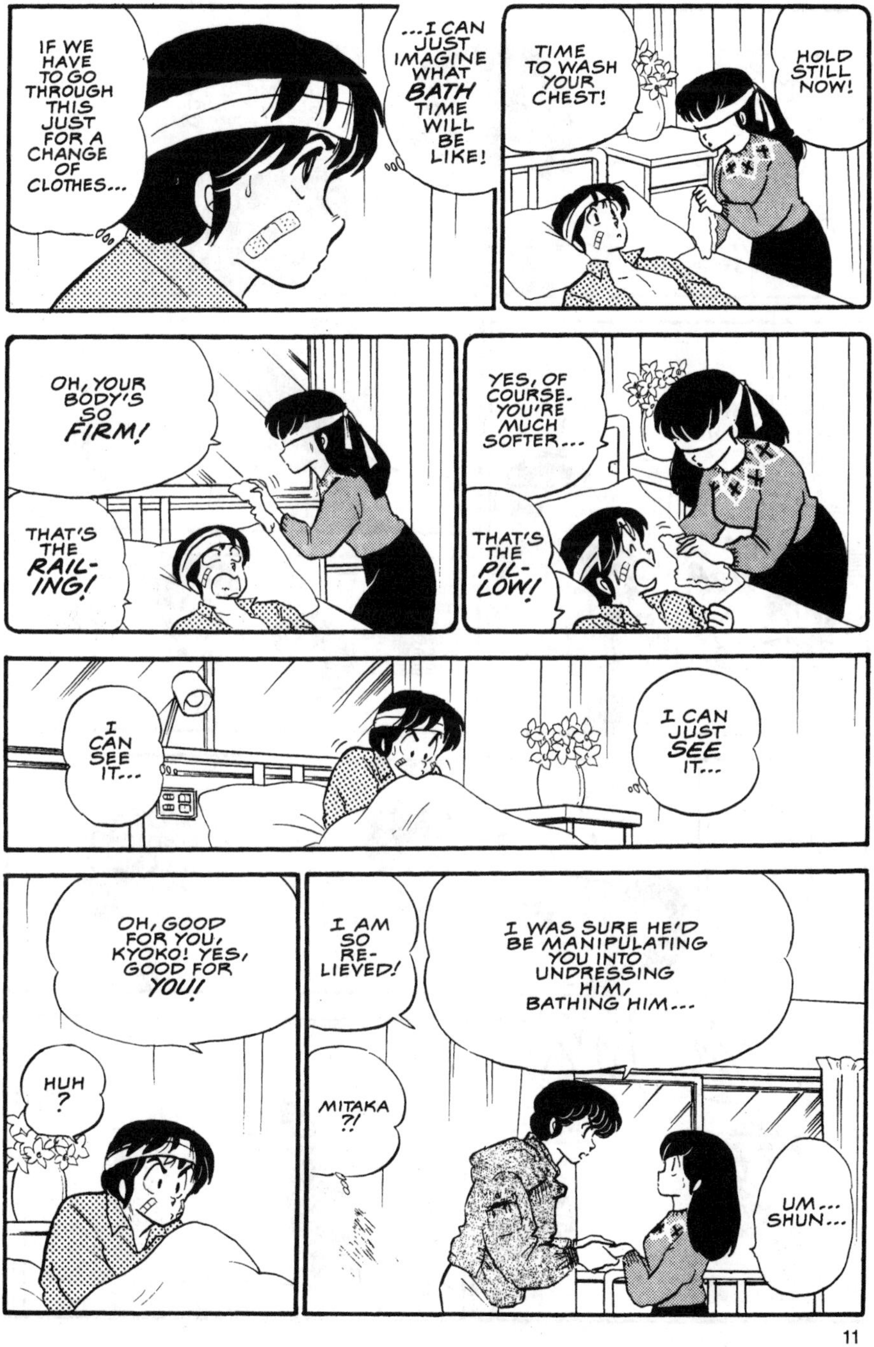
IF WE HAVE TO GO THROUGH THIS JUST FOR A CHANGE OF CLOTHES...
...I CAN JUST IMAGINE WHAT BATH TIME WILL BE LIKE!
TIME TO WASH YOUR CHEST!
HOLD STILL NOW!
OH, YOUR BODY'S SO FIRM!
THAT'S THE RAILING!
YES, OF COURSE. YOU'RE MUCH SOFTER...
THAT'S THE PILLOW!
I CAN SEE IT...
I CAN JUST SEE IT...
OH, GOOD FOR YOU, KYOKO! YES, GOOD FOR YOU!
HUH?
I AM SO RELIEVED!
I WAS SURE HE'D BE MANIPULATING YOU INTO UNDRESSING HIM, BATHING HIM...
MITAKA?!
UM... SHUN...

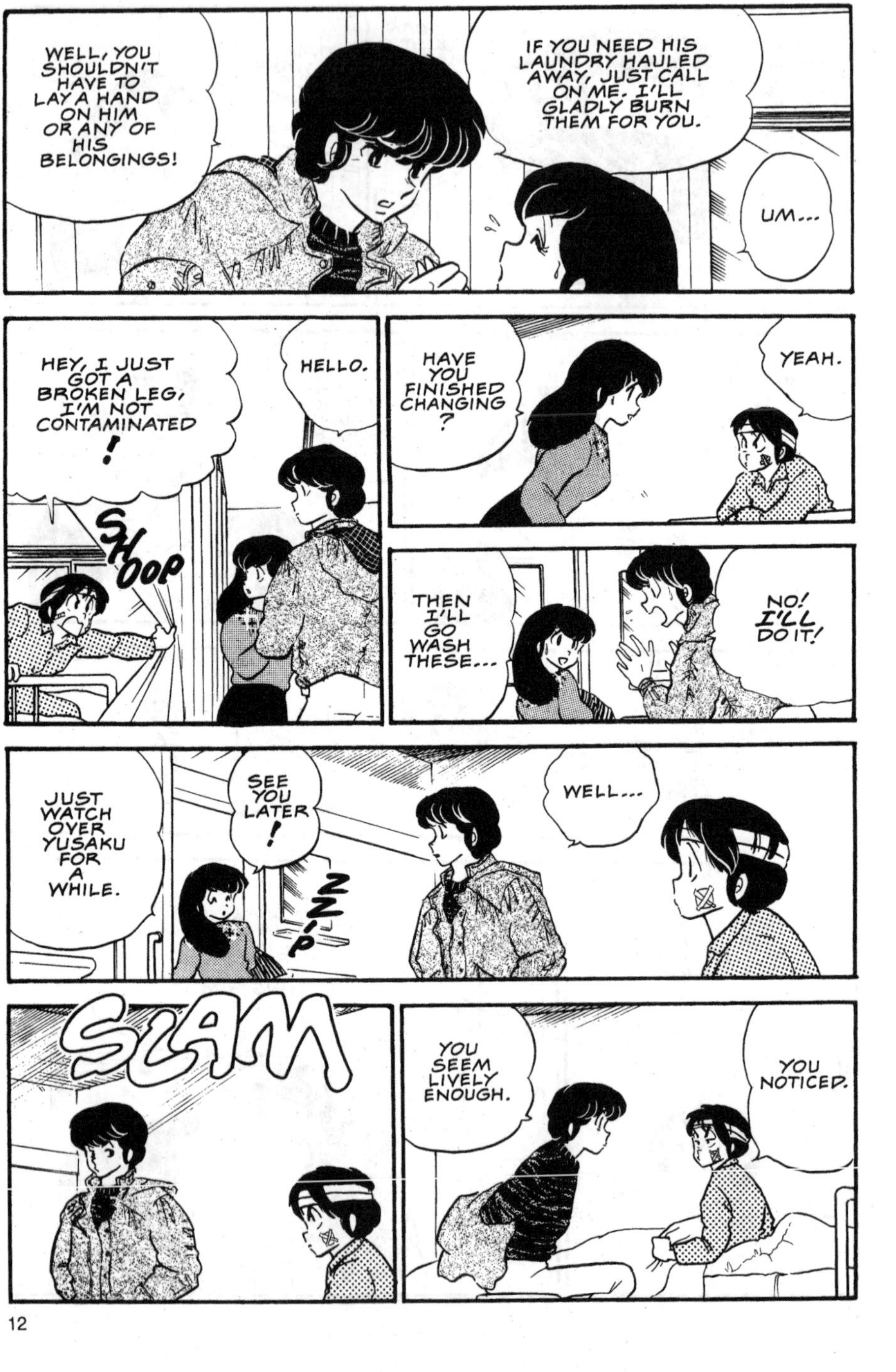
WELL, YOU SHOULDN'T HAVE TO LAY A HAND ON HIM OR ANY OF HIS BELONGINGS!
IF YOU NEED HIS LAUNDRY HAULED AWAY, JUST CALL ON ME. I'LL GLADLY BURN THEM FOR YOU.
UM...
HEY, I JUST GOT A BROKEN LEG, I'M NOT CONTAMINATED!
HELLO.
SHOOP
HAVE YOU FINISHED CHANGING?
YEAH.
THEN I'LL GO WASH THESE...
NO! I'LL DO IT!
JUST WATCH OVER YUSAKU FOR A WHILE.
SEE YOU LATER!
ZZIP
WELL...
SLAM
YOU SEEM LIVELY ENOUGH.
YOU NOTICED.

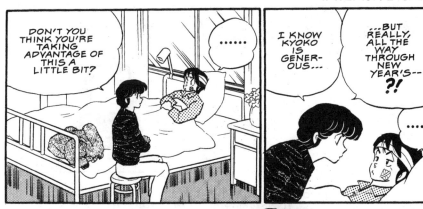

DON'T YOU THINK YOU'RE TAKING ADVANTAGE OF THIS A LITTLE BIT?

......

I KNOW KYOKO IS GENEROUS...

...BUT REALLY, ALL THE WAY THROUGH NEW YEAR'S--?!

.....

WELL, THERE WERE SOME UNUSUAL CIRCUM-STANCES, YOU KNOW.

OH?

SUCH AS WHAT?

DID YOU BREAK YOUR LEG TRYING TO RESCUE HER OR SOMETHING?

SOME-THING LIKE THAT.

NOW I SEE IT.

DEAR KYOKO, SUCH A SENSE OF DUTY!

ALL THIS JUST BECAUSE SHE FEELS RESPONSI-BLE FOR...

NOT JUST.

I'D SAY THAT'S ONLY A PART OF IT.

YOU CAN'T BE SERIOUS.

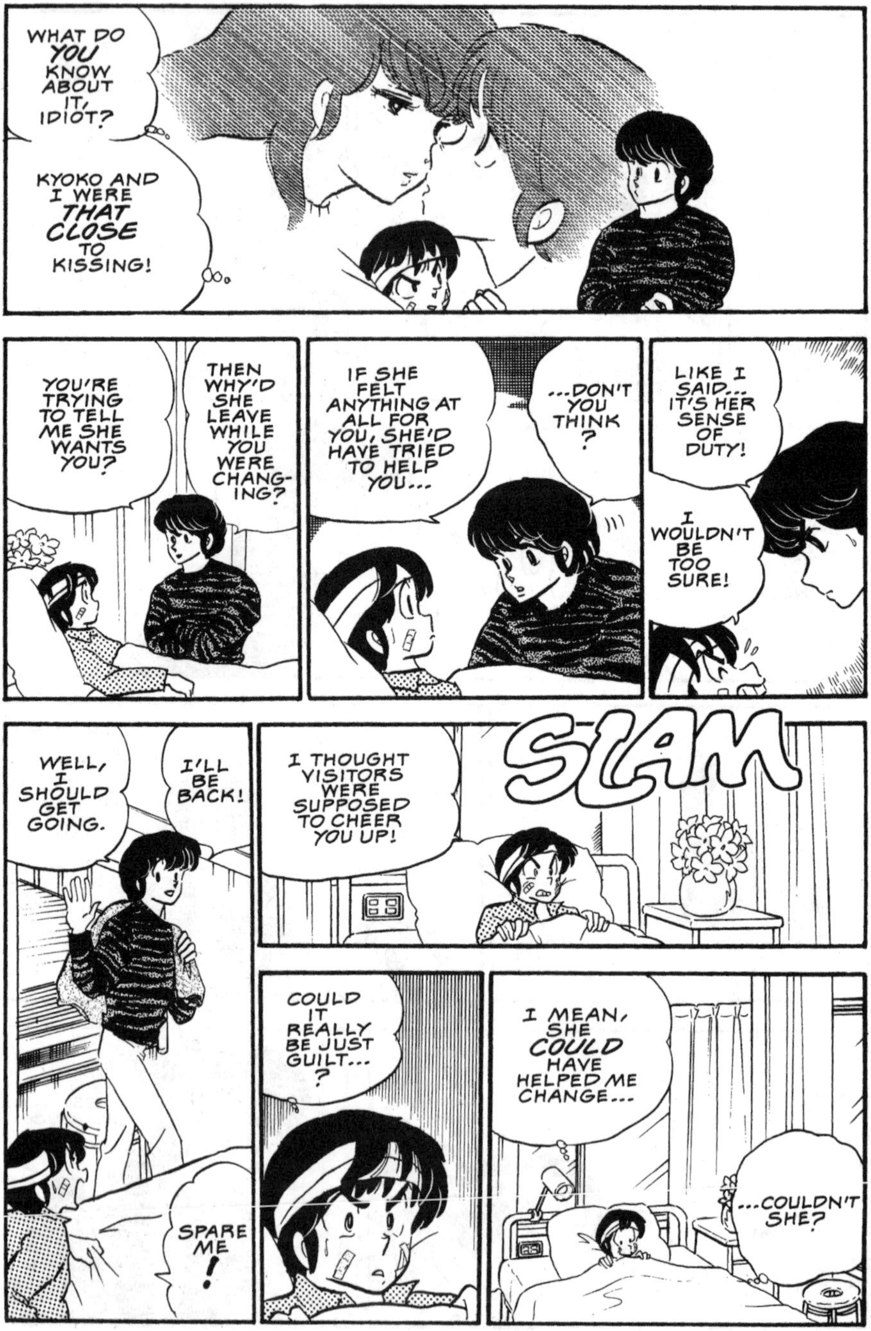
WHAT DO YOU KNOW ABOUT IT, IDIOT?
KYOKO AND I WERE THAT CLOSE TO KISSING!
YOU'RE TRYING TO TELL ME SHE WANTS YOU?
THEN WHY'D SHE LEAVE WHILE YOU WERE CHANGING?
IF SHE FELT ANYTHING AT ALL FOR YOU, SHE'D HAVE TRIED TO HELP YOU...
...DON'T YOU THINK?
LIKE I SAID... IT'S HER SENSE OF DUTY!
I WOULDN'T BE TOO SURE!
WELL, I SHOULD GET GOING.
I'LL BE BACK!
SPARE ME!
I THOUGHT VISITORS WERE SUPPOSED TO CHEER YOU UP!
SLAM
COULD IT REALLY BE JUST GUILT...?
I MEAN, SHE COULD HAVE HELPED ME CHANGE...
...COULDN'T SHE?

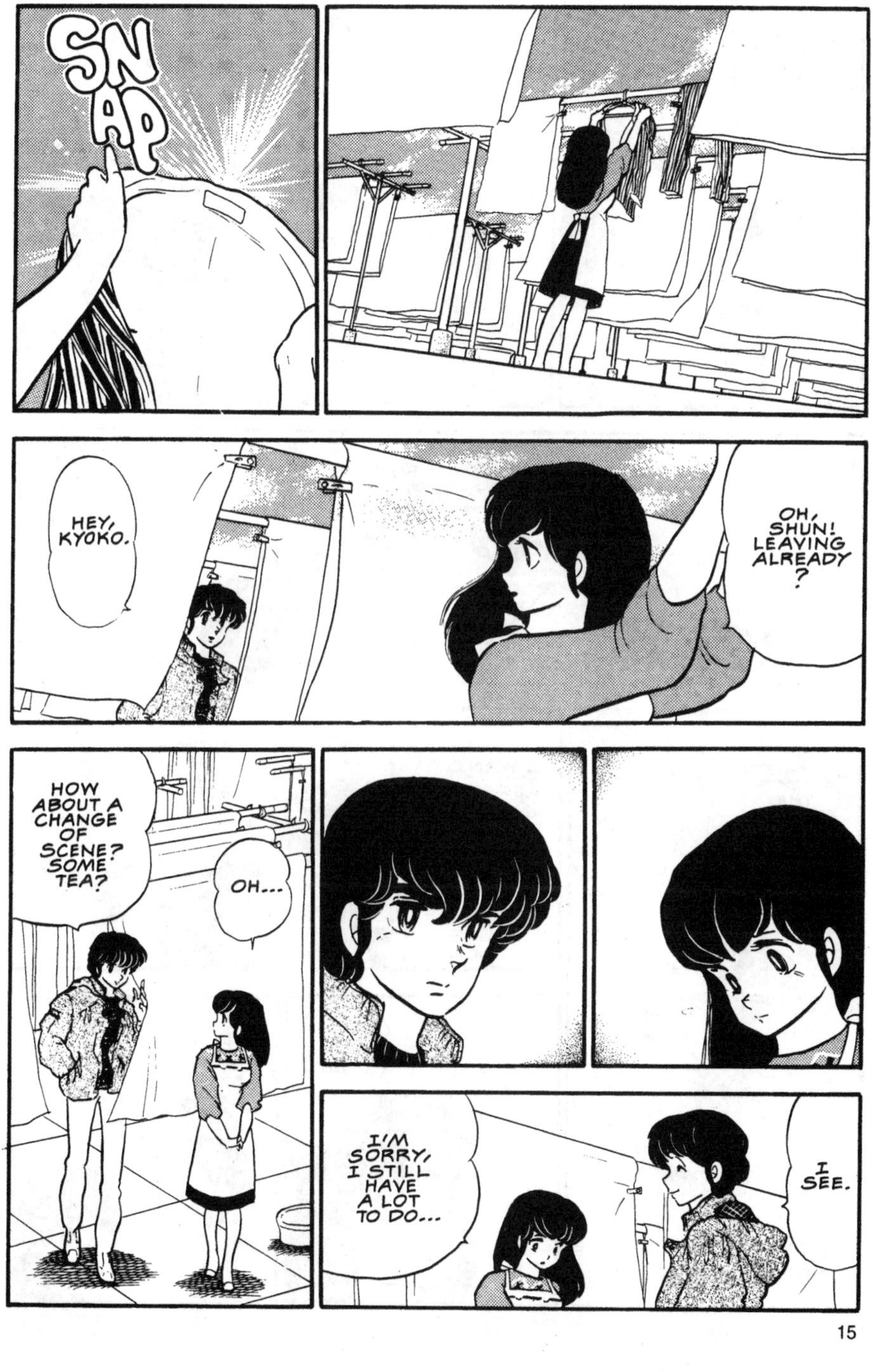
SNAP
HEY, KYOKO.
OH, SHUN! LEAVING ALREADY?
HOW ABOUT A CHANGE OF SCENE? SOME TEA?
OH...
I'M SORRY, I STILL HAVE A LOT TO DO...
I SEE.

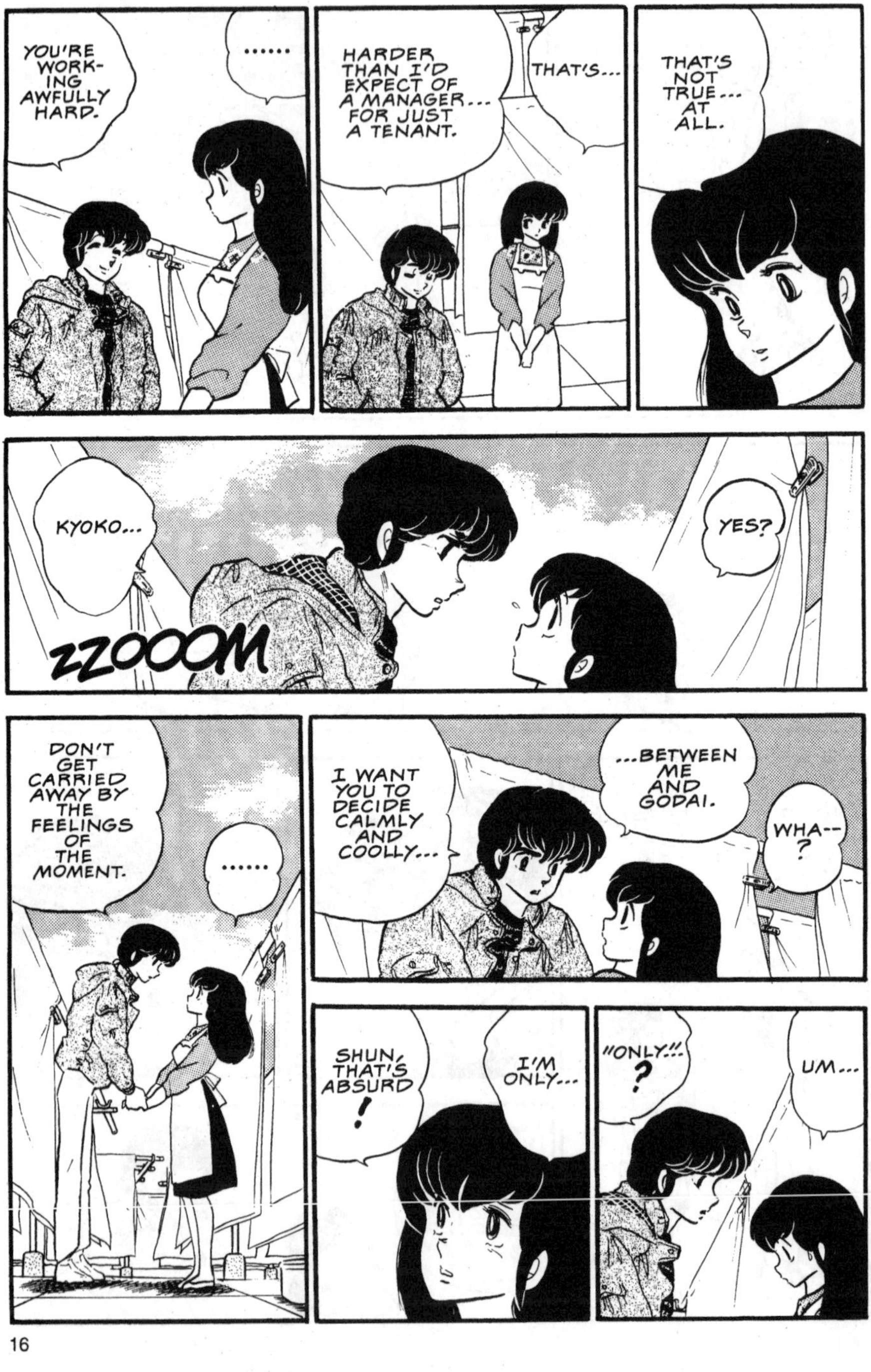
YOU'RE WORKING AWFULLY HARD.
......
HARDER THAN I'D EXPECT OF A MANAGER... FOR JUST A TENANT.
THAT'S...
THAT'S NOT TRUE... AT ALL.
KYOKO...
YES?
ZZOOOM
DON'T GET CARRIED AWAY BY THE FEELINGS OF THE MOMENT.
......
I WANT YOU TO DECIDE CALMLY AND COOLLY...
...BETWEEN ME AND GODAI.
WHA--?
SHUN, THAT'S ABSURD!
I'M ONLY...
"ONLY!!"?
UM...

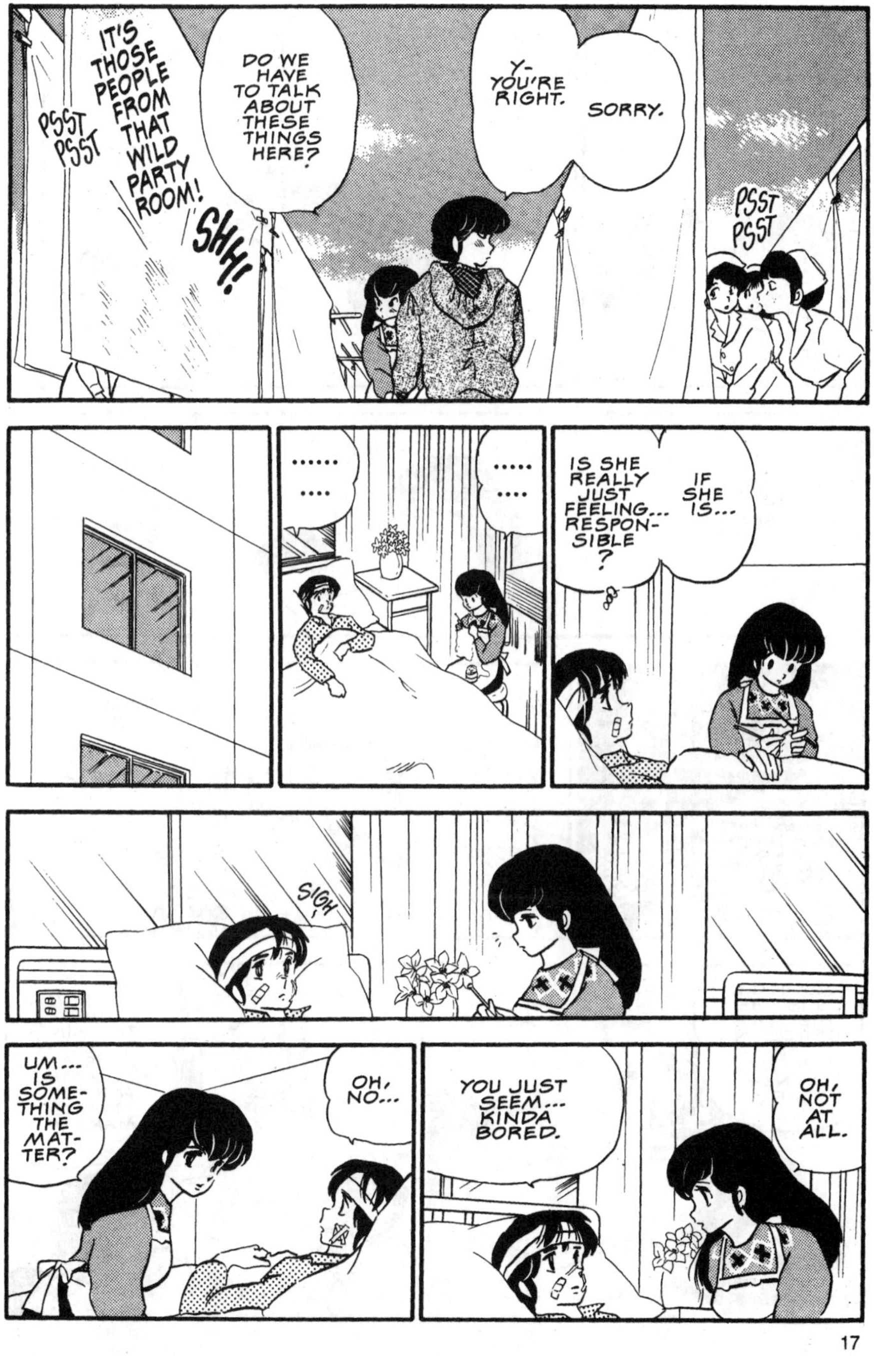
PSST PSST
IT'S THOSE PEOPLE FROM THAT WILD PARTY ROOM!
SHH!
DO WE HAVE TO TALK ABOUT THESE THINGS HERE?
Y-YOU'RE RIGHT.
SORRY.
PSST PSST
......
....
.....
....
IS SHE REALLY JUST FEELING... RESPONSIBLE?
IF SHE IS...
SIGH
UM... IS SOMETHING THE MATTER?
OH, NO...
YOU JUST SEEM... KINDA BORED.
OH, NOT AT ALL.

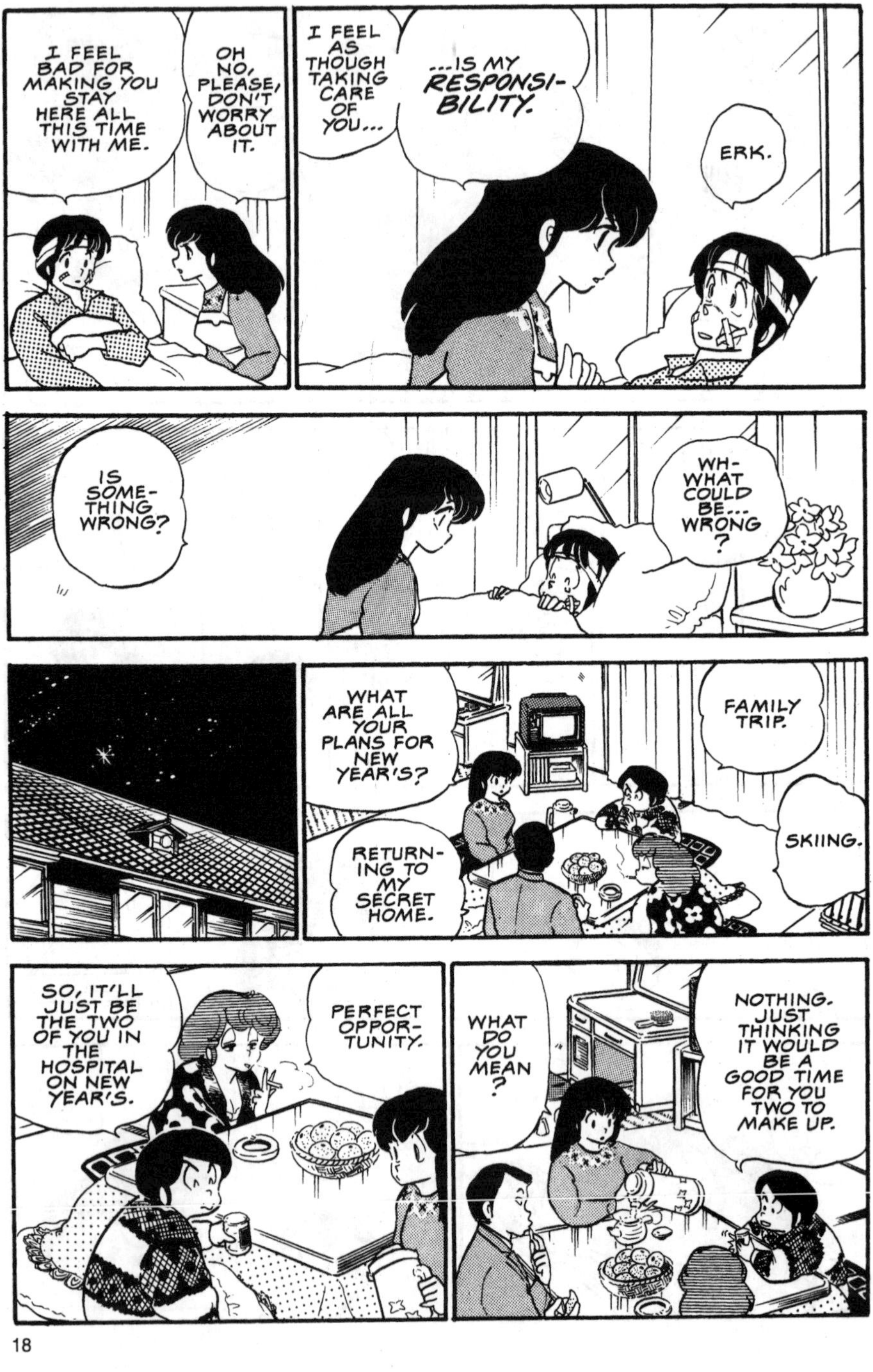
I FEEL BAD FOR MAKING YOU STAY HERE ALL THIS TIME WITH ME.
OH NO, PLEASE, DON'T WORRY ABOUT IT.
I FEEL AS THOUGH TAKING CARE OF YOU...
...IS MY RESPONSIBILITY.
ERK.
IS SOMETHING WRONG?
WH- WHAT COULD BE... WRONG?
WHAT ARE ALL YOUR PLANS FOR NEW YEAR'S?
FAMILY TRIP.
SKIING.
RETURNING TO MY SECRET HOME.
SO, IT'LL JUST BE THE TWO OF YOU IN THE HOSPITAL ON NEW YEAR'S.
PERFECT OPPORTUNITY.
WHAT DO YOU MEAN?
NOTHING. JUST THINKING IT WOULD BE A GOOD TIME FOR YOU TWO TO MAKE UP.

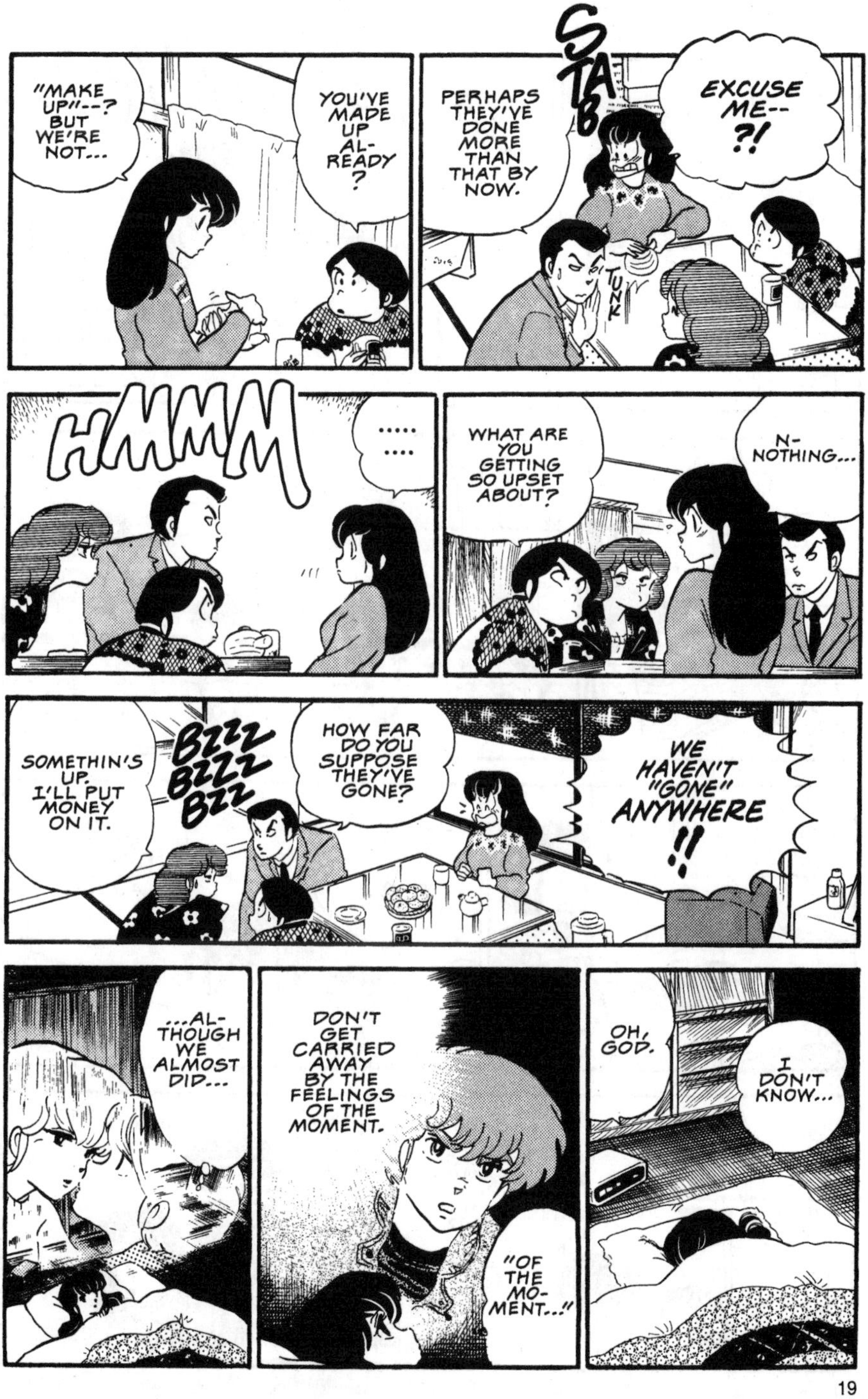
"MAKE UP"--? BUT WE'RE NOT...
YOU'VE MADE UP AL-READY?
STAB
PERHAPS THEY'VE DONE MORE THAN THAT BY NOW.
EXCUSE ME--?!
TUNK
HMMM
....
WHAT ARE YOU GETTING SO UPSET ABOUT?
N-NOTHING...
SOMETHIN'S UP. I'LL PUT MONEY ON IT.
BZZZ BZZZ BZZ
HOW FAR DO YOU SUPPOSE THEY'VE GONE?
WE HAVEN'T "GONE" ANYWHERE!!
...AL-THOUGH WE ALMOST DID...
DON'T GET CARRIED AWAY BY THE FEELINGS OF THE MOMENT.
"OF THE MO-MENT..."
OH, GOD.
I DON'T KNOW...

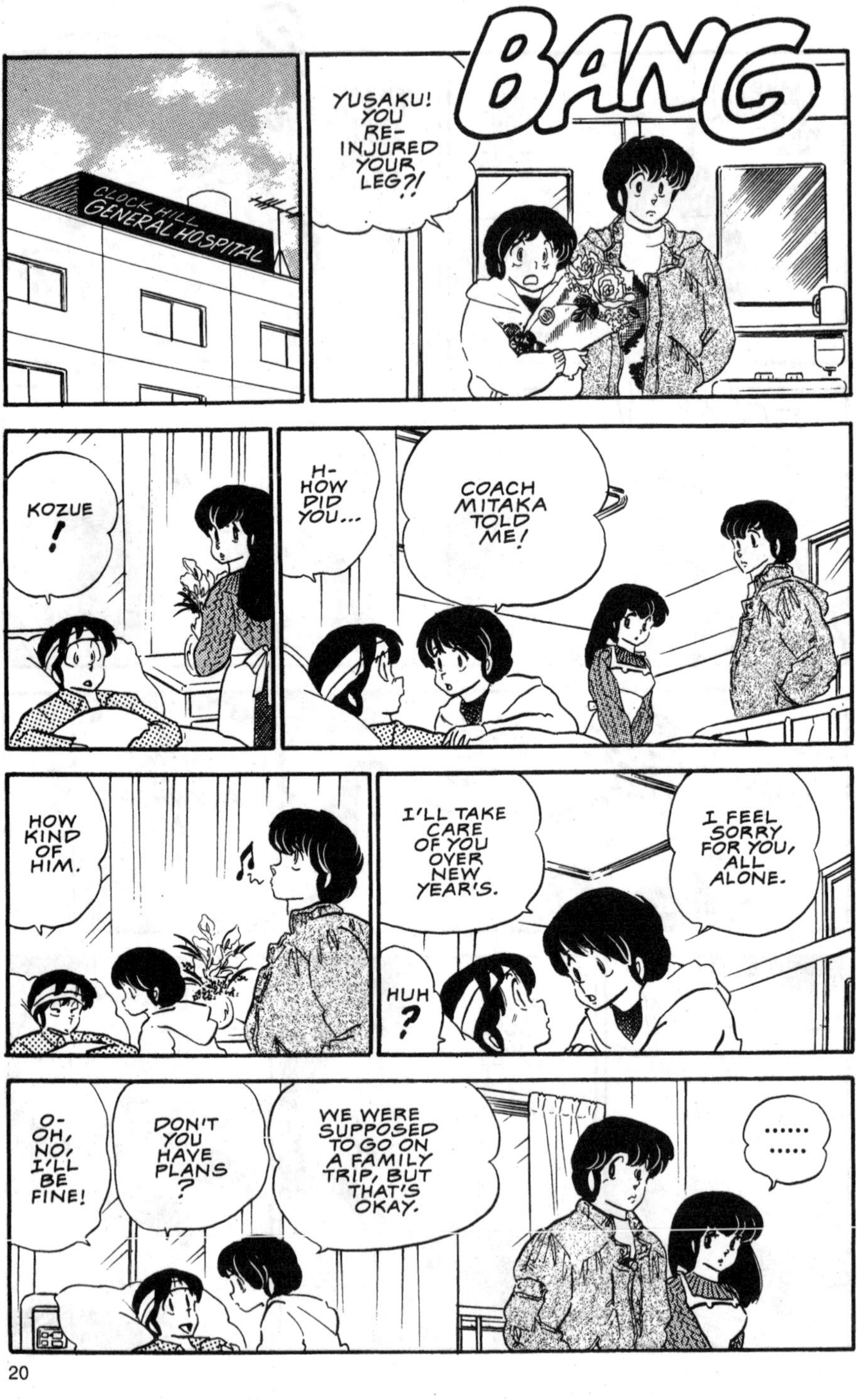
CLOCK HILL GENERAL HOSPITAL
BANG
YUSAKU! YOU RE-INJURED YOUR LEG?!
KOZUE!
H-HOW DID YOU...
COACH MITAKA TOLD ME!
HOW KIND OF HIM.
I'LL TAKE CARE OF YOU OVER NEW YEAR'S.
I FEEL SORRY FOR YOU, ALL ALONE.
HUH?
O-OH, NO, I'LL BE FINE!
DON'T YOU HAVE PLANS?
WE WERE SUPPOSED TO GO ON A FAMILY TRIP, BUT THAT'S OKAY.
....

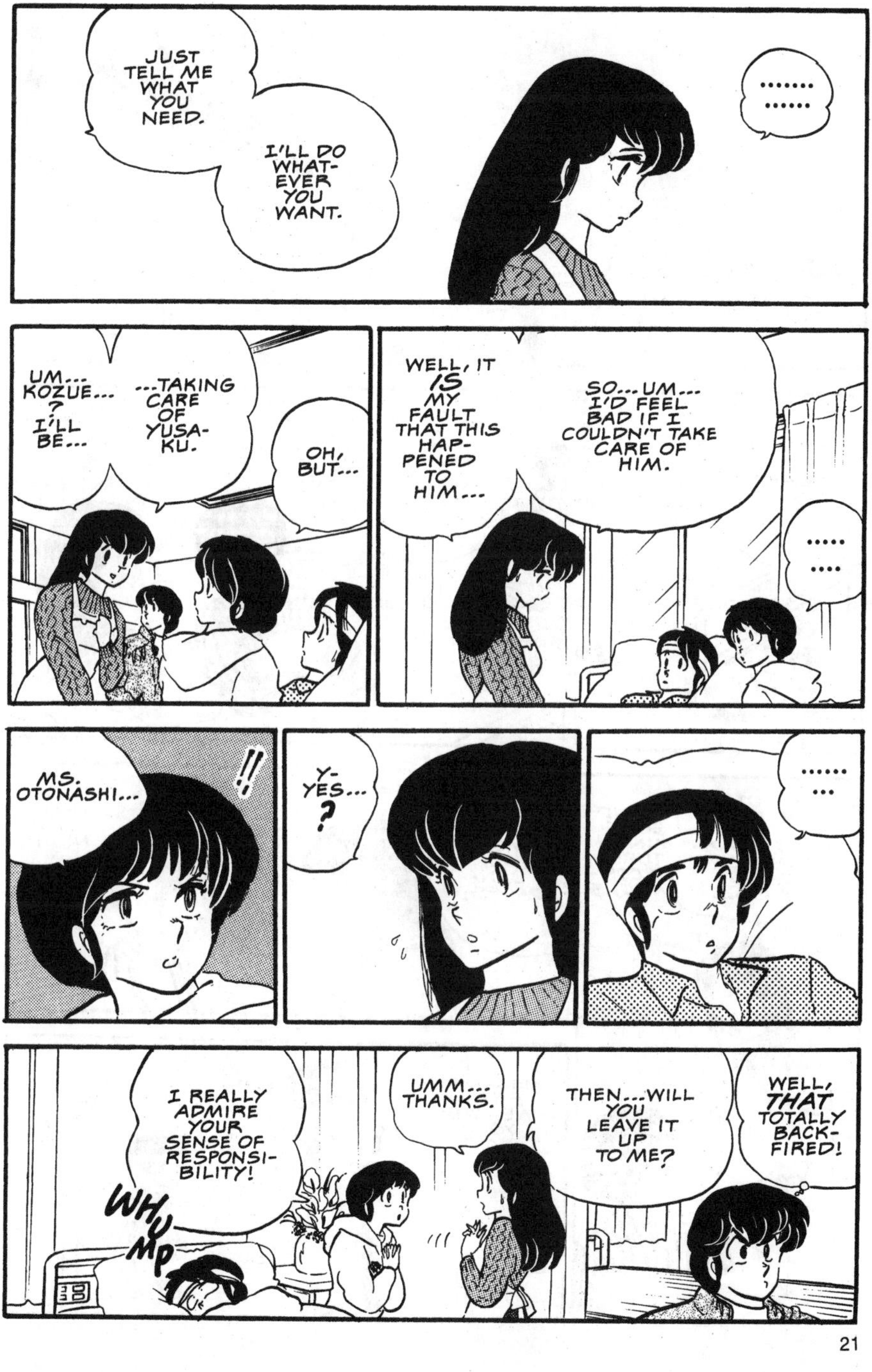
JUST TELL ME WHAT YOU NEED.
I'LL DO WHATEVER YOU WANT.
....
......
UM... KOZUE...? I'LL BE...
...TAKING CARE OF YUSAKU.
OH, BUT...
WELL, IT *IS* MY FAULT THAT THIS HAPPENED TO HIM...
SO... UM... I'D FEEL BAD IF I COULDN'T TAKE CARE OF HIM.
.....
....
MS. OTONASHI...
!!
Y-YES...?
......
...
I REALLY ADMIRE YOUR SENSE OF RESPONSIBILITY!
WHUMP
UMM... THANKS.
THEN...WILL YOU LEAVE IT UP TO ME?
WELL, *THAT* TOTALLY BACKFIRED!

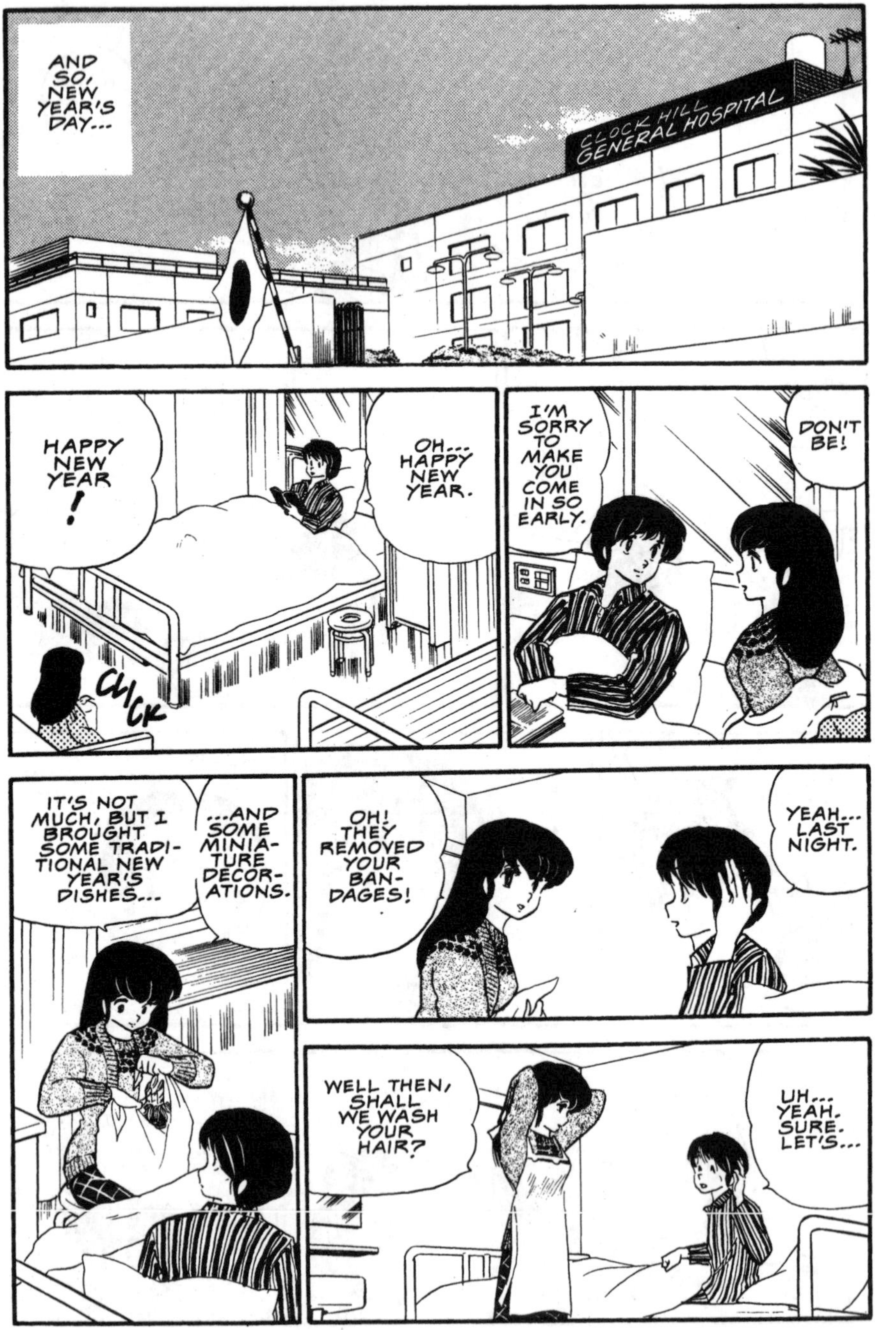
AND SO, NEW YEAR'S DAY...
CLOCK HILL GENERAL HOSPITAL
HAPPY NEW YEAR!
CLICK
OH... HAPPY NEW YEAR.
I'M SORRY TO MAKE YOU COME IN SO EARLY.
DON'T BE!
IT'S NOT MUCH, BUT I BROUGHT SOME TRADITIONAL NEW YEAR'S DISHES...
...AND SOME MINIATURE DECORATIONS.
OH! THEY REMOVED YOUR BANDAGES!
YEAH... LAST NIGHT.
WELL THEN, SHALL WE WASH YOUR HAIR?
UH... YEAH. SURE. LET'S...

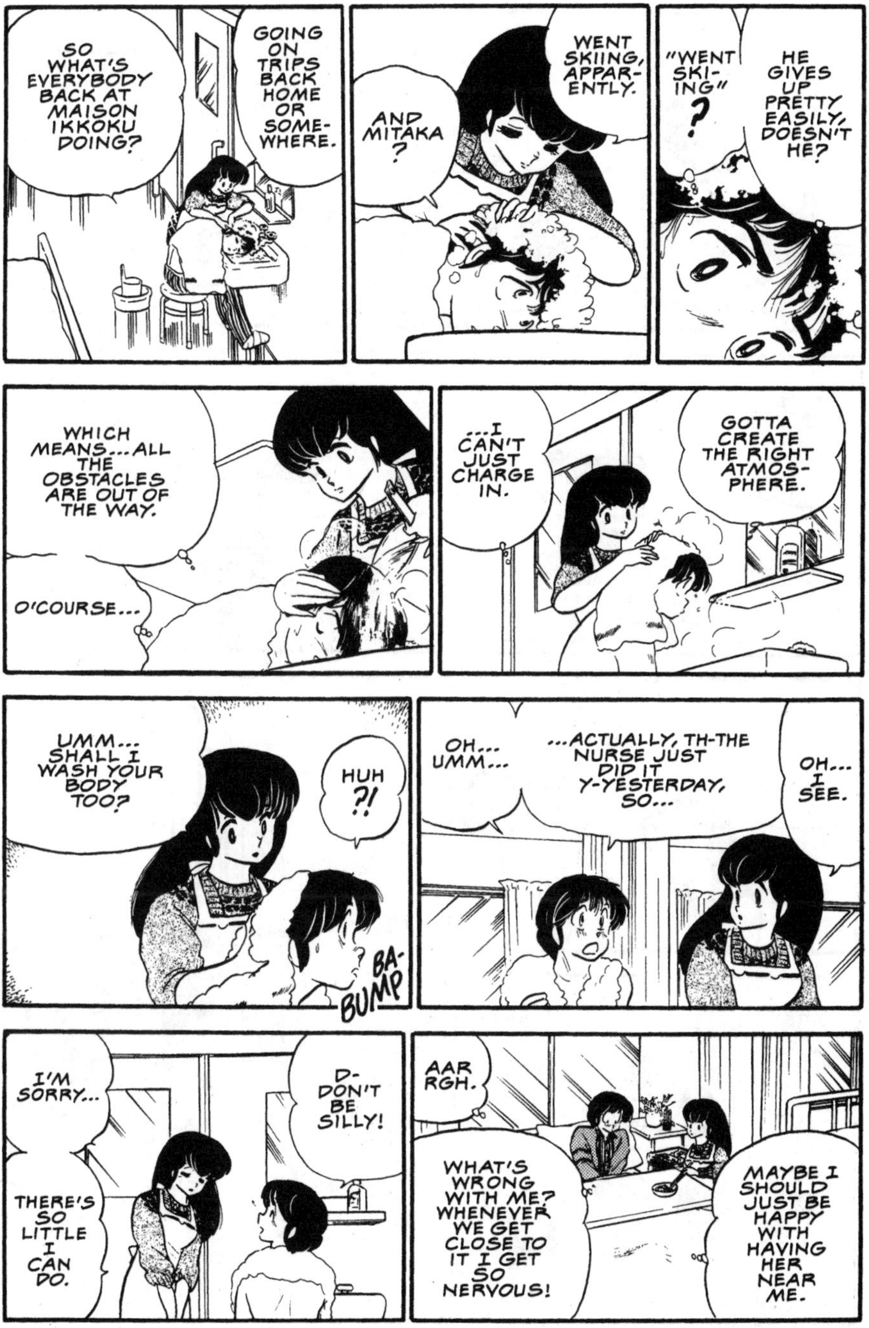
SO WHAT'S EVERYBODY BACK AT MAISON IKKOKU DOING?
GOING ON TRIPS BACK HOME OR SOMEWHERE.
AND MITAKA ?
WENT SKIING, APPARENTLY.
"WENT SKIING" ?
HE GIVES UP PRETTY EASILY, DOESN'T HE?
WHICH MEANS... ALL THE OBSTACLES ARE OUT OF THE WAY.
O'COURSE...
...I CAN'T JUST CHARGE IN.
GOTTA CREATE THE RIGHT ATMOSPHERE.
UMM... SHALL I WASH YOUR BODY TOO?
HUH ?!
BA-BUMP
OH... UMM...
...ACTUALLY, TH-THE NURSE JUST DID IT Y-YESTERDAY, SO...
OH... I SEE.
I'M SORRY...
THERE'S SO LITTLE I CAN DO.
D-DON'T BE SILLY!
AARRGH.
WHAT'S WRONG WITH ME? WHENEVER WE GET CLOSE TO IT I GET SO NERVOUS!
MAYBE I SHOULD JUST BE HAPPY WITH HAVING HER NEAR ME.

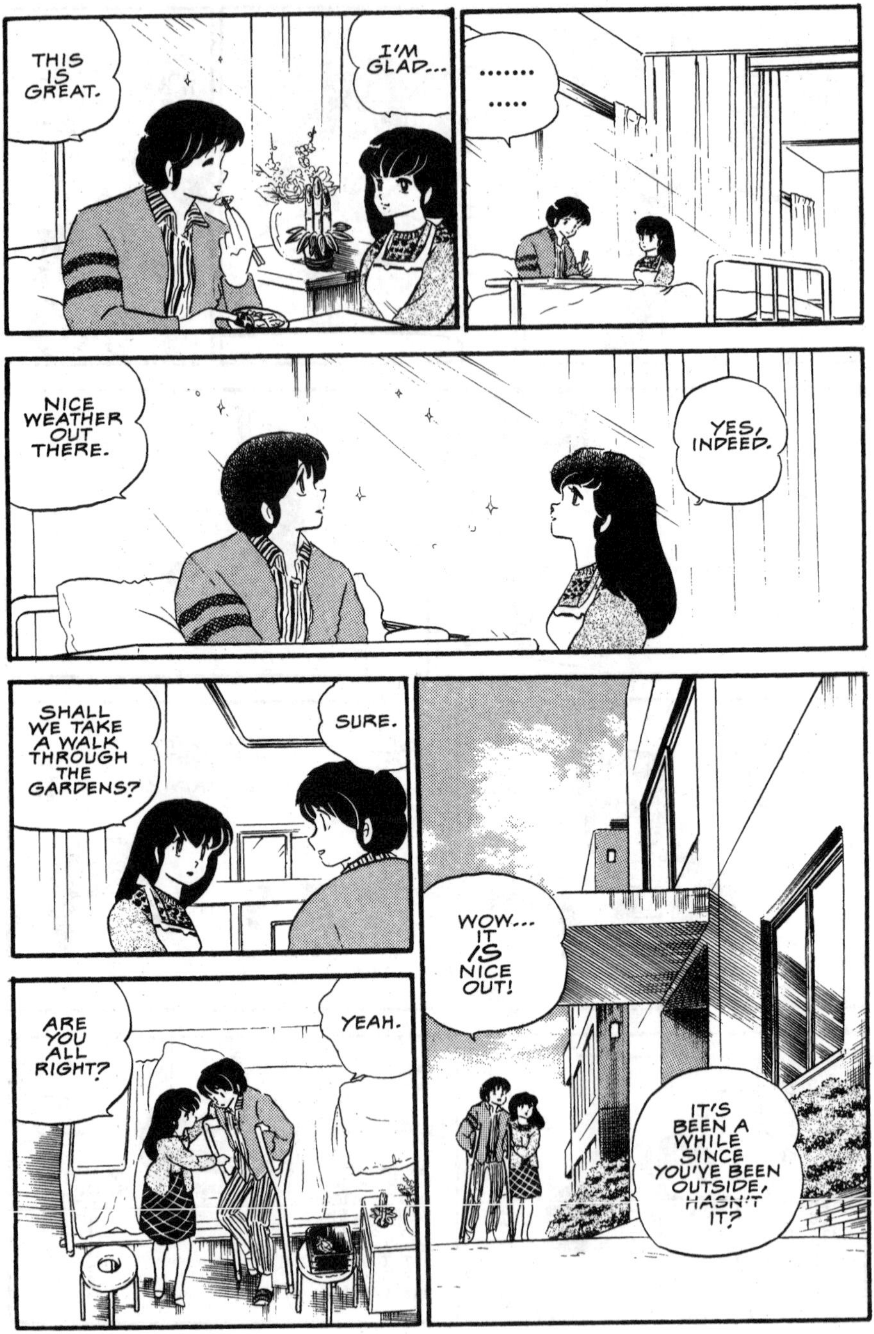
THIS IS GREAT.
I'M GLAD...
....
......
NICE WEATHER OUT THERE.
YES, INDEED.
SHALL WE TAKE A WALK THROUGH THE GARDENS?
SURE.
ARE YOU ALL RIGHT?
YEAH.
WOW... IT IS NICE OUT!
IT'S BEEN A WHILE SINCE YOU'VE BEEN OUTSIDE, HASN'T IT?

AREN'T YOU COLD?

I'M FINE, THANKS.

IT'S SO QUIET...

YES...

·······
·····

YOU'RE NOT GOING HOME TO VISIT YOUR PARENTS?

NO.

I FEEL REALLY BAD ABOUT YOU FEELING SO RESPONSIBLE FOR ME...

MY PARENTS LIVE IN TOWN, SO IT'S NOT LIKE I CAN'T SEE THEM IF I NEED TO. BESIDES...

OH, BUT DON'T!

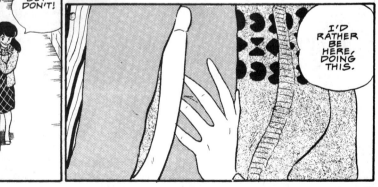

I'D RATHER BE HERE, DOING THIS.

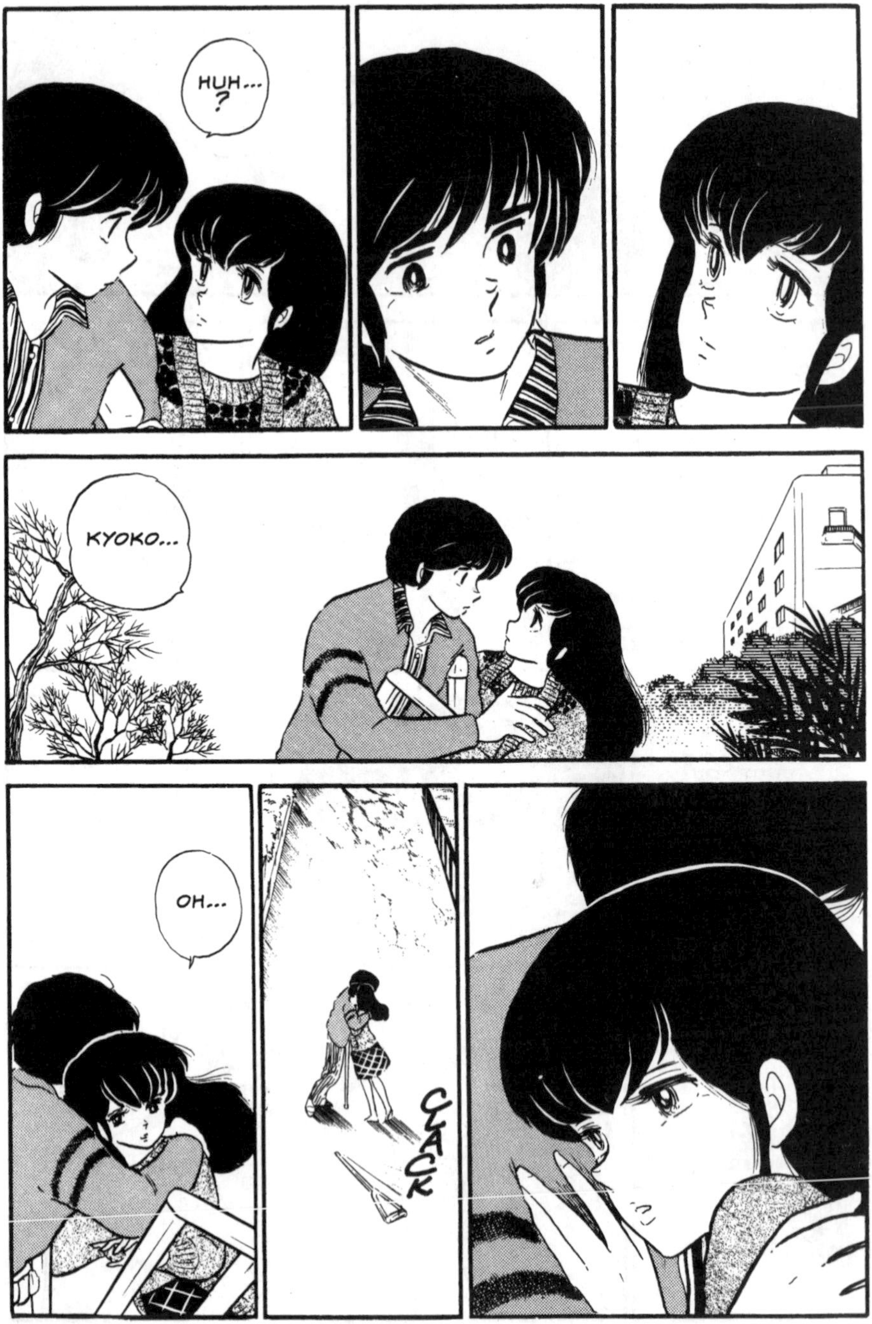
HUH...
?
KYOKO...
OH...
CLACK

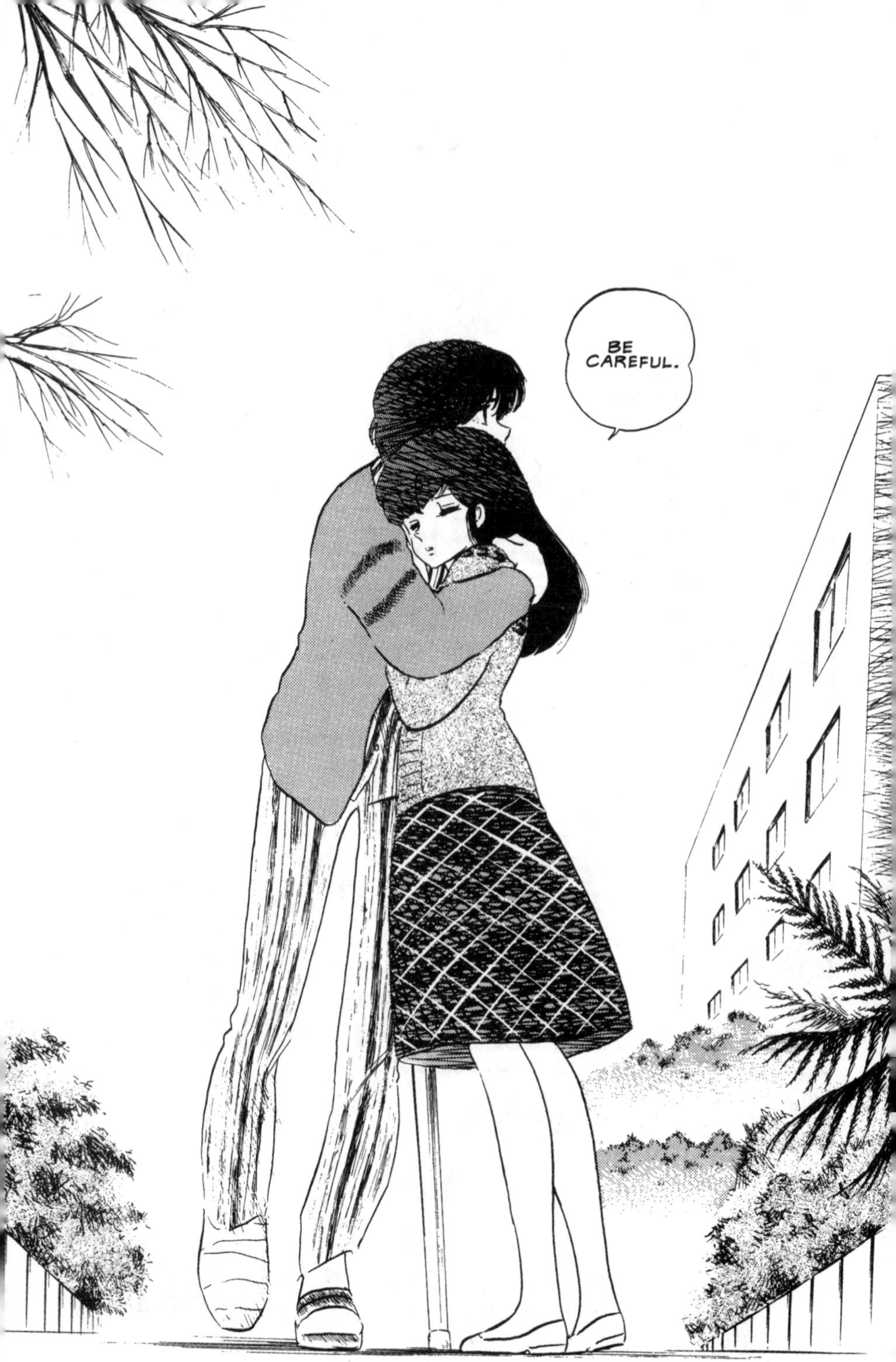
BE CAREFUL.

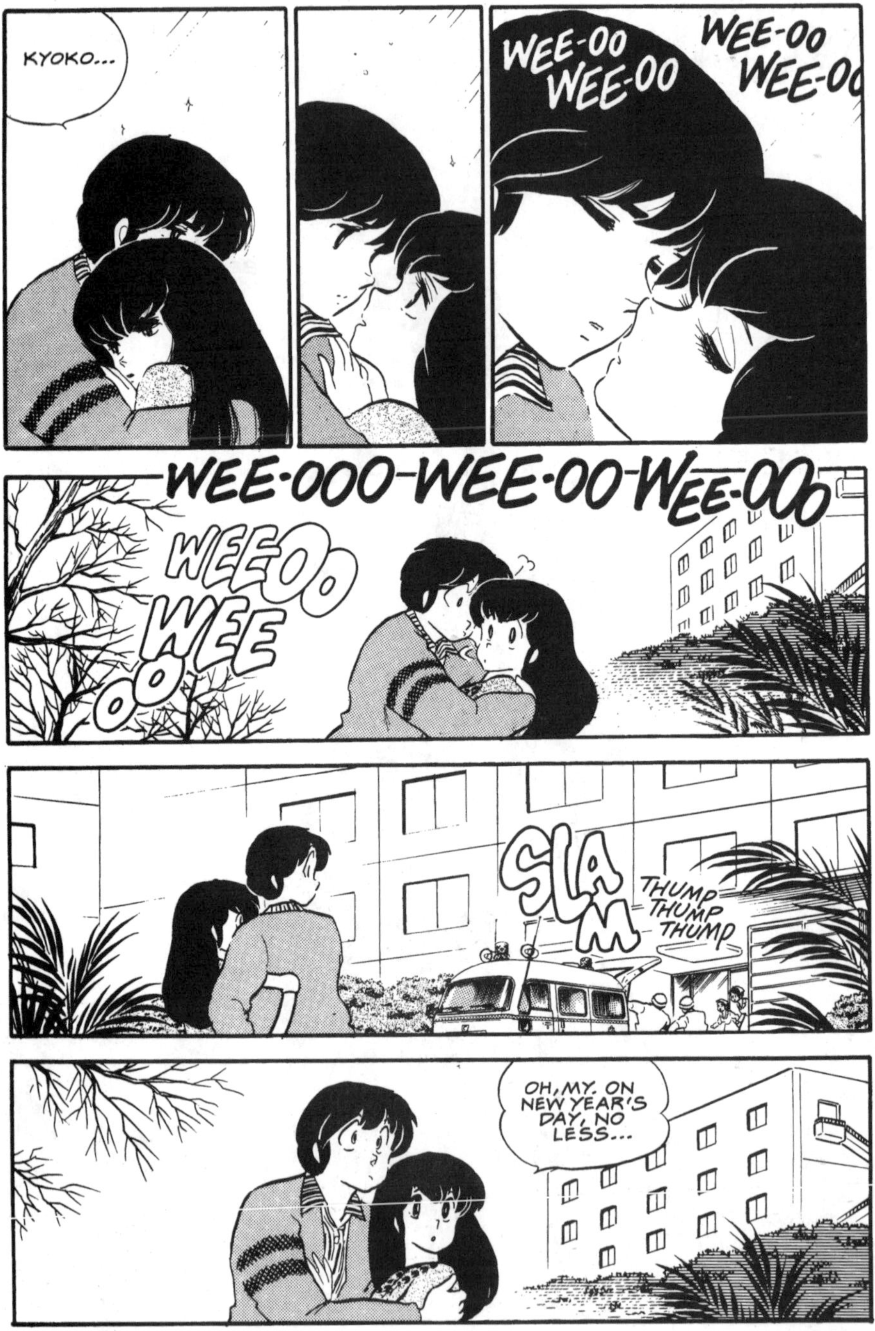
KYOKO...
WEE-OO WEE-OO
WEE-OO WEE-OO
WEE-OOO-WEE-OO-WEE-OOO
WEE-OO WEE OO
SLAM
THUMP THUMP THUMP
OH, MY. ON NEW YEAR'S DAY, NO LESS...

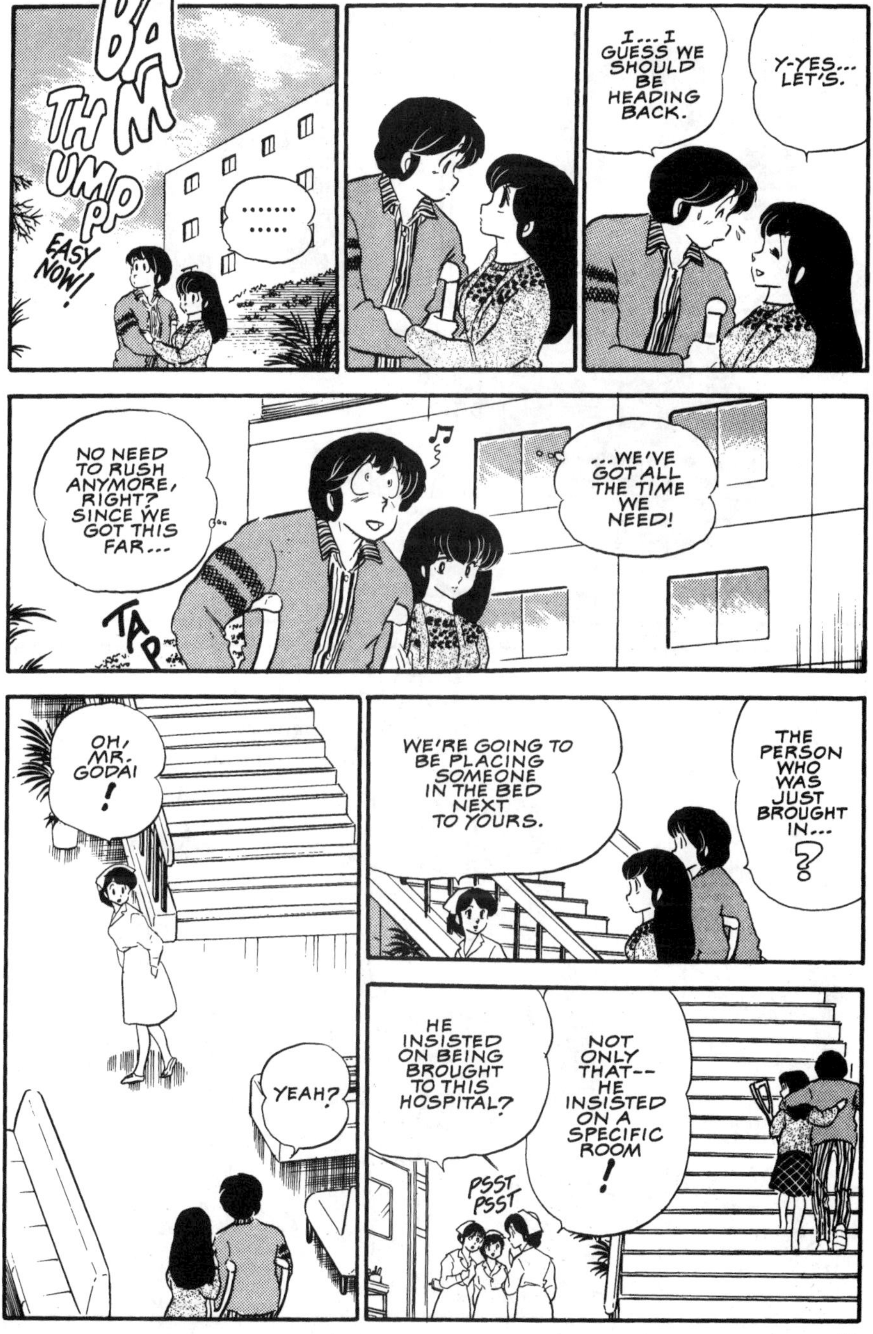
BAM
THUMPP
EASY NOW!
....
.....
I... I GUESS WE SHOULD BE HEADING BACK.
Y-YES... LET'S.
NO NEED TO RUSH ANYMORE, RIGHT? SINCE WE GOT THIS FAR...
...WE'VE GOT ALL THE TIME WE NEED!
TAP
OH, MR. GODAI!
YEAH?
WE'RE GOING TO BE PLACING SOMEONE IN THE BED NEXT TO YOURS.
THE PERSON WHO WAS JUST BROUGHT IN...?
HE INSISTED ON BEING BROUGHT TO THIS HOSPITAL?
NOT ONLY THAT-- HE INSISTED ON A SPECIFIC ROOM!
PSST PSST

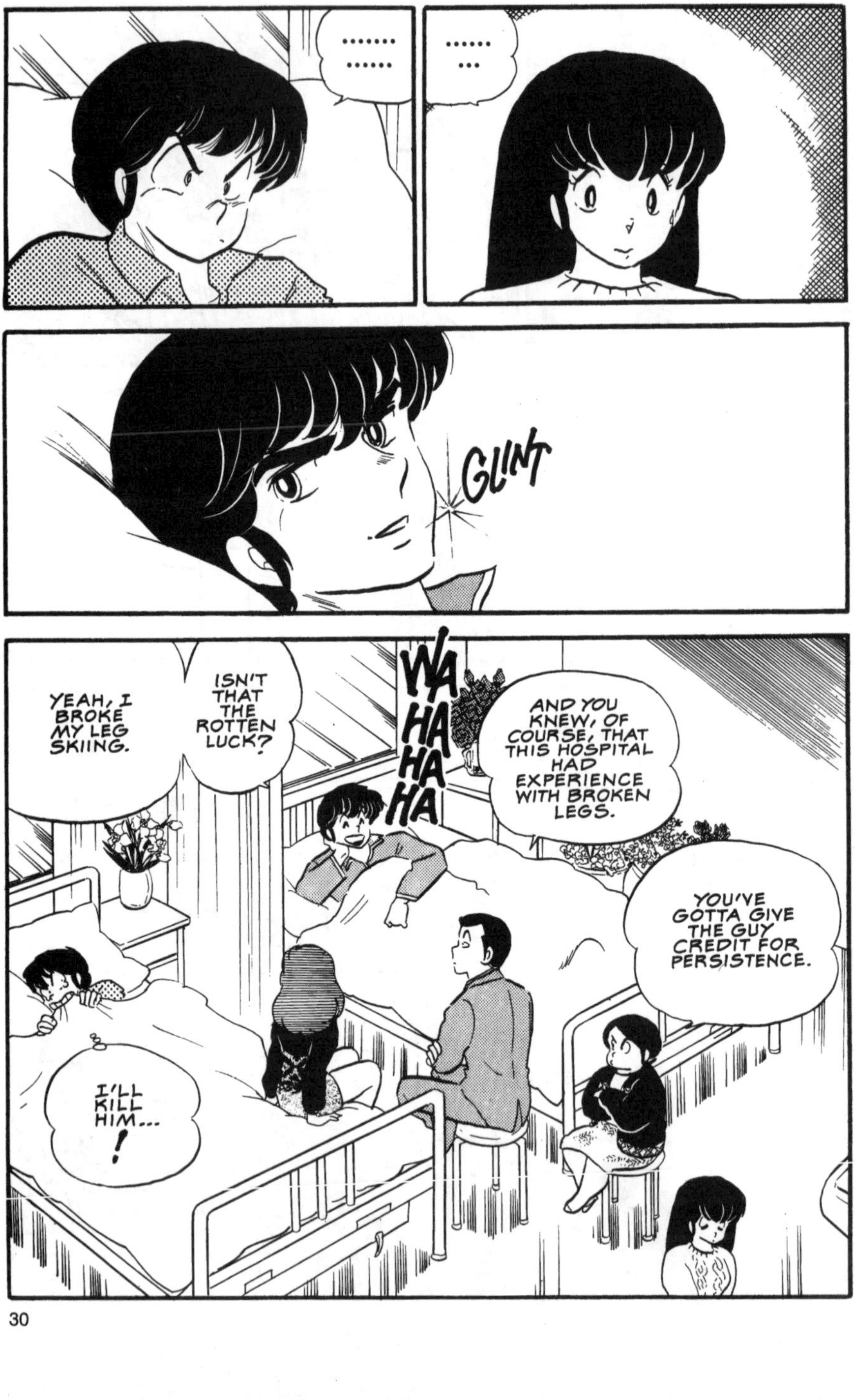

....
......
......
...
GLINT
YEAH, I BROKE MY LEG SKIING.
ISN'T THAT THE ROTTEN LUCK?
WA HA HA HA HA
AND YOU KNEW, OF COURSE, THAT THIS HOSPITAL HAD EXPERIENCE WITH BROKEN LEGS.
YOU'VE GOTTA GIVE THE GUY CREDIT FOR PERSISTENCE.
I'LL KILL HIM...!

PART 2
MESSAGE IN THE SNOW

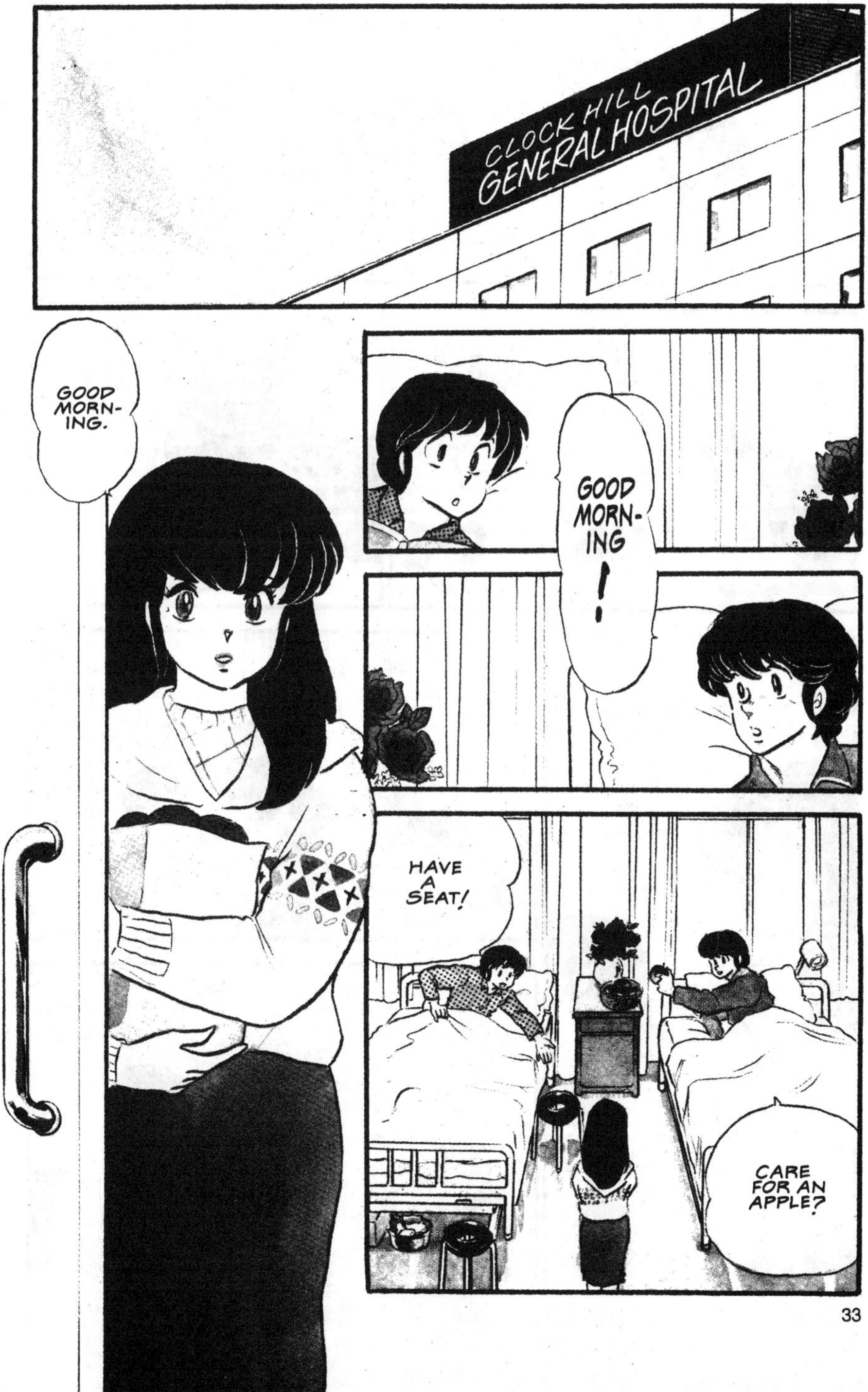
CLOCK HILL
GENERAL HOSPITAL
GOOD MORNING.
GOOD MORNING!
HAVE A SEAT!
CARE FOR AN APPLE?

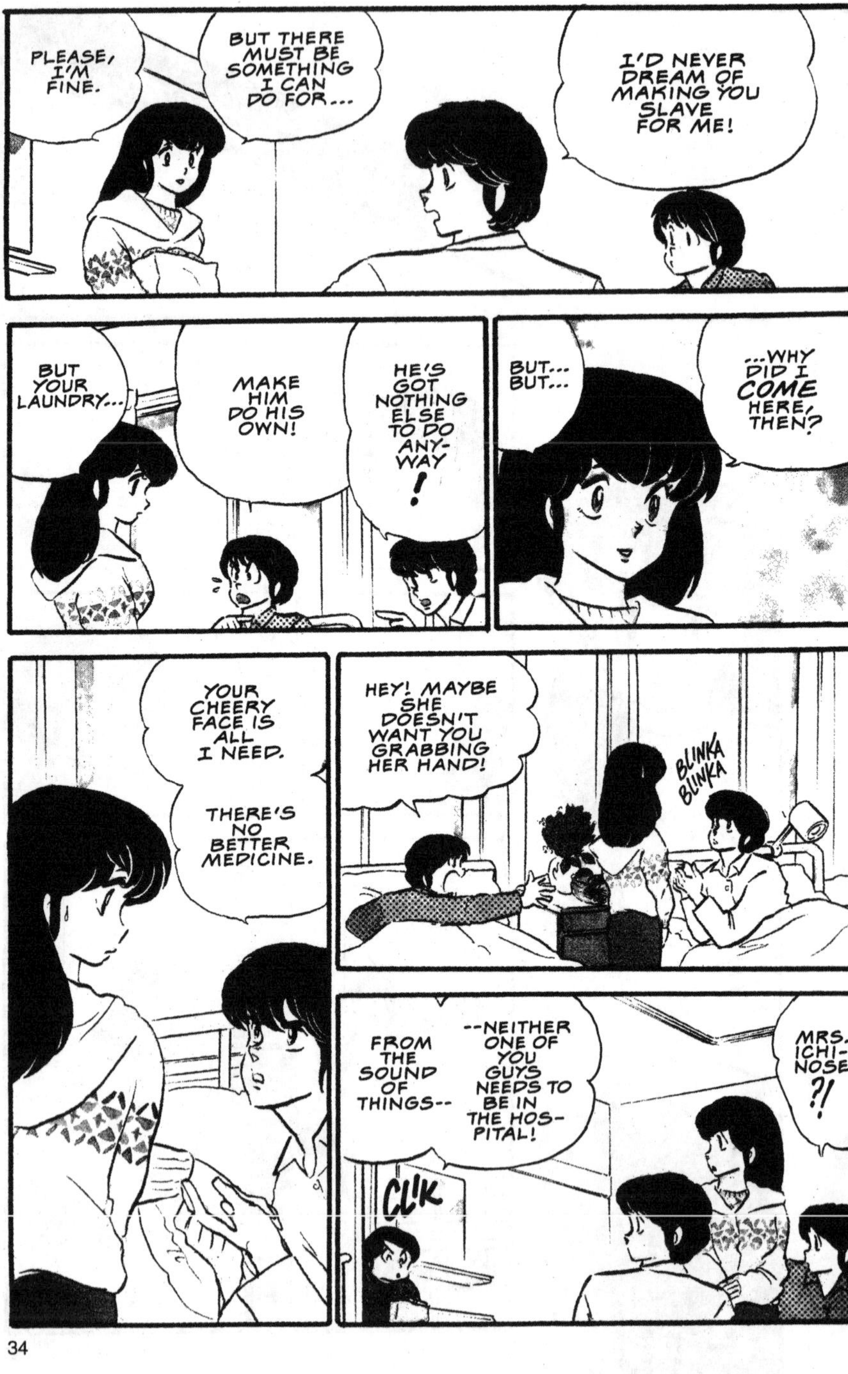
PLEASE, I'M FINE.
BUT THERE MUST BE SOMETHING I CAN DO FOR...
I'D NEVER DREAM OF MAKING YOU SLAVE FOR ME!
BUT YOUR LAUNDRY...
MAKE HIM DO HIS OWN!
HE'S GOT NOTHING ELSE TO DO ANYWAY!
BUT... BUT...
...WHY DID I COME HERE, THEN?
YOUR CHEERY FACE IS ALL I NEED.
THERE'S NO BETTER MEDICINE.
HEY! MAYBE SHE DOESN'T WANT YOU GRABBING HER HAND!
BLINKA BLINKA
FROM THE SOUND OF THINGS--
--NEITHER ONE OF YOU GUYS NEEDS TO BE IN THE HOSPITAL!
MRS. ICHINOSE ?!
CLIK

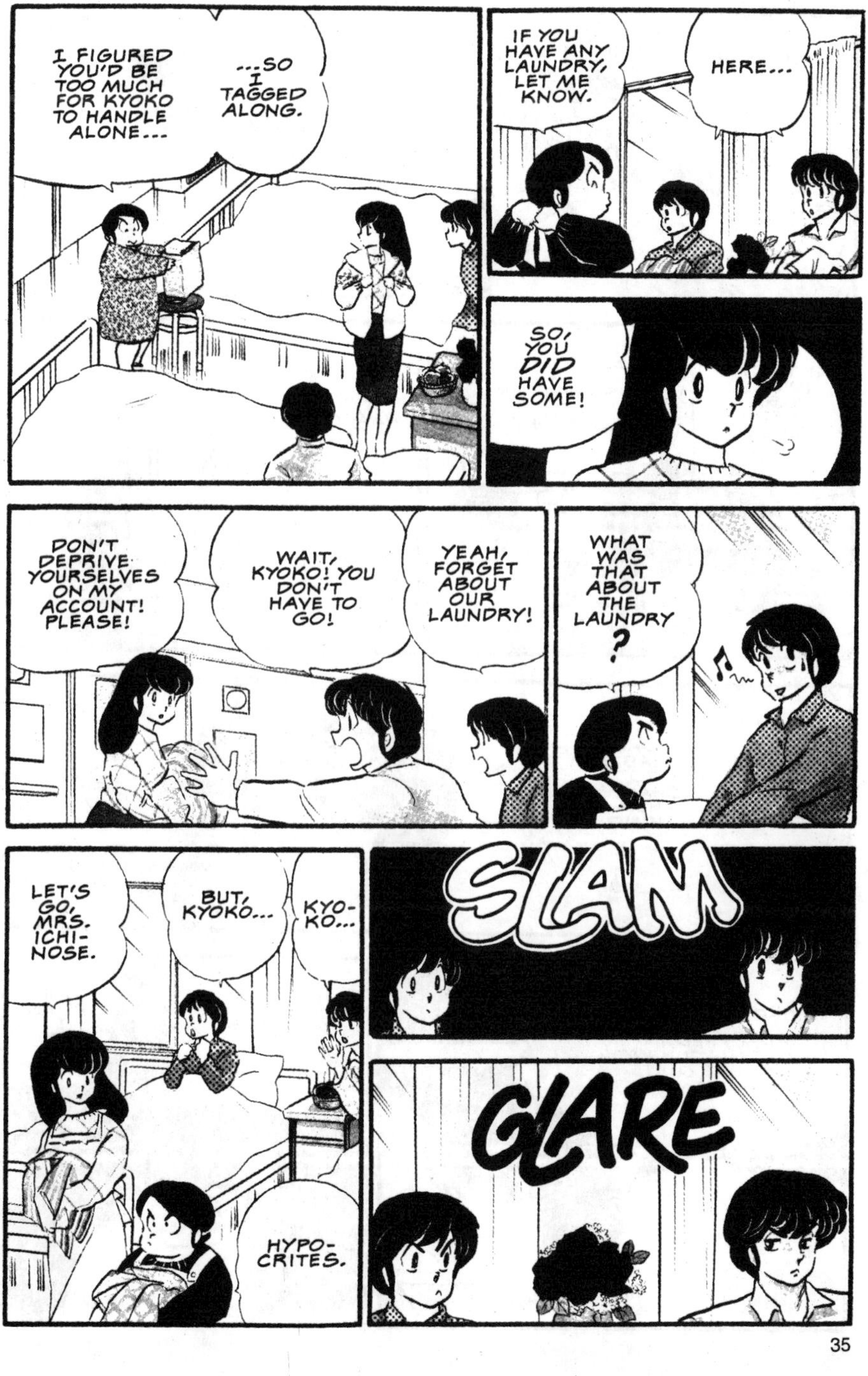
I FIGURED YOU'D BE TOO MUCH FOR KYOKO TO HANDLE ALONE...
...SO I TAGGED ALONG.
IF YOU HAVE ANY LAUNDRY, LET ME KNOW.
HERE...
SO, YOU DID HAVE SOME!
DON'T DEPRIVE YOURSELVES ON MY ACCOUNT! PLEASE!
WAIT, KYOKO! YOU DON'T HAVE TO GO!
YEAH, FORGET ABOUT OUR LAUNDRY!
WHAT WAS THAT ABOUT THE LAUNDRY ?
LET'S GO, MRS. ICHI-NOSE.
BUT, KYOKO...
KYO-KO...
HYPO-CRITES.
SLAM
GLARE

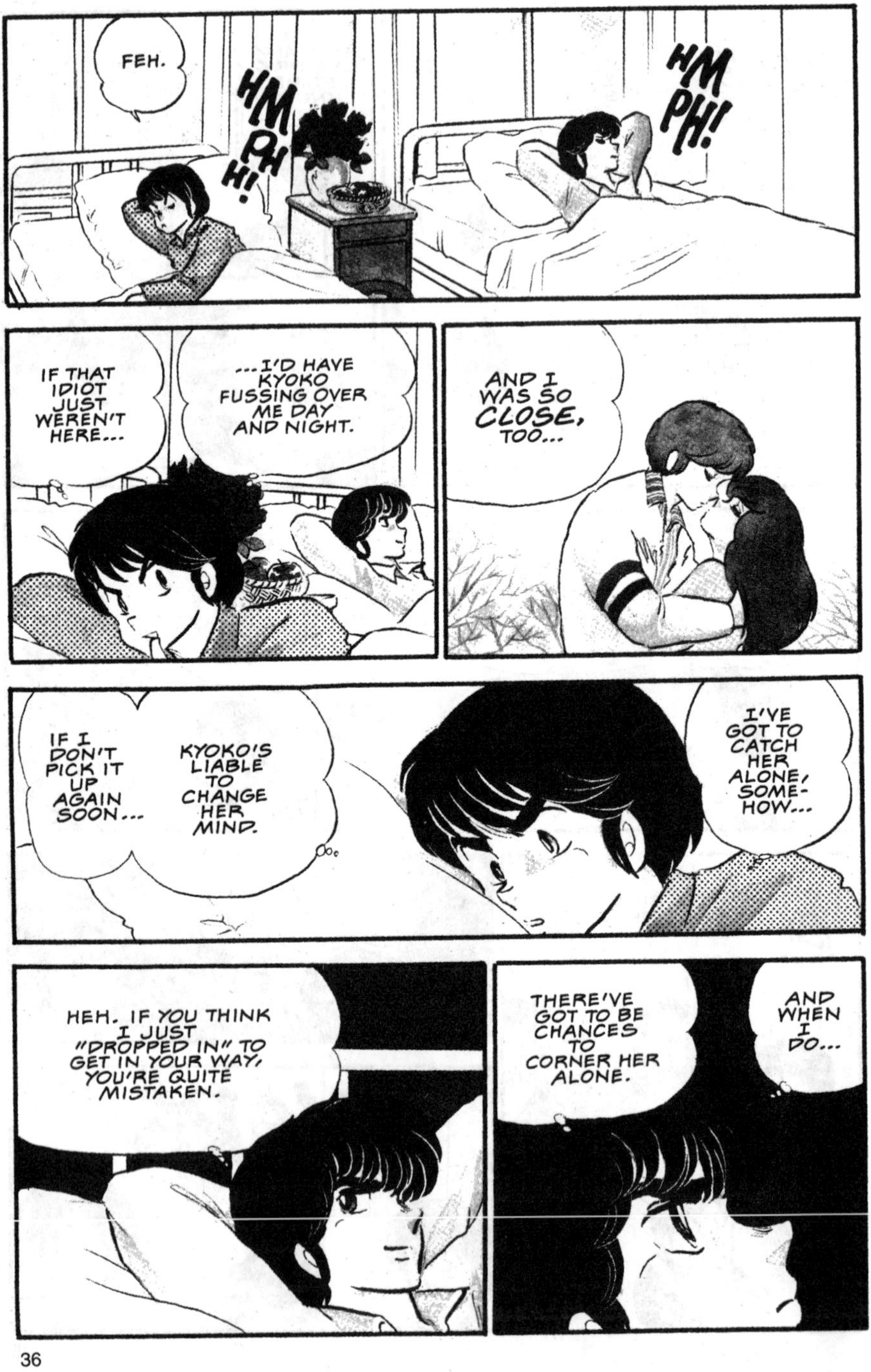
FEH.
HMPHH!
HMPH!
IF THAT IDIOT JUST WEREN'T HERE...
...I'D HAVE KYOKO FUSSING OVER ME DAY AND NIGHT.
AND I WAS SO CLOSE, TOO...
IF I DON'T PICK IT UP AGAIN SOON...
KYOKO'S LIABLE TO CHANGE HER MIND.
I'VE GOT TO CATCH HER ALONE, SOMEHOW...
HEH. IF YOU THINK I JUST "DROPPED IN" TO GET IN YOUR WAY, YOU'RE QUITE MISTAKEN.
THERE'VE GOT TO BE CHANCES TO CORNER HER ALONE.
AND WHEN I DO...

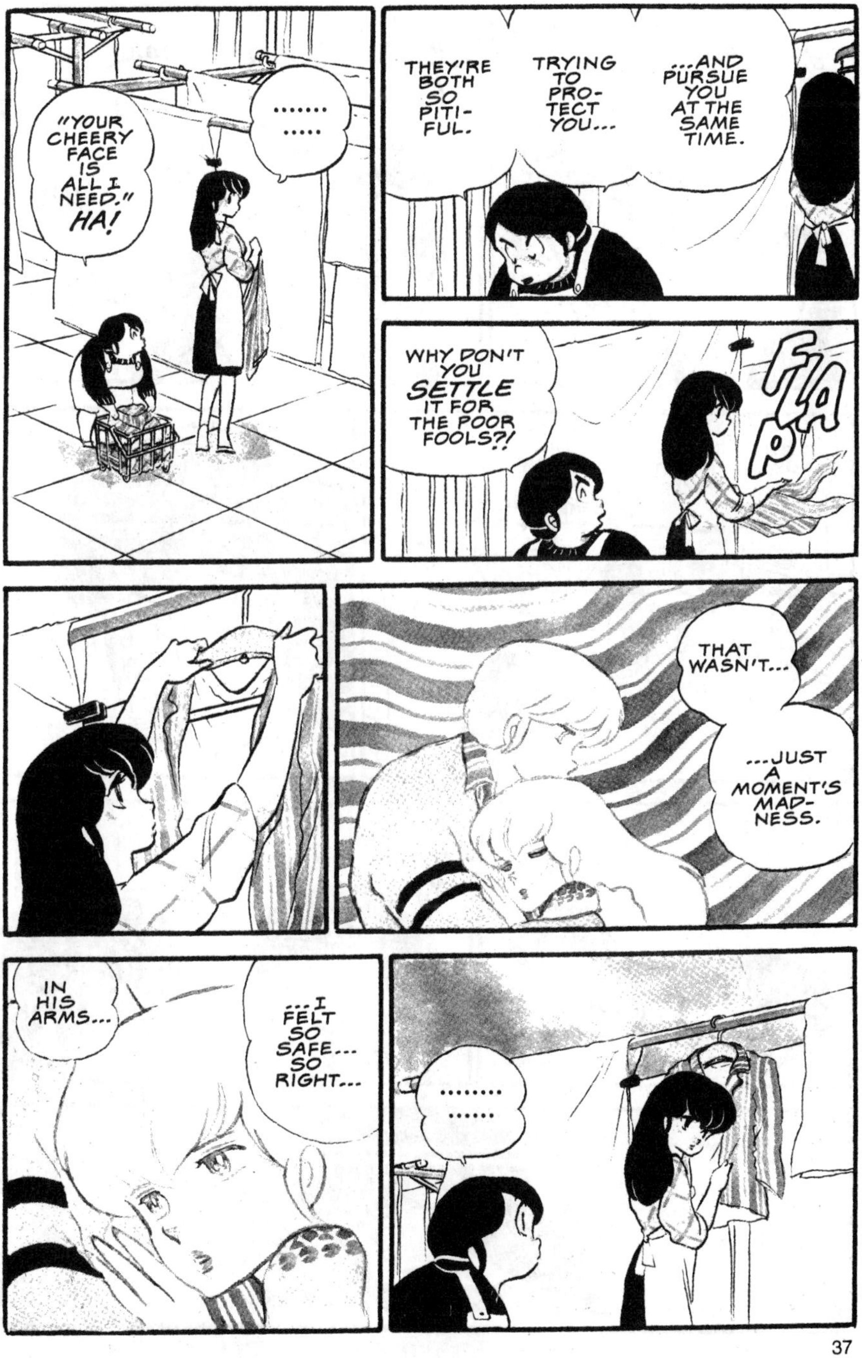
"YOUR CHEERY FACE IS ALL I NEED." HA!
....
THEY'RE BOTH SO PITIFUL.
TRYING TO PROTECT YOU...
...AND PURSUE YOU AT THE SAME TIME.
WHY DON'T YOU SETTLE IT FOR THE POOR FOOLS?!
FLAP
THAT WASN'T...
...JUST A MOMENT'S MADNESS.
IN HIS ARMS...
...I FELT SO SAFE... SO RIGHT...
....

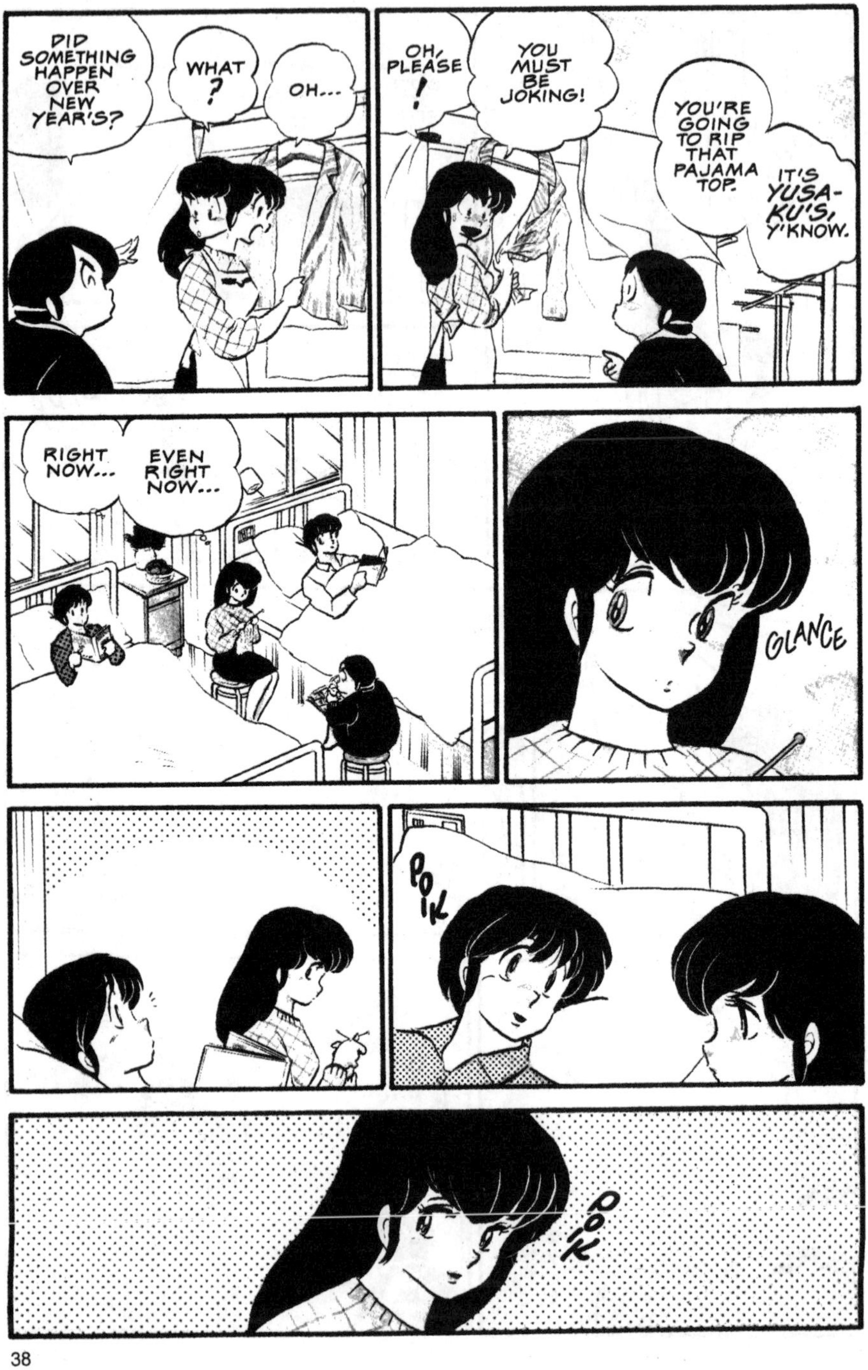
DID SOMETHING HAPPEN OVER NEW YEAR'S?
WHAT?
OH...
OH, PLEASE!
YOU MUST BE JOKING!
YOU'RE GOING TO RIP THAT PAJAMA TOP.
IT'S YUSAKU'S, Y'KNOW.
RIGHT NOW...
EVEN RIGHT NOW...
GLANCE
POIK
POOK

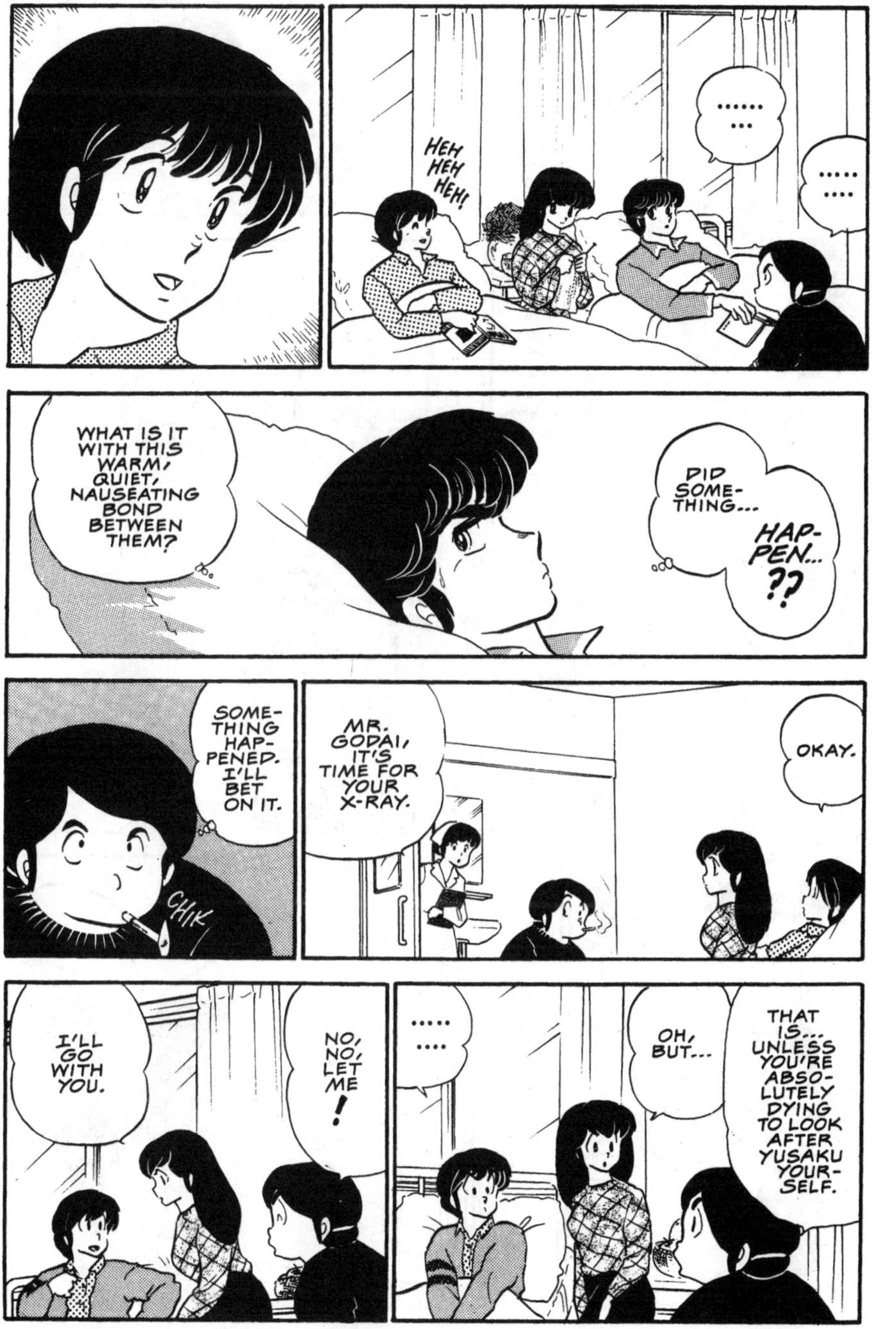
HEH HEH HEH!
....
...
.....
....
WHAT IS IT WITH THIS WARM, QUIET, NAUSEATING BOND BETWEEN THEM?
DID SOMETHING... HAPPEN...??
SOMETHING HAPPENED. I'LL BET ON IT.
CHIK
MR. GODAI, IT'S TIME FOR YOUR X-RAY.
OKAY.
I'LL GO WITH YOU.
NO, NO, LET ME!
.....
....
OH, BUT...
THAT IS... UNLESS YOU'RE ABSOLUTELY DYING TO LOOK AFTER YUSAKU YOURSELF.

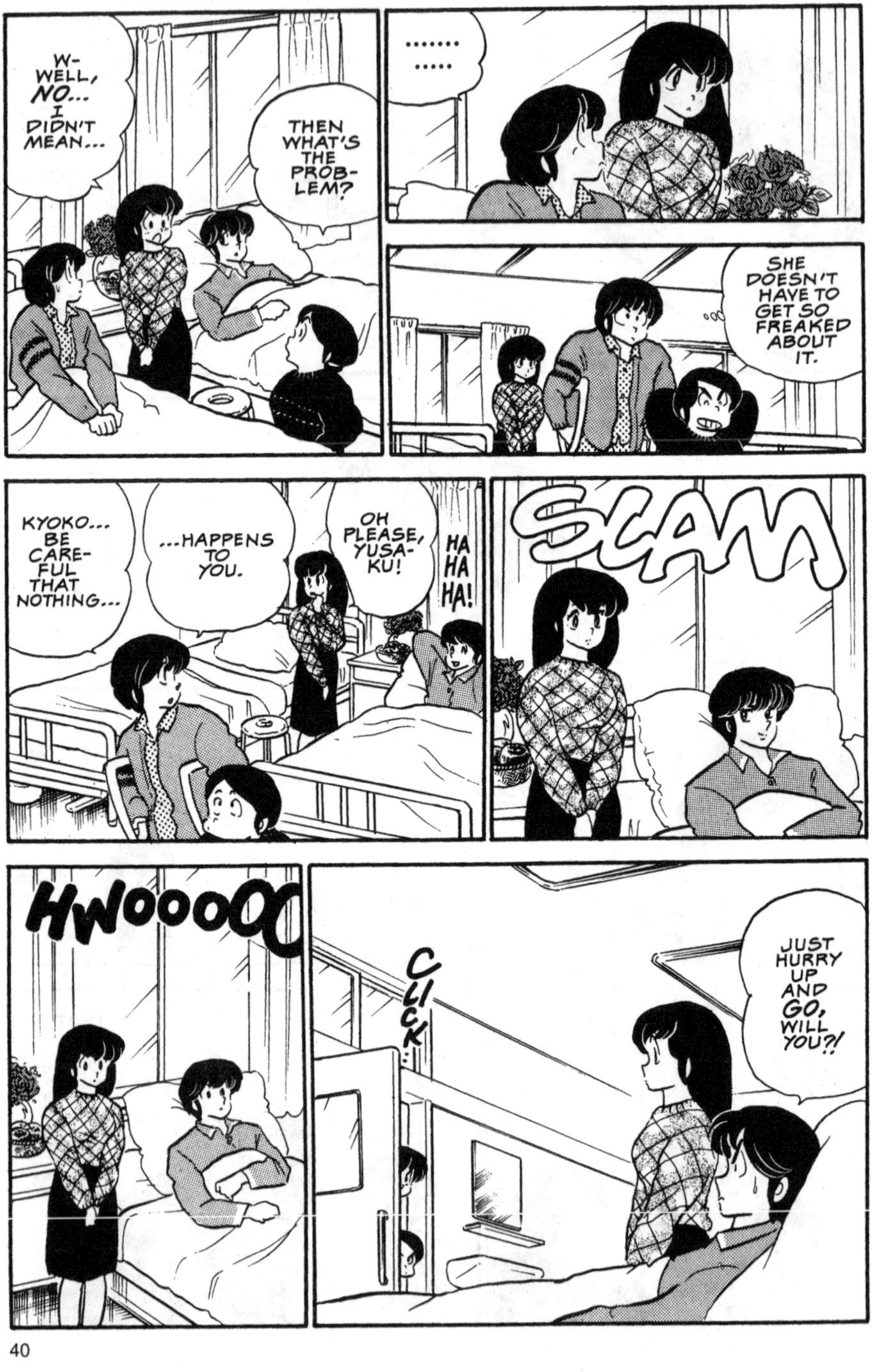
W-WELL, NO... I DIDN'T MEAN...
THEN WHAT'S THE PROB-LEM?
....
.....
SHE DOESN'T HAVE TO GET SO FREAKED ABOUT IT.
KYOKO... BE CARE-FUL THAT NOTHING...
...HAPPENS TO YOU.
OH PLEASE, YUSA-KU!
HA HA HA!
SLAM
HWOOOOO
CLICK...
JUST HURRY UP AND GO, WILL YOU?!

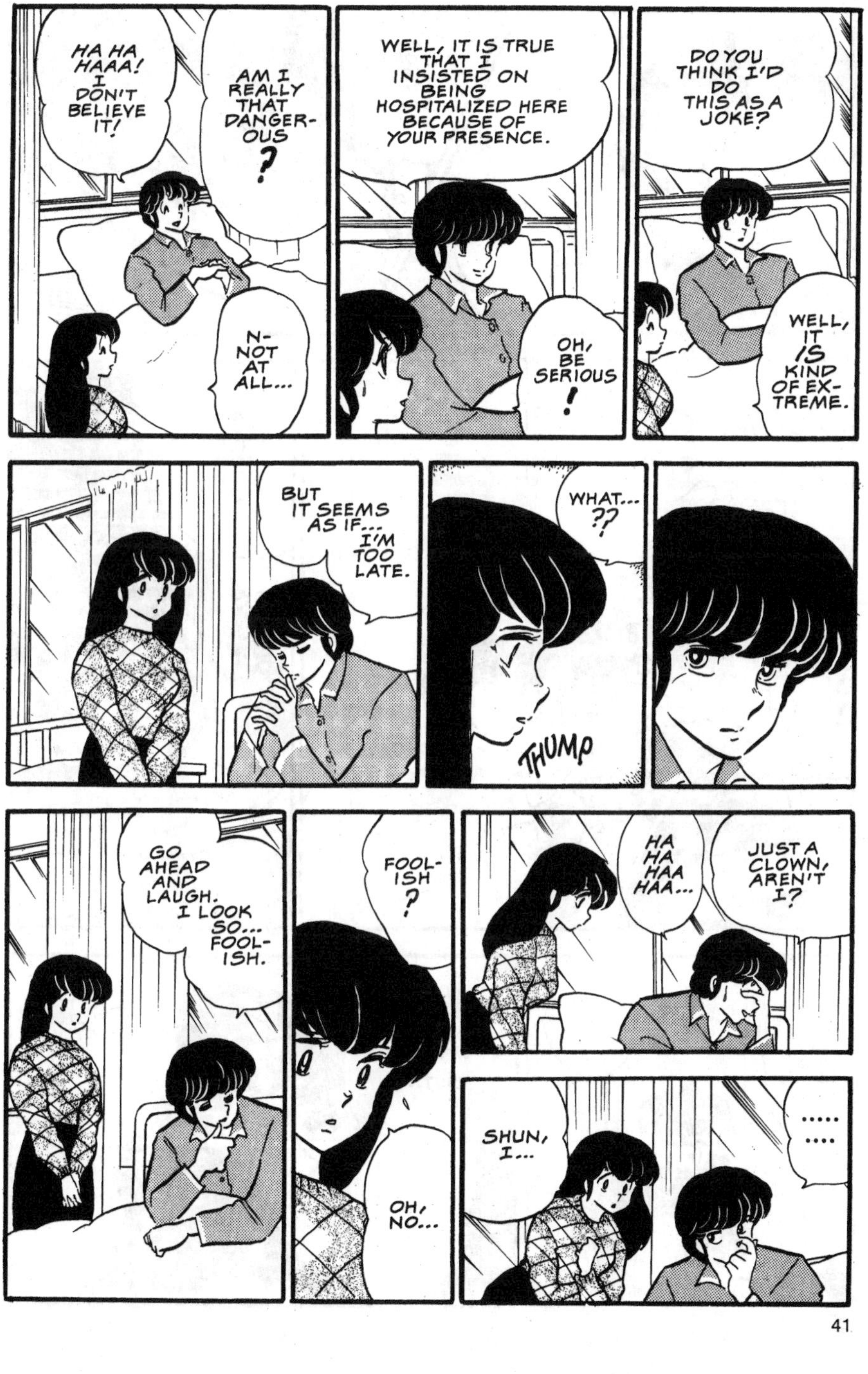
HA HA HAAA! I DON'T BELIEVE IT!
AM I REALLY THAT DANGER-OUS ?
N-NOT AT ALL...
WELL, IT IS TRUE THAT I INSISTED ON BEING HOSPITALIZED HERE BECAUSE OF YOUR PRESENCE.
OH, BE SERIOUS !
DO YOU THINK I'D DO THIS AS A JOKE?
WELL, IT IS KIND OF EX-TREME.
BUT IT SEEMS AS IF... I'M TOO LATE.
WHAT... ??
THUMP
GO AHEAD AND LAUGH. I LOOK SO... FOOL-ISH.
FOOL-ISH ?
OH, NO...
HA HA HAA HAA...
JUST A CLOWN, AREN'T I?
SHUN, I...
....

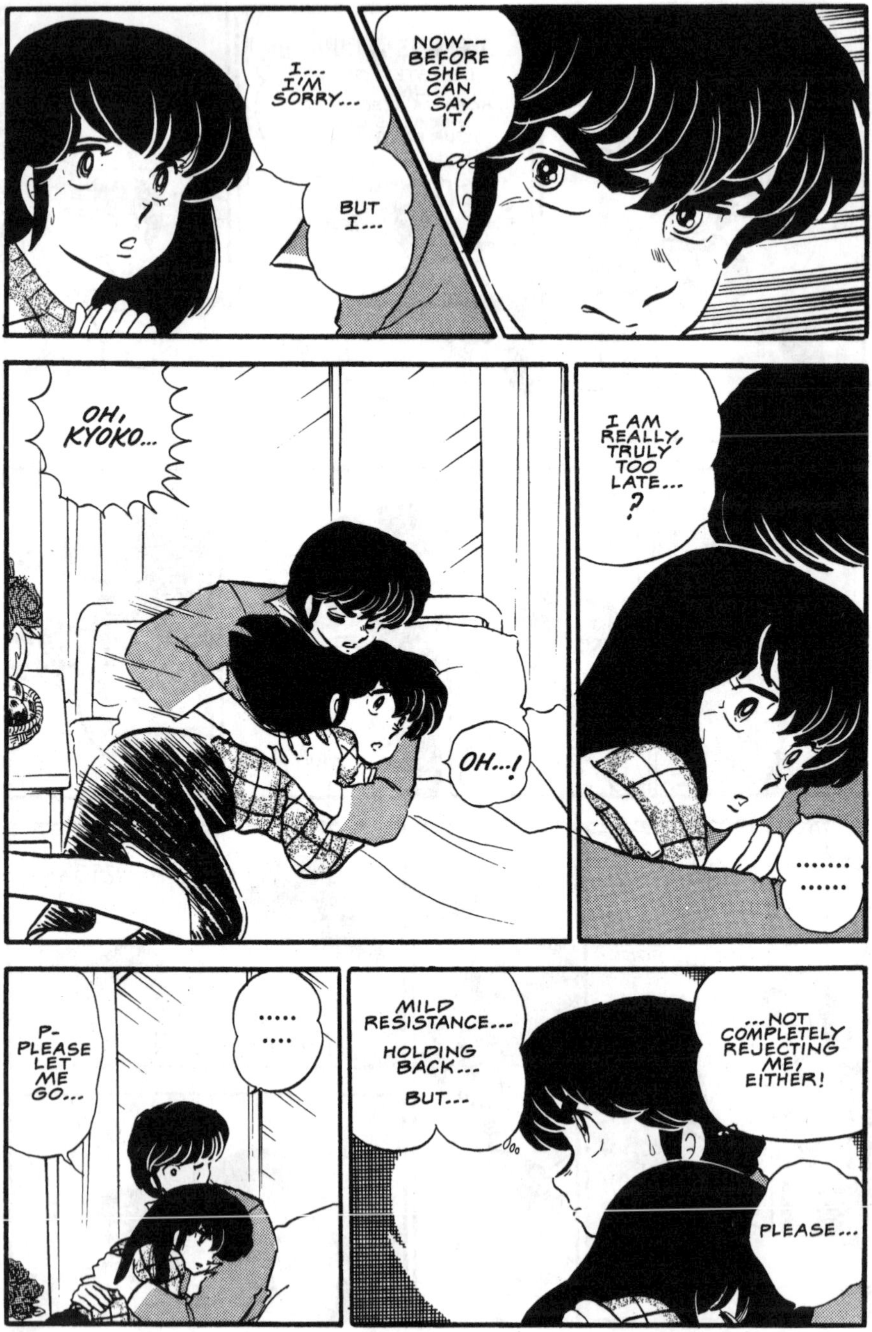
I... I'M SORRY...
BUT I...
NOW-- BEFORE SHE CAN SAY IT!
OH, KYOKO...
OH...!
I AM REALLY, TRULY TOO LATE...?
....
P-PLEASE LET ME GO...
....
MILD RESISTANCE... HOLDING BACK... BUT...
...NOT COMPLETELY REJECTING ME, EITHER!
PLEASE...

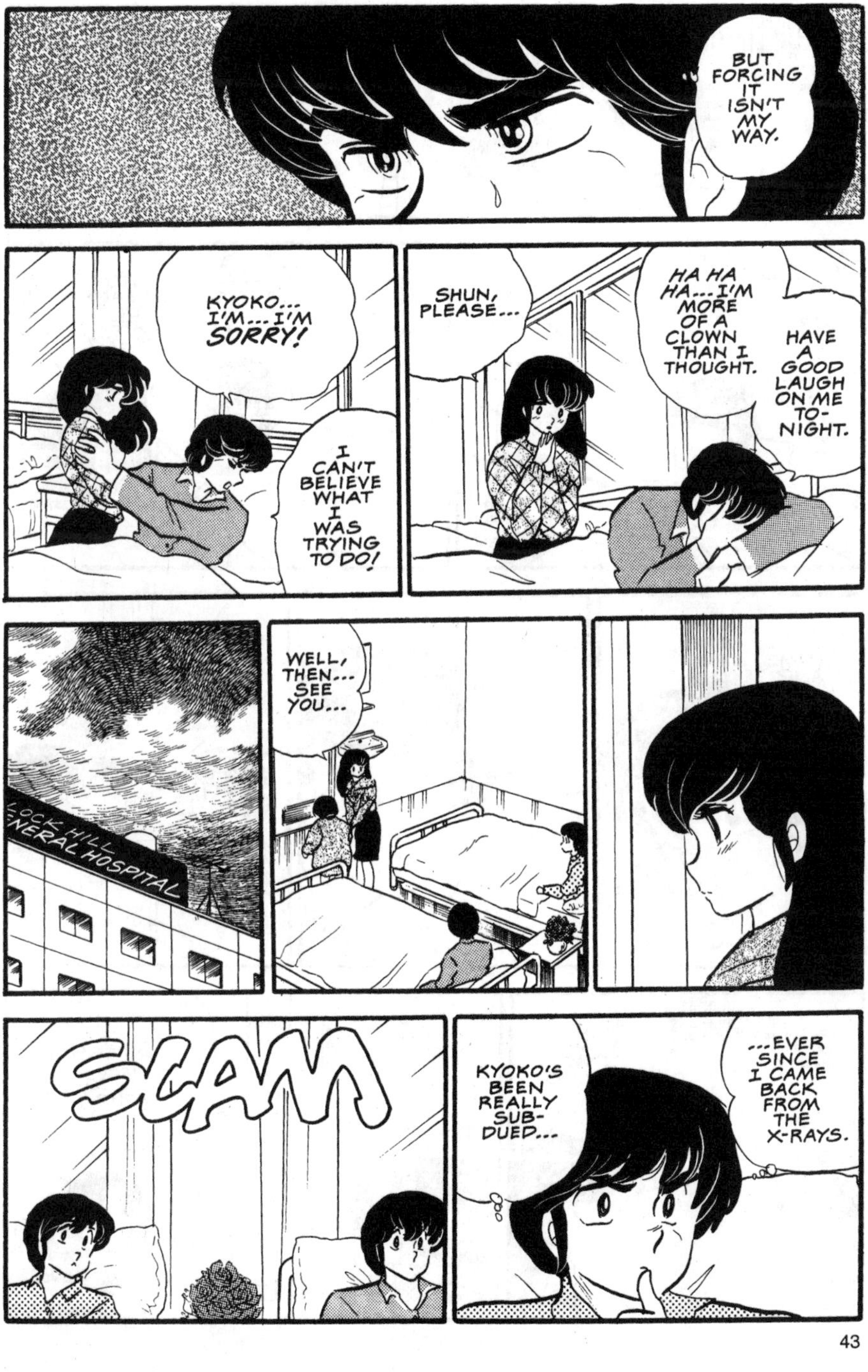
BUT FORCING IT ISN'T MY WAY.
KYOKO... I'M... I'M SORRY!
I CAN'T BELIEVE WHAT I WAS TRYING TO DO!
SHUN, PLEASE...
HA HA HA... I'M MORE OF A CLOWN THAN I THOUGHT.
HAVE A GOOD LAUGH ON ME TO-NIGHT.
LOCK HILL
ENERAL HOSPITAL
WELL, THEN... SEE YOU...
SLAM
KYOKO'S BEEN REALLY SUB-DUED...
...EVER SINCE I CAME BACK FROM THE X-RAYS.

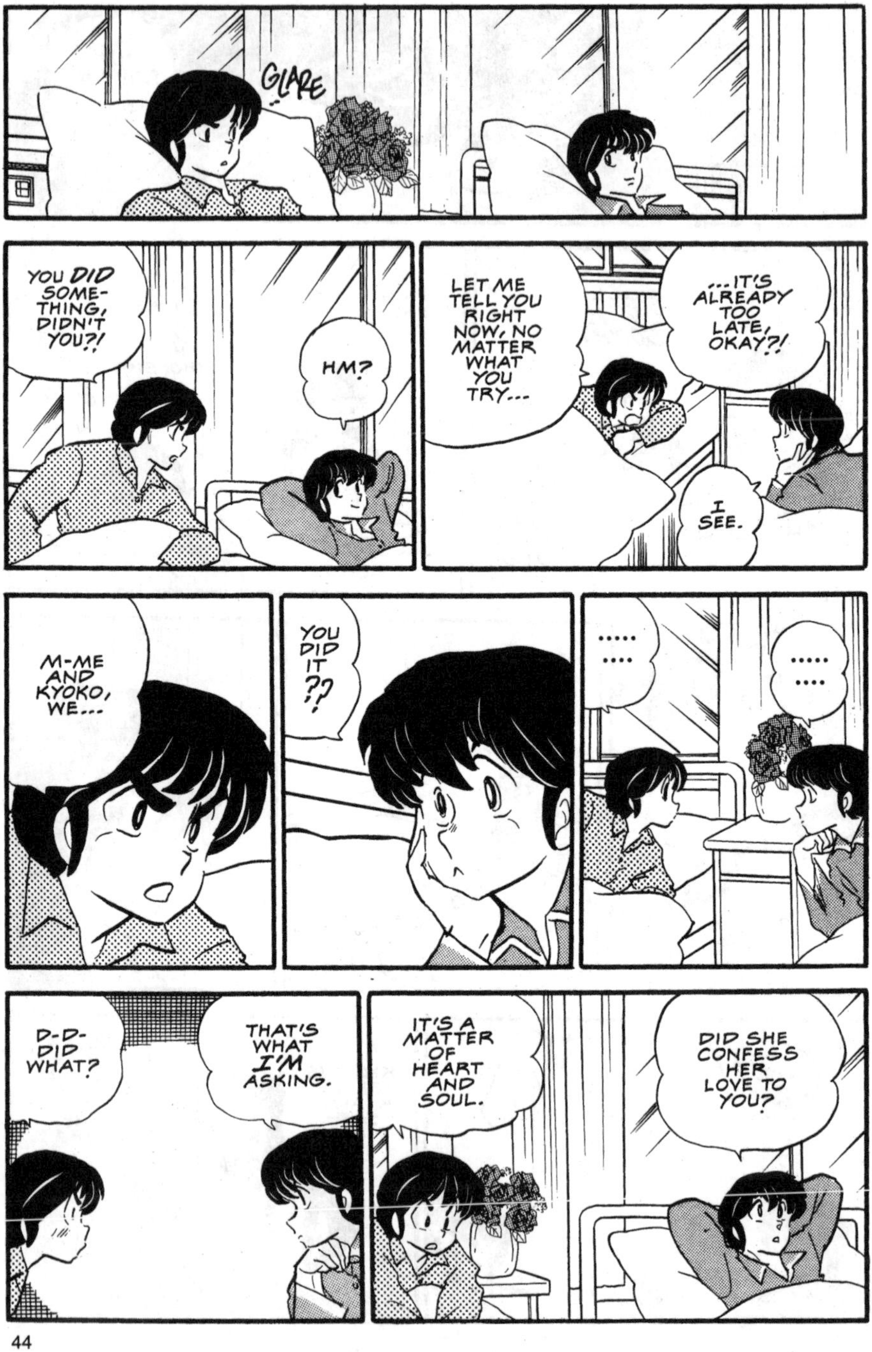
GLARE
YOU DID SOMETHING, DIDN'T YOU?!
HM?
LET ME TELL YOU RIGHT NOW, NO MATTER WHAT YOU TRY...
...IT'S ALREADY TOO LATE, OKAY?!
I SEE.
M-ME AND KYOKO, WE...
YOU DID IT??
....
....
D-D-DID WHAT?
THAT'S WHAT I'M ASKING.
IT'S A MATTER OF HEART AND SOUL.
DID SHE CONFESS HER LOVE TO YOU?

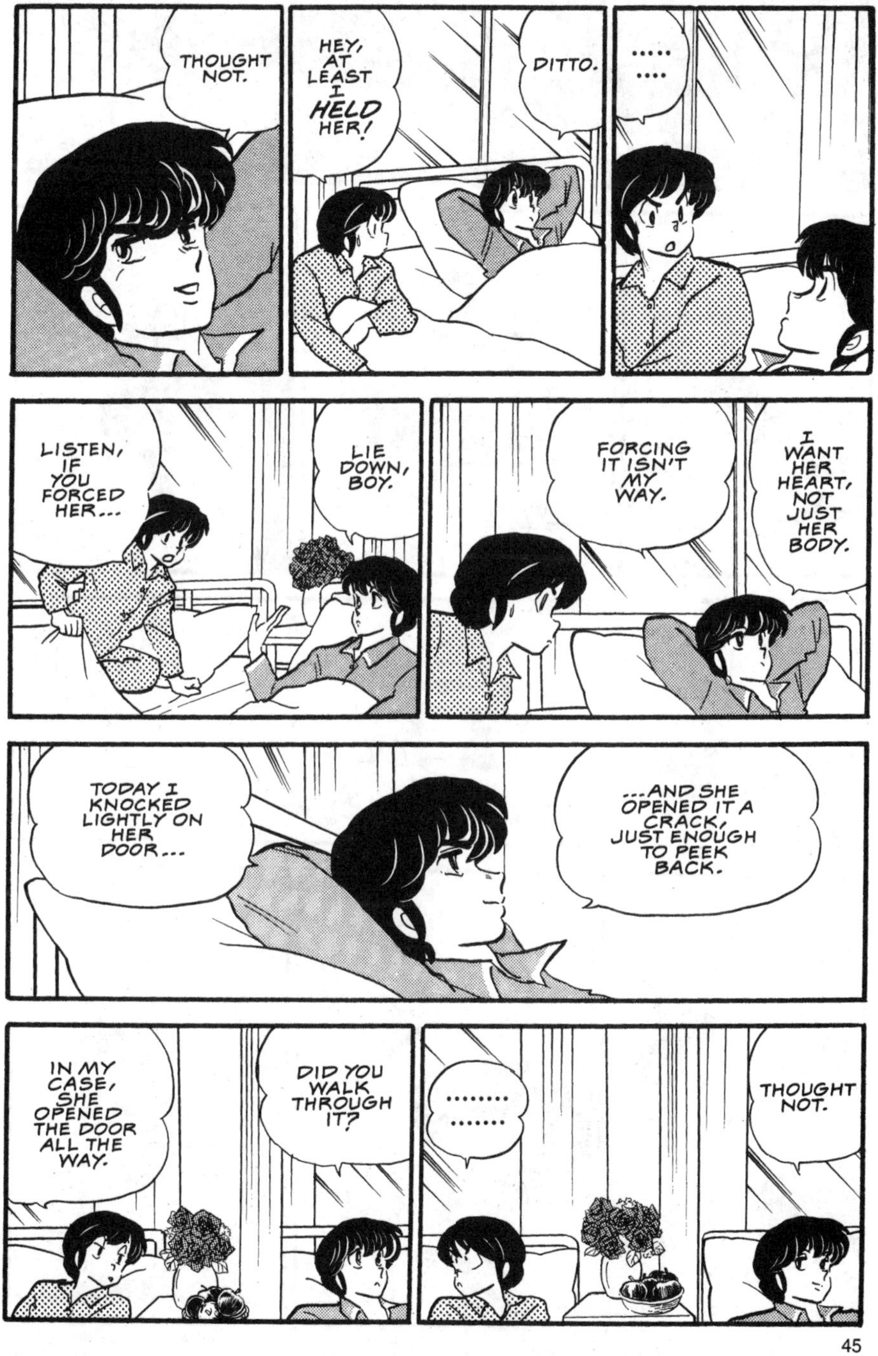
THOUGHT NOT.
HEY, AT LEAST I HELD HER!
DITTO.
....
LISTEN, IF YOU FORCED HER...
LIE DOWN, BOY.
FORCING IT ISN'T MY WAY.
I WANT HER HEART, NOT JUST HER BODY.
TODAY I KNOCKED LIGHTLY ON HER DOOR...
...AND SHE OPENED IT A CRACK, JUST ENOUGH TO PEEK BACK.
IN MY CASE, SHE OPENED THE DOOR ALL THE WAY.
DID YOU WALK THROUGH IT?
....
THOUGHT NOT.

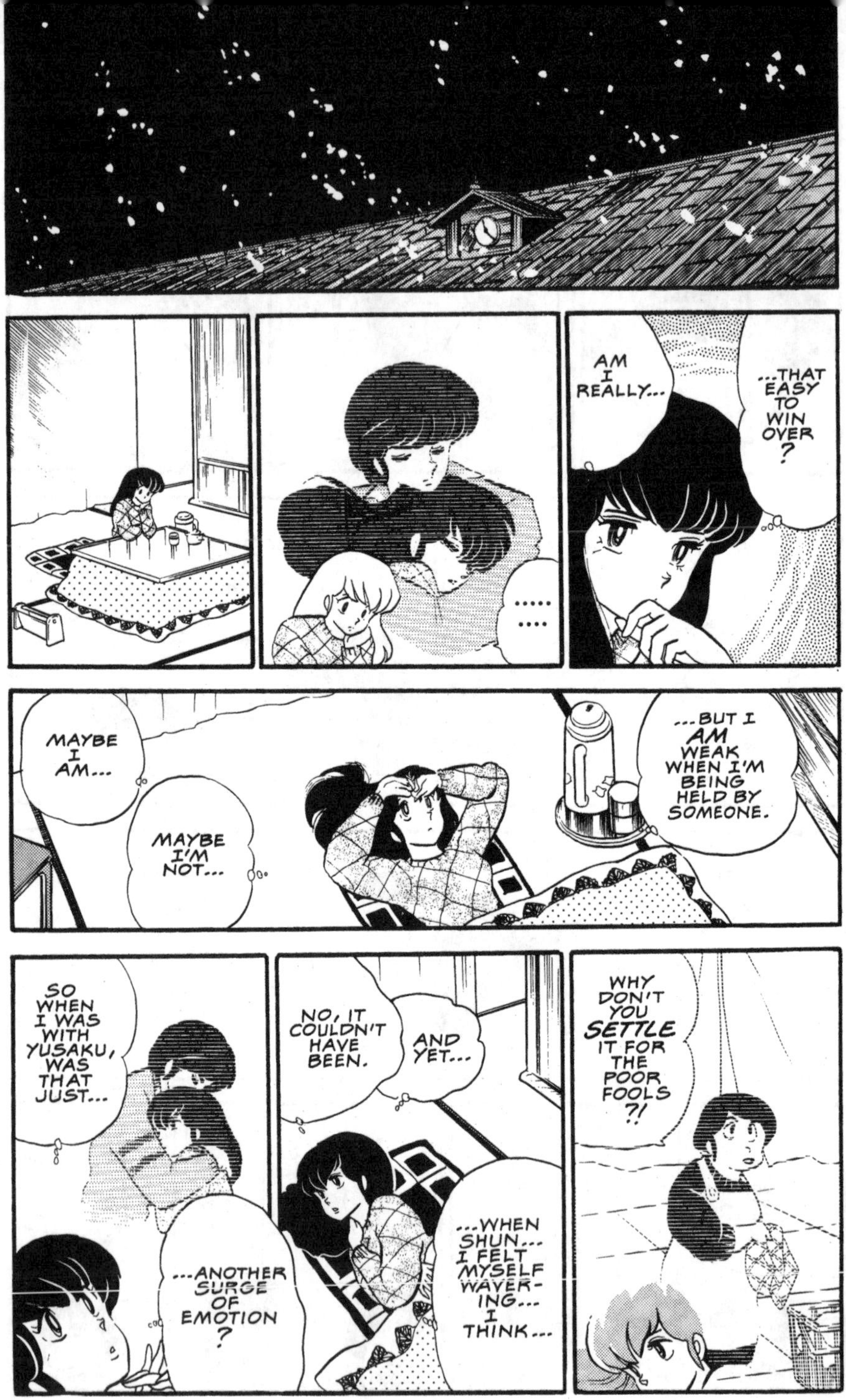

AM I REALLY...
...THAT EASY TO WIN OVER?
.....
....
MAYBE I AM...
MAYBE I'M NOT...
...BUT I AM WEAK WHEN I'M BEING HELD BY SOMEONE.
SO WHEN I WAS WITH YUSAKU, WAS THAT JUST...
...ANOTHER SURGE OF EMOTION?
NO, IT COULDN'T HAVE BEEN.
AND YET...
...WHEN SHUN... I FELT MYSELF WAVER-ING... I THINK...
WHY DON'T YOU SETTLE IT FOR THE POOR FOOLS?!

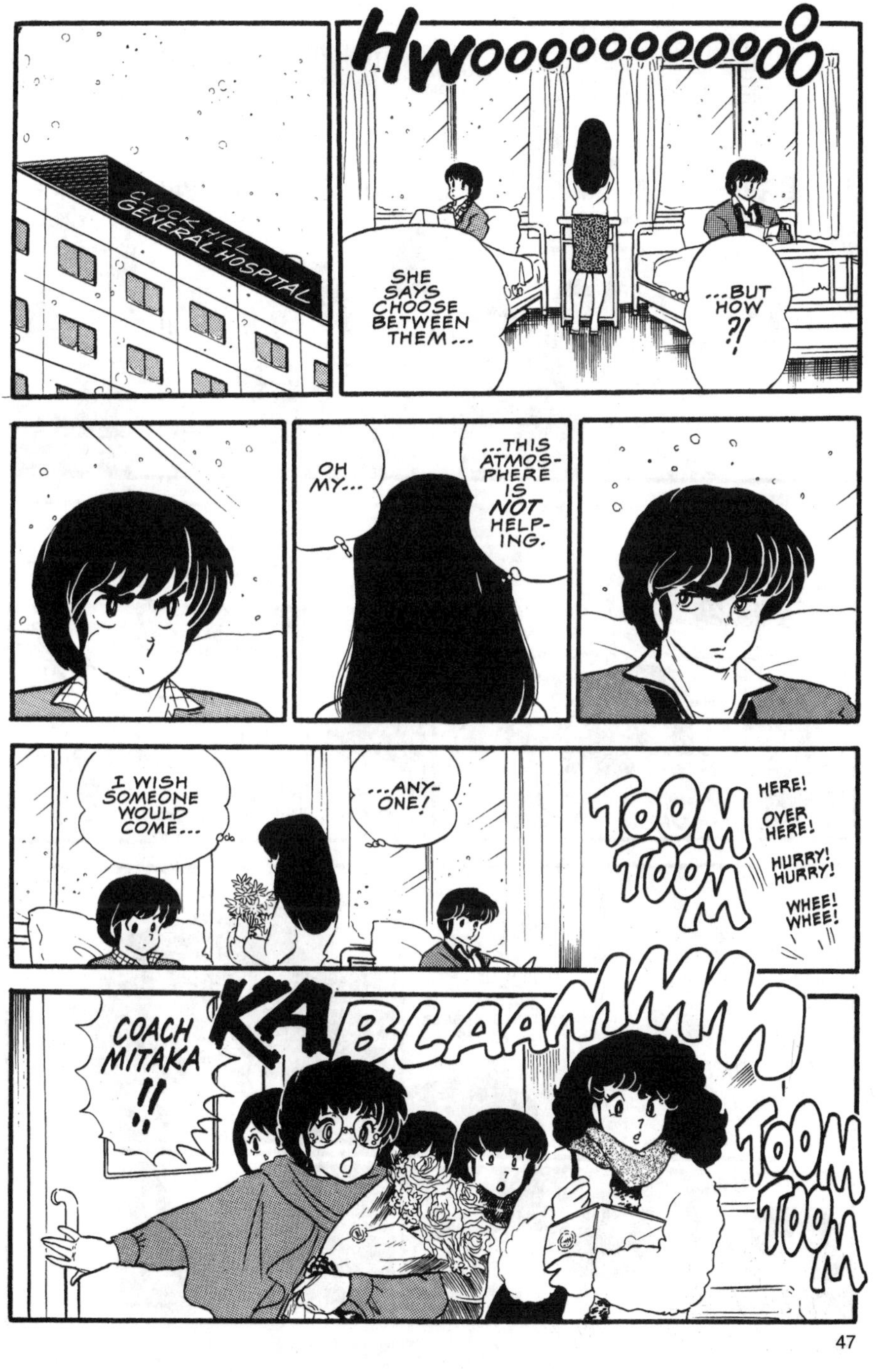
CLOCK HILL GENERAL HOSPITAL
HWOOOOOOOOOOOO
SHE SAYS CHOOSE BETWEEN THEM...
...BUT HOW ?!
OH MY...
...THIS ATMOSPHERE IS NOT HELPING.
I WISH SOMEONE WOULD COME...
...ANYONE!
TOOM TOOM
HERE!
OVER HERE!
HURRY! HURRY!
WHEE! WHEE!
KABLAAMMM
COACH MITAKA !!
TOOM TOOM

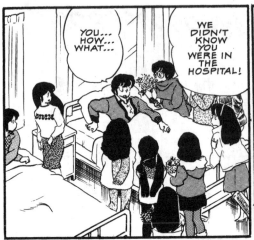

YOU... HOW... WHAT...

WE DIDN'T KNOW YOU WERE IN THE HOSPITAL!

WHEN WE SHOWED UP FOR LESSONS THEY SAID YOU WERE ON LEAVE!

YOU LOOK SO MISERABLE!

TH-THESE LADIES ARE TENNIS STUDENTS AT THE WOMEN'S COLLEGE WHERE I COACH.

HOW... NICE.

POOR BABY! SIGH!

WHOA, MITAKA! I THOUGHT YOU WERE ONLY POPULAR WITH THE OLDER LADIES, BUT IT LOOKS LIKE YOU'VE GOT A YOUNGER FOLLOWING TOO!

OH, NO, NO... NOT AT ALL--!

OH, COME ON! YOU'RE SO MODEST!

SO WHY DID IT TAKE YOU THREE MONTHS TO GET AROUND TO THAT *DATE* YOU PROMISED ME, HUH?

TEE HEE TEE HEE HEE

....

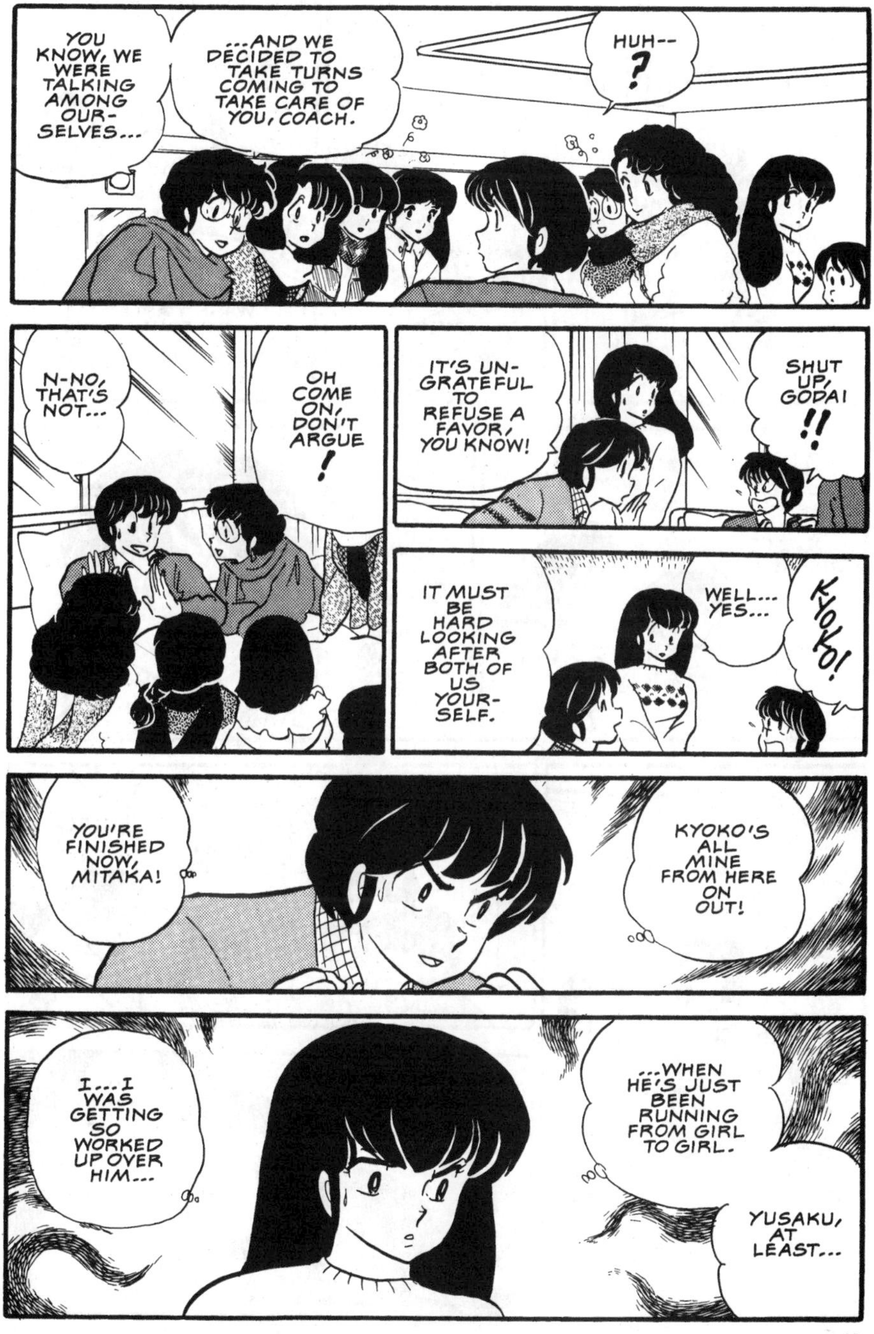
YOU KNOW, WE WERE TALKING AMONG OUR-SELVES...
...AND WE DECIDED TO TAKE TURNS COMING TO TAKE CARE OF YOU, COACH.
HUH--?
N-NO, THAT'S NOT...
OH COME ON, DON'T ARGUE!
IT'S UN-GRATEFUL TO REFUSE A FAVOR, YOU KNOW!
SHUT UP, GODAI!!
IT MUST BE HARD LOOKING AFTER BOTH OF US YOUR-SELF.
WELL... YES...
KYOKO!
YOU'RE FINISHED NOW, MITAKA!
KYOKO'S ALL MINE FROM HERE ON OUT!
I...I WAS GETTING SO WORKED UP OVER HIM...
...WHEN HE'S JUST BEEN RUNNING FROM GIRL TO GIRL.
YUSAKU, AT LEAST...

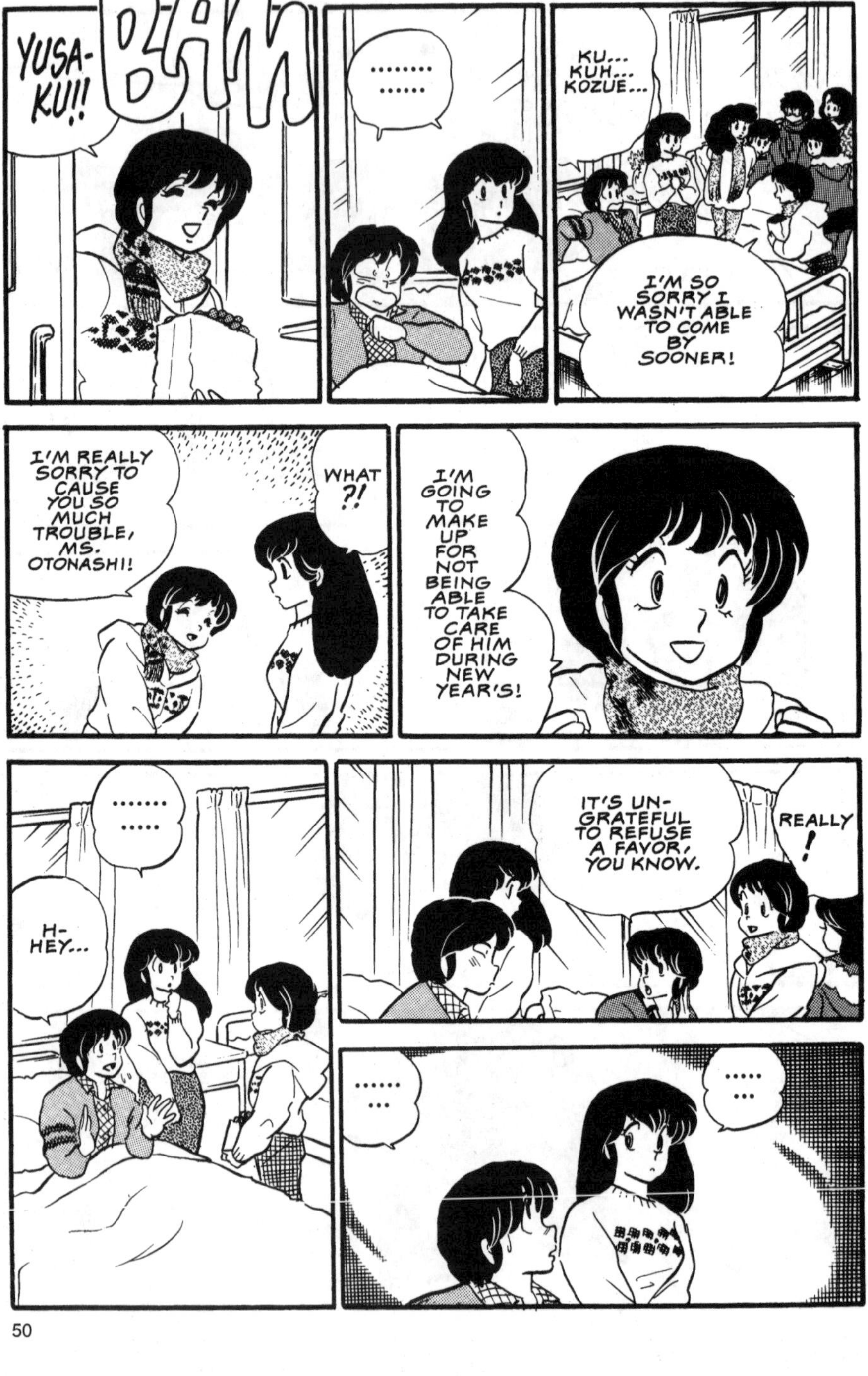
YUSA-KU!!
BAM
....
KU... KUH... KOZUE...
I'M SO SORRY I WASN'T ABLE TO COME BY SOONER!
I'M REALLY SORRY TO CAUSE YOU SO MUCH TROUBLE, MS. OTONASHI!
WHAT ?!
I'M GOING TO MAKE UP FOR NOT BEING ABLE TO TAKE CARE OF HIM DURING NEW YEAR'S!
....
H-HEY...
IT'S UN-GRATEFUL TO REFUSE A FAVOR, YOU KNOW.
REALLY !
....
....

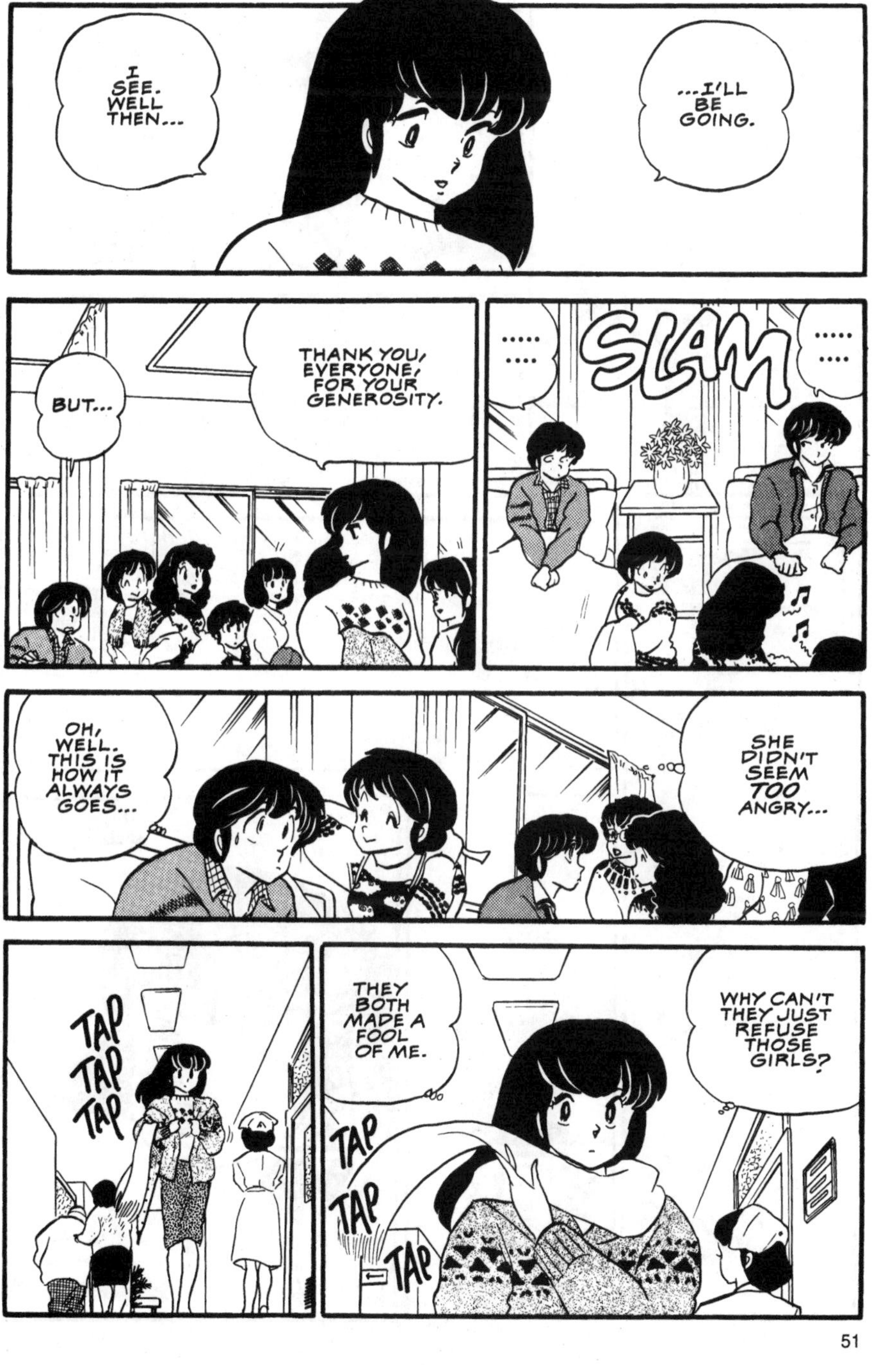
I SEE. WELL THEN...
...I'LL BE GOING.
BUT...
THANK YOU, EVERYONE, FOR YOUR GENEROSITY.
.....
.....
SLAM
.....
.....
OH, WELL. THIS IS HOW IT ALWAYS GOES...
SHE DIDN'T SEEM TOO ANGRY...
TAP TAP TAP
THEY BOTH MADE A FOOL OF ME.
WHY CAN'T THEY JUST REFUSE THOSE GIRLS?
TAP
TAP
TAP

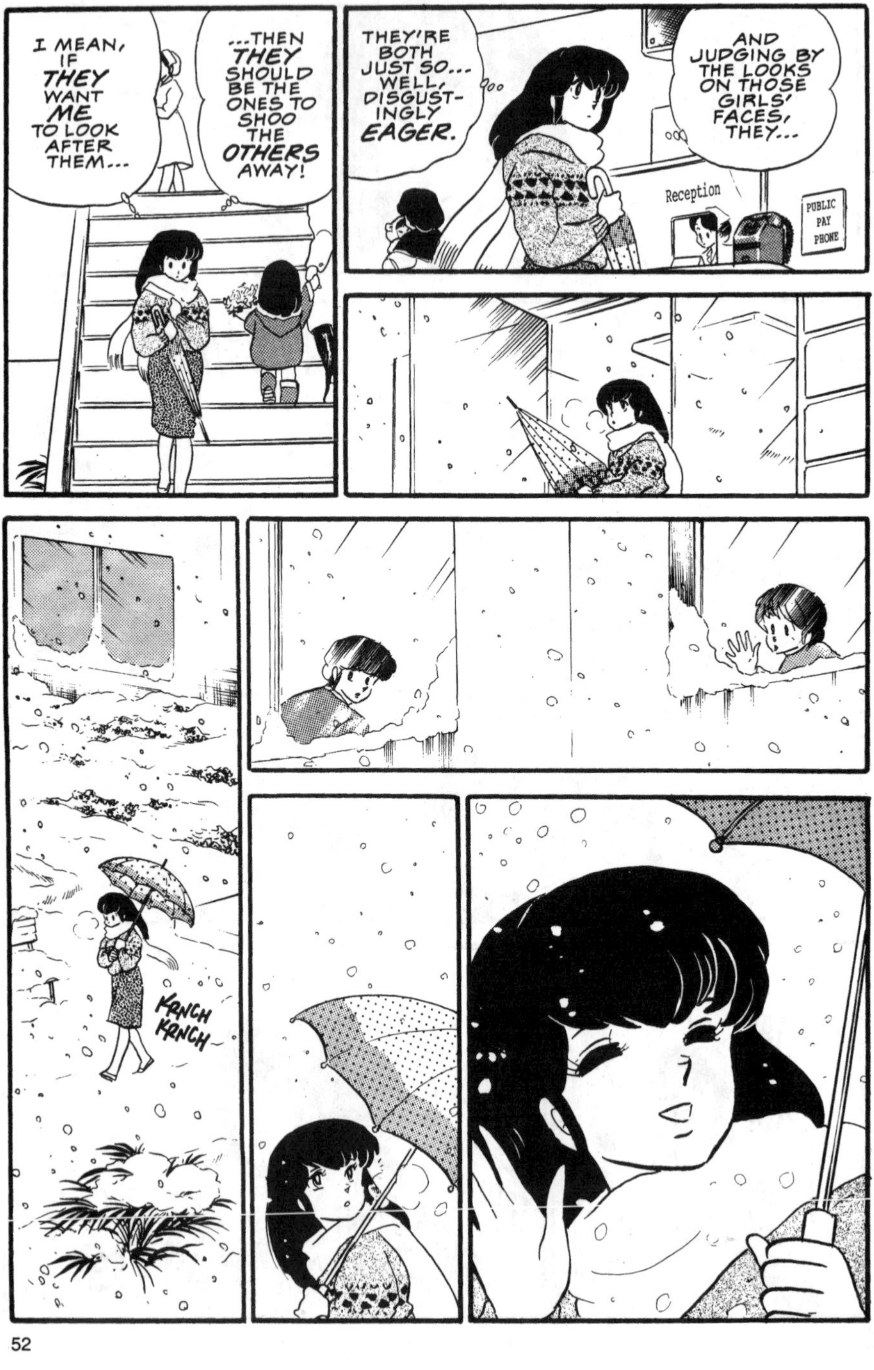
I MEAN, IF THEY WANT ME TO LOOK AFTER THEM...
...THEN THEY SHOULD BE THE ONES TO SHOO THE OTHERS AWAY!
THEY'RE BOTH JUST SO... WELL, DISGUSTINGLY EAGER.
AND JUDGING BY THE LOOKS ON THOSE GIRLS' FACES, THEY...
Reception
PUBLIC PAY PHONE
KRNCH KRNCH

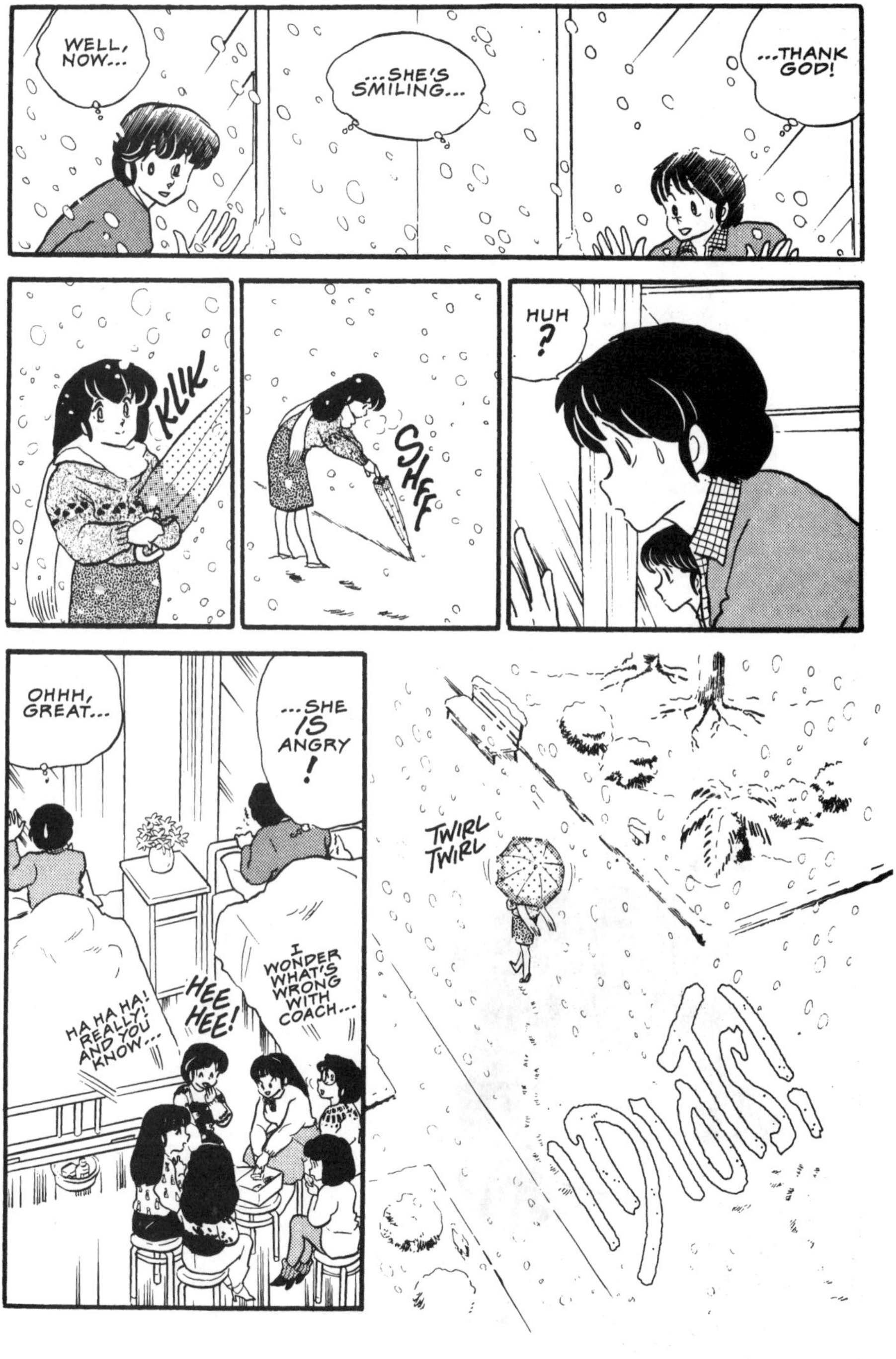
WELL, NOW...
...SHE'S SMILING...
...THANK GOD!
KLIK
SHFF
HUH ?
OHHH, GREAT...
...SHE IS ANGRY !
HA HA HA! REALLY! AND YOU KNOW...
HEE HEE!
I WONDER WHAT'S WRONG WITH COACH...
TWIRL TWIRL
IDIOTS!

PART 3

MENDING A BREAK

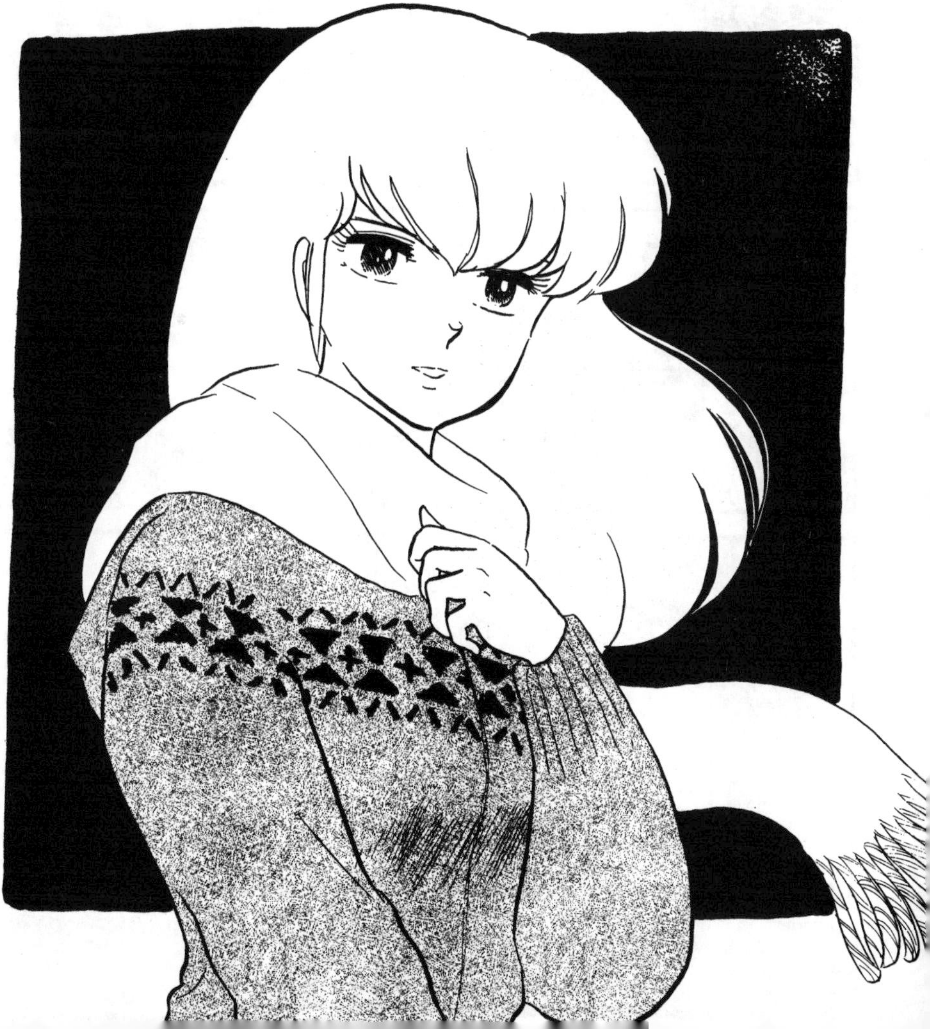

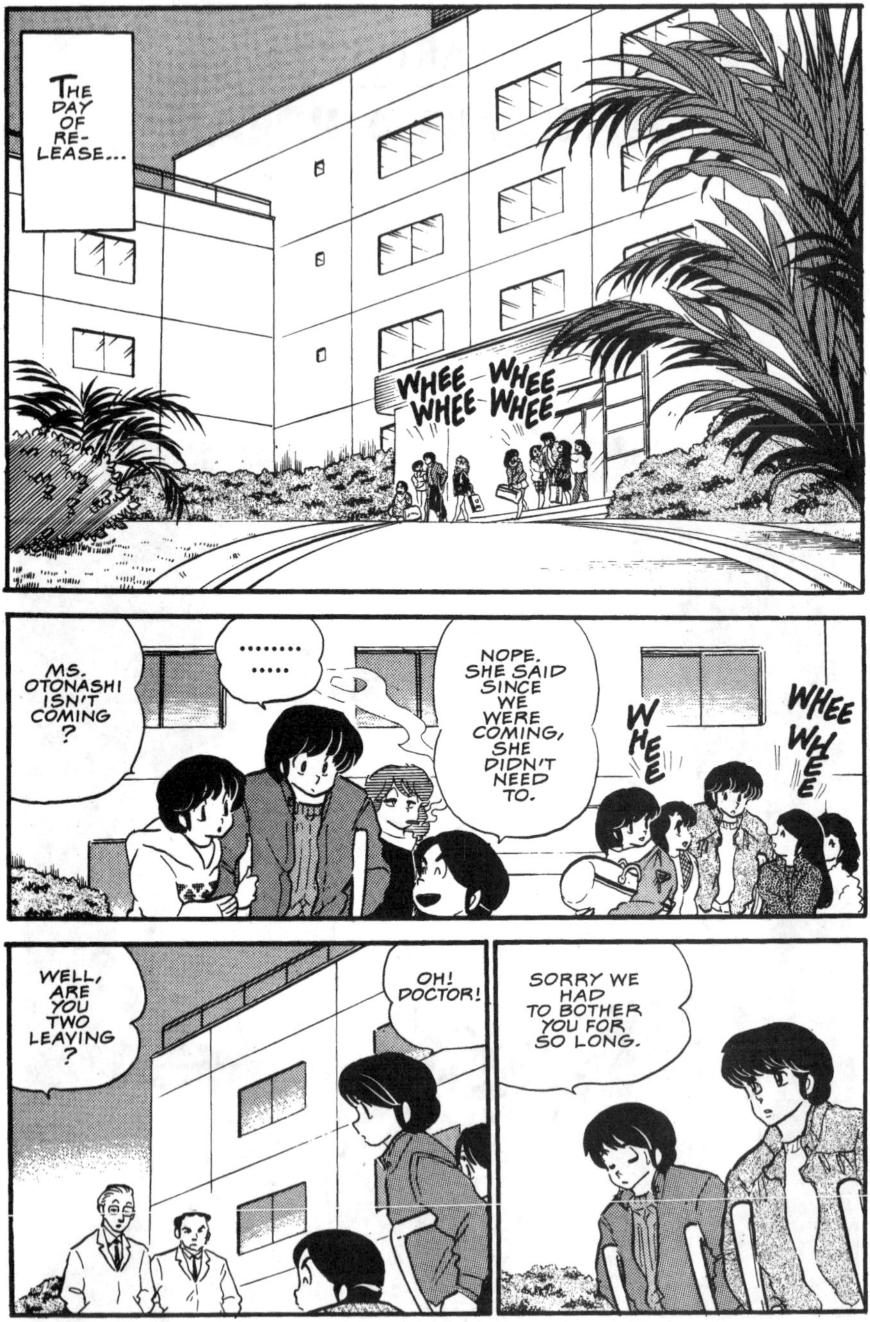
THE DAY OF RE-LEASE...
WHEE WHEE WHEE WHEE
MS. OTONASHI ISN'T COMING?
....
NOPE. SHE SAID SINCE WE WERE COMING, SHE DIDN'T NEED TO.
WHEE
WHEE WHEE
WELL, ARE YOU TWO LEAVING?
OH! DOCTOR!
SORRY WE HAD TO BOTHER YOU FOR SO LONG.

I'M JUST GLAD THAT THE TWO OF YOU ARE BEING RELEASED TOGETHER.

IF YOU'RE EVER HOSPITALIZED AGAIN, MAKE IT SOMEPLACE ELSE.

UH... GOTCHA.

WHAT DID YOU DO THIS TIME?

IT'S BECAUSE OF YOU GUYS PARTYING IN THE ROOM ALL THE TIME!

WELL, TAKE CARE, COACH MITAKA.

THANKS.

COACH, WHEN WE GET TO YOUR PLACE, CAN WE HAVE A WELCOME BACK PARTY? CAN WE?

SEE YA, YUSAKU!

SEE YA!

WELL, AREN'T YOU LUCKY, MAKING FRIENDS WITH ALL THOSE CUTE GIRLS.

KYOKO MUST STILL BE FURIOUS...

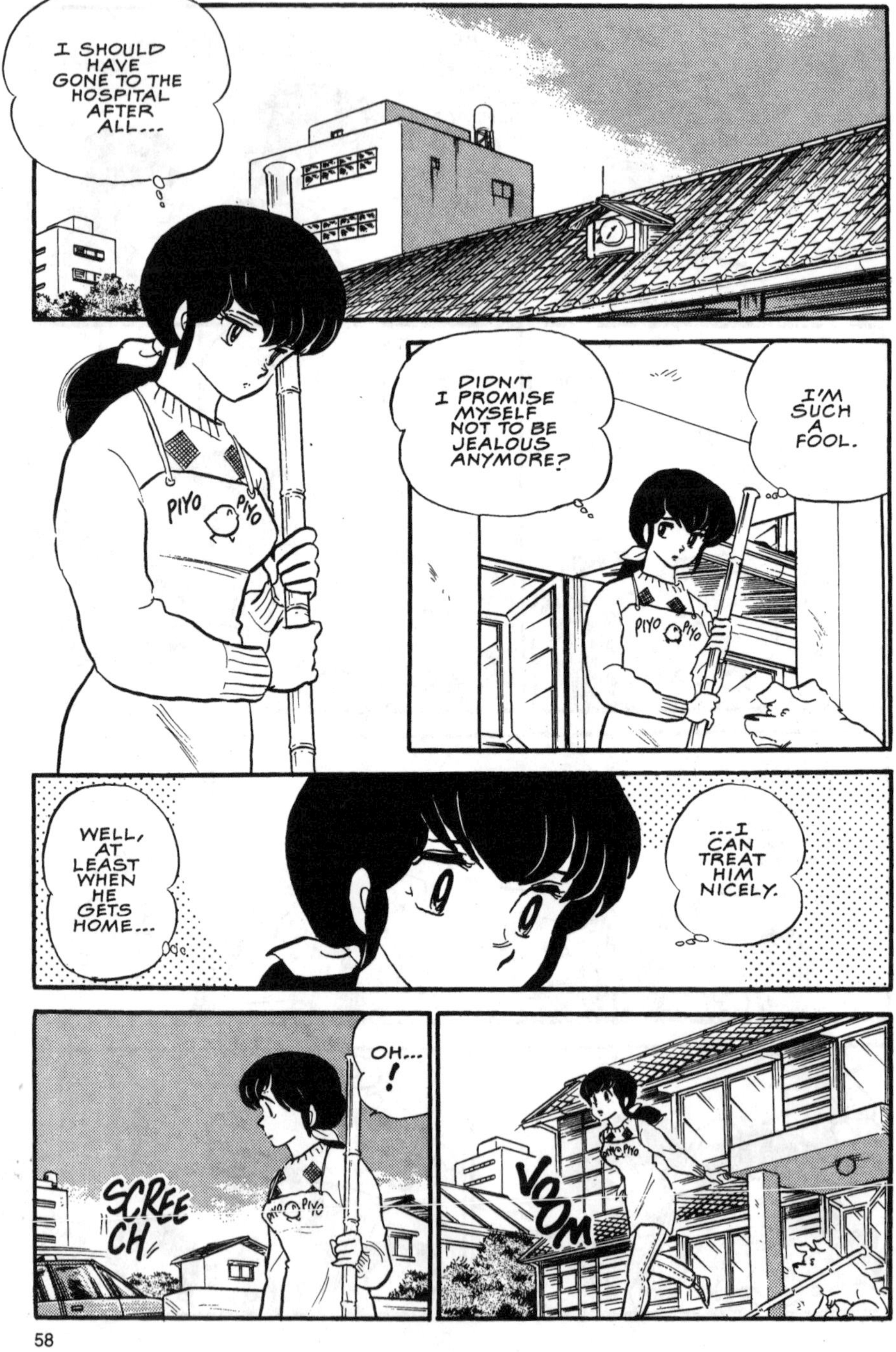
I SHOULD HAVE GONE TO THE HOSPITAL AFTER ALL...
DIDN'T I PROMISE MYSELF NOT TO BE JEALOUS ANYMORE?
I'M SUCH A FOOL.
WELL, AT LEAST WHEN HE GETS HOME...
...I CAN TREAT HIM NICELY.
SCREECH
OH...!
VOOM

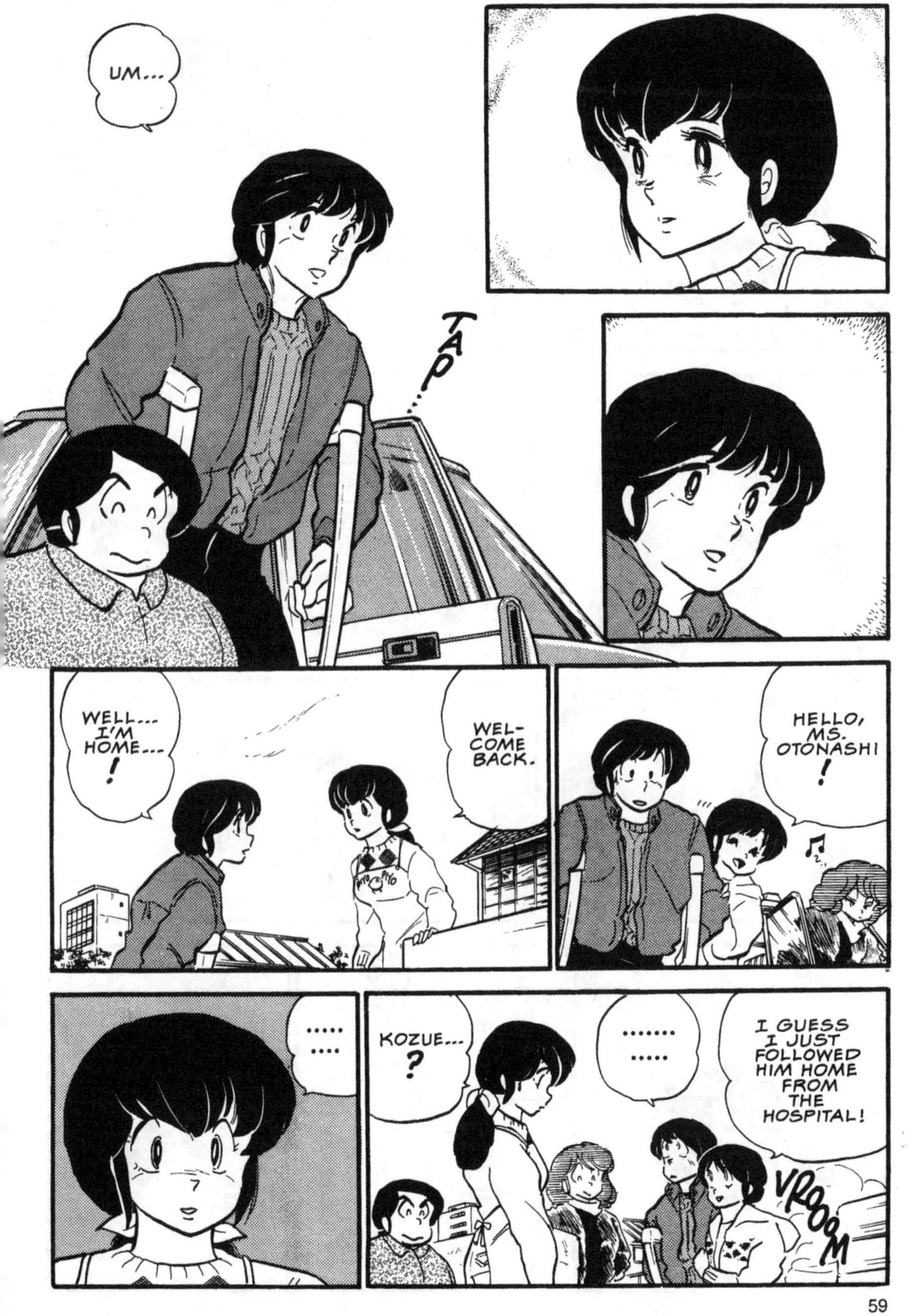
UM...
TAP...
WELL... I'M HOME...!
WEL-COME BACK.
HELLO, MS. OTONASHI!
....
KOZUE...?
....
I GUESS I JUST FOLLOWED HIM HOME FROM THE HOSPITAL!
VROOOM

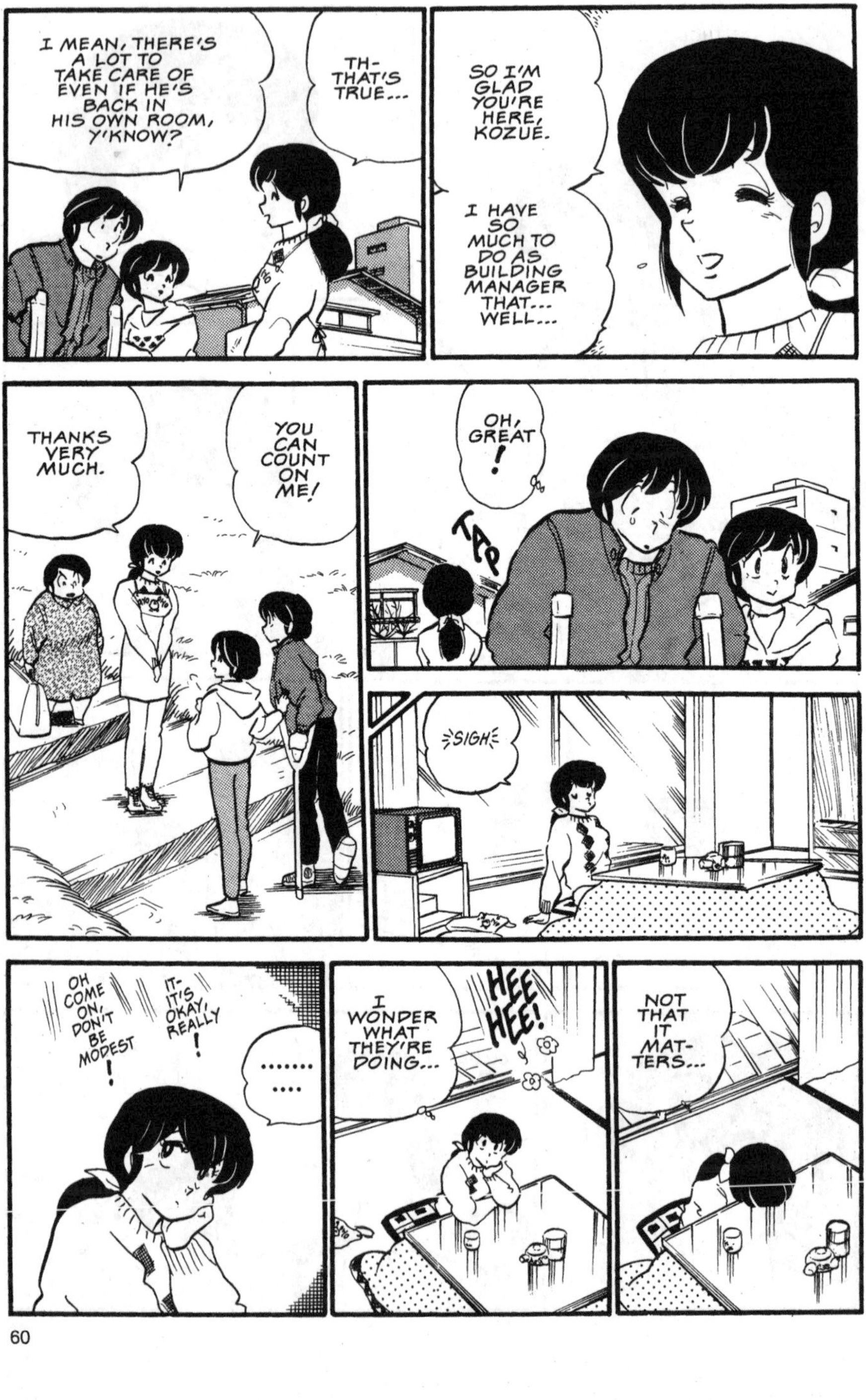
I MEAN, THERE'S A LOT TO TAKE CARE OF EVEN IF HE'S BACK IN HIS OWN ROOM, Y'KNOW?
TH-THAT'S TRUE...
SO I'M GLAD YOU'RE HERE, KOZUE.
I HAVE SO MUCH TO DO AS BUILDING MANAGER THAT... WELL...
THANKS VERY MUCH.
YOU CAN COUNT ON ME!
OH, GREAT!
TAP
SIGH
OH COME ON, DON'T BE MODEST!
IT-IT'S OKAY, REALLY!
....
I WONDER WHAT THEY'RE DOING...
HEE HEE!
NOT THAT IT MAT-TERS...

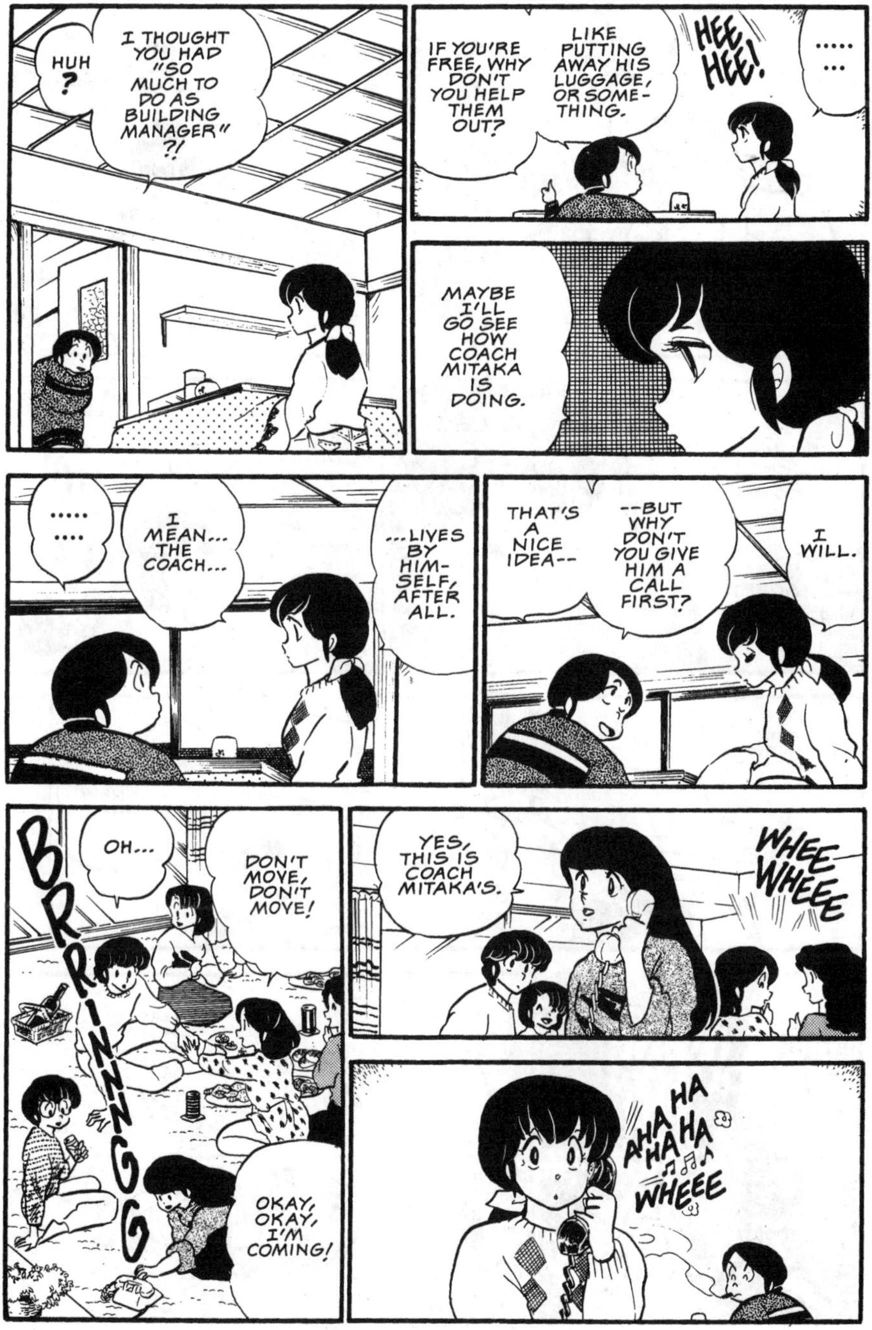
.....
...
HEE HEE!
LIKE PUTTING AWAY HIS LUGGAGE, OR SOME-THING.
IF YOU'RE FREE, WHY DON'T YOU HELP THEM OUT?
I THOUGHT YOU HAD "SO MUCH TO DO AS BUILDING MANAGER"?!
HUH?
MAYBE I'LL GO SEE HOW COACH MITAKA IS DOING.
I WILL.
--BUT WHY DON'T YOU GIVE HIM A CALL FIRST?
THAT'S A NICE IDEA--
...LIVES BY HIM-SELF, AFTER ALL.
I MEAN... THE COACH...
.....
....
WHEE WHEEE
YES, THIS IS COACH MITAKA'S.
DON'T MOVE, DON'T MOVE!
OH...
BRRRINNNGG
OKAY, OKAY, I'M COMING!
AHAHA HAHA WHEEE

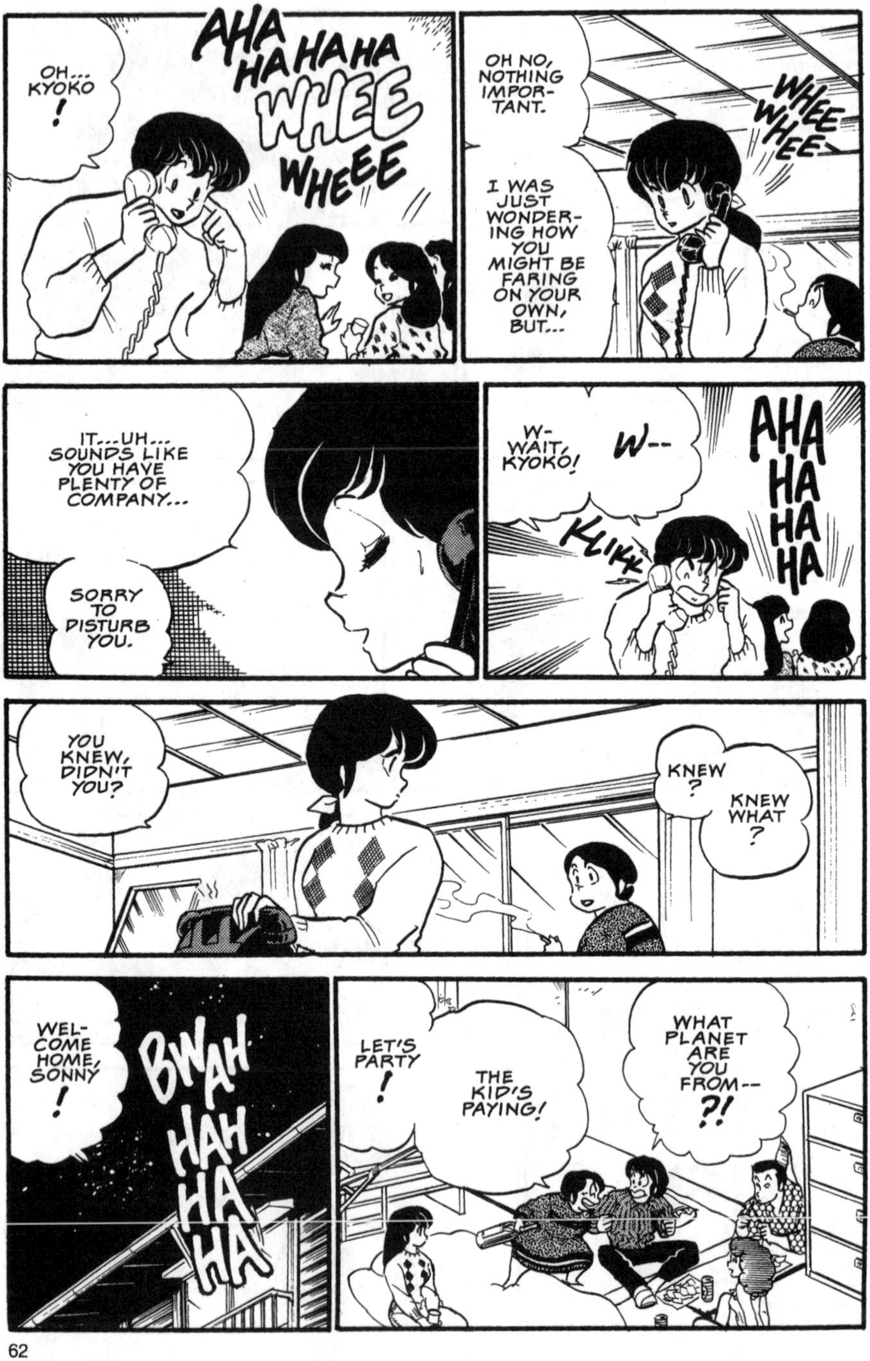
OH... KYOKO!
AHA HAHAHA WHEE WHEEE
OH NO, NOTHING IMPORTANT.
WHEE WHEE
I WAS JUST WONDERING HOW YOU MIGHT BE FARING ON YOUR OWN, BUT...
IT...UH... SOUNDS LIKE YOU HAVE PLENTY OF COMPANY...
SORRY TO DISTURB YOU.
W-WAIT, KYOKO!
W--
AHA HA HA HA HA
KLIKK
YOU KNEW, DIDN'T YOU?
KNEW?
KNEW WHAT?
WEL-COME HOME, SONNY!
BWAH HAH HA HA HA
LET'S PARTY!
THE KID'S PAYING!
WHAT PLANET ARE YOU FROM--?!

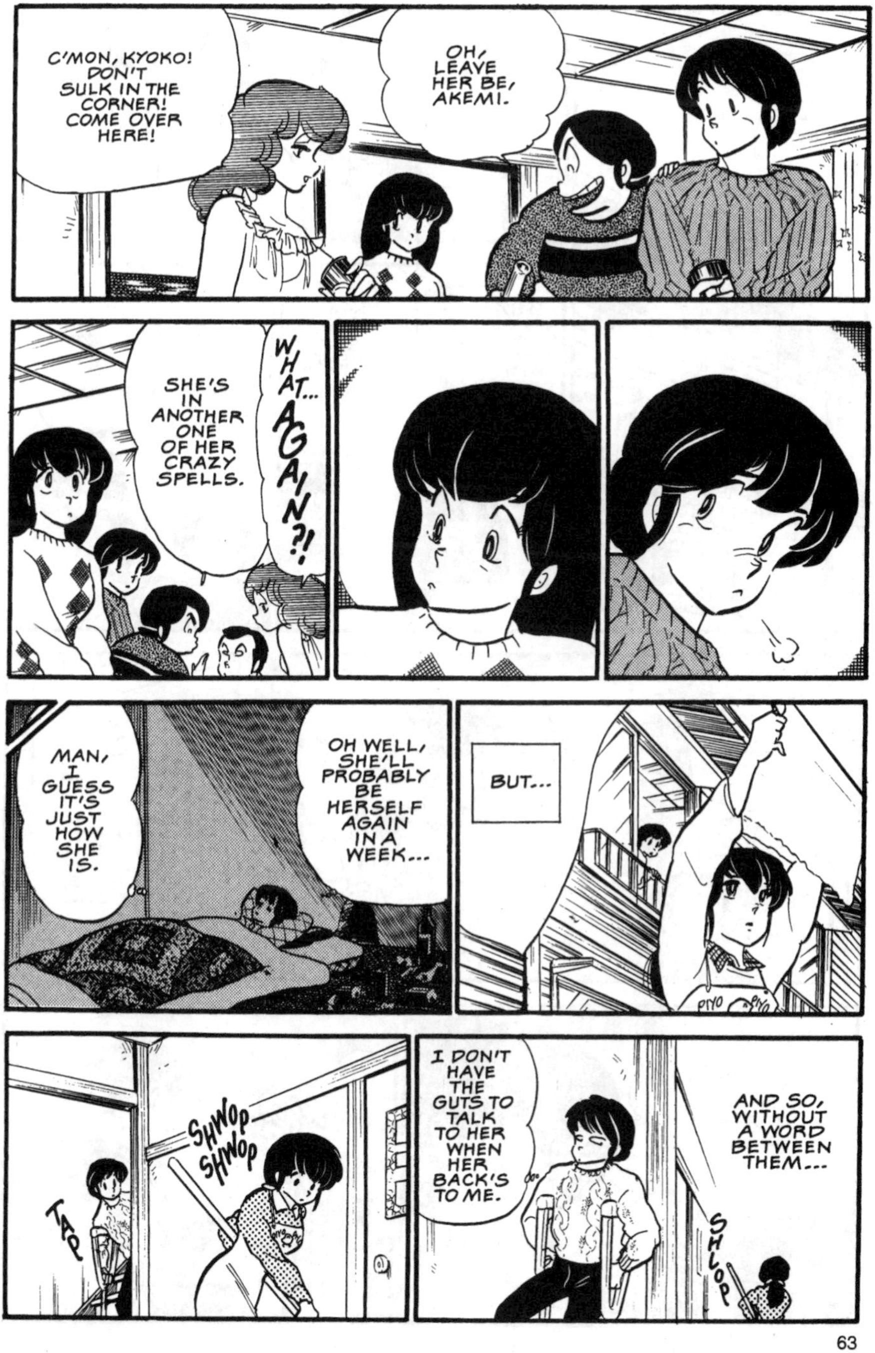
C'MON, KYOKO! DON'T SULK IN THE CORNER! COME OVER HERE!
OH, LEAVE HER BE, AKEMI.
SHE'S IN ANOTHER ONE OF HER CRAZY SPELLS.
WHAT... AGAIN?!
MAN, I GUESS IT'S JUST HOW SHE IS.
OH WELL, SHE'LL PROBABLY BE HERSELF AGAIN IN A WEEK...
BUT...
PIYO PIYO
TAP
SHWOP SHWOP
I DON'T HAVE THE GUTS TO TALK TO HER WHEN HER BACK'S TO ME.
AND SO, WITHOUT A WORD BETWEEN THEM...
SHLOP

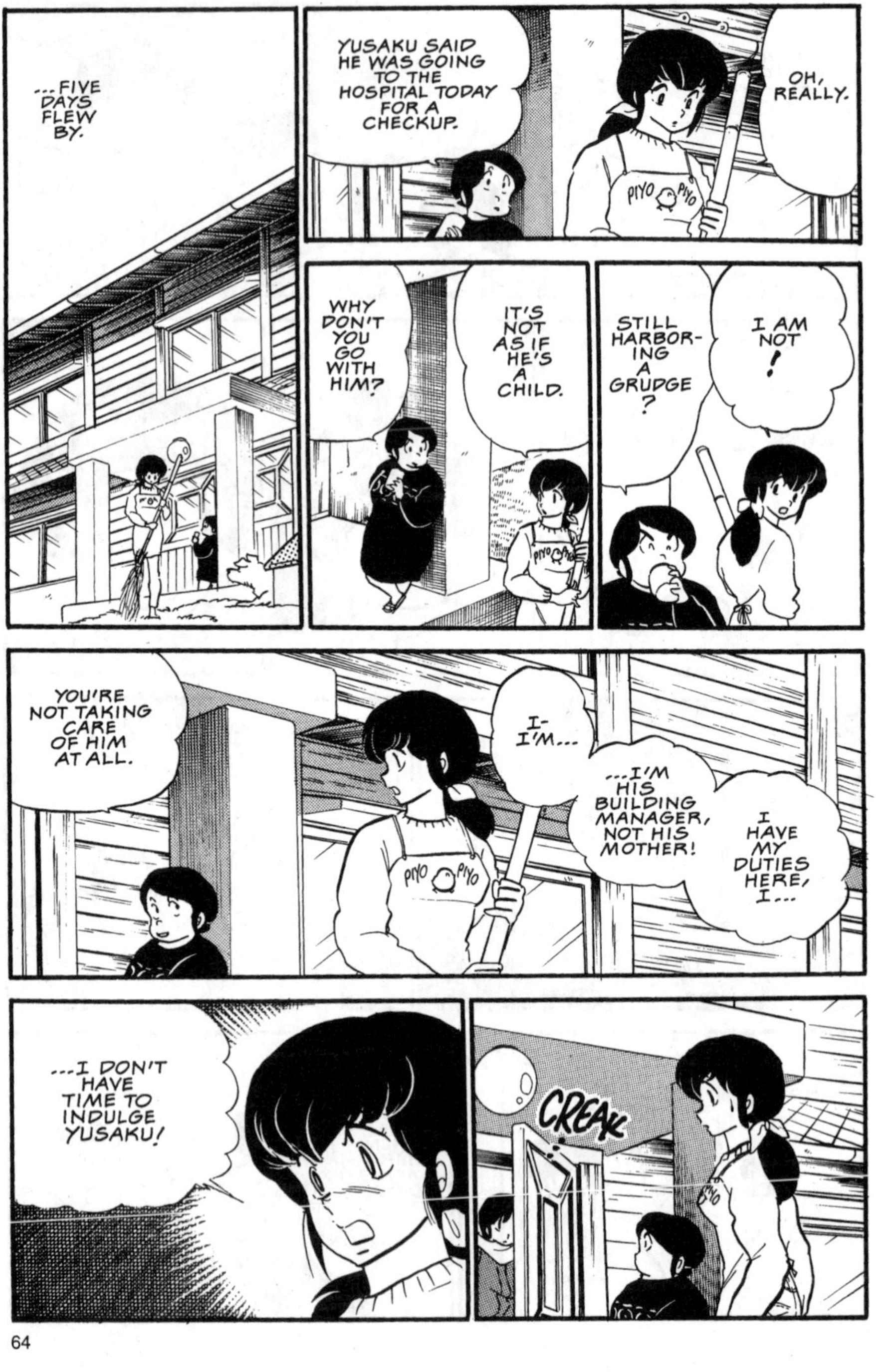
...FIVE DAYS FLEW BY.
YUSAKU SAID HE WAS GOING TO THE HOSPITAL TODAY FOR A CHECKUP.
OH, REALLY.
PIYO PIYO
WHY DON'T YOU GO WITH HIM?
IT'S NOT AS IF HE'S A CHILD.
STILL HARBOR-ING A GRUDGE?
I AM NOT!
YOU'RE NOT TAKING CARE OF HIM AT ALL.
I- I'M...
...I'M HIS BUILDING MANAGER, NOT HIS MOTHER!
I HAVE MY DUTIES HERE, I...
...I DON'T HAVE TIME TO INDULGE YUSAKU!
CREAK

OH...

TAP

HE'S PRETTY DE-PRESSED.

TAP

SWIp

YOU *KNEW* HE WAS THERE, DIDN'T YOU!?

THIS TIME WAS AN ACCIDENT! I SWEAR!

HE SEEMED AWFUL HURT, THOUGH.

POOR KID...

CLOCK HILL GENERAL HOSPITAL

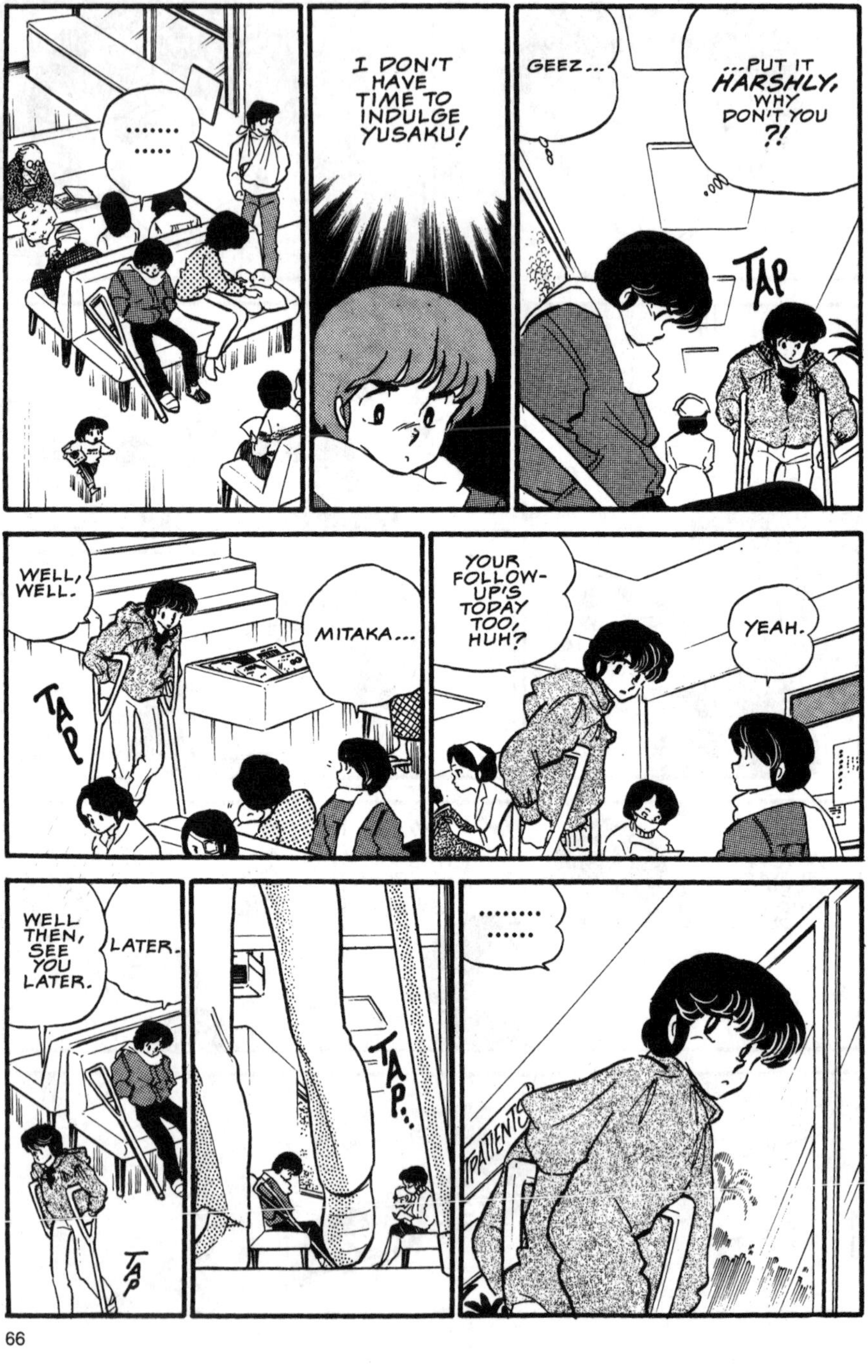

....
......
I DON'T HAVE TIME TO INDULGE YUSAKU!
GEEZ...
...PUT IT HARSHLY, WHY DON'T YOU ?!
TAP
WELL, WELL.
TAP
MITAKA...
YOUR FOLLOW-UP'S TODAY TOO, HUH?
YEAH.
WELL THEN, SEE YOU LATER.
LATER.
TAP
TAP...
....
......

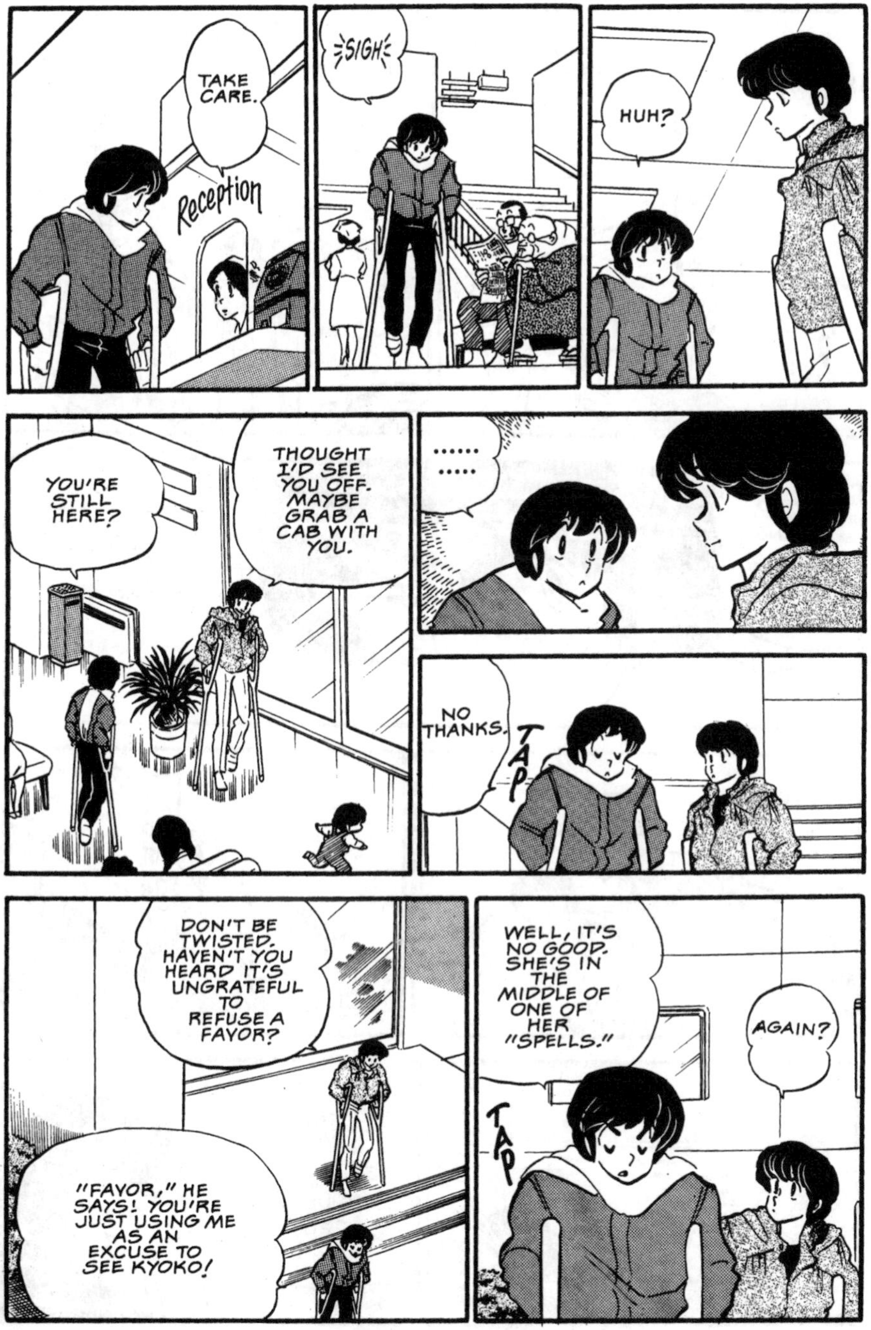
TAKE CARE.
Reception
SIGH
HUH?
YOU'RE STILL HERE?
THOUGHT I'D SEE YOU OFF. MAYBE GRAB A CAB WITH YOU.
......
.....
NO THANKS.
TAP
DON'T BE TWISTED. HAVEN'T YOU HEARD IT'S UNGRATEFUL TO REFUSE A FAVOR?
"FAVOR," HE SAYS! YOU'RE JUST USING ME AS AN EXCUSE TO SEE KYOKO!
WELL, IT'S NO GOOD. SHE'S IN THE MIDDLE OF ONE OF HER "SPELLS."
TAP
AGAIN?

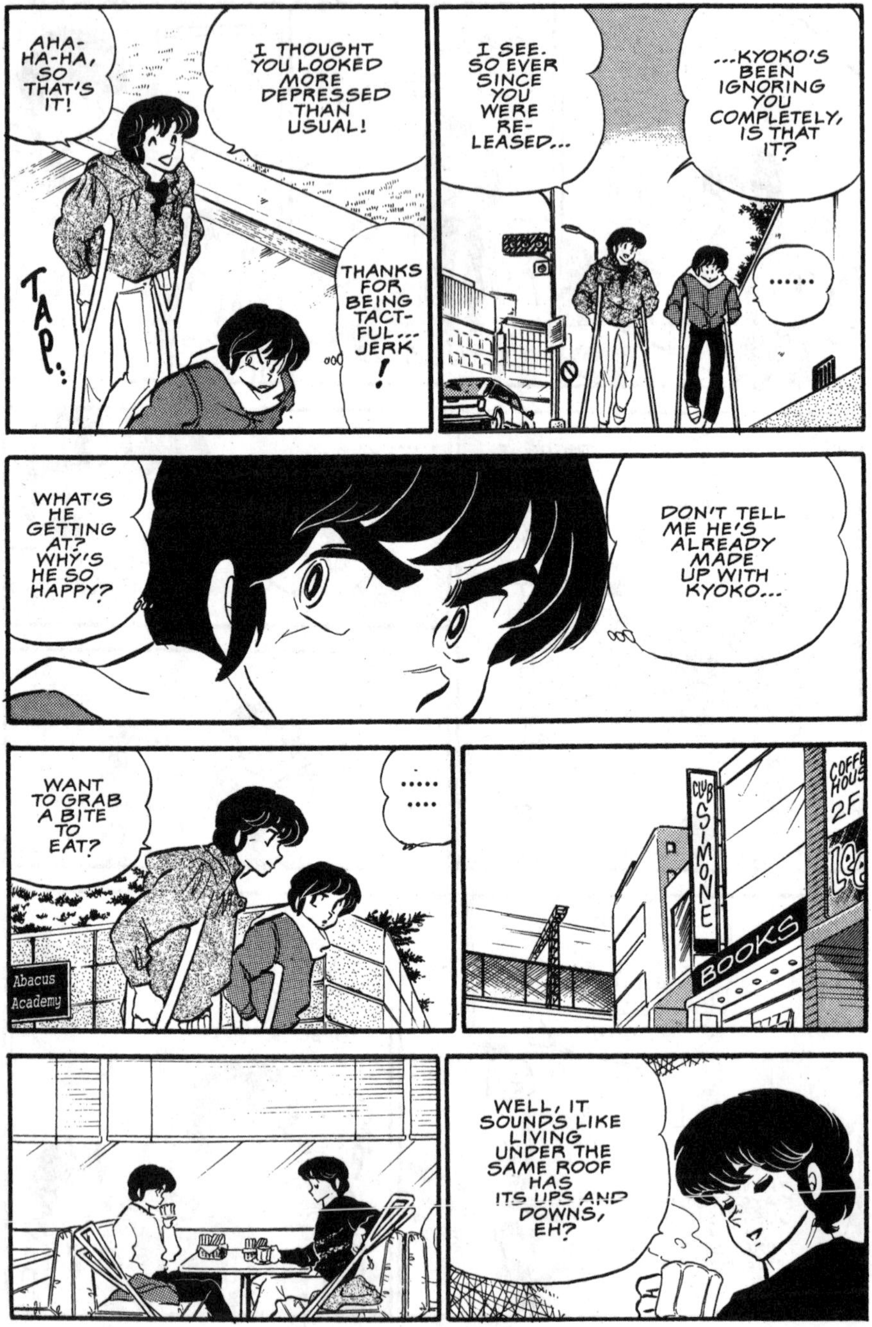
AHA-HA-HA, SO THAT'S IT!
I THOUGHT YOU LOOKED MORE DEPRESSED THAN USUAL!
TAP...
THANKS FOR BEING TACT-FUL... JERK!
I SEE. SO EVER SINCE YOU WERE RE-LEASED...
...KYOKO'S BEEN IGNORING YOU COMPLETELY, IS THAT IT?
......
WHAT'S HE GETTING AT? WHY'S HE SO HAPPY?
DON'T TELL ME HE'S ALREADY MADE UP WITH KYOKO...
WANT TO GRAB A BITE TO EAT?
....
Abacus Academy
CLUB SIMONE
BOOKS
COFFEE HOUS 2F
WELL, IT SOUNDS LIKE LIVING UNDER THE SAME ROOF HAS ITS UPS AND DOWNS, EH?

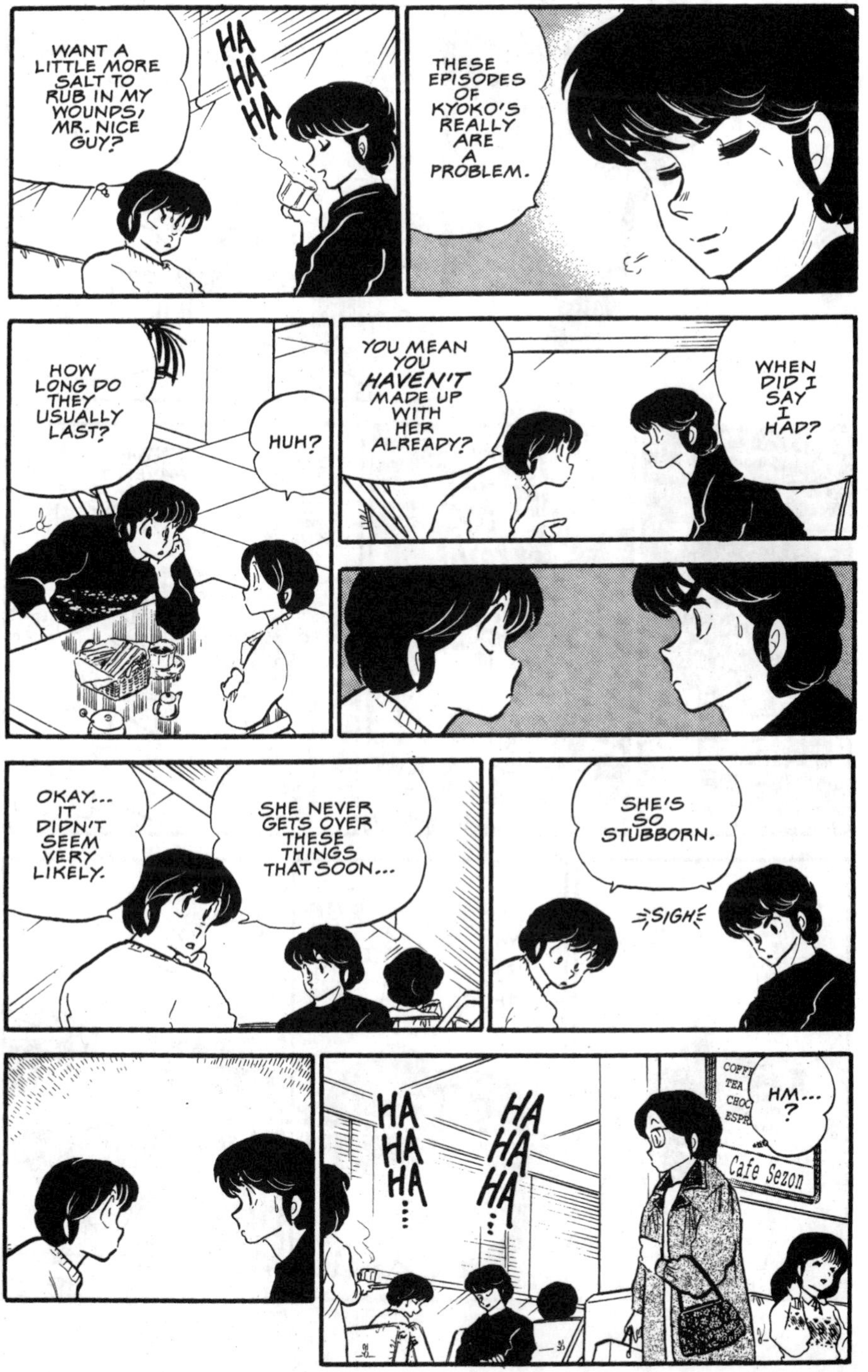
WANT A LITTLE MORE SALT TO RUB IN MY WOUNDS, MR. NICE GUY?
HA HA HA
THESE EPISODES OF KYOKO'S REALLY ARE A PROBLEM.
HOW LONG DO THEY USUALLY LAST?
HUH?
YOU MEAN YOU HAVEN'T MADE UP WITH HER ALREADY?
WHEN DID I SAY I HAD?
OKAY... IT DIDN'T SEEM VERY LIKELY.
SHE NEVER GETS OVER THESE THINGS THAT SOON...
SHE'S SO STUBBORN.
SIGH
HA HA HA...
HA HA HA...
COFF
TEA
CHOC
ESPR
HM...?
Cafe Sezon

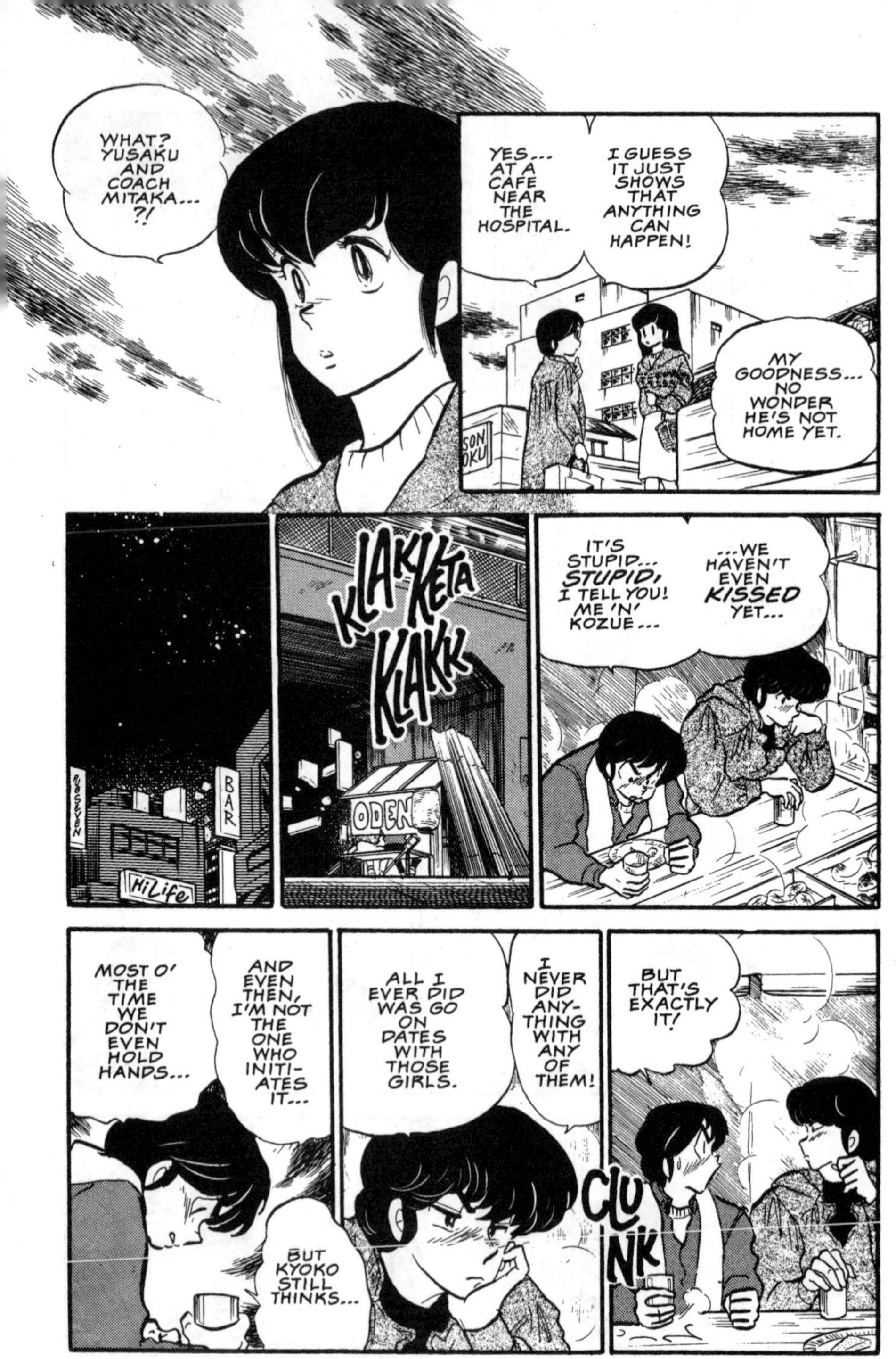
WHAT? YUSAKU AND COACH MITAKA...?!
YES... AT A CAFE NEAR THE HOSPITAL.
I GUESS IT JUST SHOWS THAT ANYTHING CAN HAPPEN!
MY GOODNESS... NO WONDER HE'S NOT HOME YET.
BAR
HiLife
KLAKKETA KLAKK
ODEN
IT'S STUPID... STUPID, I TELL YOU! ME 'N' KOZUE...
...WE HAVEN'T EVEN KISSED YET...
MOST O' THE TIME WE DON'T EVEN HOLD HANDS...
AND EVEN THEN, I'M NOT THE ONE WHO INITI-ATES IT...
BUT KYOKO STILL THINKS...
ALL I EVER DID WAS GO ON DATES WITH THOSE GIRLS.
I NEVER DID ANY-THING WITH ANY OF THEM!
BUT THAT'S EXACTLY IT!
CLUNK

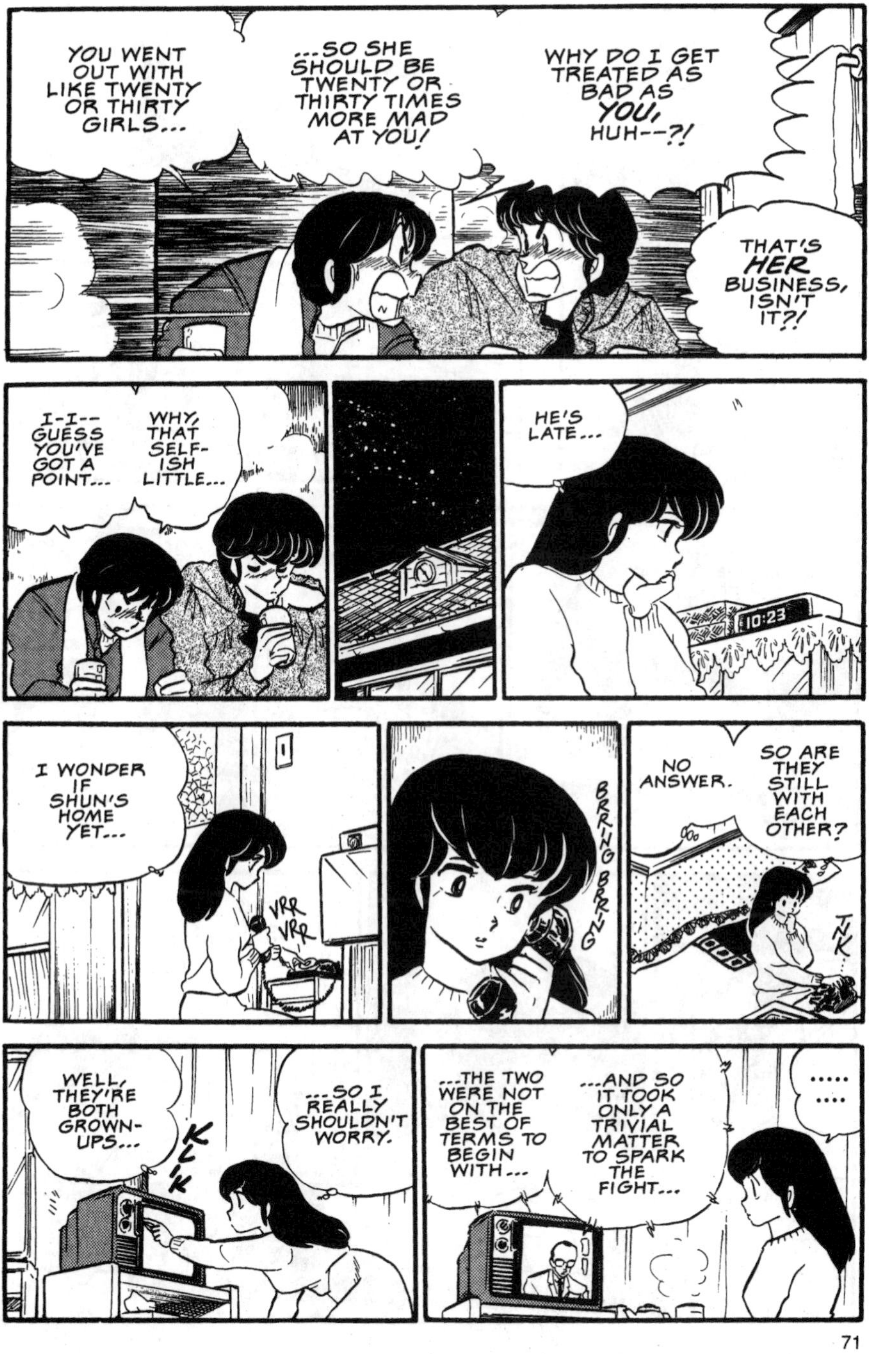
YOU WENT OUT WITH LIKE TWENTY OR THIRTY GIRLS...
...SO SHE SHOULD BE TWENTY OR THIRTY TIMES MORE MAD AT YOU!
WHY DO I GET TREATED AS BAD AS YOU, HUH--?!
THAT'S HER BUSINESS, ISN'T IT?!
I-I--GUESS YOU'VE GOT A POINT...
WHY, THAT SELF-ISH LITTLE...
HE'S LATE...
10:23
I WONDER IF SHUN'S HOME YET...
VRR VRR
BRRING BRRING
NO ANSWER.
SO ARE THEY STILL WITH EACH OTHER?
TNK...
WELL, THEY'RE BOTH GROWN-UPS...
KLIK
...SO I REALLY SHOULDN'T WORRY.
...THE TWO WERE NOT ON THE BEST OF TERMS TO BEGIN WITH...
...AND SO IT TOOK ONLY A TRIVIAL MATTER TO SPARK THE FIGHT...
.....
....

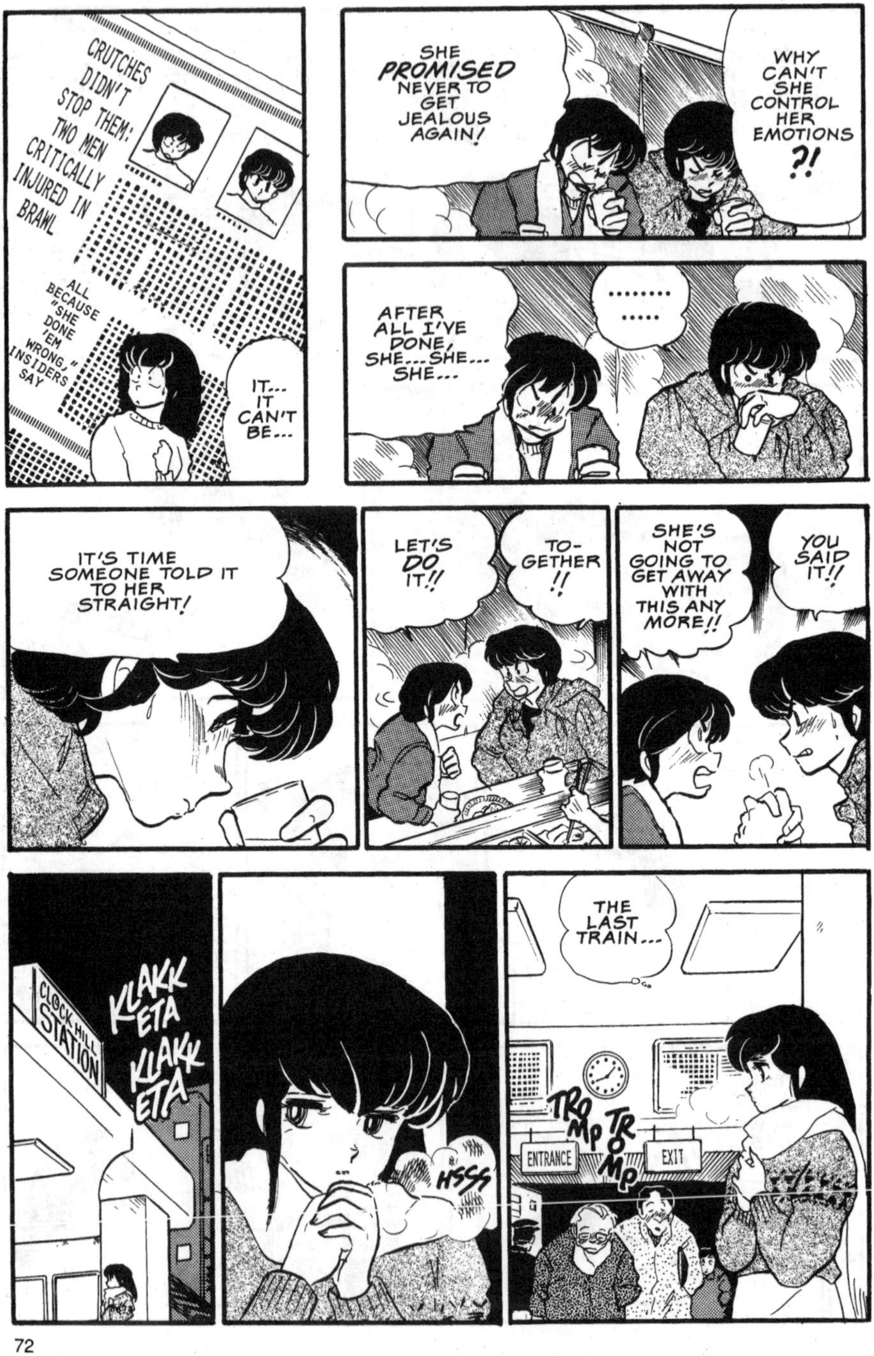
CRUTCHES DIDN'T STOP THEM: TWO MEN CRITICALLY INJURED IN BRAWL
ALL BECAUSE "SHE DONE 'EM WRONG," INSIDERS SAY
IT... IT CAN'T BE...
SHE PROMISED NEVER TO GET JEALOUS AGAIN!
WHY CAN'T SHE CONTROL HER EMOTIONS ?!
AFTER ALL I'VE DONE, SHE...SHE... SHE...
....
IT'S TIME SOMEONE TOLD IT TO HER STRAIGHT!
LET'S DO IT!!
TO-GETHER !!
SHE'S NOT GOING TO GET AWAY WITH THIS ANY MORE!!
YOU SAID IT!!
CLOCK HILL STATION
KLAKK ETA KLAKK ETA
HSSS
THE LAST TRAIN...
TROMP TROMP
ENTRANCE
EXIT

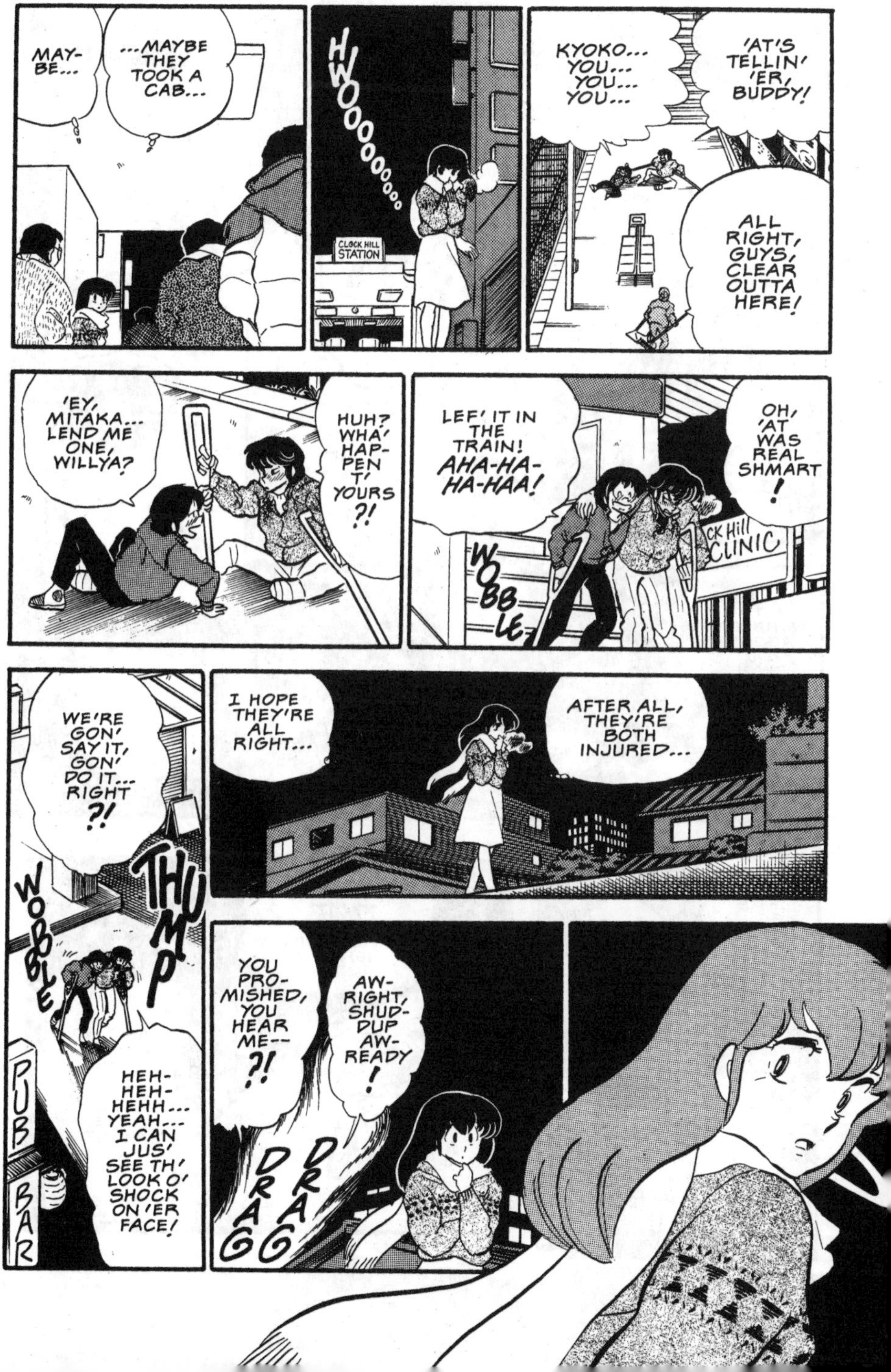
MAY-BE...
...MAYBE THEY TOOK A CAB...
HWOOOOOOoooo
CLOCK HILL STATION
KYOKO... YOU... YOU... YOU...
'AT'S TELLIN' 'ER, BUDDY!
ALL RIGHT, GUYS, CLEAR OUTTA HERE!
'EY, MITAKA... LEND ME ONE, WILLYA?
HUH? WHA' HAP-PEN T' YOURS ?!
LEF' IT IN THE TRAIN! AHA-HA-HA-HAA!
OH, 'AT WAS REAL SHMART !
CK Hill CLINIC
WOBBLE
WE'RE GON' SAY IT, GON' DO IT... RIGHT ?!
THUMP
WOBBLE
PUB BAR
I HOPE THEY'RE ALL RIGHT...
AFTER ALL, THEY'RE BOTH INJURED...
YOU PRO-MISHED, YOU HEAR ME-- ?!
AW-RIGHT, SHUD-DUP AW-READY !
HEH-HEH-HEHH... YEAH... I CAN JUS' SEE TH' LOOK O' SHOCK ON 'ER FACE!
DRAG
DRAG

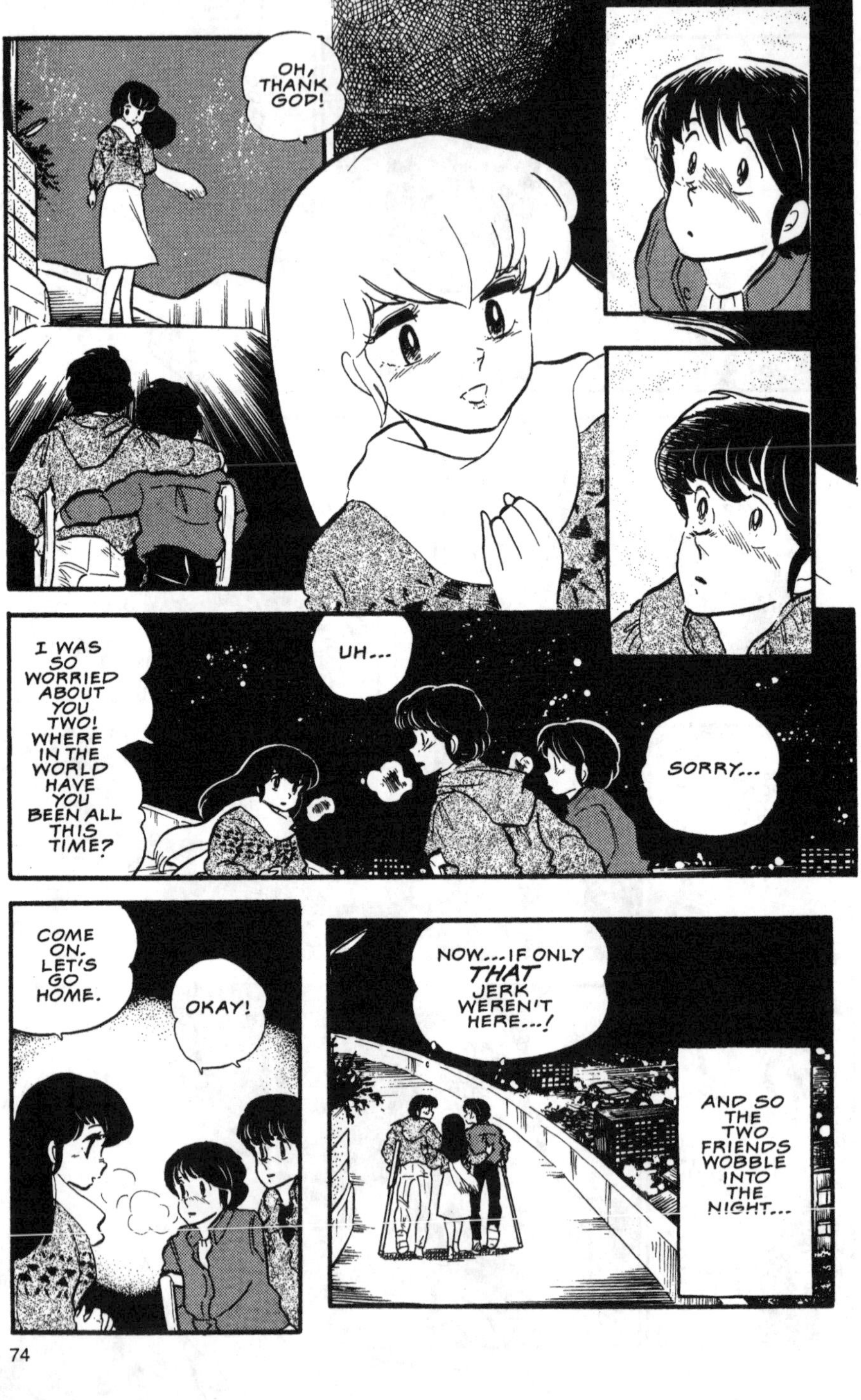
OH, THANK GOD!
I WAS SO WORRIED ABOUT YOU TWO! WHERE IN THE WORLD HAVE YOU BEEN ALL THIS TIME?
UH...
SORRY...
COME ON. LET'S GO HOME.
OKAY!
NOW...IF ONLY THAT JERK WEREN'T HERE...!
AND SO THE TWO FRIENDS WOBBLE INTO THE NIGHT...

PART 4

JUST DO YOUR BEST!

CUT ON DOTTED LINE

TO PASS YOUR TESTS

AMULET
BEST OF LUCK, ______!!!
YOU PASSED!

JUST CUT OUT, INSERT YOUR NAME, AND CARRY IN YOUR WALLET ON EXAM DAY!

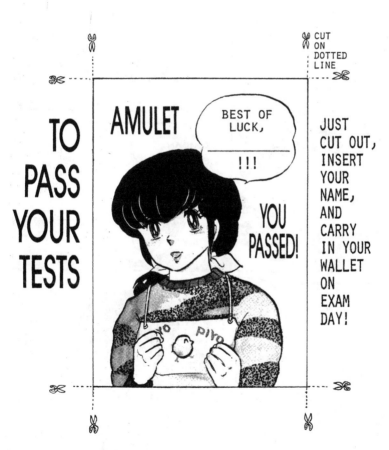

Good Luck!

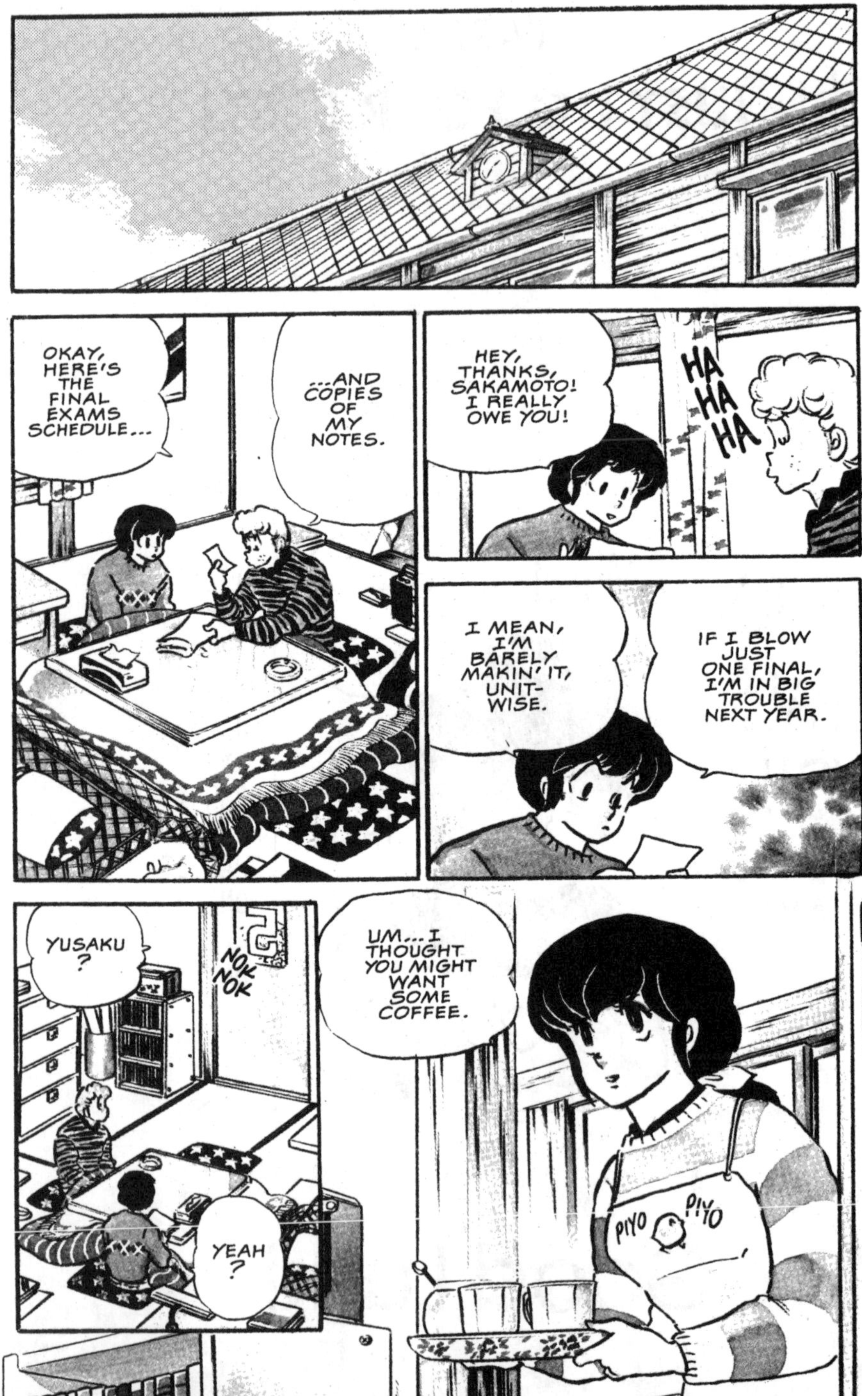

OKAY, HERE'S THE FINAL EXAMS SCHEDULE...
...AND COPIES OF MY NOTES.
HEY, THANKS, SAKAMOTO! I REALLY OWE YOU!
HA HA HA
I MEAN, I'M BARELY MAKIN' IT, UNIT-WISE.
IF I BLOW JUST ONE FINAL, I'M IN BIG TROUBLE NEXT YEAR.
YUSAKU?
NOK NOK
YEAH?
UM... I THOUGHT YOU MIGHT WANT SOME COFFEE.
PIYO PIYO

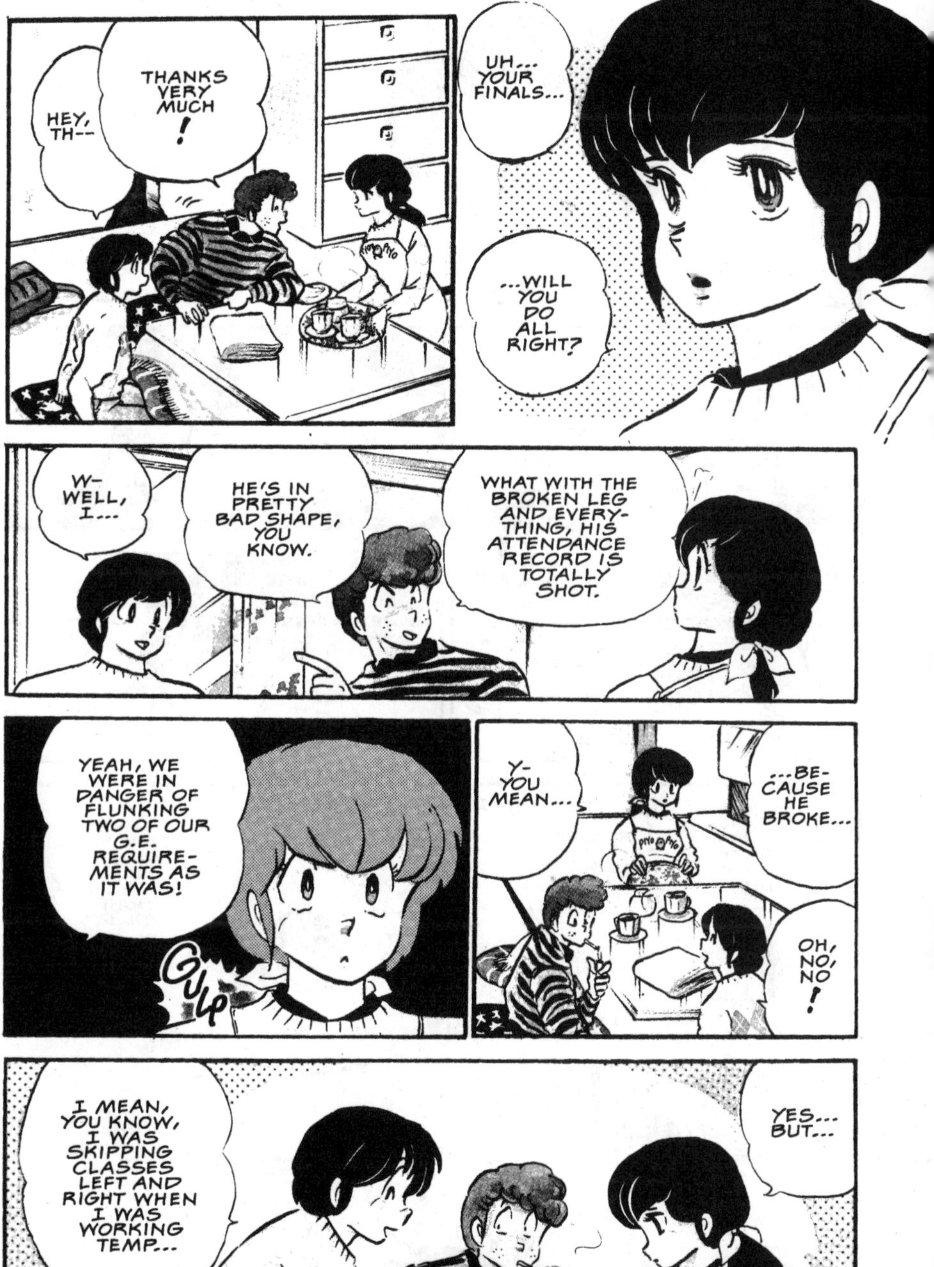
HEY, TH--
THANKS VERY MUCH!
UH... YOUR FINALS...
...WILL YOU DO ALL RIGHT?
W-WELL, I...
HE'S IN PRETTY BAD SHAPE, YOU KNOW.
WHAT WITH THE BROKEN LEG AND EVERY-THING, HIS ATTENDANCE RECORD IS TOTALLY SHOT.
YEAH, WE WERE IN DANGER OF FLUNKING TWO OF OUR G.E. REQUIRE-MENTS AS IT WAS!
GULP
Y-YOU MEAN...
...BE-CAUSE HE BROKE...
OH, NO, NO!
I MEAN, YOU KNOW, I WAS SKIPPING CLASSES LEFT AND RIGHT WHEN I WAS WORKING TEMP...
YES... BUT...

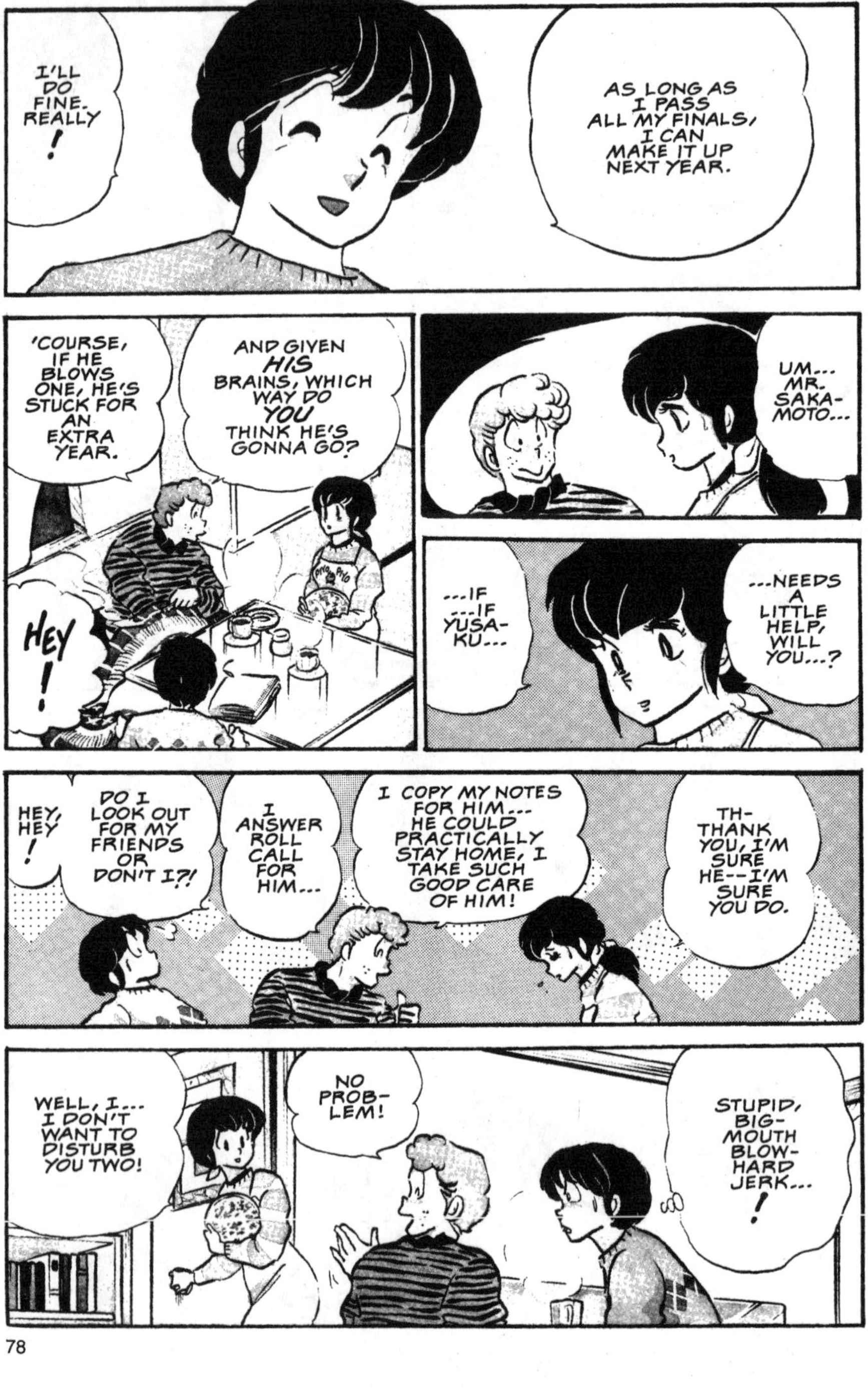
I'LL DO FINE. REALLY!
AS LONG AS I PASS ALL MY FINALS, I CAN MAKE IT UP NEXT YEAR.
'COURSE, IF HE BLOWS ONE, HE'S STUCK FOR AN EXTRA YEAR.
AND GIVEN HIS BRAINS, WHICH WAY DO YOU THINK HE'S GONNA GO?
HEY!
UM... MR. SAKAMOTO...
...IF ...IF YUSAKU...
...NEEDS A LITTLE HELP, WILL YOU...?
HEY, HEY!
DO I LOOK OUT FOR MY FRIENDS OR DON'T I?!
I ANSWER ROLL CALL FOR HIM...
I COPY MY NOTES FOR HIM... HE COULD PRACTICALLY STAY HOME, I TAKE SUCH GOOD CARE OF HIM!
TH-THANK YOU, I'M SURE HE--I'M SURE YOU DO.
WELL, I... I DON'T WANT TO DISTURB YOU TWO!
NO PROBLEM!
STUPID, BIG-MOUTH BLOW-HARD JERK...!

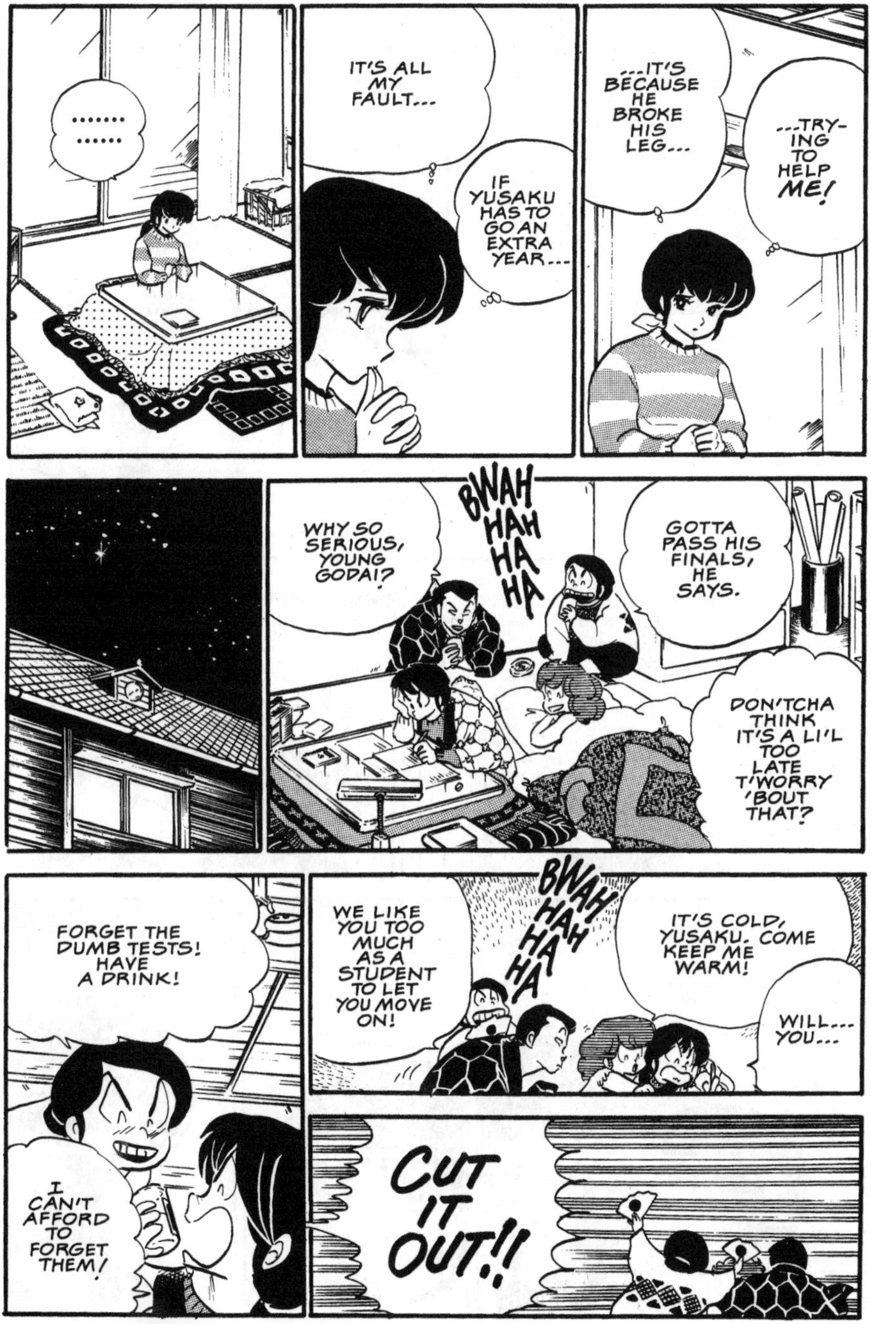
....
......
IT'S ALL MY FAULT...
IF YUSAKU HAS TO GO AN EXTRA YEAR...
...IT'S BECAUSE HE BROKE HIS LEG...
...TRYING TO HELP ME!
BWAH HAH HA HA
WHY SO SERIOUS, YOUNG GODAI?
GOTTA PASS HIS FINALS, HE SAYS.
DON'TCHA THINK IT'S A LI'L TOO LATE T'WORRY 'BOUT THAT?
FORGET THE DUMB TESTS! HAVE A DRINK!
I CAN'T AFFORD TO FORGET THEM!
BWAH HAH HA HA
WE LIKE YOU TOO MUCH AS A STUDENT TO LET YOU MOVE ON!
IT'S COLD, YUSAKU. COME KEEP ME WARM!
WILL... YOU...
CUT IT OUT!!

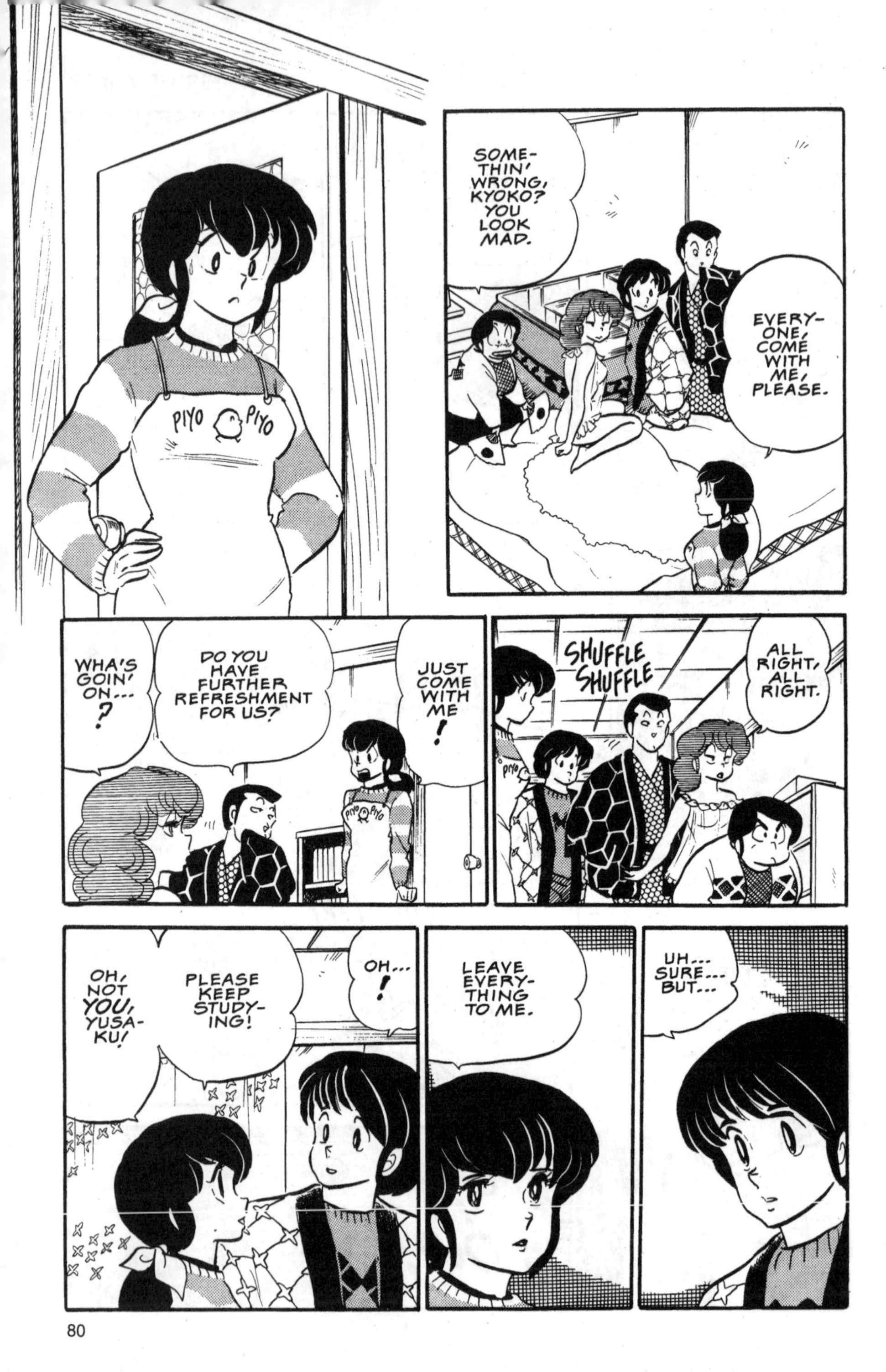
PIYO PIYO
SOME-THIN' WRONG, KYOKO? YOU LOOK MAD.
EVERY-ONE, COME WITH ME, PLEASE.
WHA'S GOIN' ON...?
DO YOU HAVE FURTHER REFRESHMENT FOR US?
JUST COME WITH ME!
SHUFFLE SHUFFLE
ALL RIGHT, ALL RIGHT.
OH, NOT *YOU*, YUSA-KU!
PLEASE KEEP STUDY-ING!
OH...!
LEAVE EVERY-THING TO ME.
UH... SURE... BUT...

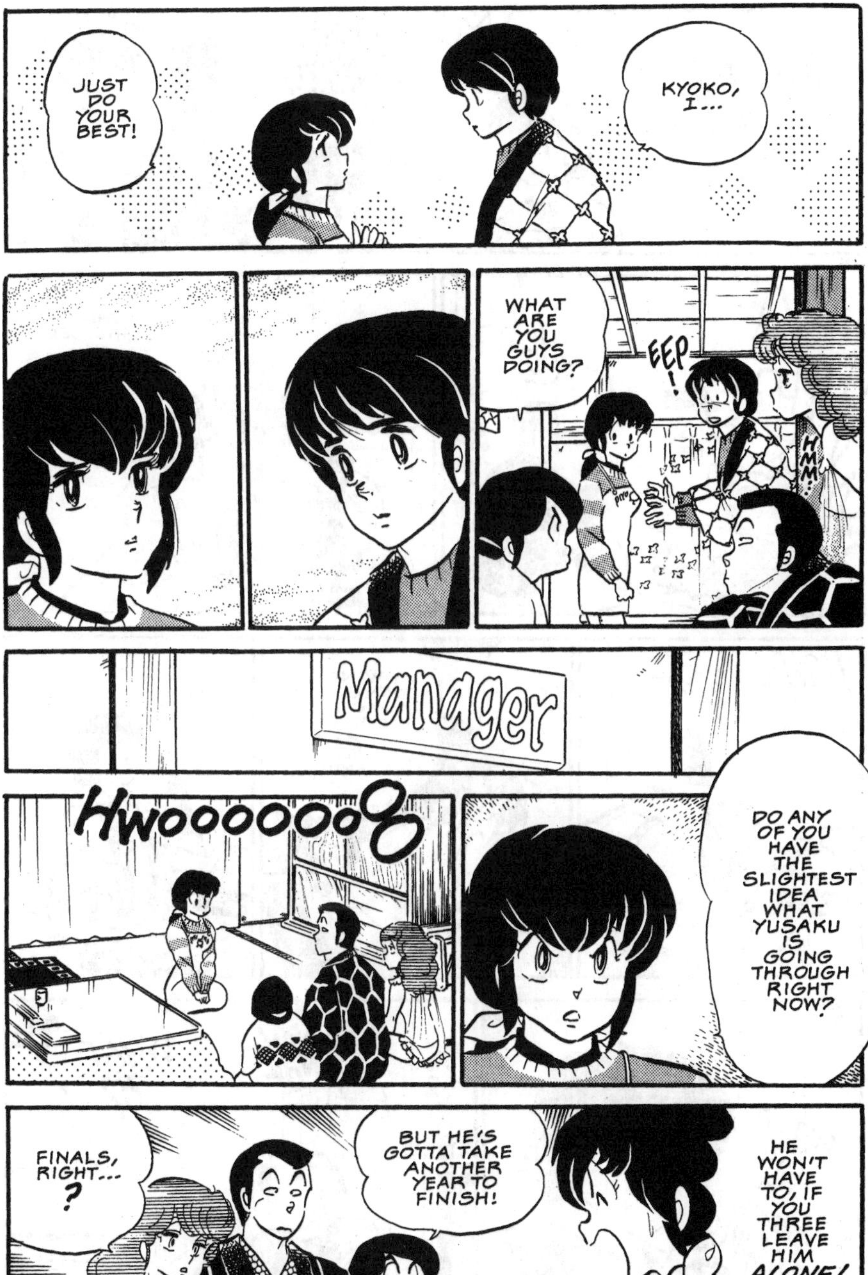
JUST DO YOUR BEST!
KYOKO, I...
WHAT ARE YOU GUYS DOING?
EEP!
HMM.
Manager
Hwoooooo
DO ANY OF YOU HAVE THE SLIGHTEST IDEA WHAT YUSAKU IS GOING THROUGH RIGHT NOW?
FINALS, RIGHT...?
BUT HE'S GOTTA TAKE ANOTHER YEAR TO FINISH!
HE WON'T HAVE TO, IF YOU THREE LEAVE HIM ALONE!

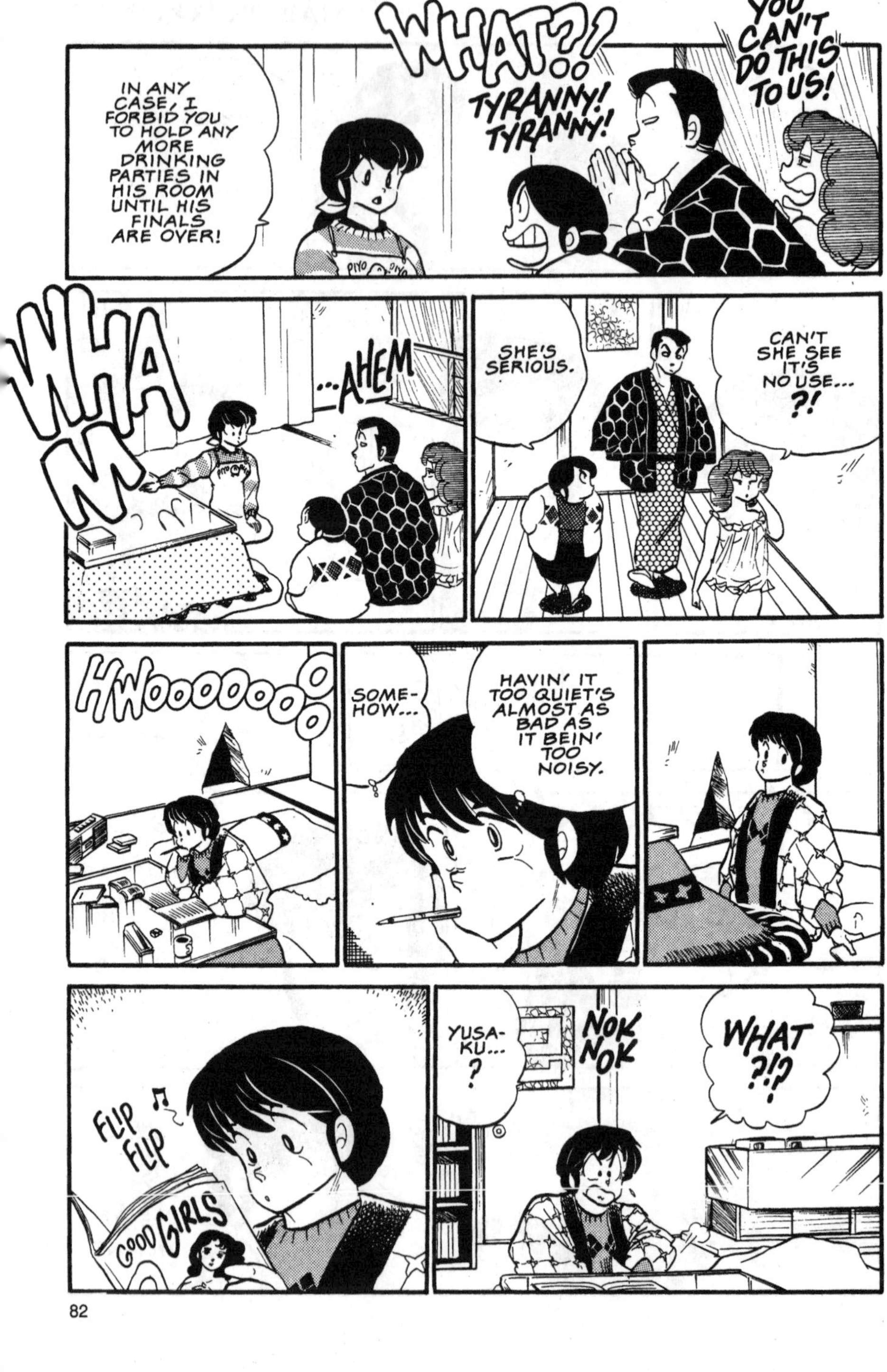
IN ANY CASE, I FORBID YOU TO HOLD ANY MORE DRINKING PARTIES IN HIS ROOM UNTIL HIS FINALS ARE OVER!
PIYO PIYO
WHAT?!
TYRANNY! TYRANNY!
YOU CAN'T DO THIS TO US!
WHAM
...AHEM
SHE'S SERIOUS.
CAN'T SHE SEE IT'S NO USE... ?!
HWOOOOOOOOOO
SOME-HOW...
HAVIN' IT TOO QUIET'S ALMOST AS BAD AS IT BEIN' TOO NOISY.
FLIP FLIP
GOOD GIRLS
YUSA-KU... ?
NOK NOK
WHAT ?!?

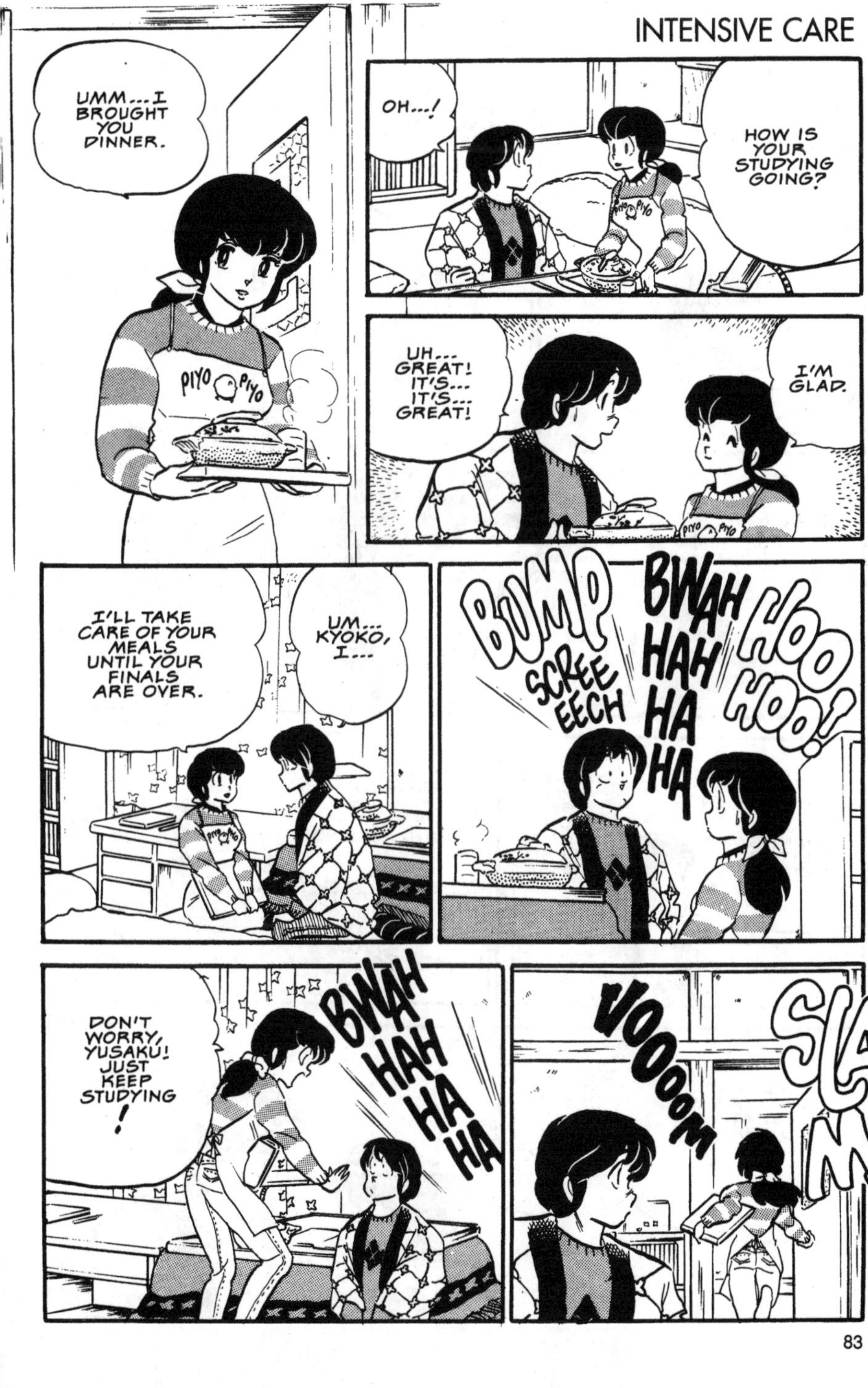
UMM...I BROUGHT YOU DINNER.
OH...!
HOW IS YOUR STUDYING GOING?
PIYO PIYO
UH... GREAT! IT'S... IT'S... GREAT!
I'M GLAD.
I'LL TAKE CARE OF YOUR MEALS UNTIL YOUR FINALS ARE OVER.
UM... KYOKO, I...
BUMP
SCREEEECH
BWAH HAH HAH HA HA
HOO HOO!
DON'T WORRY, YUSAKU! JUST KEEP STUDYING!
BWAH HAH HA HA HA
VOOOOOM
SLAM

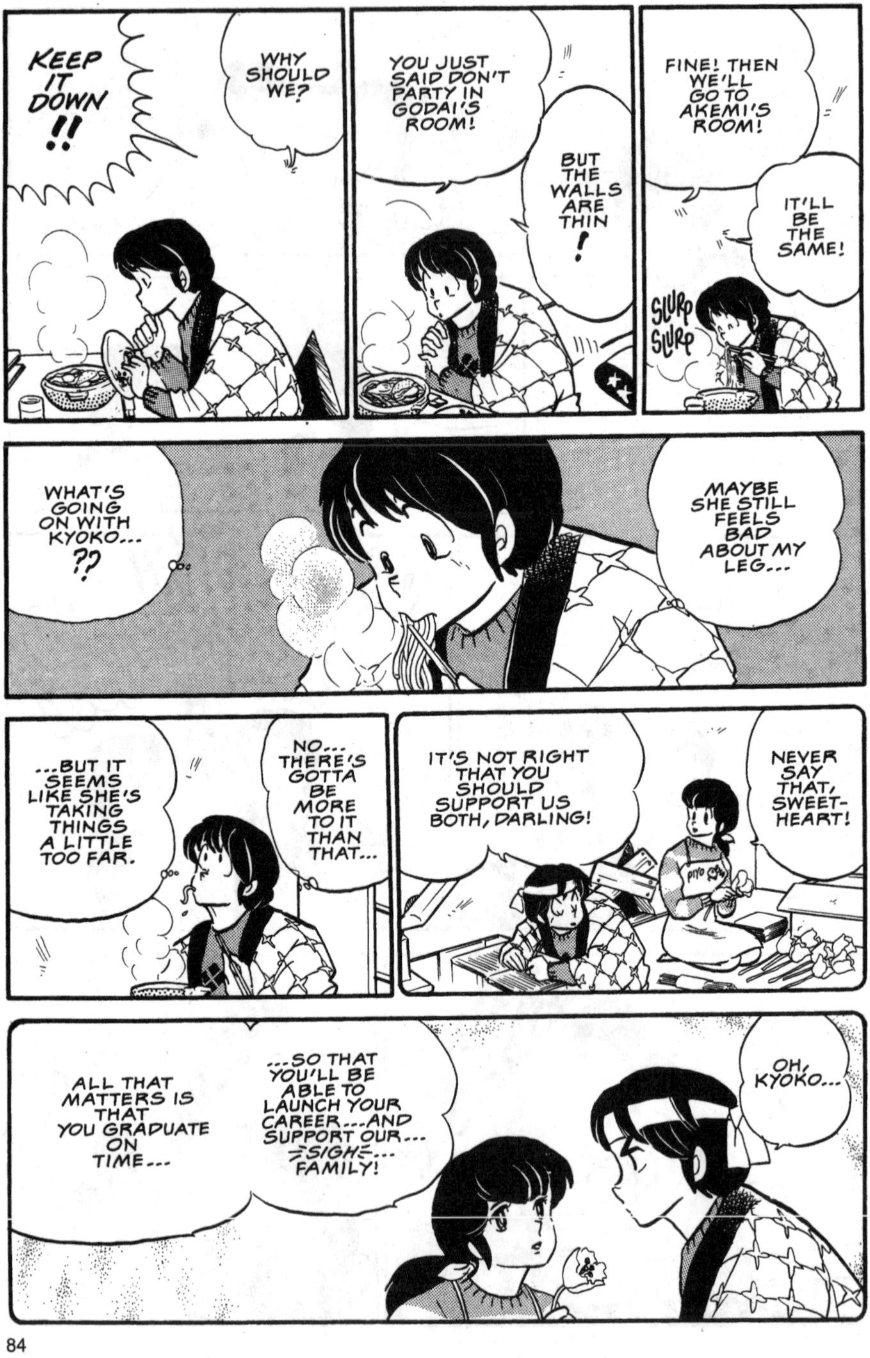
KEEP IT DOWN!!
WHY SHOULD WE?
YOU JUST SAID DON'T PARTY IN GODAI'S ROOM!
BUT THE WALLS ARE THIN!
FINE! THEN WE'LL GO TO AKEMI'S ROOM!
IT'LL BE THE SAME!
SLURP SLURP
WHAT'S GOING ON WITH KYOKO...??
MAYBE SHE STILL FEELS BAD ABOUT MY LEG...
...BUT IT SEEMS LIKE SHE'S TAKING THINGS A LITTLE TOO FAR.
NO... THERE'S GOTTA BE MORE TO IT THAN THAT...
IT'S NOT RIGHT THAT YOU SHOULD SUPPORT US BOTH, DARLING!
NEVER SAY THAT, SWEET-HEART!
PIYO
ALL THAT MATTERS IS THAT YOU GRADUATE ON TIME...
...SO THAT YOU'LL BE ABLE TO LAUNCH YOUR CAREER...AND SUPPORT OUR... =SIGH=... FAMILY!
OH, KYOKO...

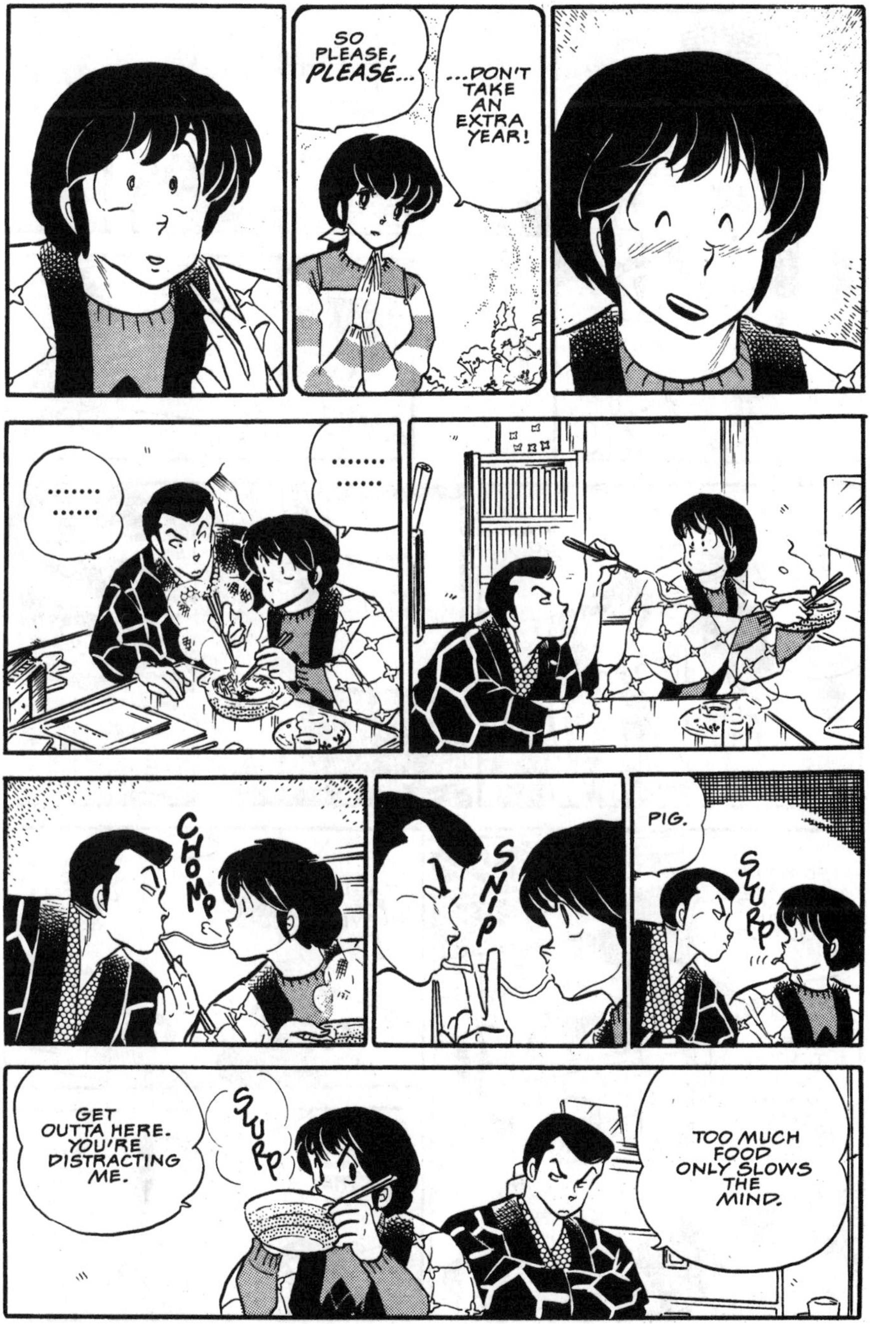
SO PLEASE, PLEASE...
...DON'T TAKE AN EXTRA YEAR!
....
....
....
......
CHOMP
SNIP
PIG.
SLURP
GET OUTTA HERE. YOU'RE DISTRACTING ME.
SLURP
TOO MUCH FOOD ONLY SLOWS THE MIND.

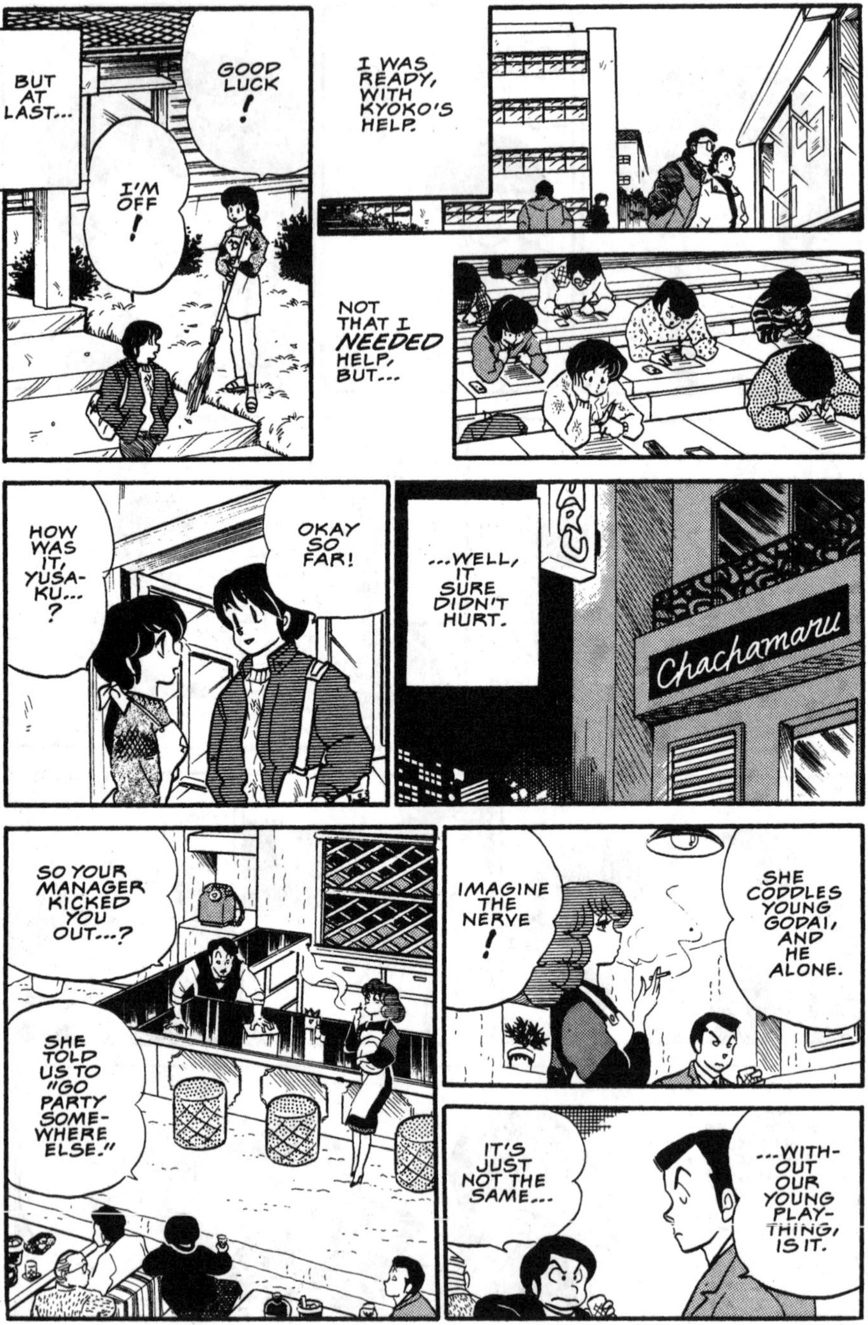
BUT AT LAST...
GOOD LUCK!
I'M OFF!
I WAS READY, WITH KYOKO'S HELP.
NOT THAT I *NEEDED* HELP, BUT...
HOW WAS IT, YUSAKU...?
OKAY SO FAR!
...WELL, IT SURE DIDN'T HURT.
Chachamaru
SO YOUR MANAGER KICKED YOU OUT...?
SHE TOLD US TO "GO PARTY SOMEWHERE ELSE."
IMAGINE THE NERVE!
SHE CODDLES YOUNG GODAI, AND HE ALONE.
IT'S JUST NOT THE SAME...
...WITHOUT OUR YOUNG PLAYTHING, IS IT.

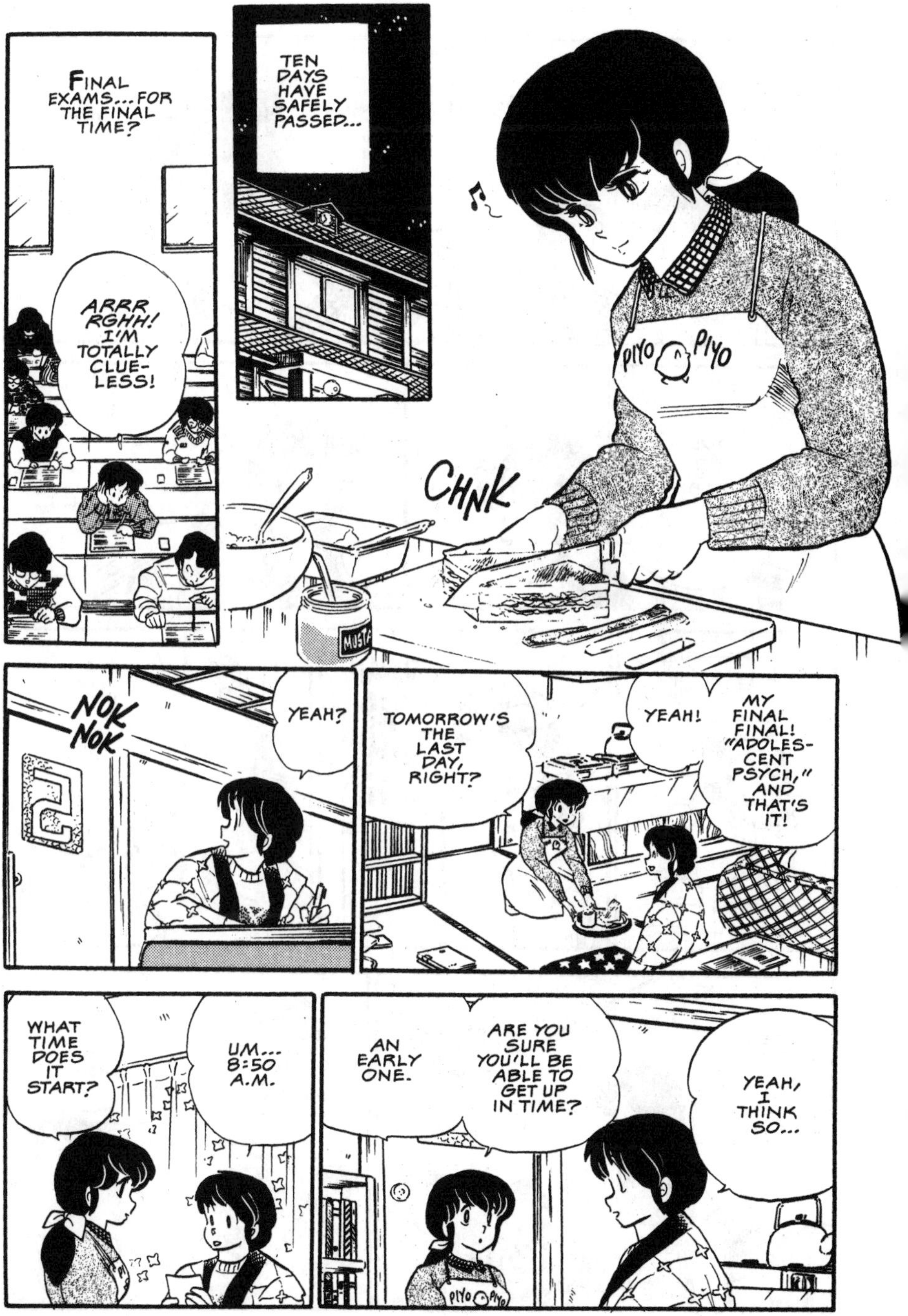
FINAL EXAMS... FOR THE FINAL TIME?
ARRRRGHH! I'M TOTALLY CLUELESS!
TEN DAYS HAVE SAFELY PASSED...
PIYO PIYO
CHNK
MUSTA
NOK NOK
YEAH?
TOMORROW'S THE LAST DAY, RIGHT?
YEAH!
MY FINAL FINAL! "ADOLESCENT PSYCH," AND THAT'S IT!
WHAT TIME DOES IT START?
UM... 8:50 A.M.
AN EARLY ONE.
ARE YOU SURE YOU'LL BE ABLE TO GET UP IN TIME?
YEAH, I THINK SO...

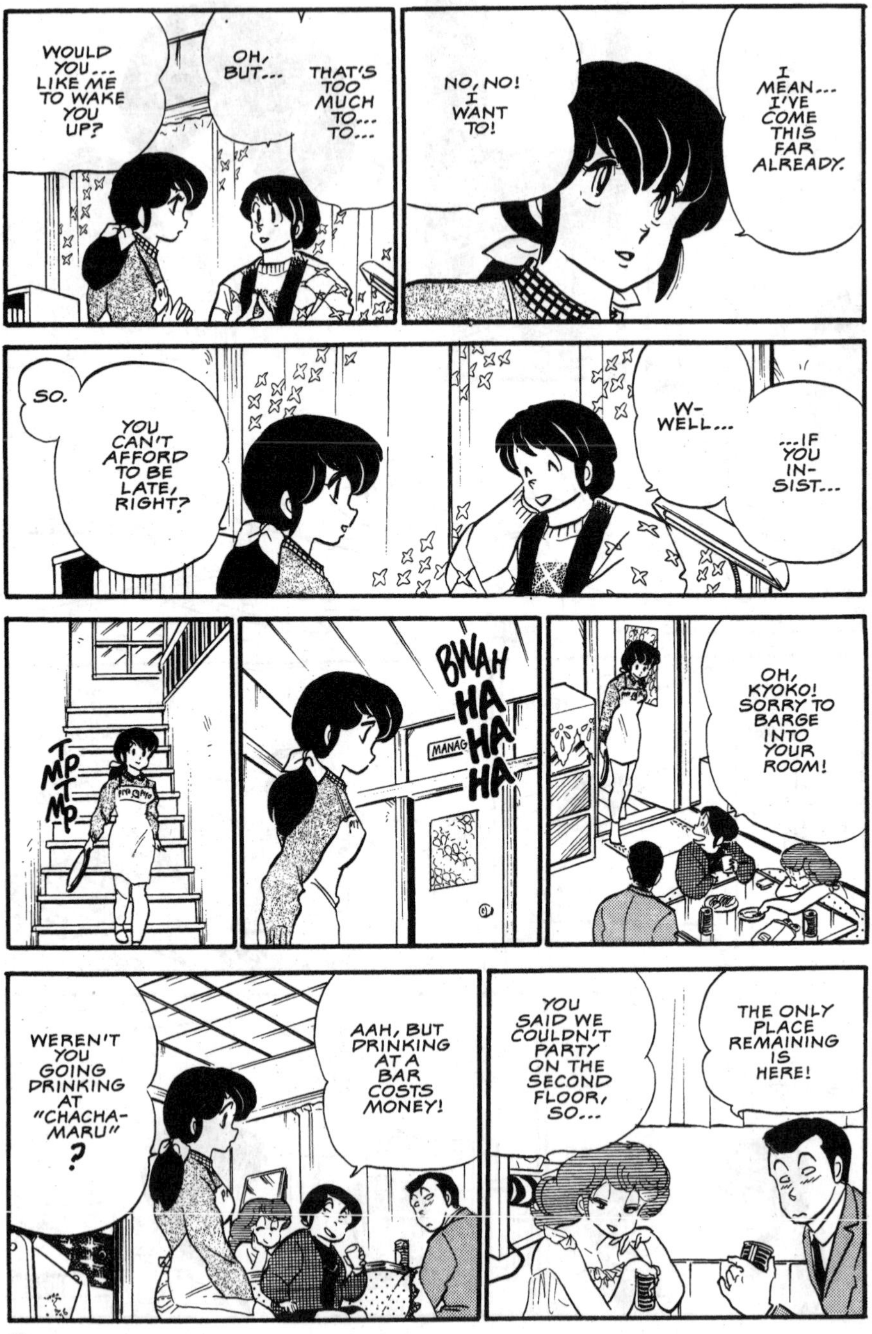

WOULD YOU... LIKE ME TO WAKE YOU UP?
OH, BUT...
THAT'S TOO MUCH TO... TO...
NO, NO! I WANT TO!
I MEAN... I'VE COME THIS FAR ALREADY.
SO.
YOU CAN'T AFFORD TO BE LATE, RIGHT?
W-WELL...
...IF YOU IN-SIST...
TMP TMP
BWAH HA HA HA HA
MANAG
OH, KYOKO! SORRY TO BARGE INTO YOUR ROOM!
WEREN'T YOU GOING DRINKING AT "CHACHA-MARU" ?
AAH, BUT DRINKING AT A BAR COSTS MONEY!
YOU SAID WE COULDN'T PARTY ON THE SECOND FLOOR, SO...
THE ONLY PLACE REMAINING IS HERE!

WELL, FOR YUSAKU'S SAKE...

AND SURELY YOU MUST JOIN YOUR GUESTS IN A TOAST!

BWAH HAHAHA

HEE HEE!

BWAH HA HA HA

12:36

UM...WE SHOULD PROBABLY CALL IT A NIGHT SOON...

WHAT ARE YOU TALKING ABOUT? THE NIGHT'S JUST BEGUN!

BUT I HAVE TO WAKE YUSAKU UP TOMORROW MORNING...

HEY, DID YOU HEAR THAT?! UNFAIR, I TELL YOU, UNFAIR!!

YOU'RE TELLING ME YOU CAN WAKE UP THAT PUTZ GODAI BUT YOU CAN'T STAY AWAKE WITH US?!

W-WELL, MAYBE A LITTLE LONGER...

2 A.M., HUH?

MAYBE I OUGHTTA CRASH SOON.

NAH. KYOKO SAID SHE'D WAKE ME UP, SO...

JUST A LITTLE LONGER...

BWAH HAHAHA

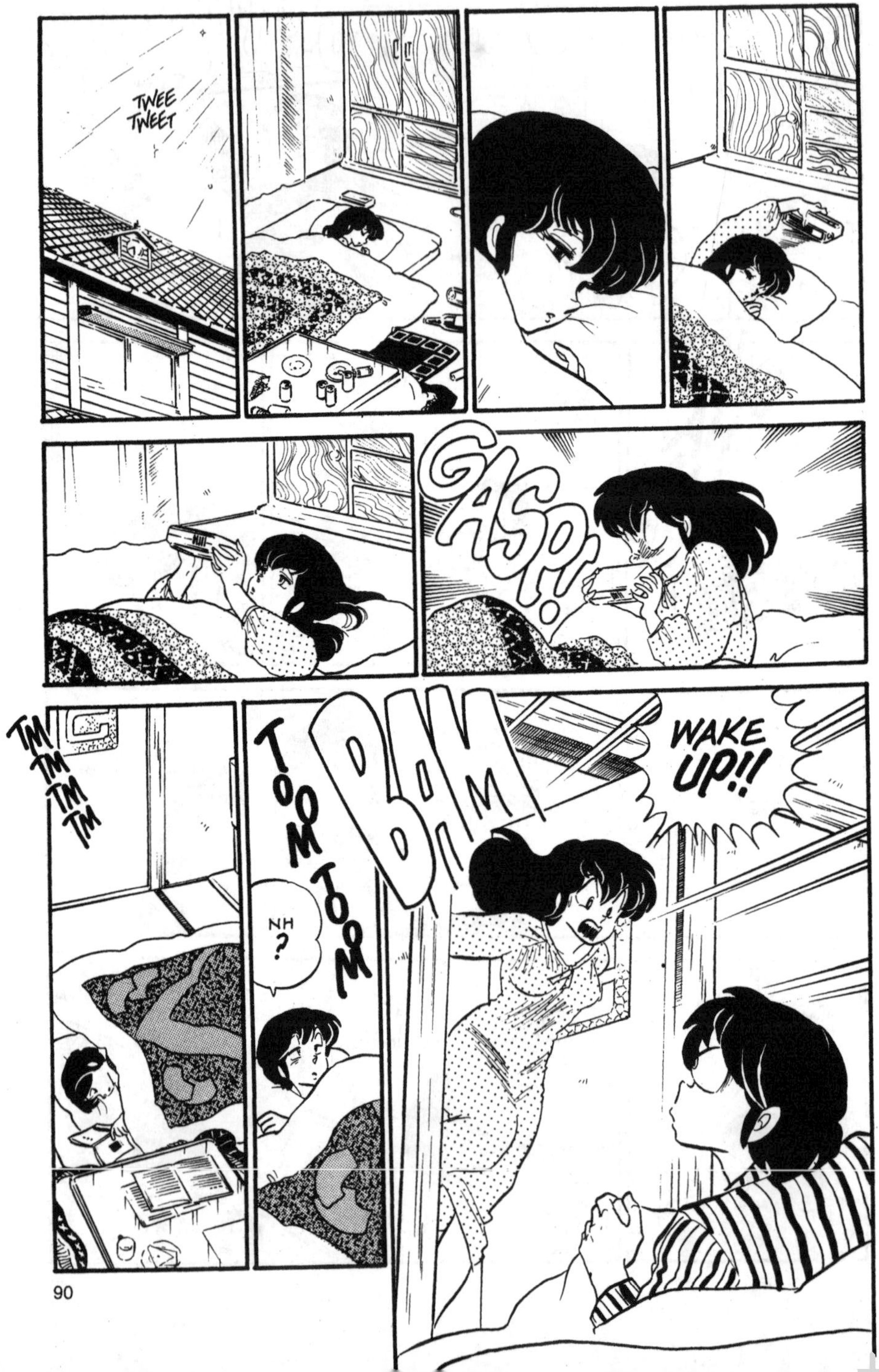

TWEE TWEET
GASP!!
TM TM TM TM
TOOM TOOM
NH ?
BAM
WAKE UP!!

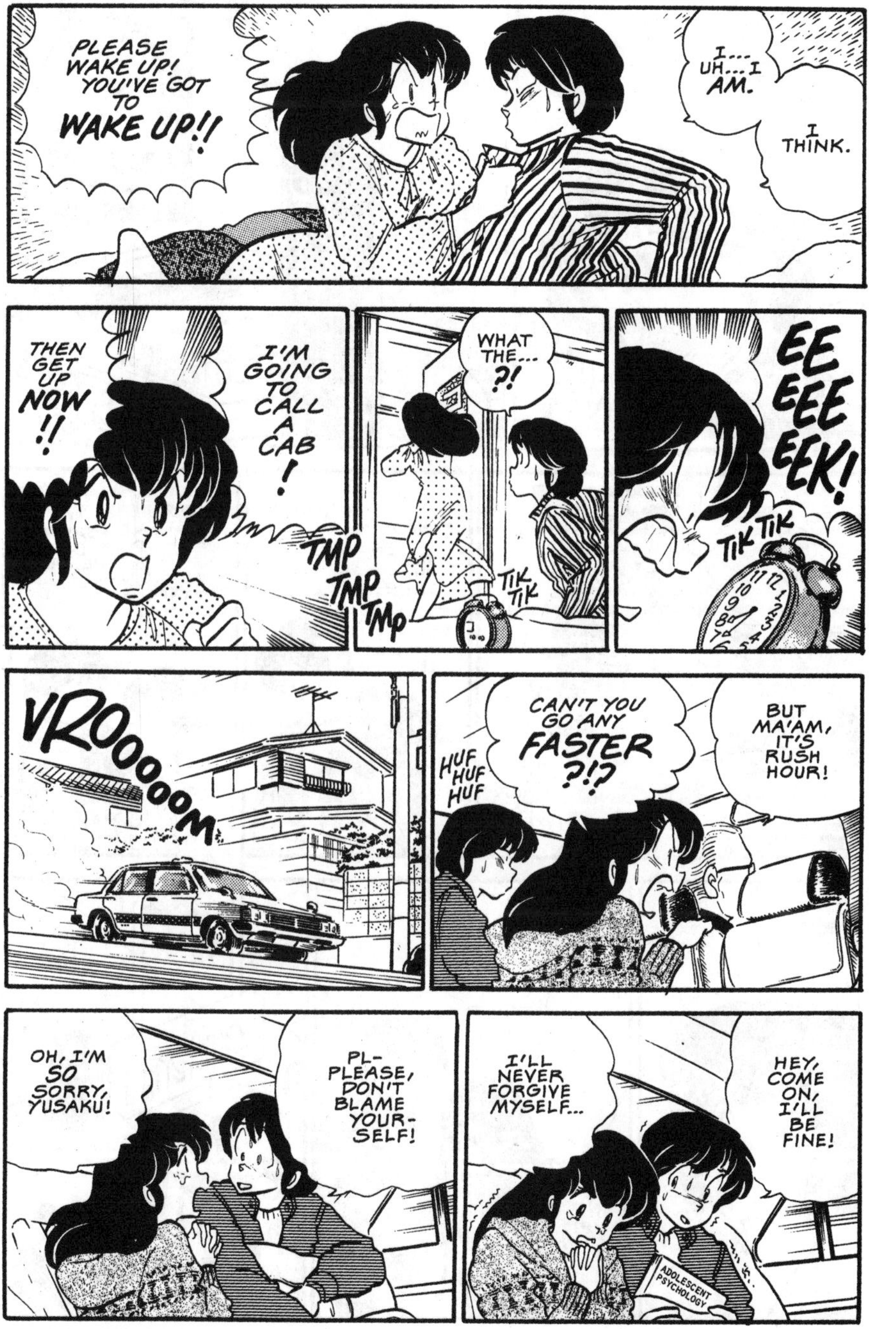
PLEASE WAKE UP! YOU'VE GOT TO WAKE UP!!
I... UH... I AM.
I THINK.
THEN GET UP NOW!!
I'M GOING TO CALL A CAB!
TMP TMP TMP
WHAT THE...?!
TIK TIK
EE EEE EEEK!
TIK TIK
VROOOOOOM
HUF HUF HUF
CAN'T YOU GO ANY FASTER?!?
BUT MA'AM, IT'S RUSH HOUR!
OH, I'M SO SORRY, YUSAKU!
PL-PLEASE, DON'T BLAME YOURSELF!
I'LL NEVER FORGIVE MYSELF...
HEY, COME ON, I'LL BE FINE!
ADOLESCENT PSYCHOLOGY

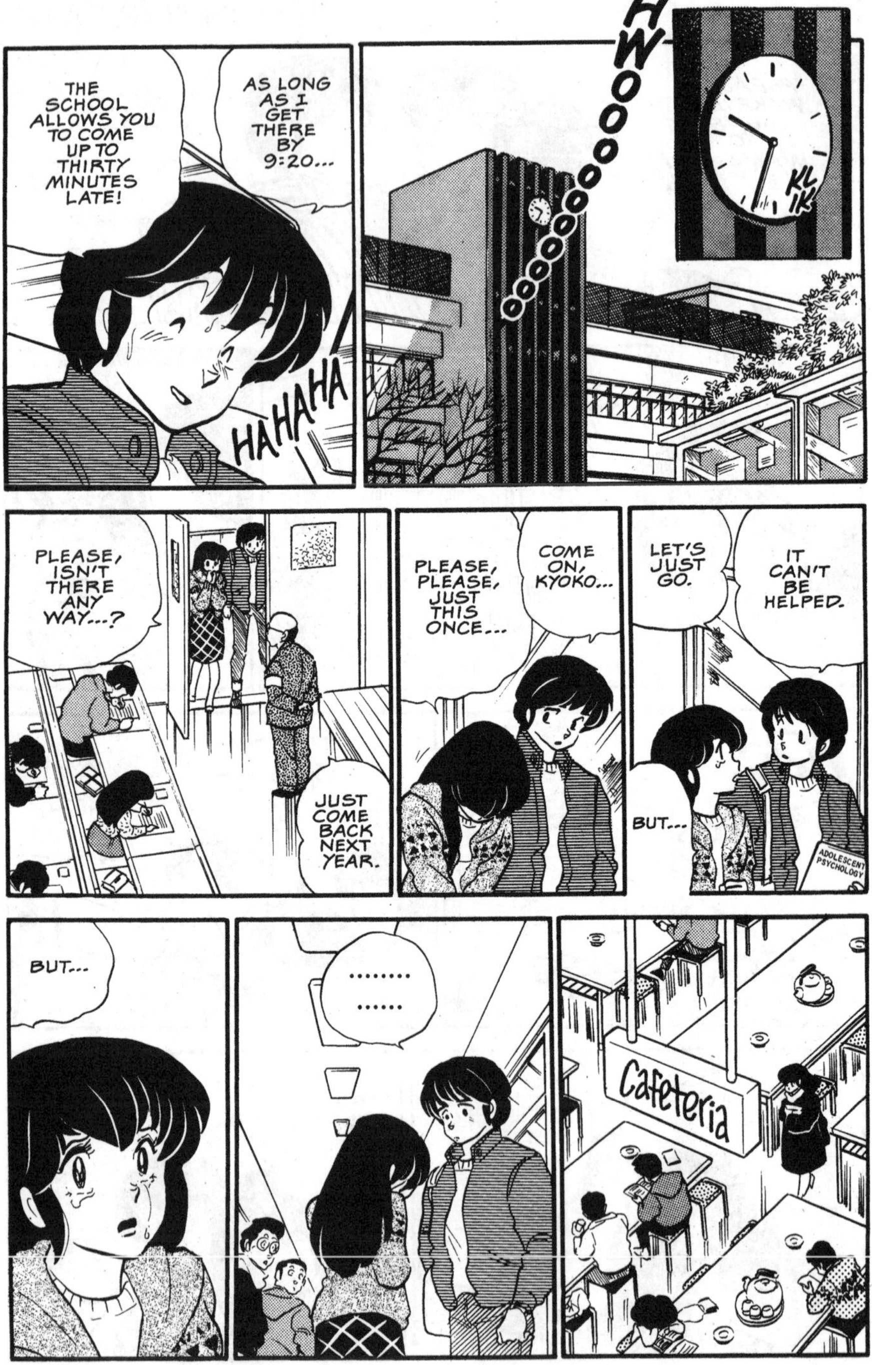
THE SCHOOL ALLOWS YOU TO COME UP TO THIRTY MINUTES LATE!
AS LONG AS I GET THERE BY 9:20...
HAHAHA
HWOOOOOOOOOOOOOO
KLIK
PLEASE, ISN'T THERE ANY WAY...?
JUST COME BACK NEXT YEAR.
PLEASE, PLEASE, JUST THIS ONCE...
COME ON, KYOKO...
LET'S JUST GO.
IT CAN'T BE HELPED.
BUT...
ADOLESCENT PSYCHOLOGY
BUT...
....
......
Cafeteria

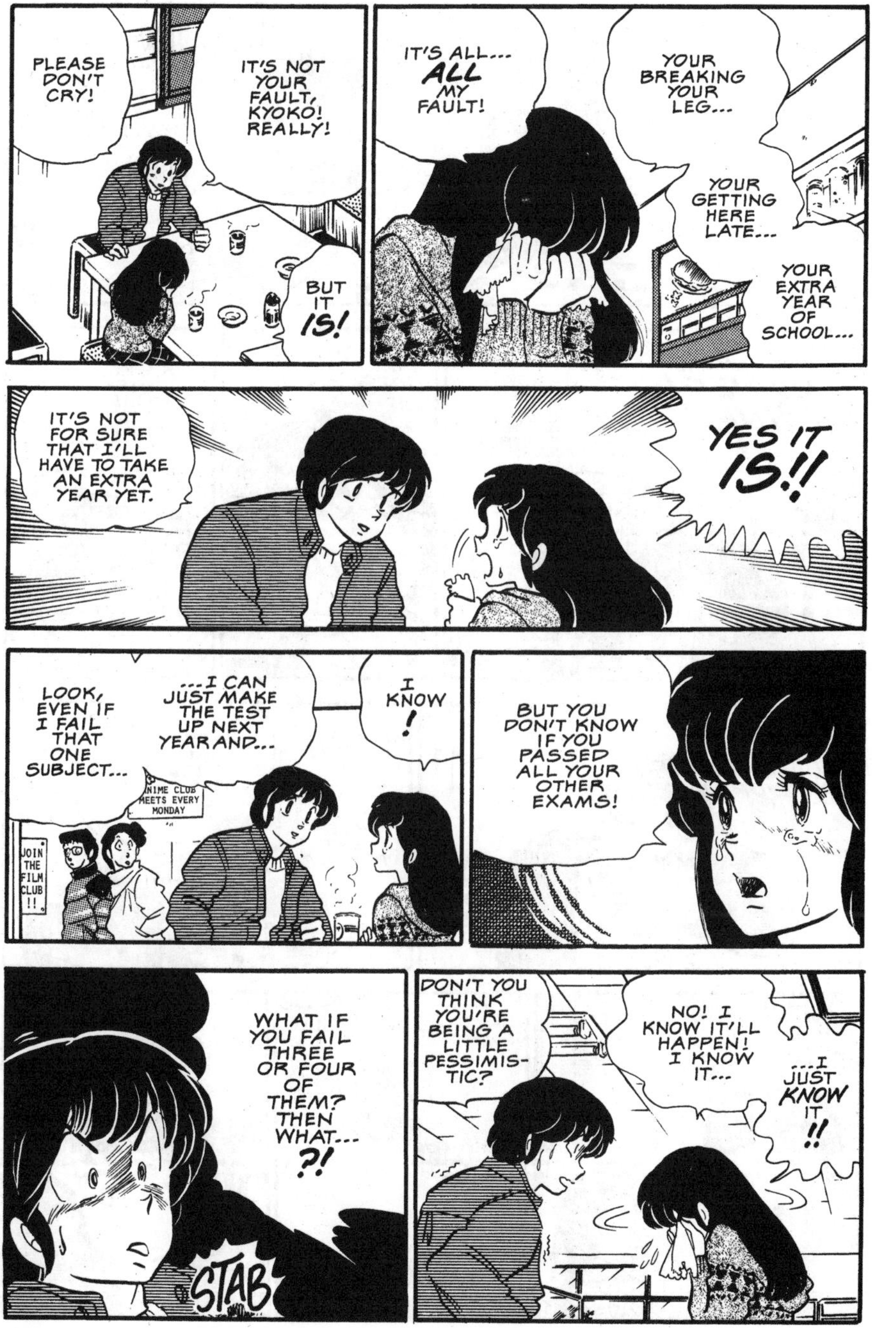
PLEASE DON'T CRY!
IT'S NOT YOUR FAULT, KYOKO! REALLY!
BUT IT IS!
IT'S ALL... ALL MY FAULT!
YOUR BREAKING YOUR LEG...
YOUR GETTING HERE LATE...
YOUR EXTRA YEAR OF SCHOOL...
IT'S NOT FOR SURE THAT I'LL HAVE TO TAKE AN EXTRA YEAR YET.
YES IT IS!!
LOOK, EVEN IF I FAIL THAT ONE SUBJECT...
...I CAN JUST MAKE THE TEST UP NEXT YEAR AND...
I KNOW!
JOIN THE FILM CLUB !!
NIME CLUB MEETS EVERY MONDAY
BUT YOU DON'T KNOW IF YOU PASSED ALL YOUR OTHER EXAMS!
WHAT IF YOU FAIL THREE OR FOUR OF THEM? THEN WHAT...?!
STAB
DON'T YOU THINK YOU'RE BEING A LITTLE PESSIMIS-TIC?
NO! I KNOW IT'LL HAPPEN! I KNOW IT...
...I JUST KNOW IT!!

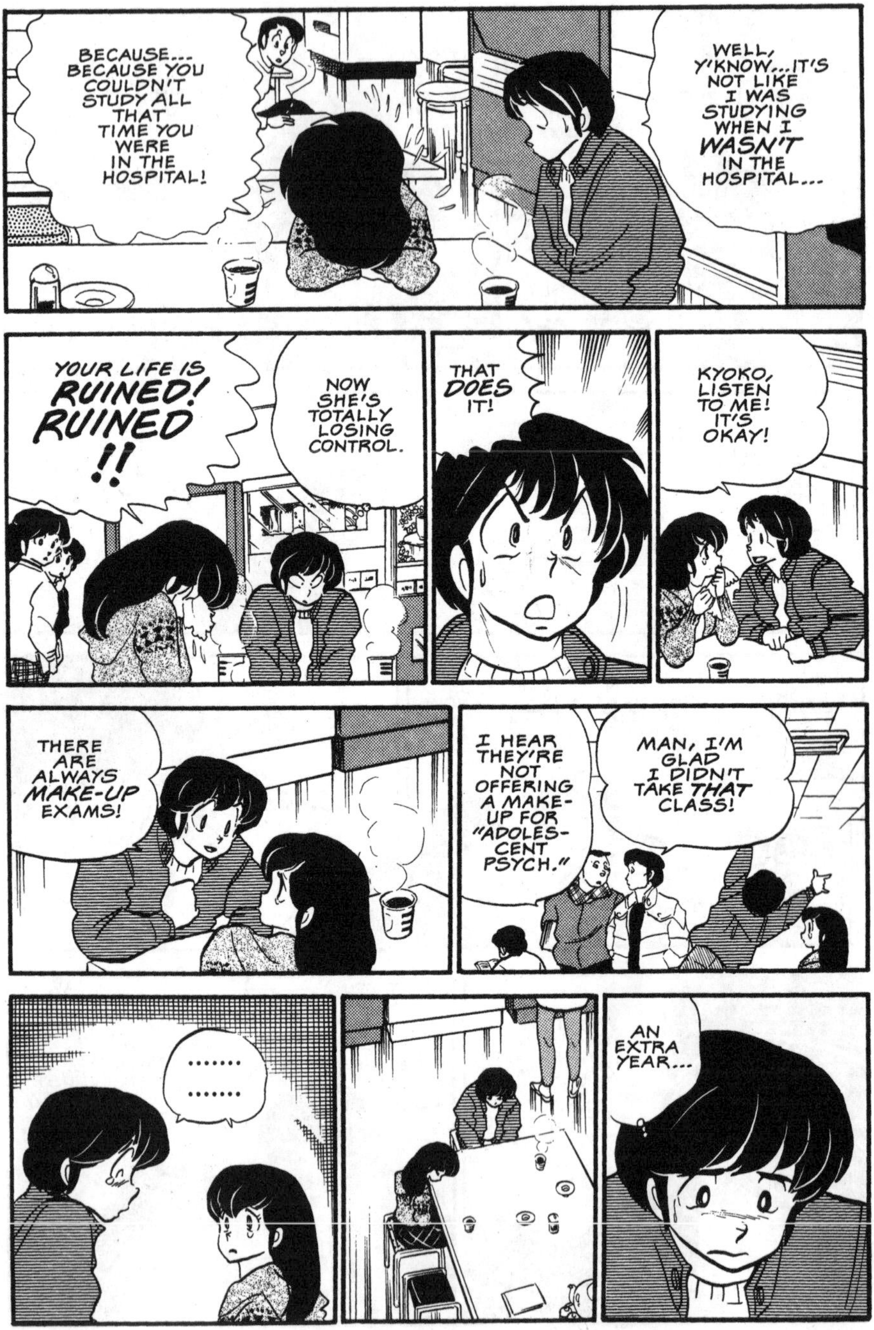
BECAUSE... BECAUSE YOU COULDN'T STUDY ALL THAT TIME YOU WERE IN THE HOSPITAL!
WELL, Y'KNOW... IT'S NOT LIKE I WAS STUDYING WHEN I WASN'T IN THE HOSPITAL...
YOUR LIFE IS RUINED! RUINED !!
NOW SHE'S TOTALLY LOSING CONTROL.
THAT DOES IT!
KYOKO, LISTEN TO ME! IT'S OKAY!
THERE ARE ALWAYS MAKE-UP EXAMS!
I HEAR THEY'RE NOT OFFERING A MAKE-UP FOR "ADOLESCENT PSYCH."
MAN, I'M GLAD I DIDN'T TAKE THAT CLASS!
....
AN EXTRA YEAR...

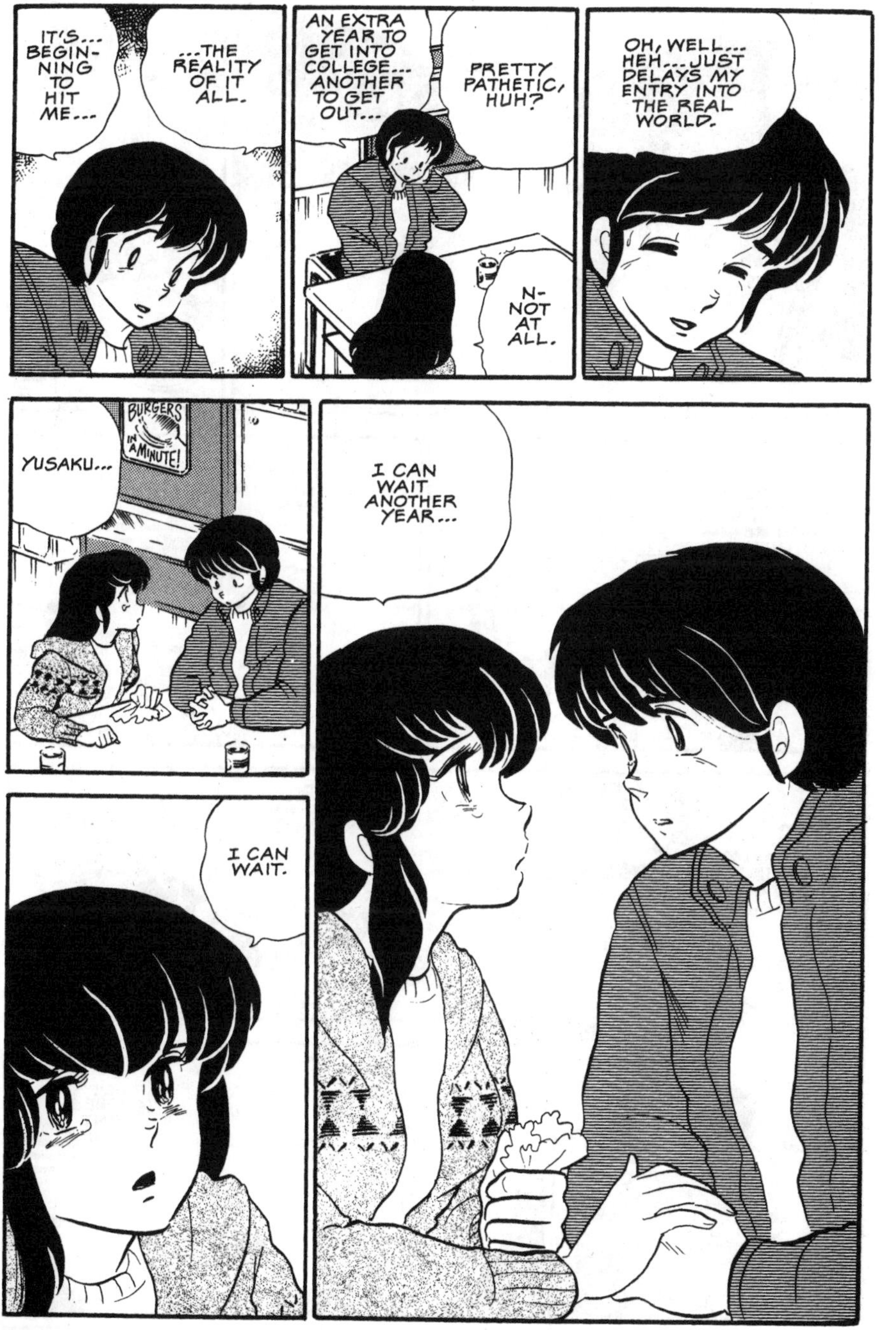
IT'S... BEGIN-NING TO HIT ME...
...THE REALITY OF IT ALL.
AN EXTRA YEAR TO GET INTO COLLEGE... ANOTHER TO GET OUT...
PRETTY PATHETIC, HUH?
N-NOT AT ALL.
OH, WELL... HEH... JUST DELAYS MY ENTRY INTO THE REAL WORLD.
BURGERS IN A MINUTE!
YUSAKU...
I CAN WAIT.
I CAN WAIT ANOTHER YEAR...

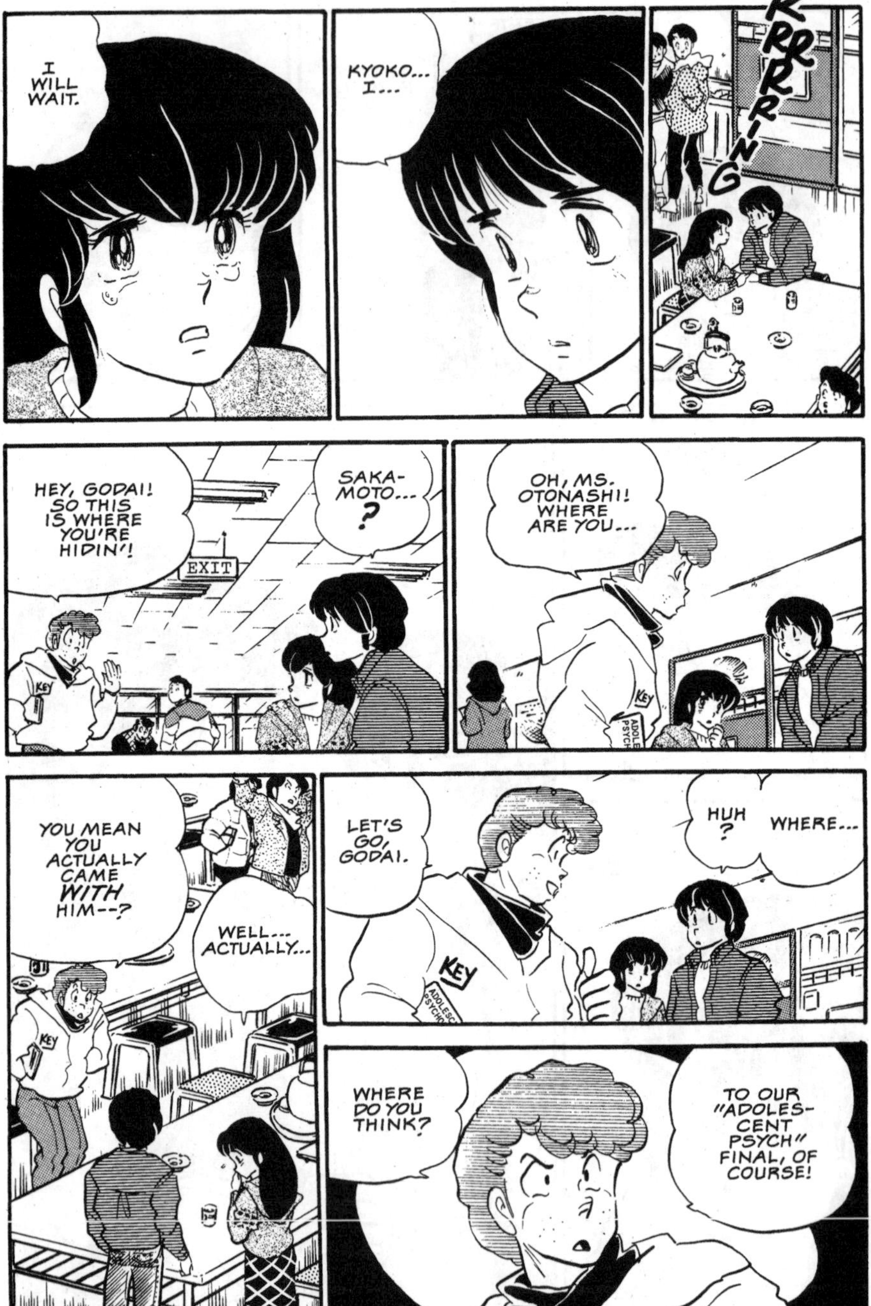
I WILL WAIT.
KYOKO... I...
RRRRRRING
HEY, GODAI! SO THIS IS WHERE YOU'RE HIDIN'!
SAKAMOTO...?
EXIT
OH, MS. OTONASHI! WHERE ARE YOU...
KEY
YOU MEAN YOU ACTUALLY CAME WITH HIM--?
WELL... ACTUALLY...
LET'S GO, GODAI.
HUH?
WHERE...
WHERE DO YOU THINK?
TO OUR "ADOLESCENT PSYCH" FINAL, OF COURSE!

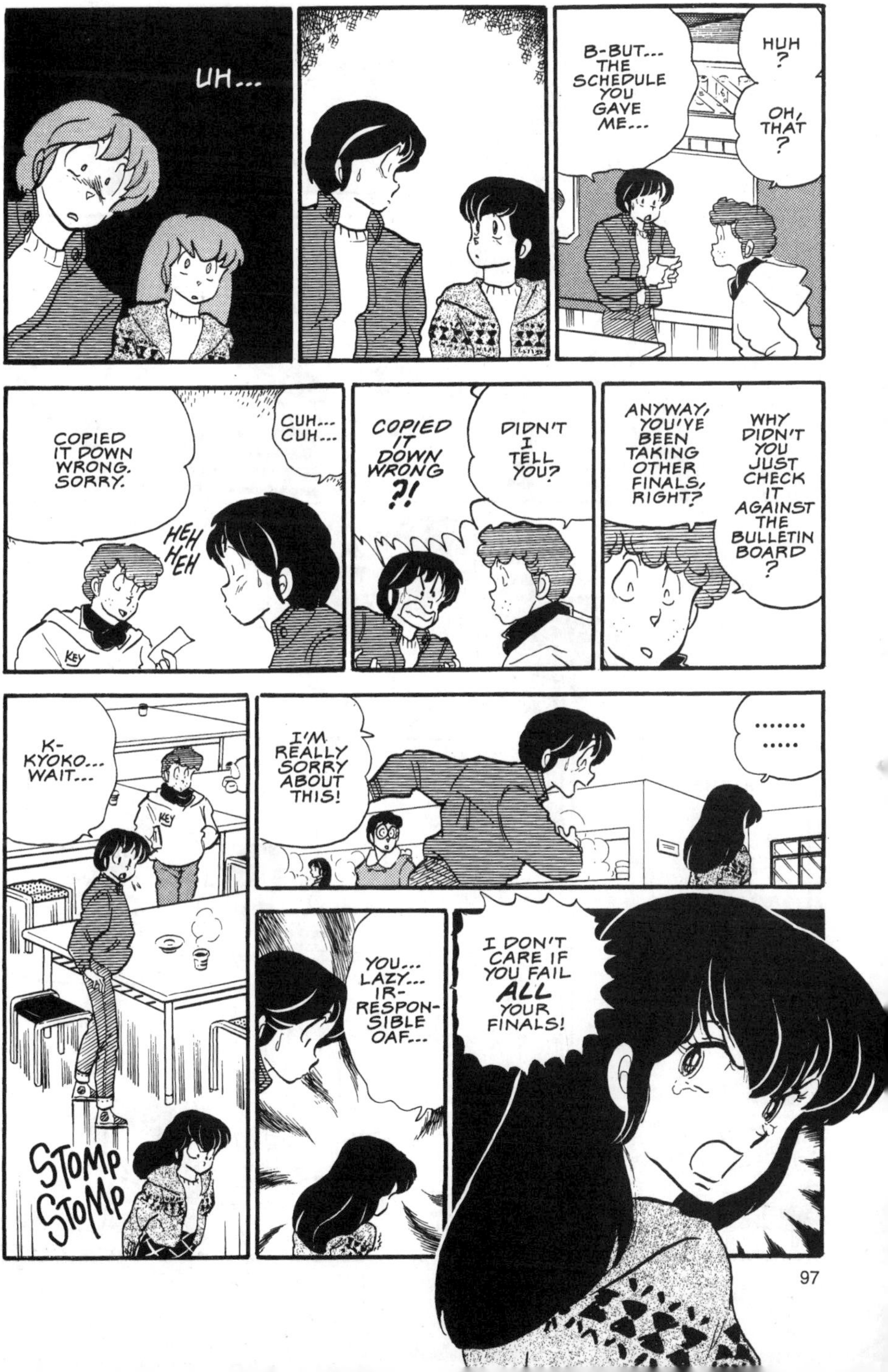
UH...
B-BUT... THE SCHEDULE YOU GAVE ME...
HUH?
OH, THAT?
COPIED IT DOWN WRONG. SORRY.
CUH... CUH...
HEH HEH
COPIED IT DOWN WRONG ?!
DIDN'T I TELL YOU?
ANYWAY, YOU'VE BEEN TAKING OTHER FINALS, RIGHT?
WHY DIDN'T YOU JUST CHECK IT AGAINST THE BULLETIN BOARD?
K-KYOKO... WAIT...
STOMP STOMP
I'M REALLY SORRY ABOUT THIS!
....
.....
YOU... LAZY... IR-RESPONSIBLE OAF...
I DON'T CARE IF YOU FAIL ALL YOUR FINALS!

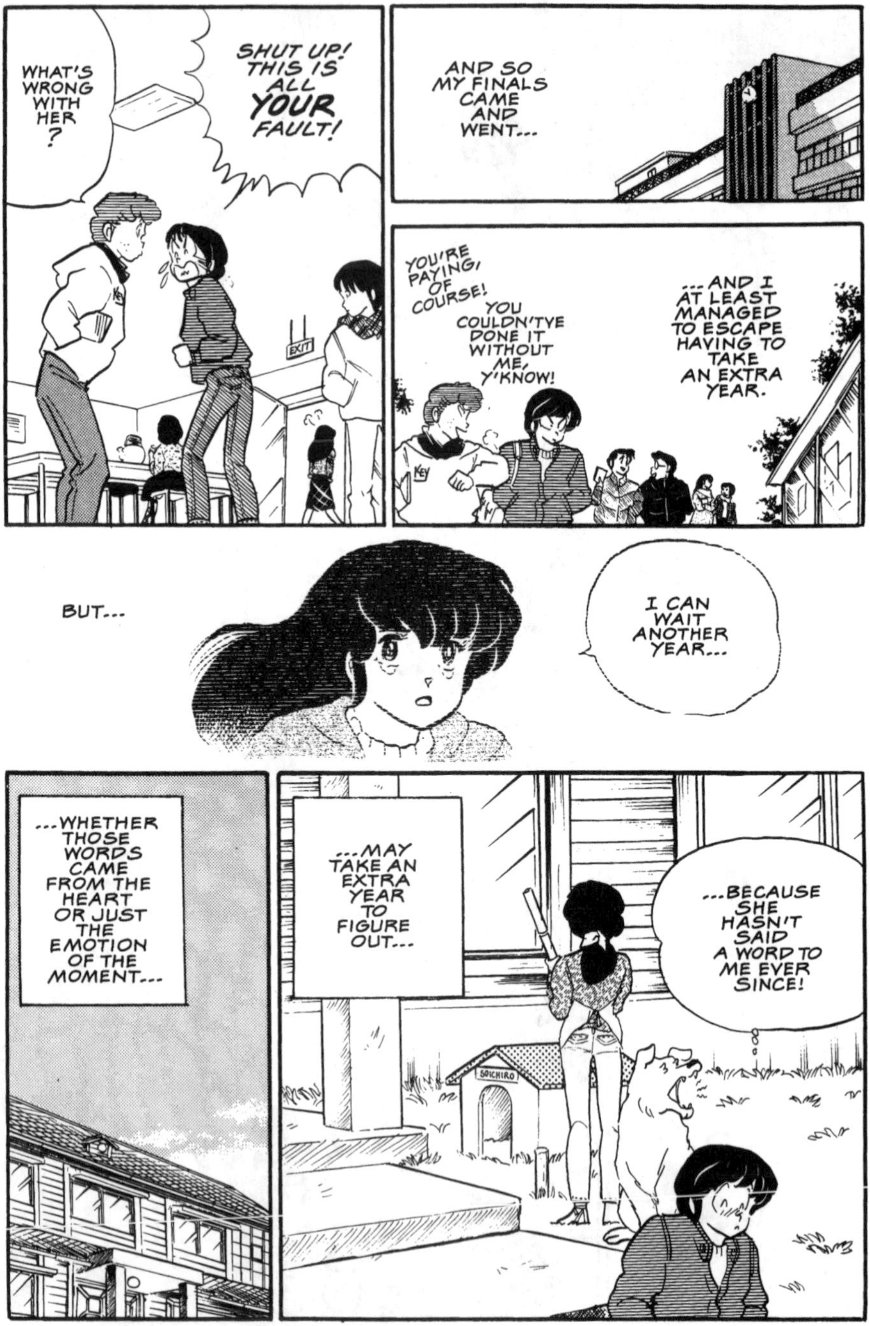

WHAT'S WRONG WITH HER ?
SHUT UP! THIS IS ALL YOUR FAULT!
AND SO MY FINALS CAME AND WENT...
YOU'RE PAYING, OF COURSE!
YOU COULDN'TVE DONE IT WITHOUT ME, Y'KNOW!
...AND I AT LEAST MANAGED TO ESCAPE HAVING TO TAKE AN EXTRA YEAR.
BUT...
I CAN WAIT ANOTHER YEAR...
...WHETHER THOSE WORDS CAME FROM THE HEART OR JUST THE EMOTION OF THE MOMENT...
...MAY TAKE AN EXTRA YEAR TO FIGURE OUT...
...BECAUSE SHE HASN'T SAID A WORD TO ME EVER SINCE!
SOICHIRO

PART 5
IN HOT WATER

HOT SPRINGS

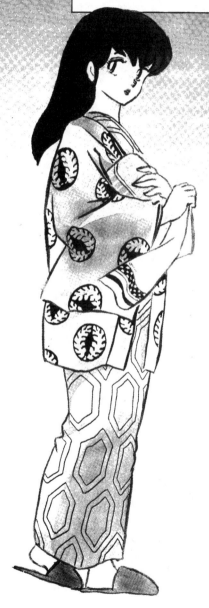

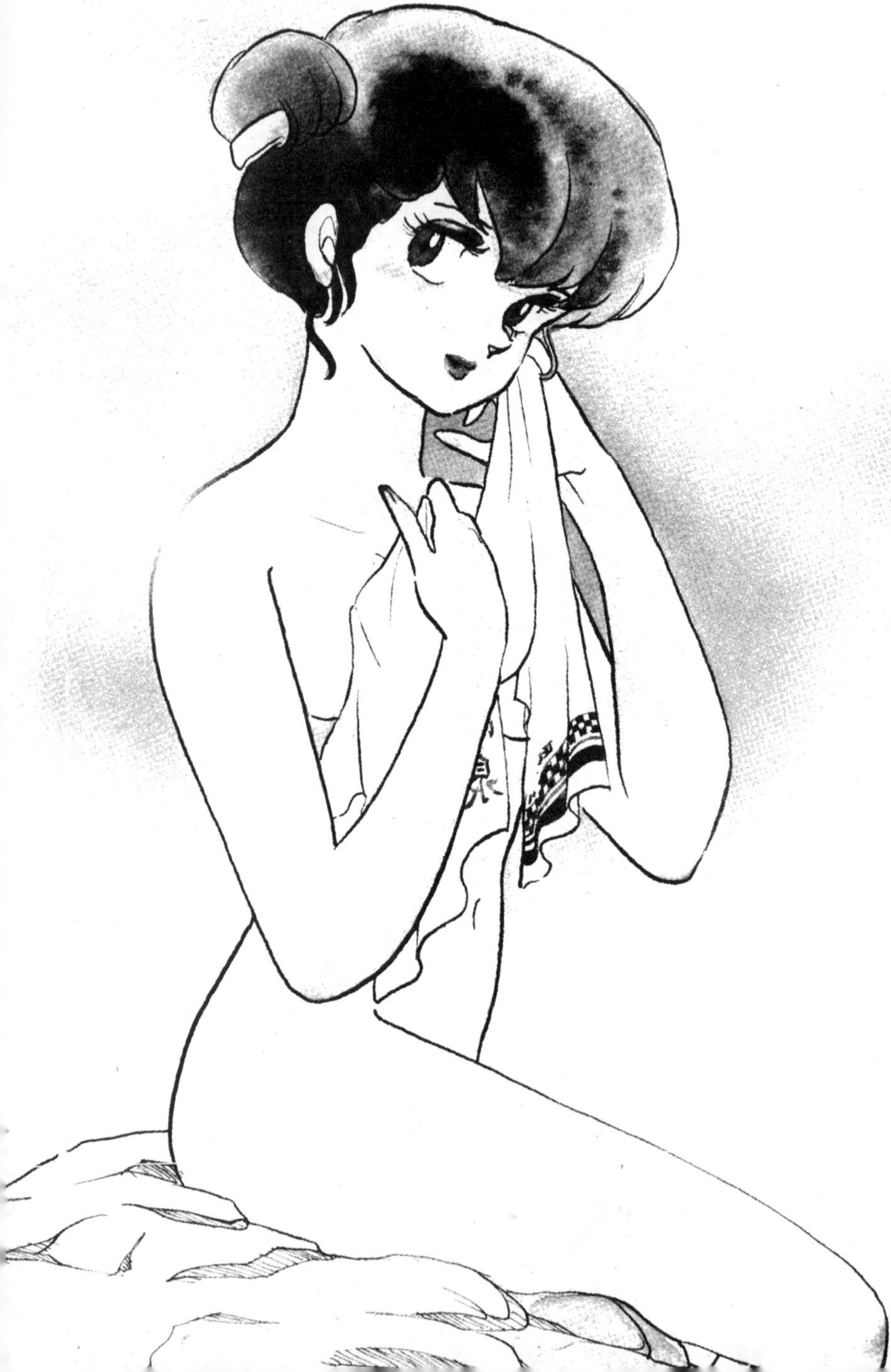

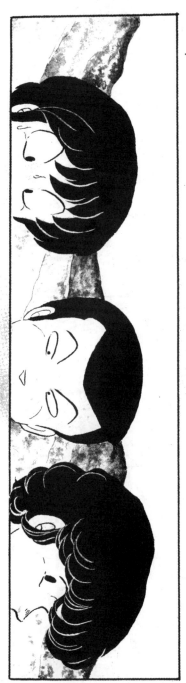

PART 5
IN HOT WATER

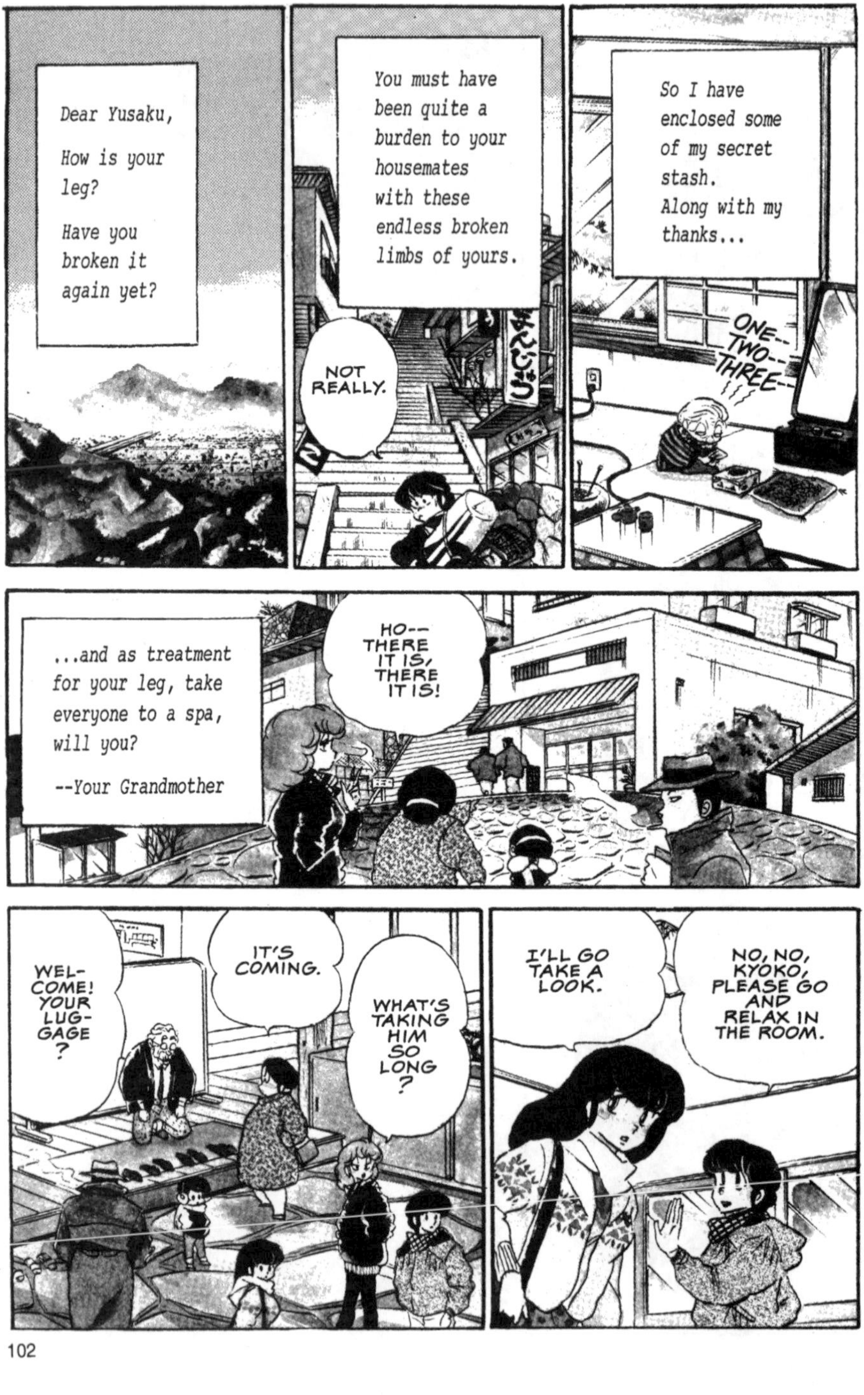
Dear Yusaku,
How is your leg?
Have you broken it again yet?
You must have been quite a burden to your housemates with these endless broken limbs of yours.
NOT REALLY.
まんじゅう
So I have enclosed some of my secret stash.
Along with my thanks...
ONE-- TWO-- THREE--
...and as treatment for your leg, take everyone to a spa, will you?
--Your Grandmother
HO-- THERE IT IS, THERE IT IS!
WEL-COME! YOUR LUG-GAGE?
IT'S COMING.
WHAT'S TAKING HIM SO LONG?
I'LL GO TAKE A LOOK.
NO, NO, KYOKO, PLEASE GO AND RELAX IN THE ROOM.

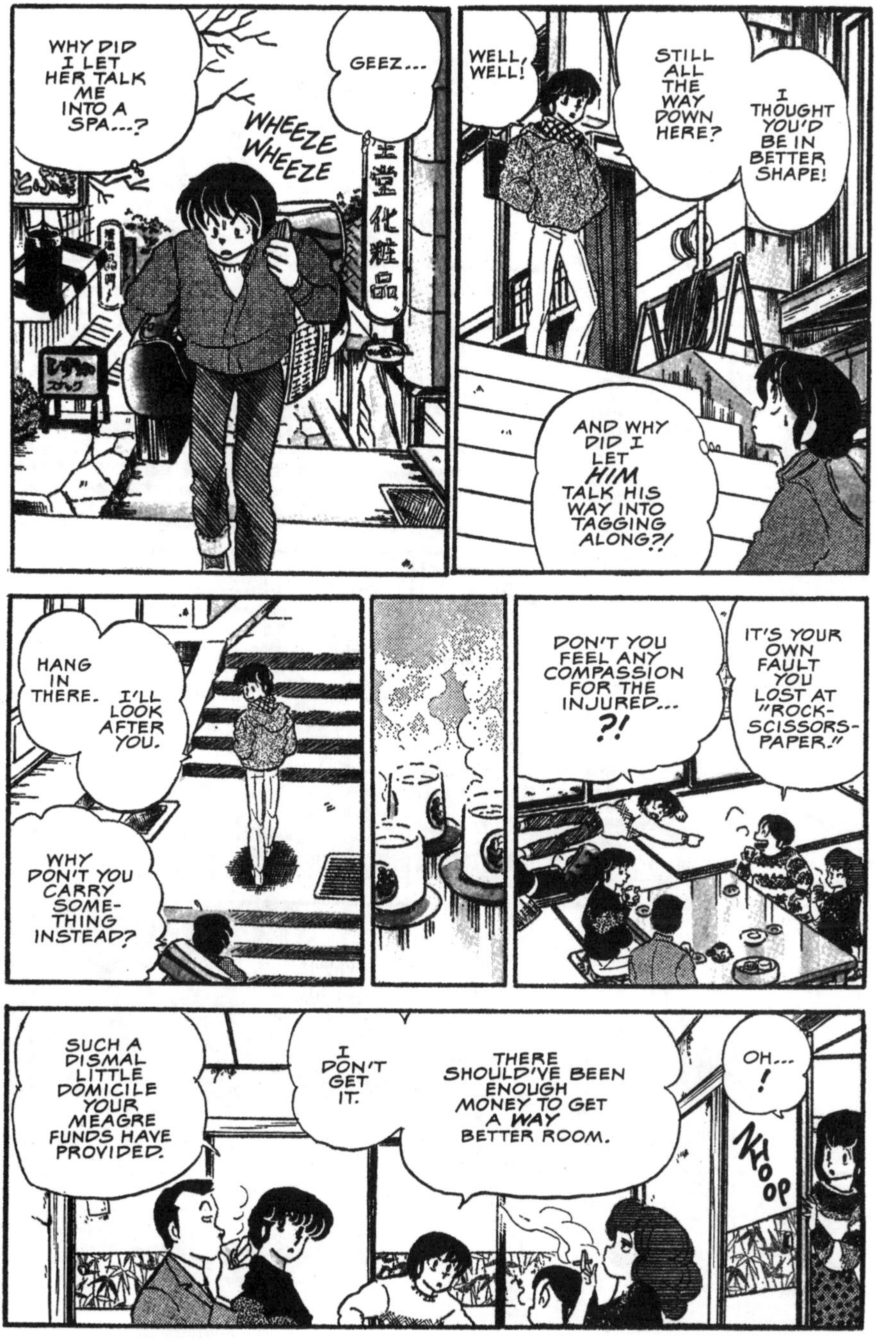
WHY DID I LET HER TALK ME INTO A SPA...?
GEEZ...
WHEEZE WHEEZE
WELL, WELL!
STILL ALL THE WAY DOWN HERE?
I THOUGHT YOU'D BE IN BETTER SHAPE!
AND WHY DID I LET *HIM* TALK HIS WAY INTO TAGGING ALONG?!
HANG IN THERE.
I'LL LOOK AFTER YOU.
WHY DON'T YOU CARRY SOME-THING INSTEAD?
DON'T YOU FEEL ANY COMPASSION FOR THE INJURED...?!
IT'S YOUR OWN FAULT YOU LOST AT "ROCK-SCISSORS-PAPER."
SUCH A DISMAL LITTLE DOMICILE YOUR MEAGRE FUNDS HAVE PROVIDED.
I DON'T GET IT.
THERE SHOULD'VE BEEN ENOUGH MONEY TO GET A *WAY* BETTER ROOM.
OH...!
WHOOP

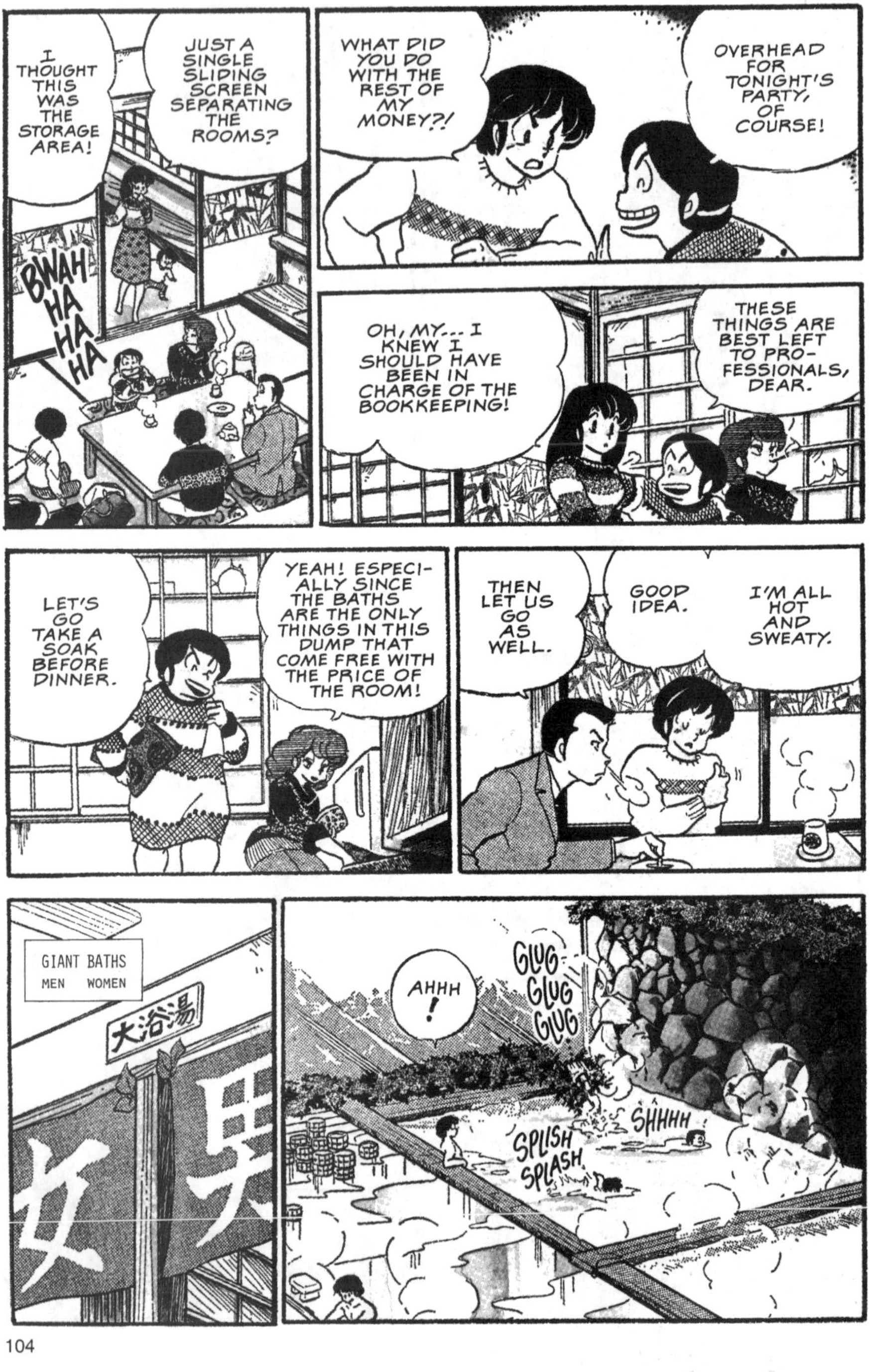

I THOUGHT THIS WAS THE STORAGE AREA!
JUST A SINGLE SLIDING SCREEN SEPARATING THE ROOMS?
BWAH HA HA HA HA
WHAT DID YOU DO WITH THE REST OF MY MONEY?!
OVERHEAD FOR TONIGHT'S PARTY, OF COURSE!
OH, MY... I KNEW I SHOULD HAVE BEEN IN CHARGE OF THE BOOKKEEPING!
THESE THINGS ARE BEST LEFT TO PRO-FESSIONALS, DEAR.
LET'S GO TAKE A SOAK BEFORE DINNER.
YEAH! ESPECI-ALLY SINCE THE BATHS ARE THE ONLY THINGS IN THIS DUMP THAT COME FREE WITH THE PRICE OF THE ROOM!
THEN LET US GO AS WELL.
GOOD IDEA.
I'M ALL HOT AND SWEATY.
GIANT BATHS
MEN WOMEN
大浴場
AHHH !
GLUG GLUG GLUG
SHHHH
SPLISH SPLASH

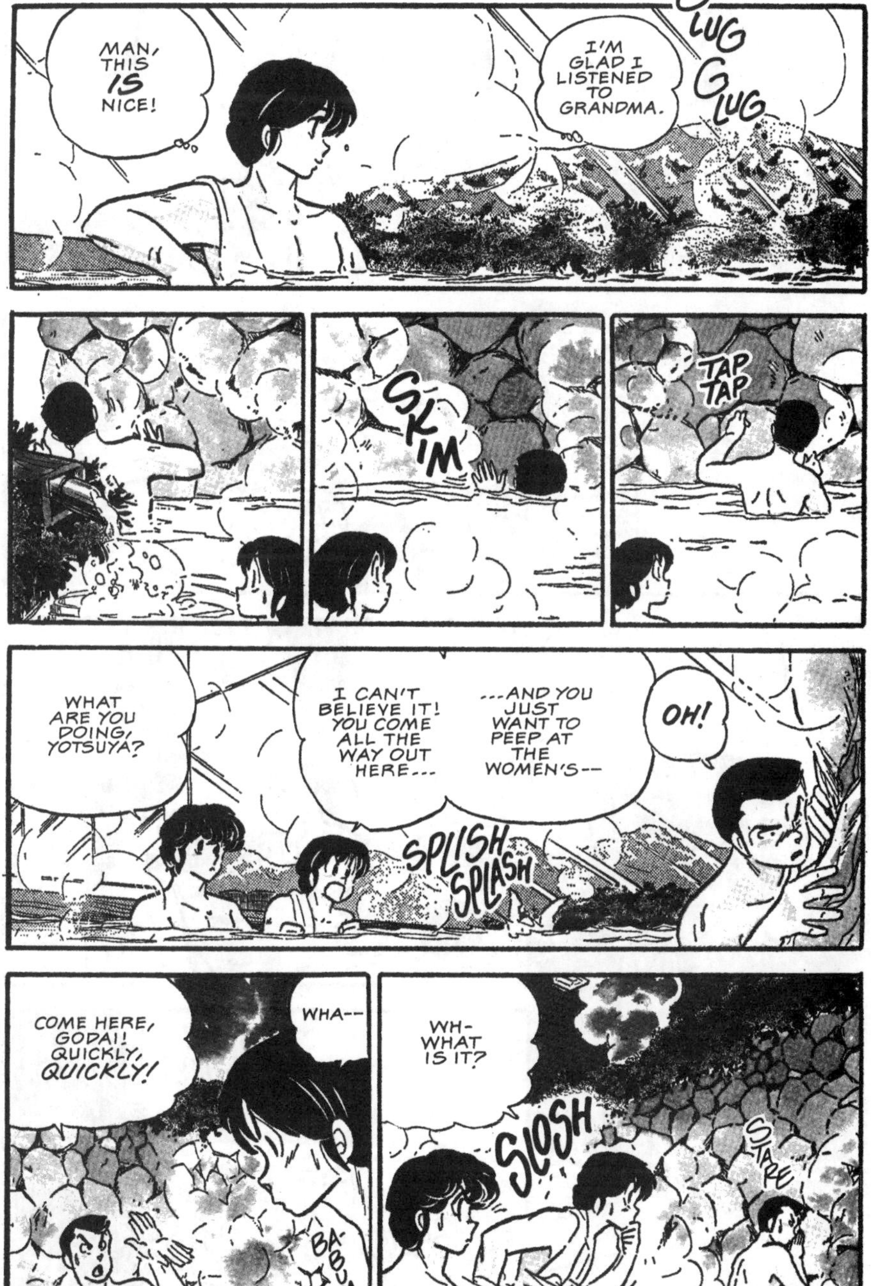
MAN, THIS IS NICE!
I'M GLAD I LISTENED TO GRANDMA.
GLUG GLUG
SKIM
TAP TAP
WHAT ARE YOU DOING, YOTSUYA?
I CAN'T BELIEVE IT! YOU COME ALL THE WAY OUT HERE--- ---AND YOU JUST WANT TO PEEP AT THE WOMEN'S--
OH!
SPLISH SPLASH
COME HERE, GODAI! QUICKLY, QUICKLY!
WHA--
BA-BUMP
WH-WHAT IS IT?
SLOSH
STARE

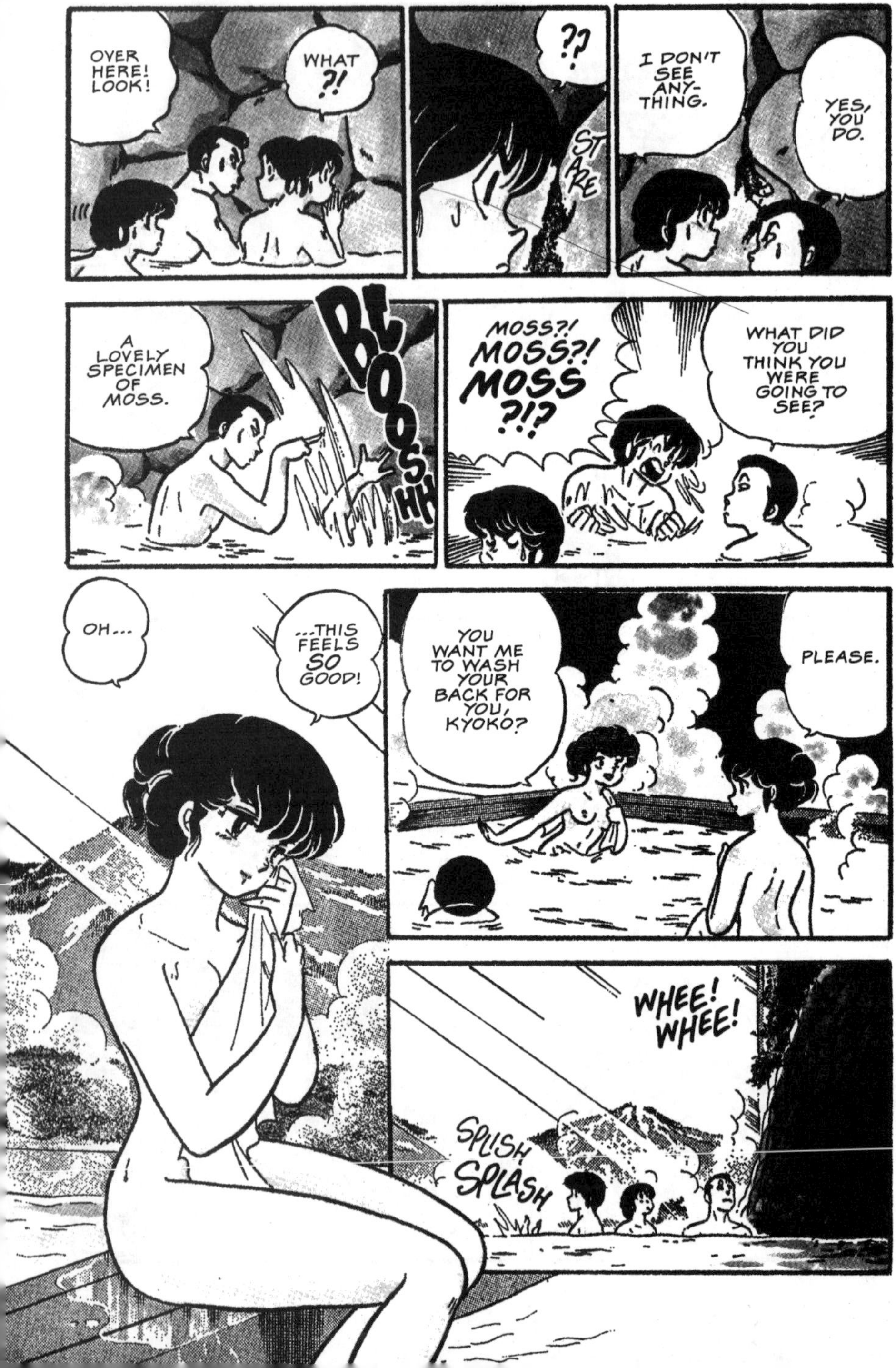

OVER HERE! LOOK!
WHAT ?!
??
STARE
I DON'T SEE ANY-THING.
YES, YOU DO.
A LOVELY SPECIMEN OF MOSS.
BLOOOSHH
MOSS?! MOSS?! MOSS ?!?
WHAT DID YOU THINK YOU WERE GOING TO SEE?
OH...
...THIS FEELS SO GOOD!
YOU WANT ME TO WASH YOUR BACK FOR YOU, KYOKO?
PLEASE.
WHEE! WHEE!
SPLISH SPLASH

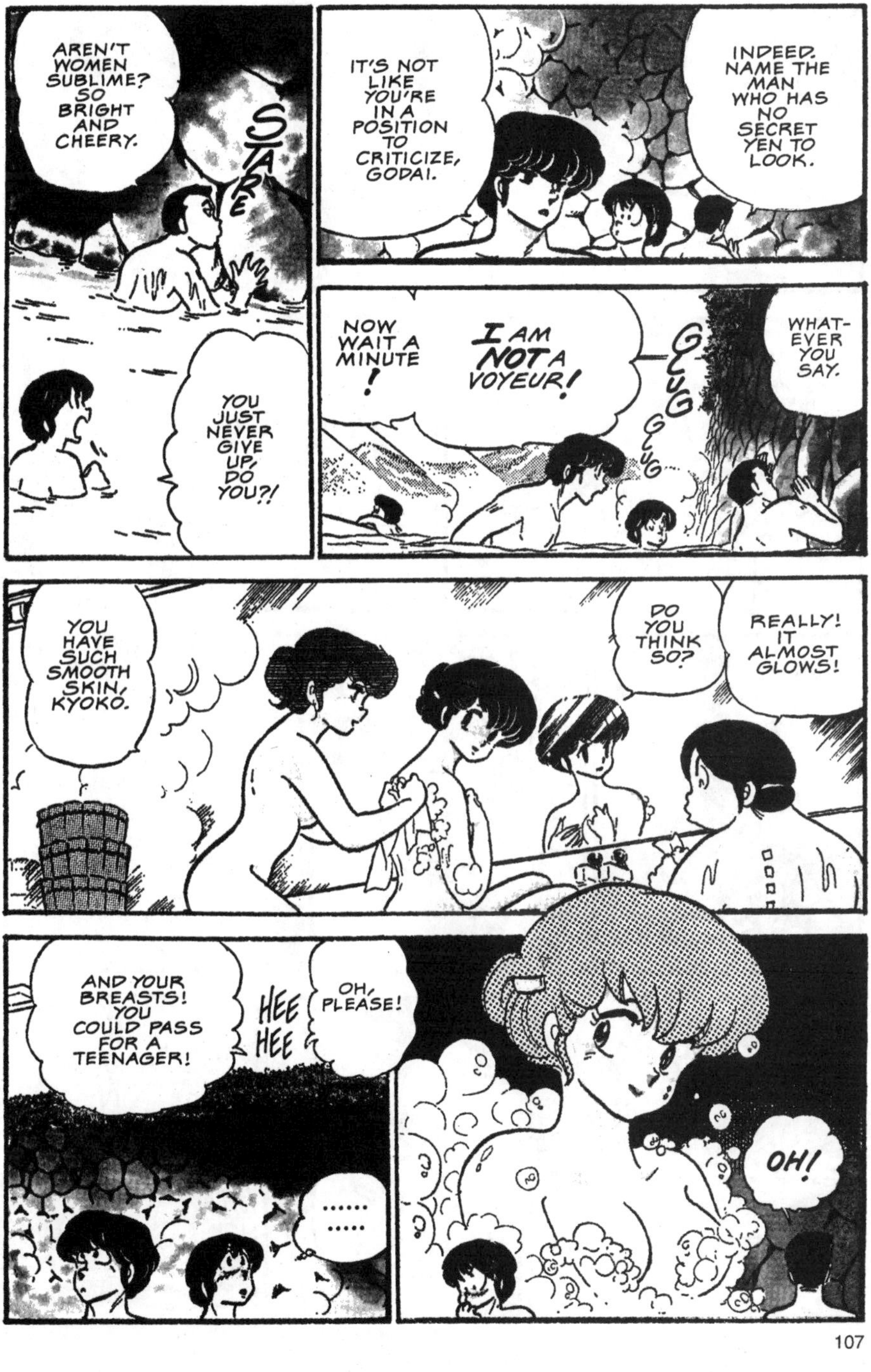
AREN'T WOMEN SUBLIME? SO BRIGHT AND CHEERY.
STARE
YOU JUST NEVER GIVE UP, DO YOU?!
IT'S NOT LIKE YOU'RE IN A POSITION TO CRITICIZE, GODAI.
INDEED. NAME THE MAN WHO HAS NO SECRET YEN TO LOOK.
NOW WAIT A MINUTE!
I AM NOT A VOYEUR!
GLUG GLUG
WHAT-EVER YOU SAY.
YOU HAVE SUCH SMOOTH SKIN, KYOKO.
DO YOU THINK SO?
REALLY! IT ALMOST GLOWS!
AND YOUR BREASTS! YOU COULD PASS FOR A TEENAGER!
HEE HEE
OH, PLEASE!
....
OH!

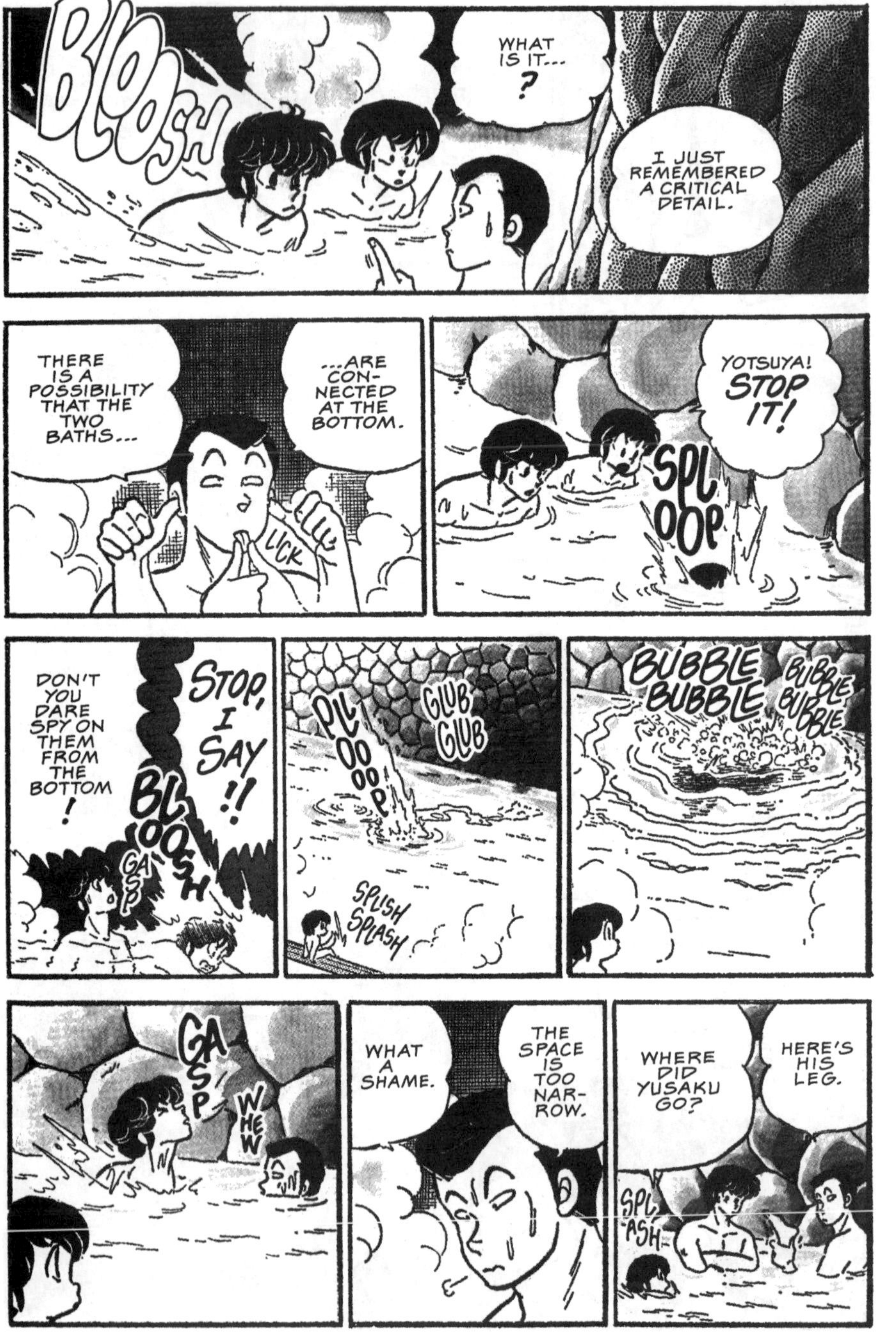
BLOOSH
WHAT IS IT... ?
I JUST REMEMBERED A CRITICAL DETAIL.
THERE IS A POSSIBILITY THAT THE TWO BATHS...
...ARE CONNECTED AT THE BOTTOM.
LICK
YOTSUYA! STOP IT!
SPLOOP
DON'T YOU DARE SPY ON THEM FROM THE BOTTOM!
STOP, I SAY!!
BLOOSH
GASP
PLOOOOP
GLUB GLUB
SPLISH SPLASH
BUBBLE BUBBLE
BUBBLE BUBBLE
GASP
WHEW
WHAT A SHAME.
THE SPACE IS TOO NARROW.
WHERE DID YUSAKU GO?
HERE'S HIS LEG.
SPLASH

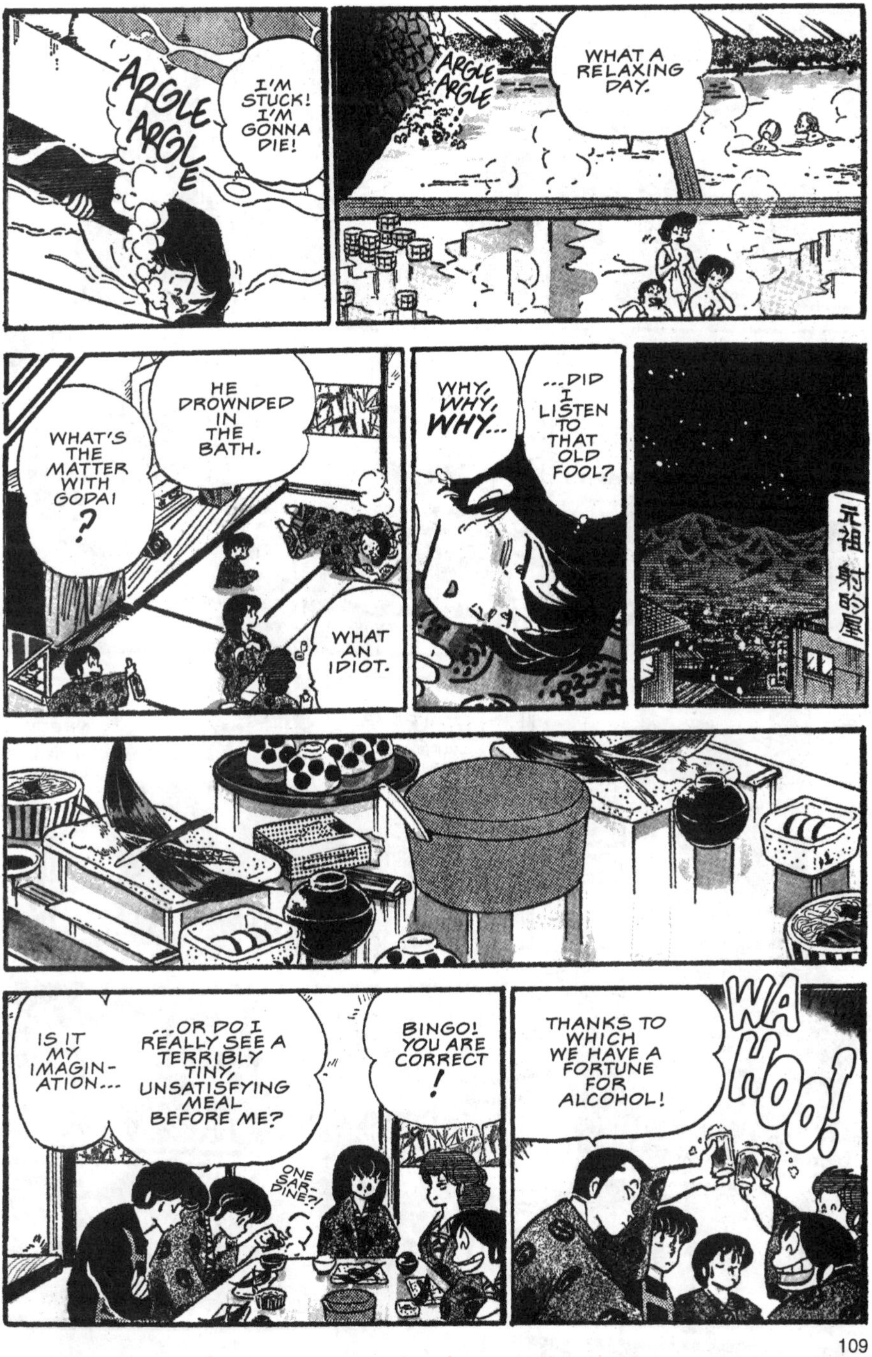
ARGLE ARGLE
I'M STUCK! I'M GONNA DIE!
ARGLE ARGLE
WHAT A RELAXING DAY.
WHAT'S THE MATTER WITH GODAI?
HE DROWNED IN THE BATH.
WHAT AN IDIOT.
WHY, WHY, WHY...
...DID I LISTEN TO THAT OLD FOOL?
元祖 射的屋
IS IT MY IMAGINATION...
...OR DO I REALLY SEE A TERRIBLY TINY, UNSATISFYING MEAL BEFORE ME?
ONE SARDINE?!
BINGO! YOU ARE CORRECT!
THANKS TO WHICH WE HAVE A FORTUNE FOR ALCOHOL!
WA HOO!

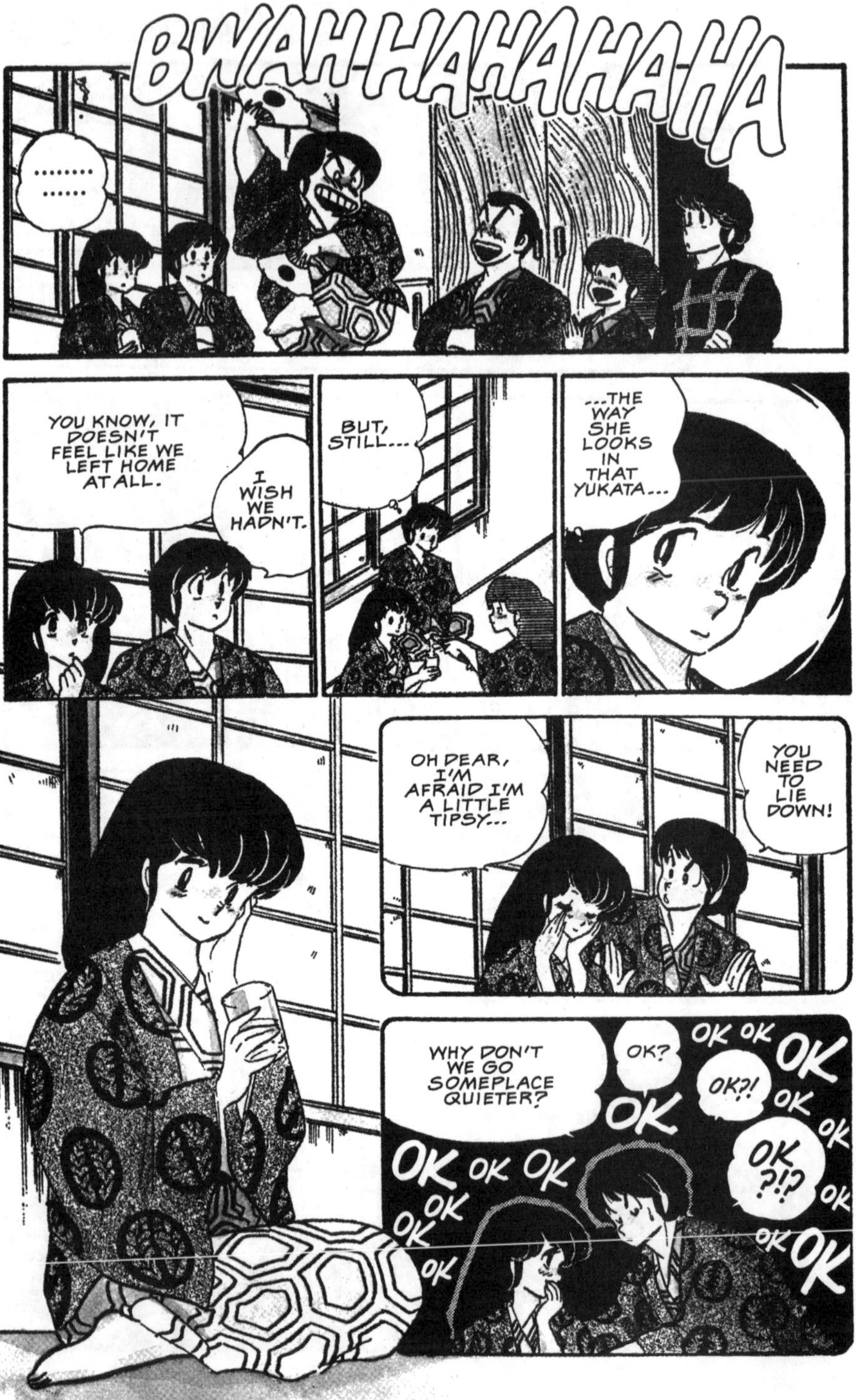
BWAHHAHAHAHAHA
....
YOU KNOW, IT DOESN'T FEEL LIKE WE LEFT HOME AT ALL.
I WISH WE HADN'T.
BUT, STILL...
...THE WAY SHE LOOKS IN THAT YUKATA...
OH DEAR, I'M AFRAID I'M A LITTLE TIPSY...
YOU NEED TO LIE DOWN!
WHY DON'T WE GO SOMEPLACE QUIETER?
OK?
OK OK OK
OK?!
OK OK
OK
OK OK OK
OK ?!?
OK
OK OK OK OK
OK OK

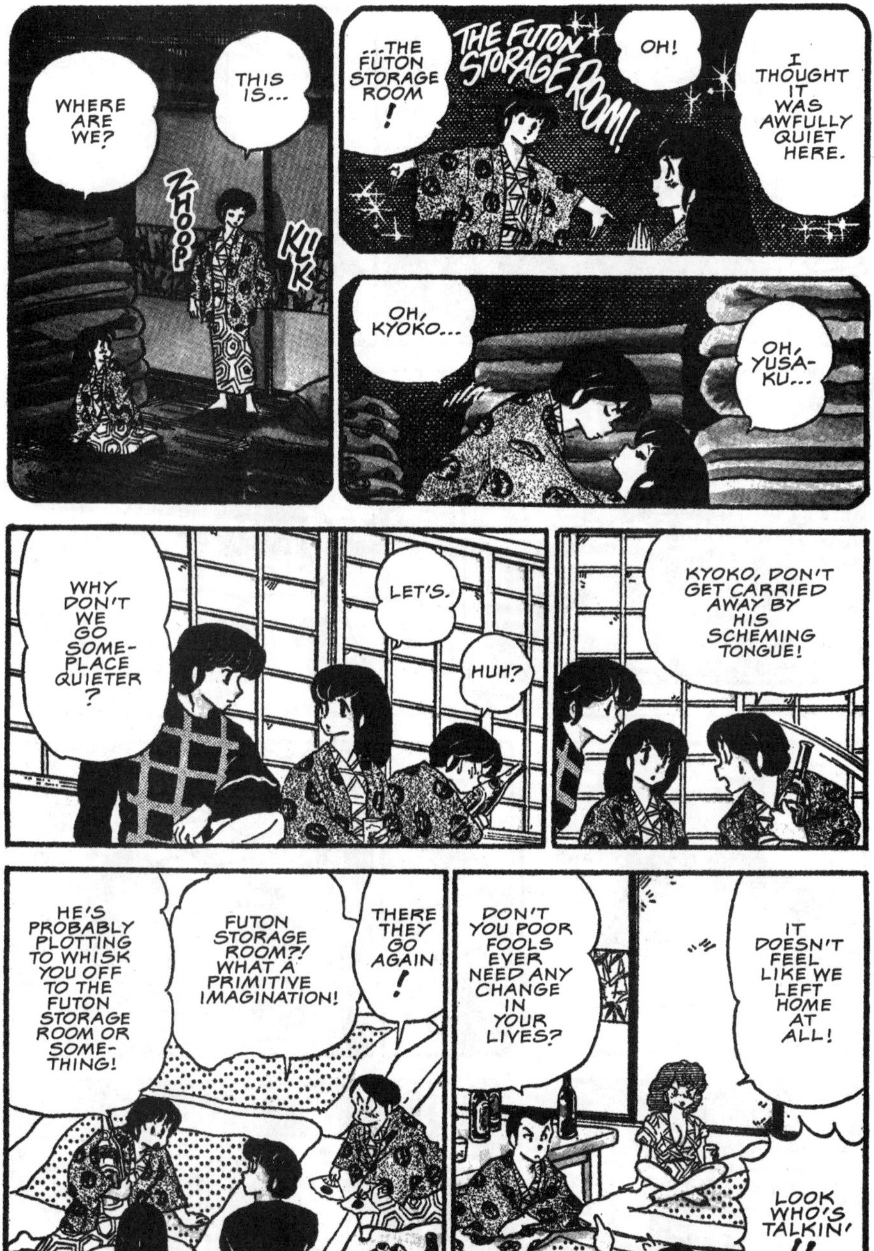
WHERE ARE WE?
THIS IS...
ZHOOP
KLIK
...THE FUTON STORAGE ROOM!
THE FUTON STORAGE ROOM!!
OH!
I THOUGHT IT WAS AWFULLY QUIET HERE.
OH, KYOKO...
OH, YUSAKU...
WHY DON'T WE GO SOMEPLACE QUIETER?
LET'S.
HUH?
KYOKO, DON'T GET CARRIED AWAY BY HIS SCHEMING TONGUE!
HE'S PROBABLY PLOTTING TO WHISK YOU OFF TO THE FUTON STORAGE ROOM OR SOMETHING!
FUTON STORAGE ROOM?! WHAT A PRIMITIVE IMAGINATION!
THERE THEY GO AGAIN!
DON'T YOU POOR FOOLS EVER NEED ANY CHANGE IN YOUR LIVES?
IT DOESN'T FEEL LIKE WE LEFT HOME AT ALL!
LOOK WHO'S TALKIN'!!

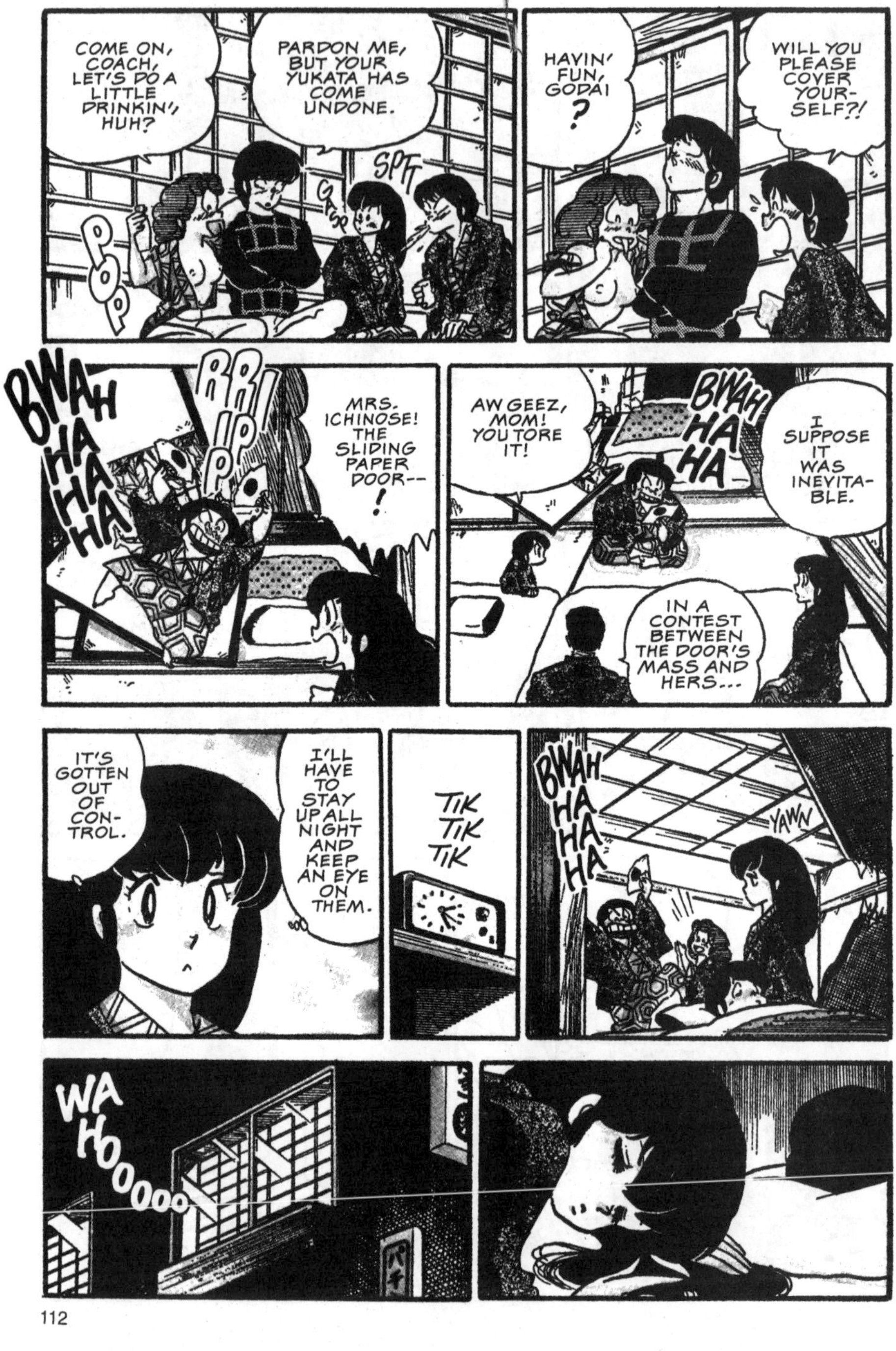
COME ON, COACH, LET'S DO A LITTLE DRINKIN', HUH?
PARDON ME, BUT YOUR YUKATA HAS COME UNDONE.
POP
GASP
SPFT
HAVIN' FUN, GODAI?
WILL YOU PLEASE COVER YOURSELF?!
BWAH HA HA HA HA HA
RRIPP
MRS. ICHINOSE! THE SLIDING PAPER DOOR--!
AW GEEZ, MOM! YOU TORE IT!
BWAH HA HA
I SUPPOSE IT WAS INEVITABLE.
IN A CONTEST BETWEEN THE DOOR'S MASS AND HERS...
IT'S GOTTEN OUT OF CONTROL.
I'LL HAVE TO STAY UP ALL NIGHT AND KEEP AN EYE ON THEM.
TIK TIK TIK
BWAH HA HA HA HA
YAWN
WA HOOOOOO

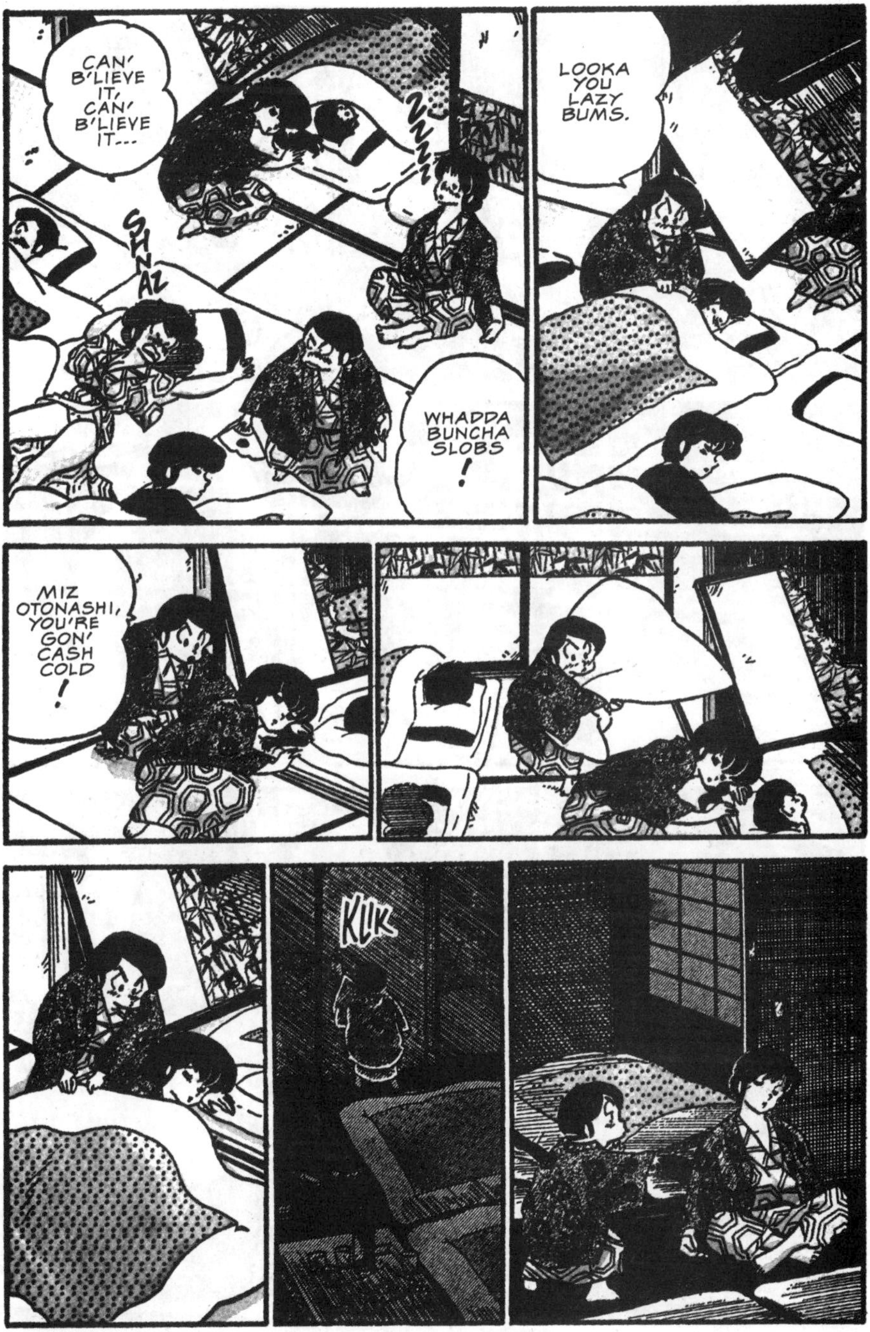
CAN' B'LIEVE IT, CAN' B'LIEVE IT...
SHNAZ
WHADDA BUNCHA SLOBS!
LOOKA YOU LAZY BUMS.
MIZ OTONASHI, YOU'RE GON' CASH COLD!
KLIK

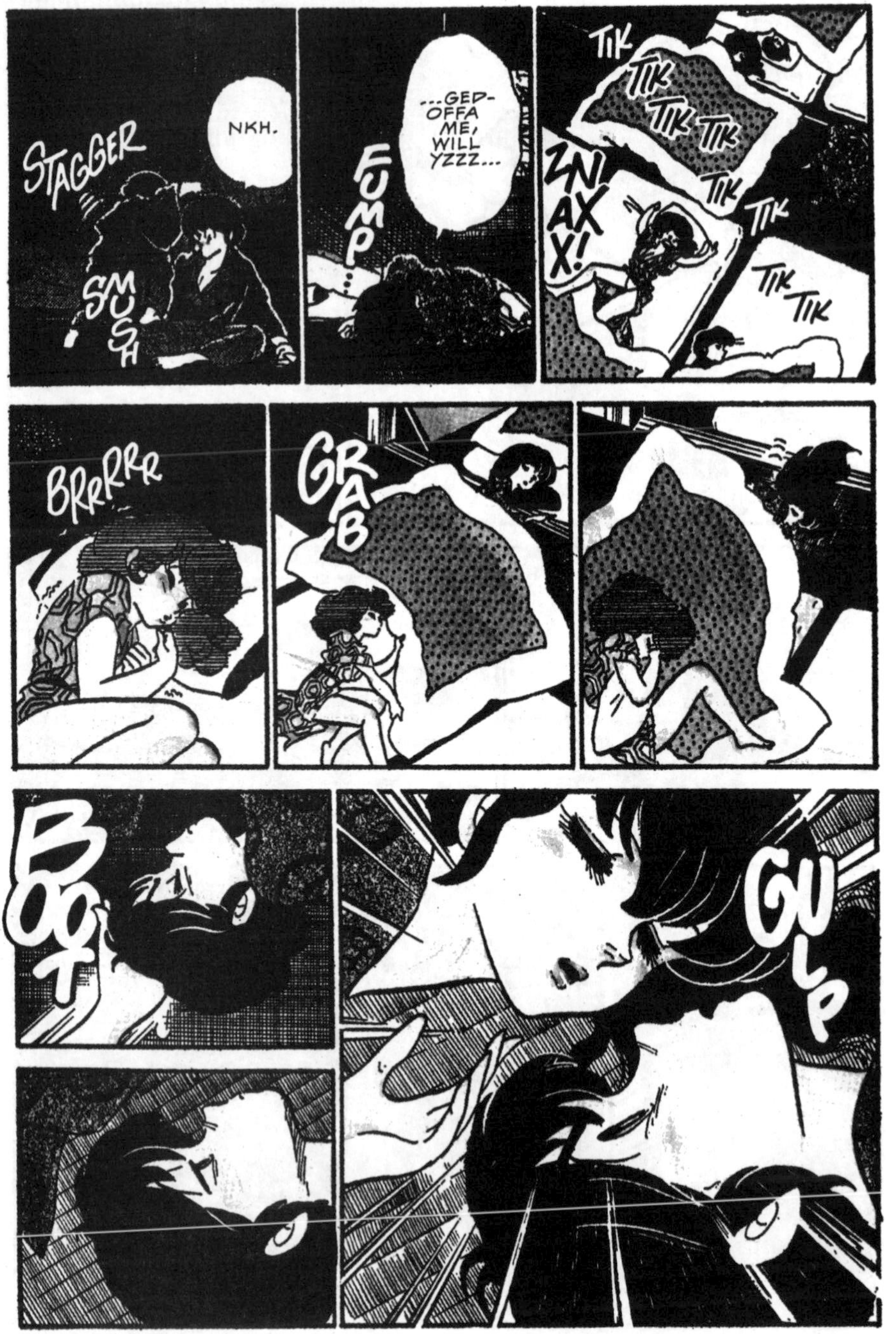
NKH.
STAGGER
SMUSH
...GED-OFFA ME, WILL YZZZ...
FUMP...
TIK
TIK
TIK
TIK
TIK
ZNAX X!
TIK
TIK TIK
BRRRRR
GRAB
BOOT
GULP

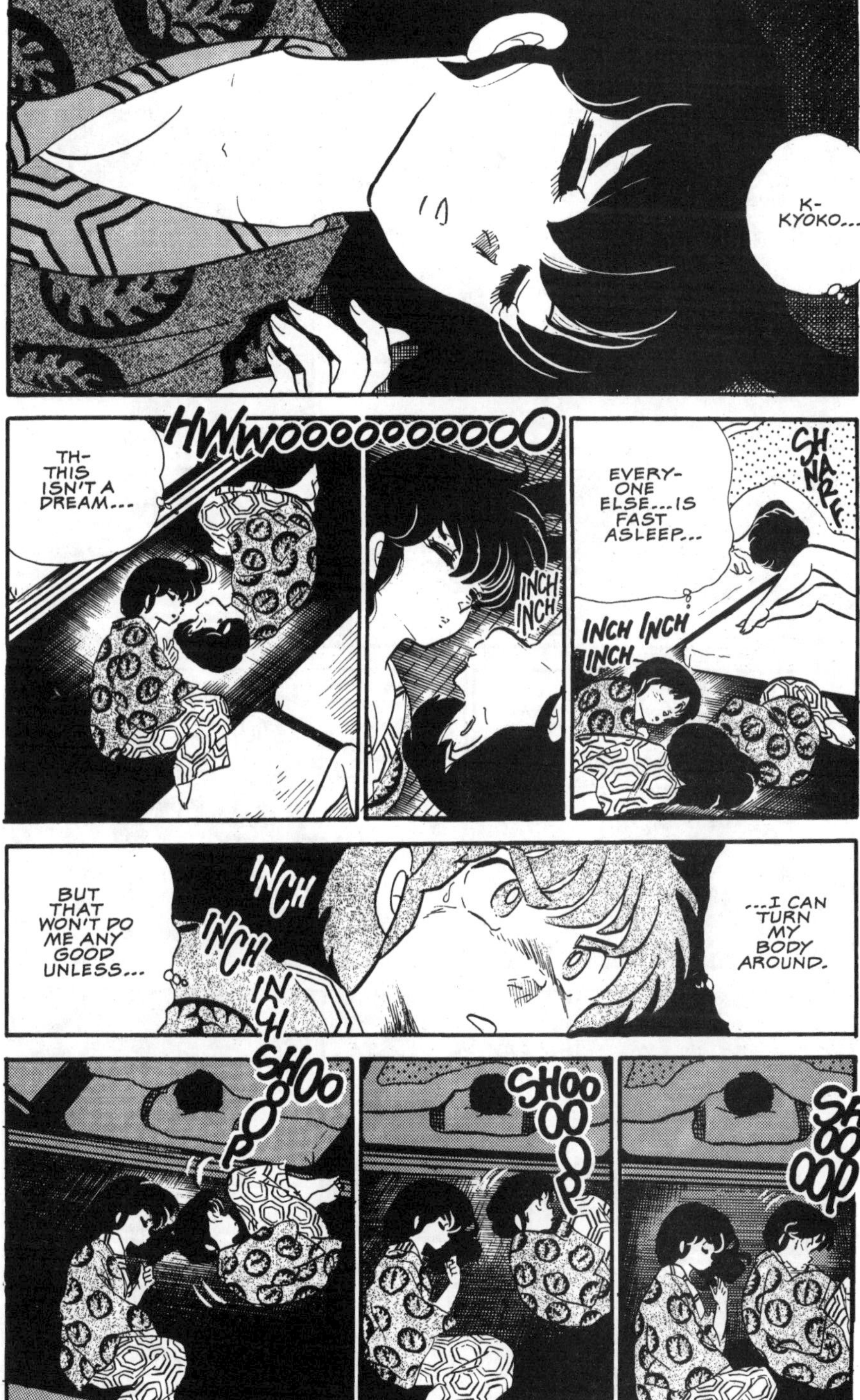
K-KYOKO...
HWWOOOOOOOOOO
TH-THIS ISN'T A DREAM...
INCH INCH
EVERY-ONE ELSE...IS FAST ASLEEP...
SNARK
INCH INCH INCH
BUT THAT WON'T DO ME ANY GOOD UNLESS...
INCH INCH INCH
...I CAN TURN MY BODY AROUND.
SHOOOOP
SHOOOOOP
SHOOOOP

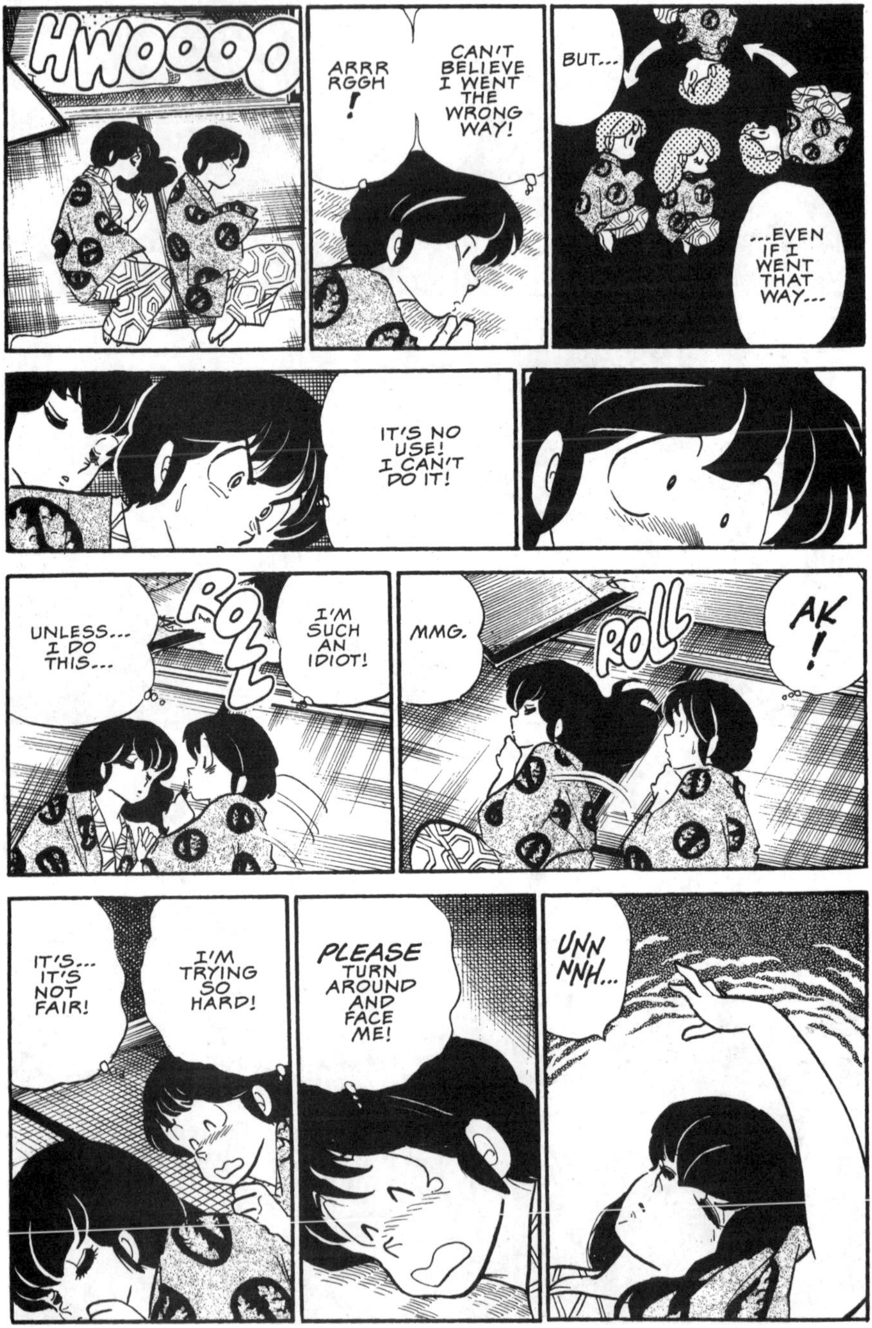
HWOOOO
ARRRRGGH!
CAN'T BELIEVE I WENT THE WRONG WAY!
BUT...
...EVEN IF I WENT THAT WAY...
IT'S NO USE! I CAN'T DO IT!
UNLESS... I DO THIS...
ROLL
I'M SUCH AN IDIOT!
MMG.
ROLL
AK!
IT'S... IT'S NOT FAIR!
I'M TRYING SO HARD!
PLEASE TURN AROUND AND FACE ME!
UNNNNH...

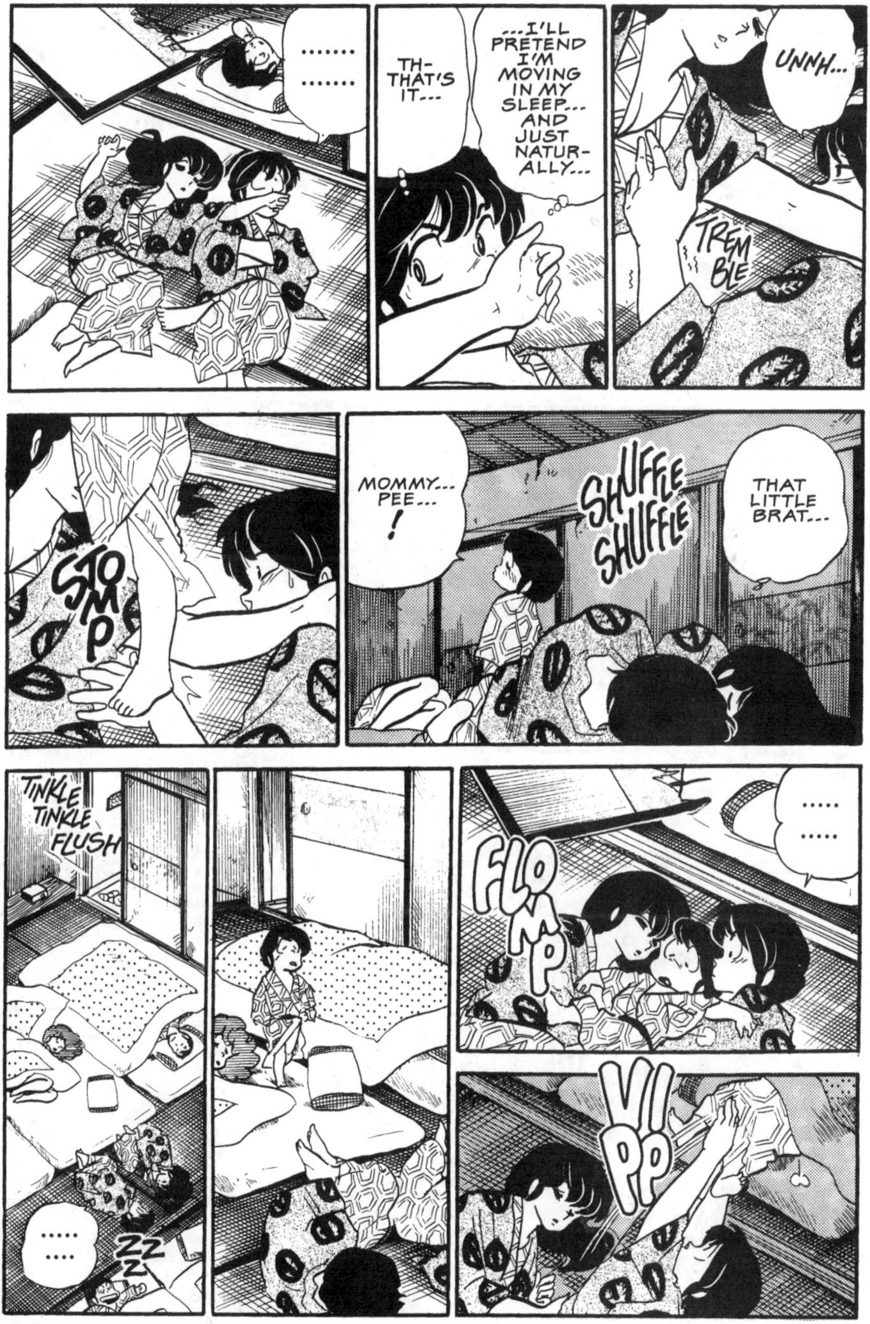
....
....
TH-THAT'S IT...
...I'LL PRETEND I'M MOVING IN MY SLEEP... AND JUST NATURALLY...
UNNH...
TREMBLE
STOMP
MOMMY... PEE...
!
SHUFFLE SHUFFLE
THAT LITTLE BRAT...
TINKLE TINKLE FLUSH
.....
.....
ZZZ
.....
.....
FLOMP
VIPP

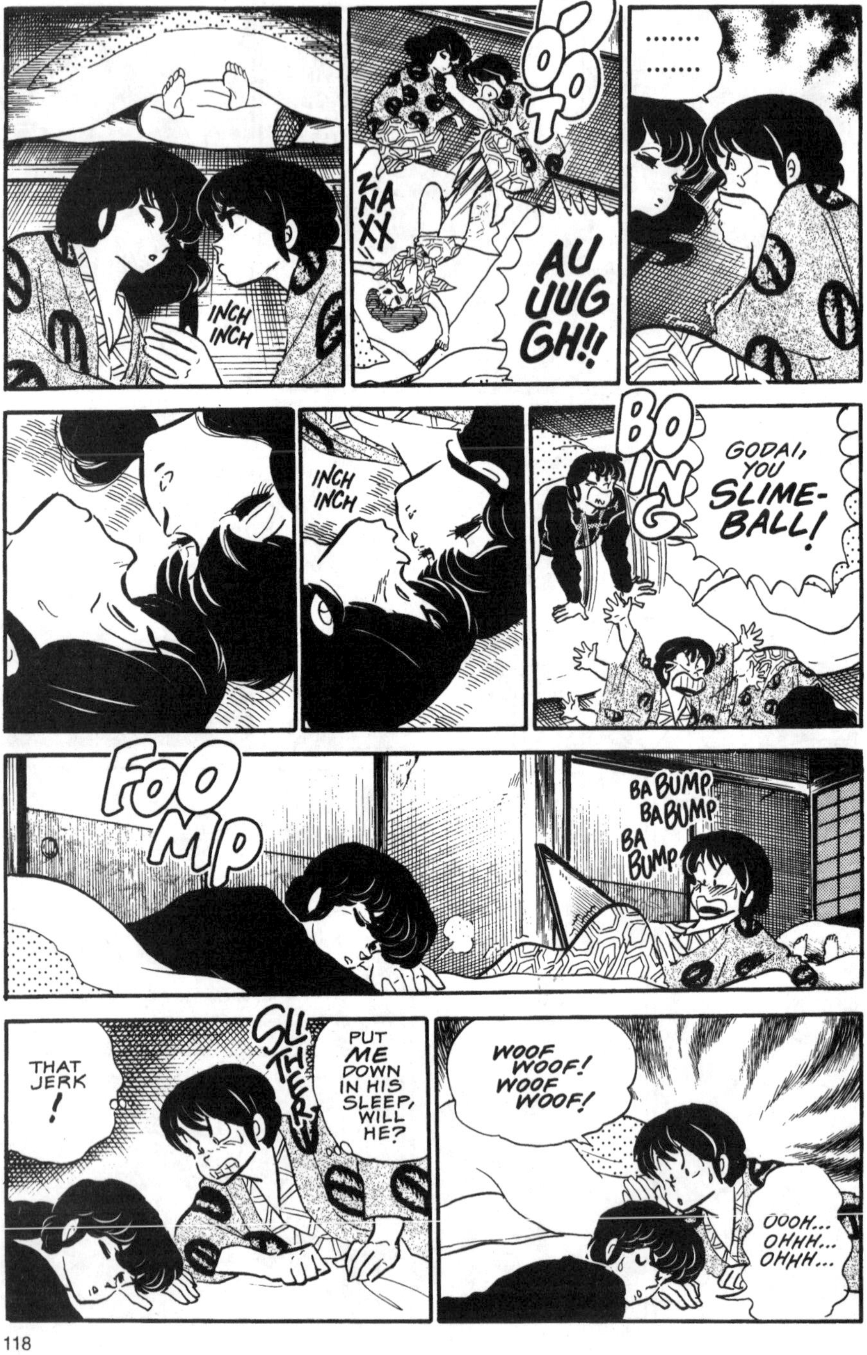
INCH INCH
BOOT
ZNAXX
AUUUGGH!!
....
....
INCH INCH
BOING
GODAI, YOU SLIME-BALL!
FOOMP
BA BUMP BA BUMP BA BUMP
THAT JERK!
SLITHER
PUT ME DOWN IN HIS SLEEP, WILL HE?
WOOF WOOF! WOOF WOOF!
OOOH... OHHH... OHHH...

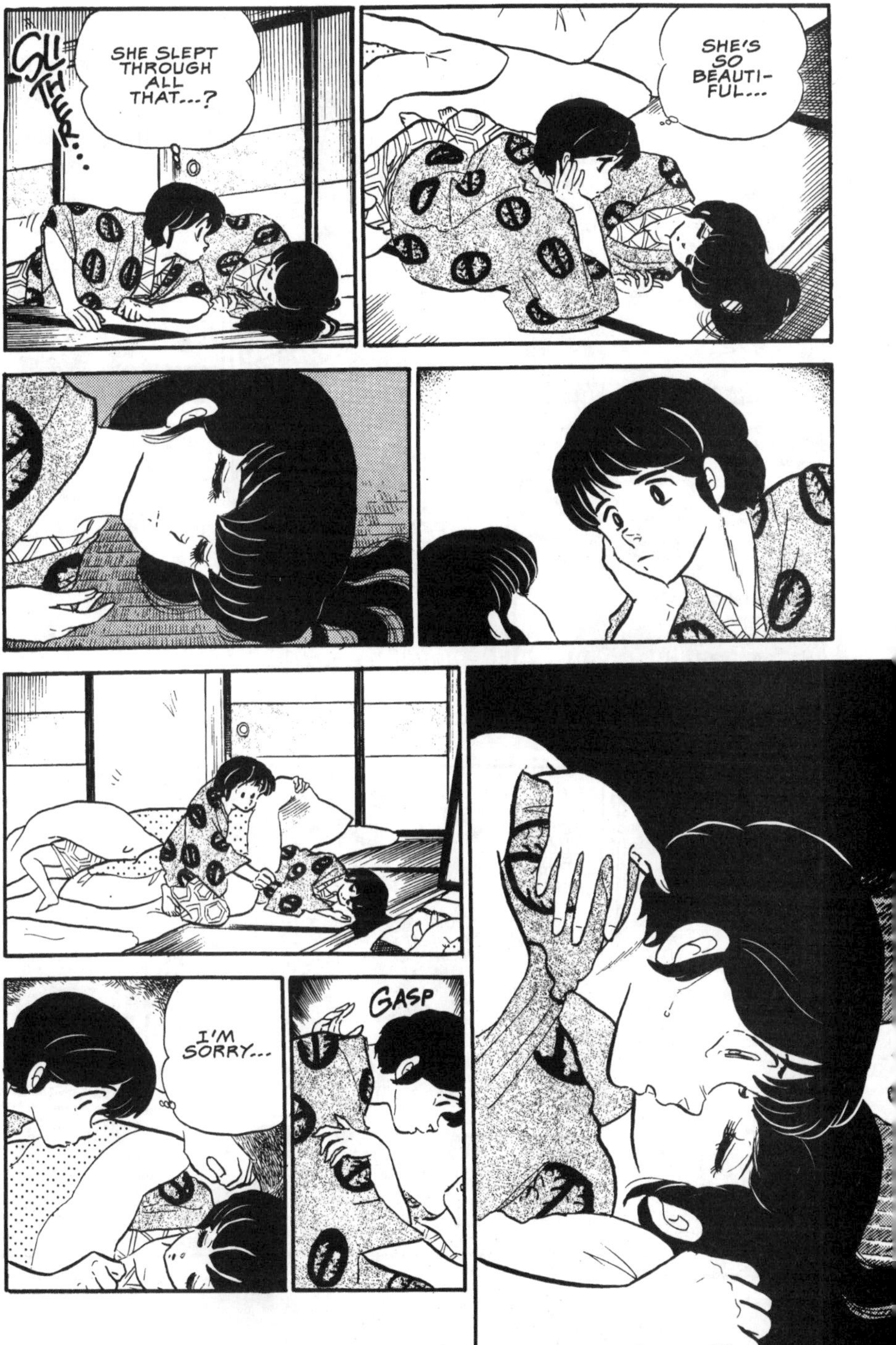
SLITHER...
SHE SLEPT THROUGH ALL THAT...?
SHE'S SO BEAUTIFUL...
I'M SORRY...
GASP

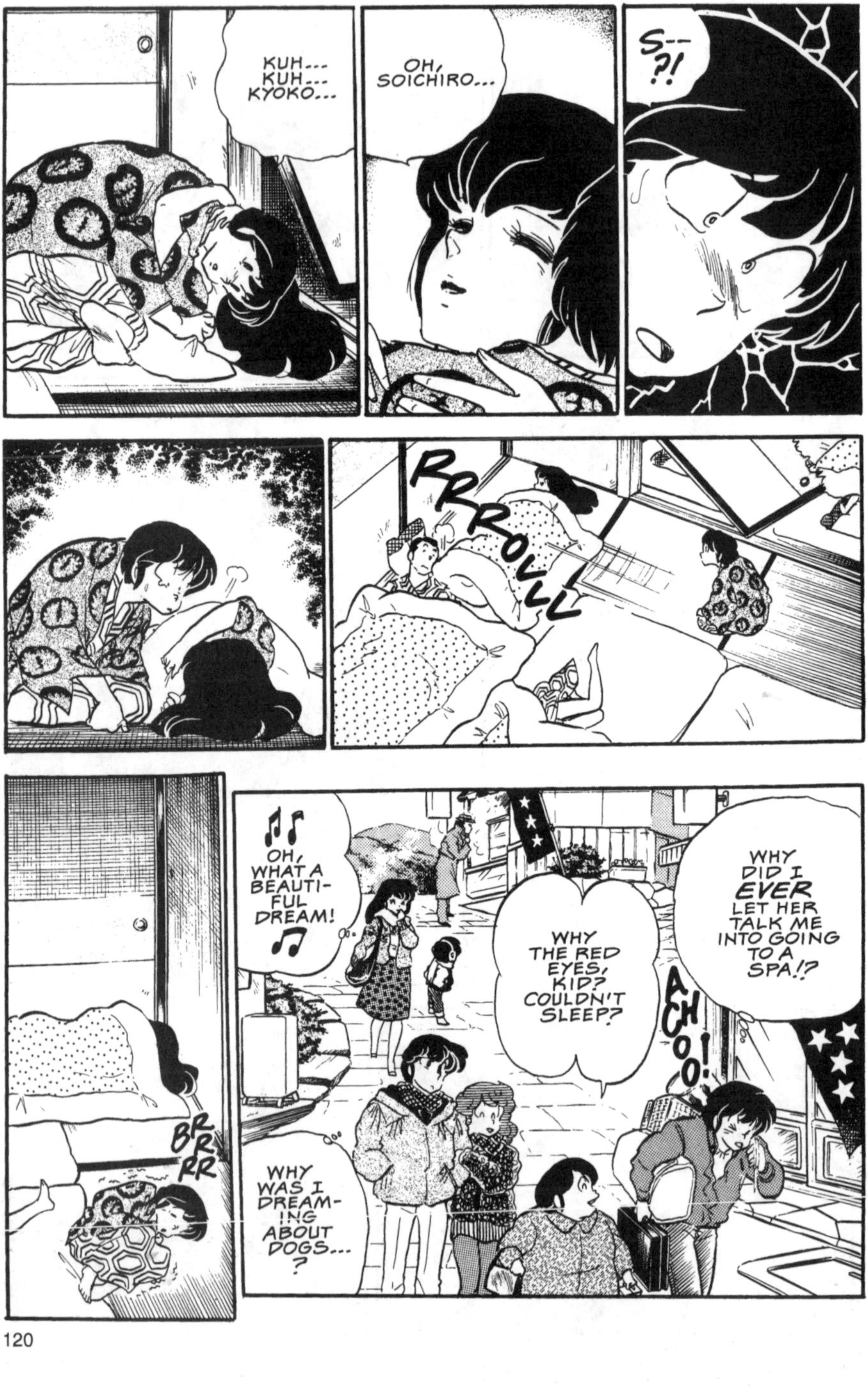
KUH... KUH... KYOKO...
OH, SOICHIRO...
S-- ?!
RRROVVV
OH, WHAT A BEAUTIFUL DREAM!
WHY THE RED EYES, KID? COULDN'T SLEEP?
WHY DID I EVER LET HER TALK ME INTO GOING TO A SPA!?
BRRRR
WHY WAS I DREAMING ABOUT DOGS...?
ACHOO!

PART 6

GOING SHOPPING IN A SUIT

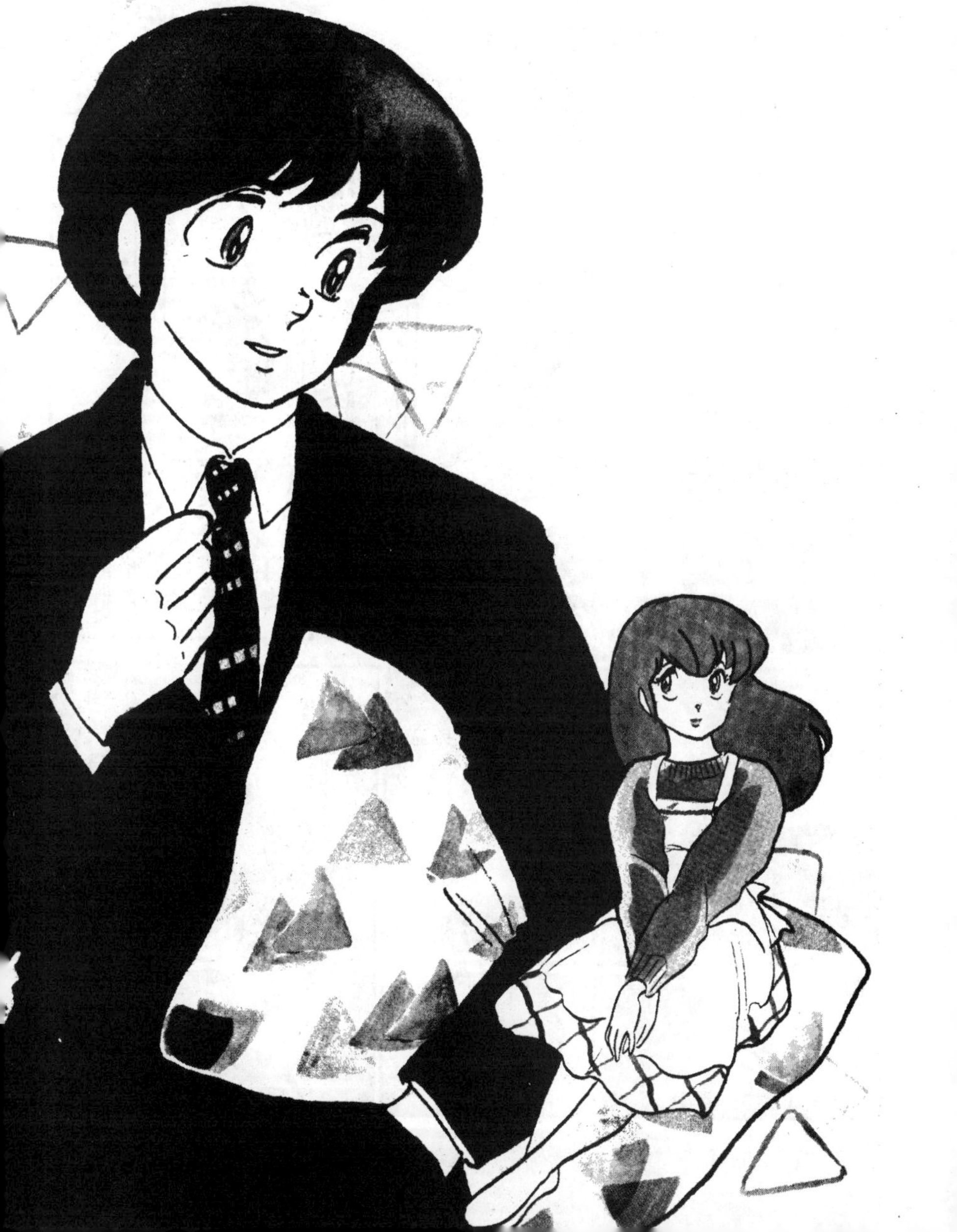

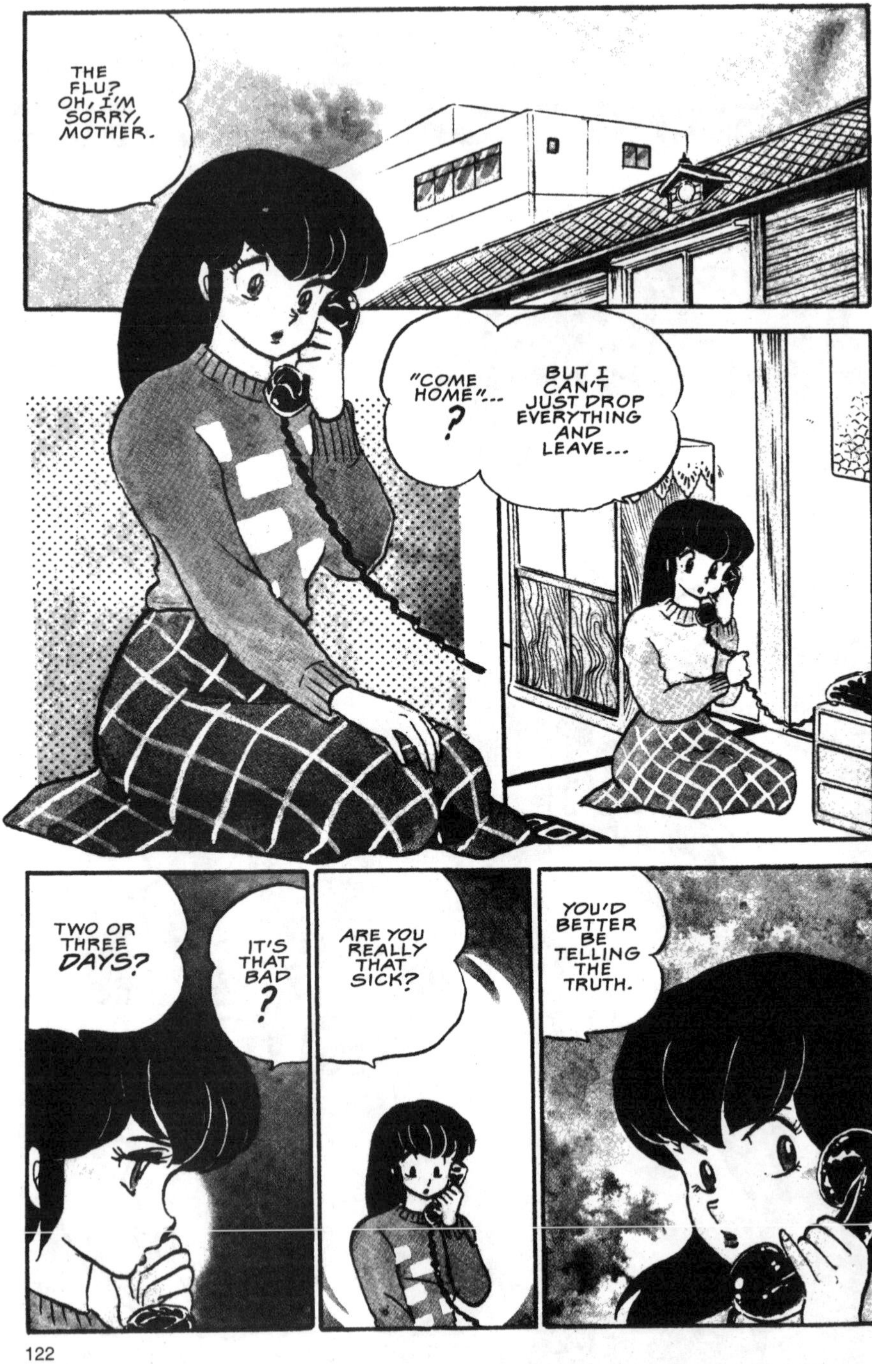
THE FLU? OH, I'M SORRY, MOTHER.
"COME HOME"...?
BUT I CAN'T JUST DROP EVERYTHING AND LEAVE...
TWO OR THREE DAYS?
IT'S THAT BAD?
ARE YOU REALLY THAT SICK?
YOU'D BETTER BE TELLING THE TRUTH.

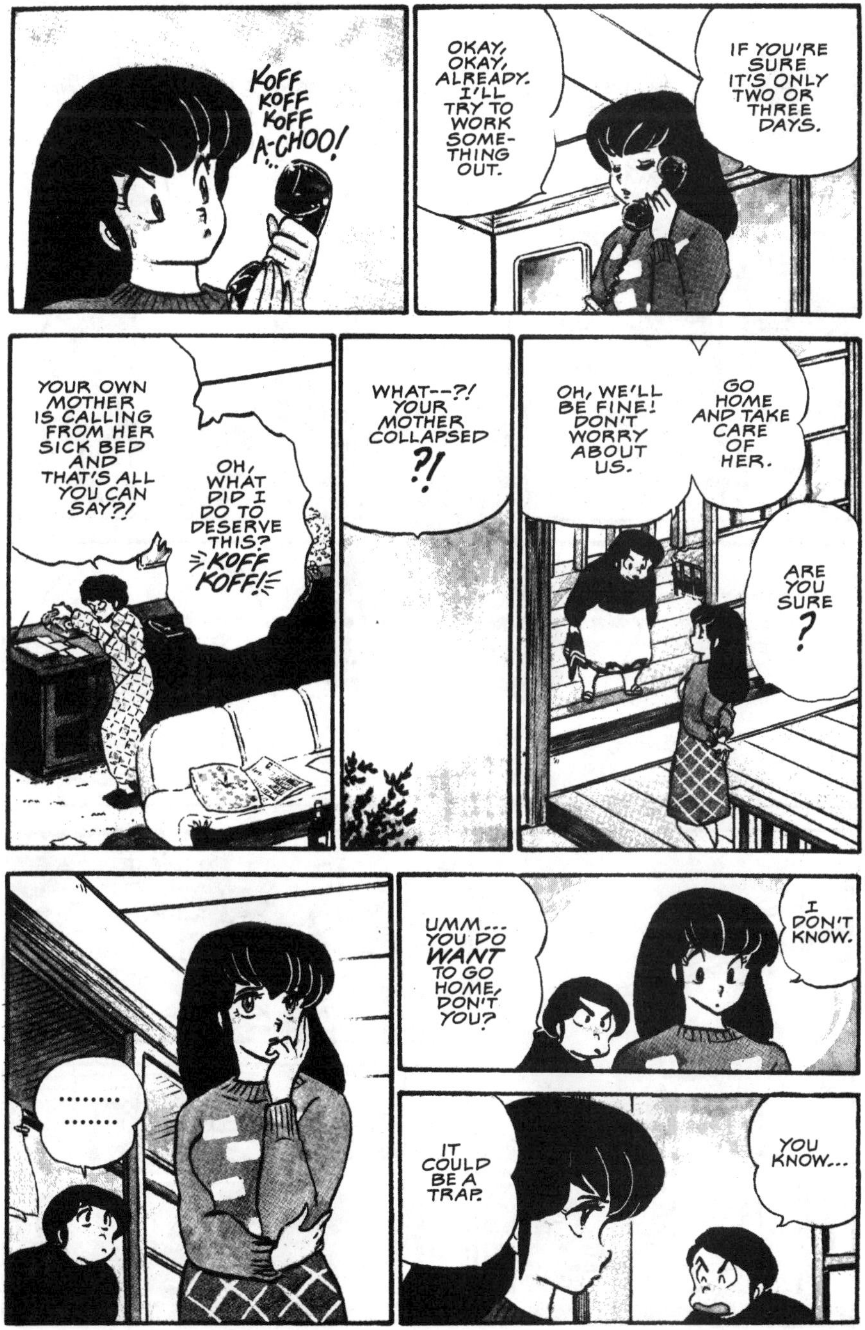
KOFF KOFF KOFF A-CHOO!
OKAY, OKAY, ALREADY. I'LL TRY TO WORK SOMETHING OUT.
IF YOU'RE SURE IT'S ONLY TWO OR THREE DAYS.
YOUR OWN MOTHER IS CALLING FROM HER SICK BED AND THAT'S ALL YOU CAN SAY?!
OH, WHAT DID I DO TO DESERVE THIS? KOFF KOFF!
WHAT--?! YOUR MOTHER COLLAPSED ?!
OH, WE'LL BE FINE! DON'T WORRY ABOUT US.
GO HOME AND TAKE CARE OF HER.
ARE YOU SURE ?
....
UMM... YOU DO WANT TO GO HOME, DON'T YOU?
I DON'T KNOW.
IT COULD BE A TRAP.
YOU KNOW...

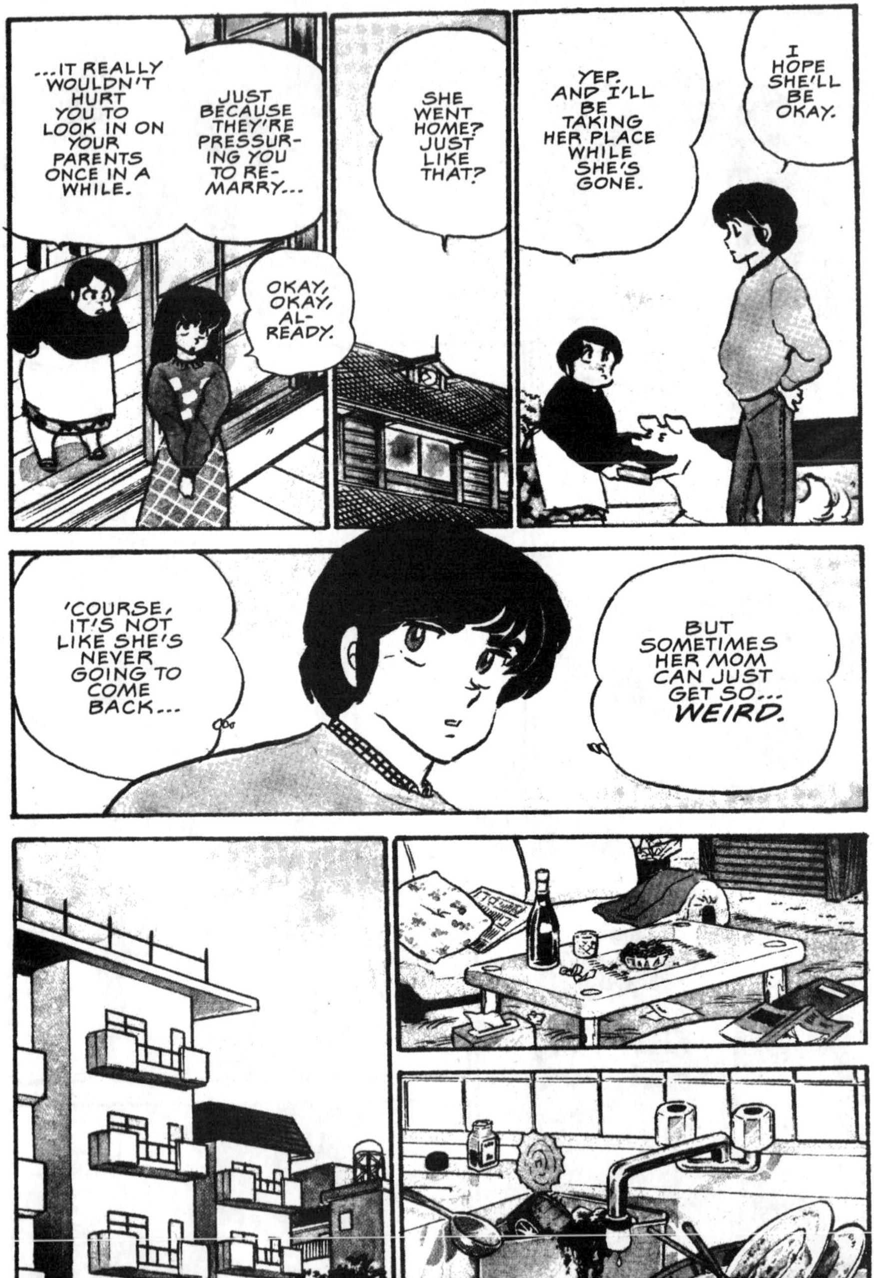

...IT REALLY WOULDN'T HURT YOU TO LOOK IN ON YOUR PARENTS ONCE IN A WHILE.
JUST BECAUSE THEY'RE PRESSURING YOU TO RE-MARRY...
OKAY, OKAY, AL-READY.
SHE WENT HOME? JUST LIKE THAT?
YEP. AND I'LL BE TAKING HER PLACE WHILE SHE'S GONE.
I HOPE SHE'LL BE OKAY.
'COURSE, IT'S NOT LIKE SHE'S NEVER GOING TO COME BACK...
BUT SOMETIMES HER MOM CAN JUST GET SO... *WEIRD.*

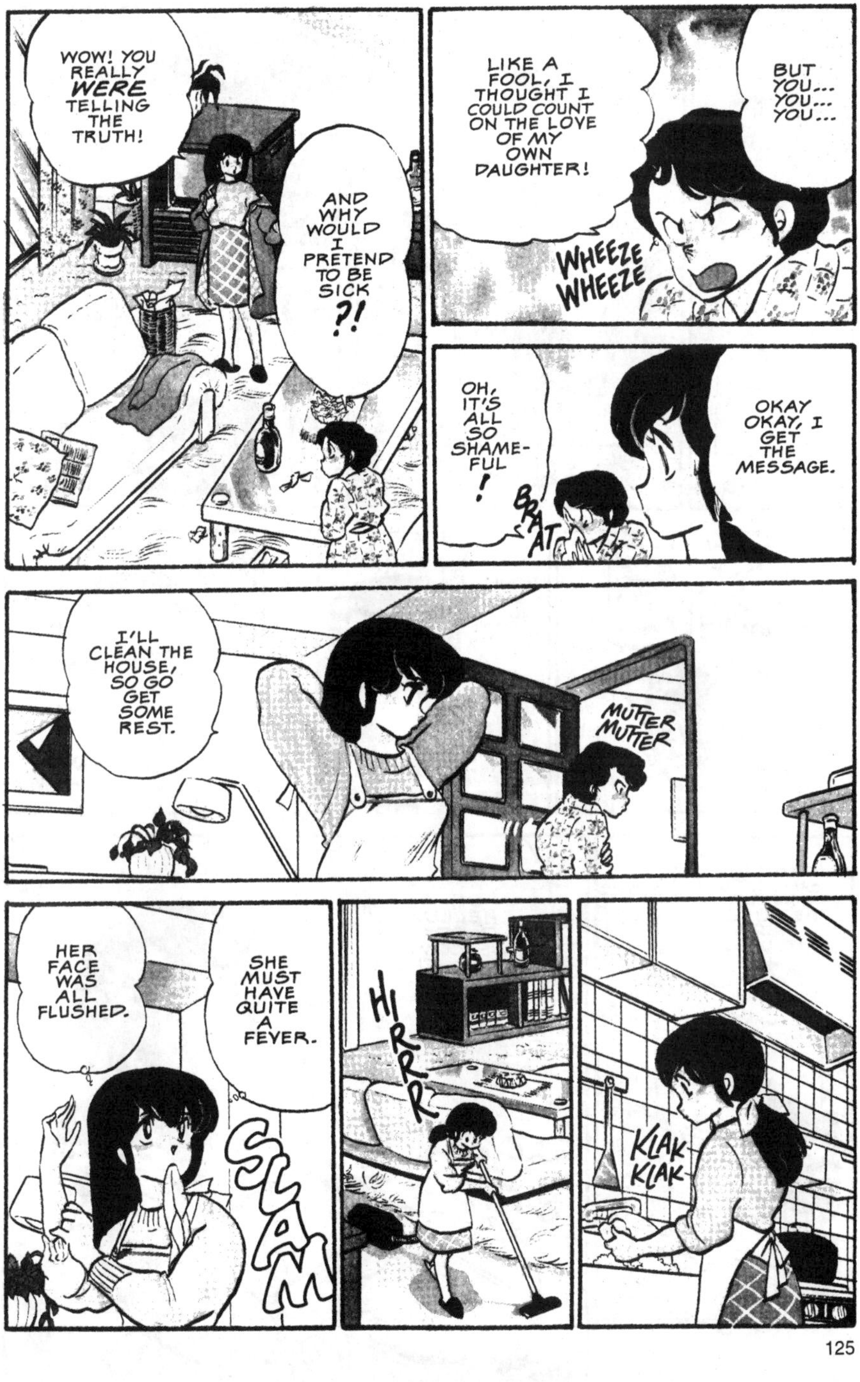
WOW! YOU REALLY WERE TELLING THE TRUTH!
AND WHY WOULD I PRETEND TO BE SICK ?!
LIKE A FOOL, I THOUGHT I COULD COUNT ON THE LOVE OF MY OWN DAUGHTER!
BUT YOU... YOU... YOU...
WHEEZE WHEEZE
OH, IT'S ALL SO SHAME-FUL!
BRAAT
OKAY OKAY, I GET THE MESSAGE.
I'LL CLEAN THE HOUSE, SO GO GET SOME REST.
MUTTER MUTTER
HER FACE WAS ALL FLUSHED.
SHE MUST HAVE QUITE A FEVER.
SLAM
HIRRR
KLAK KLAK

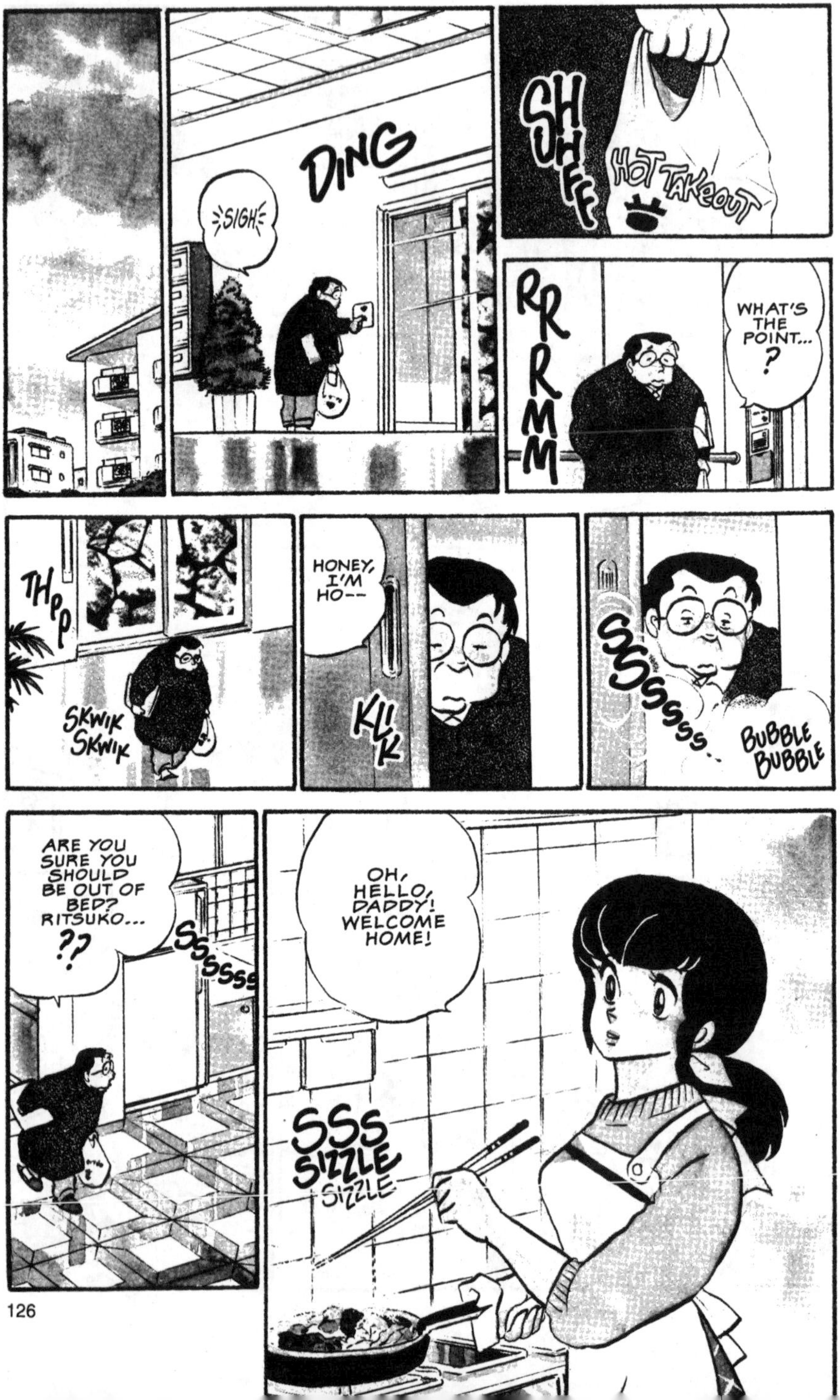
SIGH
DING
SHUHFF
HOT TAKEOUT
RRRMM
WHAT'S THE POINT...?
THPP
SKWIK SKWIK
HONEY, I'M HO--
KLIK
SSSSSS..
BUBBLE BUBBLE
ARE YOU SURE YOU SHOULD BE OUT OF BED? RITSUKO... ??
SSSSSS
OH, HELLO, DADDY! WELCOME HOME!
SSS SIZZLE SIZZLE

KYOKO!

WHAT ARE YOU DOING HERE?!

WHAT AM I...?

ISN'T IT OBVIOUS?

O' COURSE, O' COURSE!

YOU CAME HOME TO TAKE CARE OF YOUR MOTHER!

GOSH, THIS PLACE IS IMMACULATE!

DUM DE DUM

I NEVER THOUGHT A CLEAN APARTMENT MEANT SO MUCH TO HIM...

MMM, IT'S DELICIOUS!

I'M SO GLAD YOU CAME HOME, KYOKO!

YES, YES, SO GLAD!

127

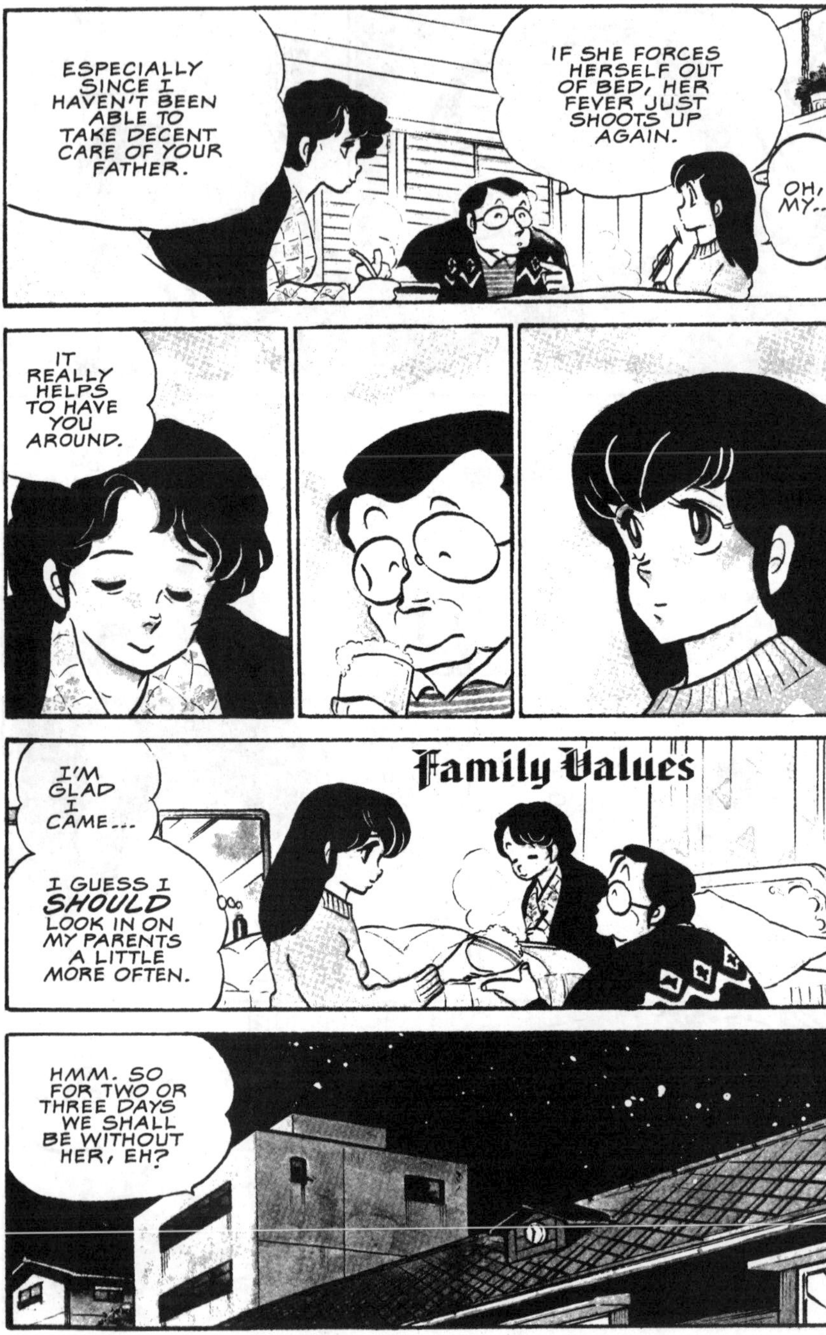
ESPECIALLY SINCE I HAVEN'T BEEN ABLE TO TAKE DECENT CARE OF YOUR FATHER.
IF SHE FORCES HERSELF OUT OF BED, HER FEVER JUST SHOOTS UP AGAIN.
OH, MY...
IT REALLY HELPS TO HAVE YOU AROUND.
Family Values
I'M GLAD I CAME...
I GUESS I ***SHOULD*** LOOK IN ON MY PARENTS A LITTLE MORE OFTEN.
HMM. SO FOR TWO OR THREE DAYS WE SHALL BE WITHOUT HER, EH?

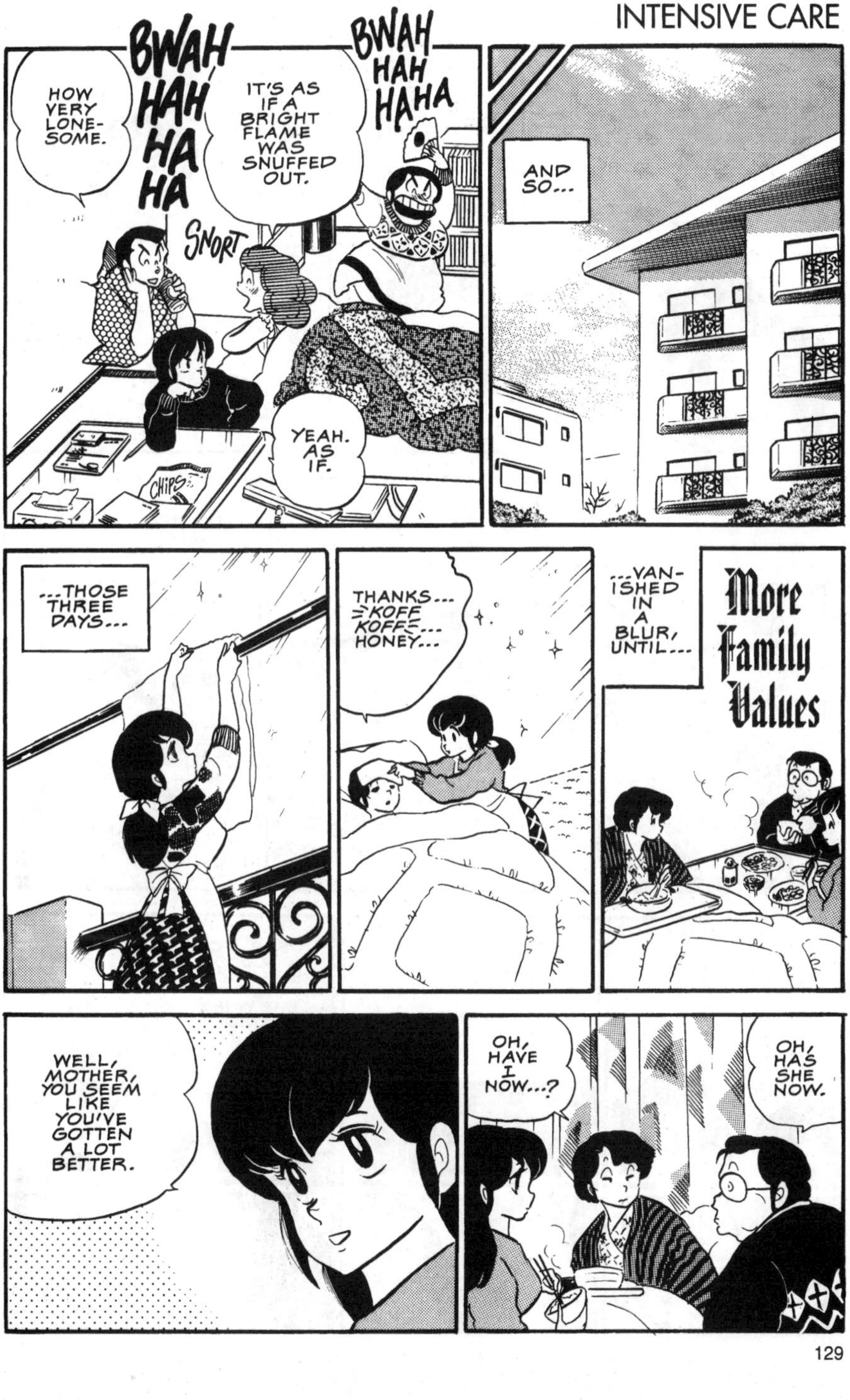
HOW VERY LONE-SOME.
BWAH HAH HA HA HA
IT'S AS IF A BRIGHT FLAME WAS SNUFFED OUT.
BWAH HAH HAHA
SNORT
YEAH. AS IF.
AND SO...
...THOSE THREE DAYS...
THANKS... KOFF KOFF... HONEY...
...VAN-ISHED IN A BLUR, UNTIL...
More Family Values
WELL, MOTHER, YOU SEEM LIKE YOU'VE GOTTEN A LOT BETTER.
OH, HAVE I NOW...?
OH, HAS SHE NOW.

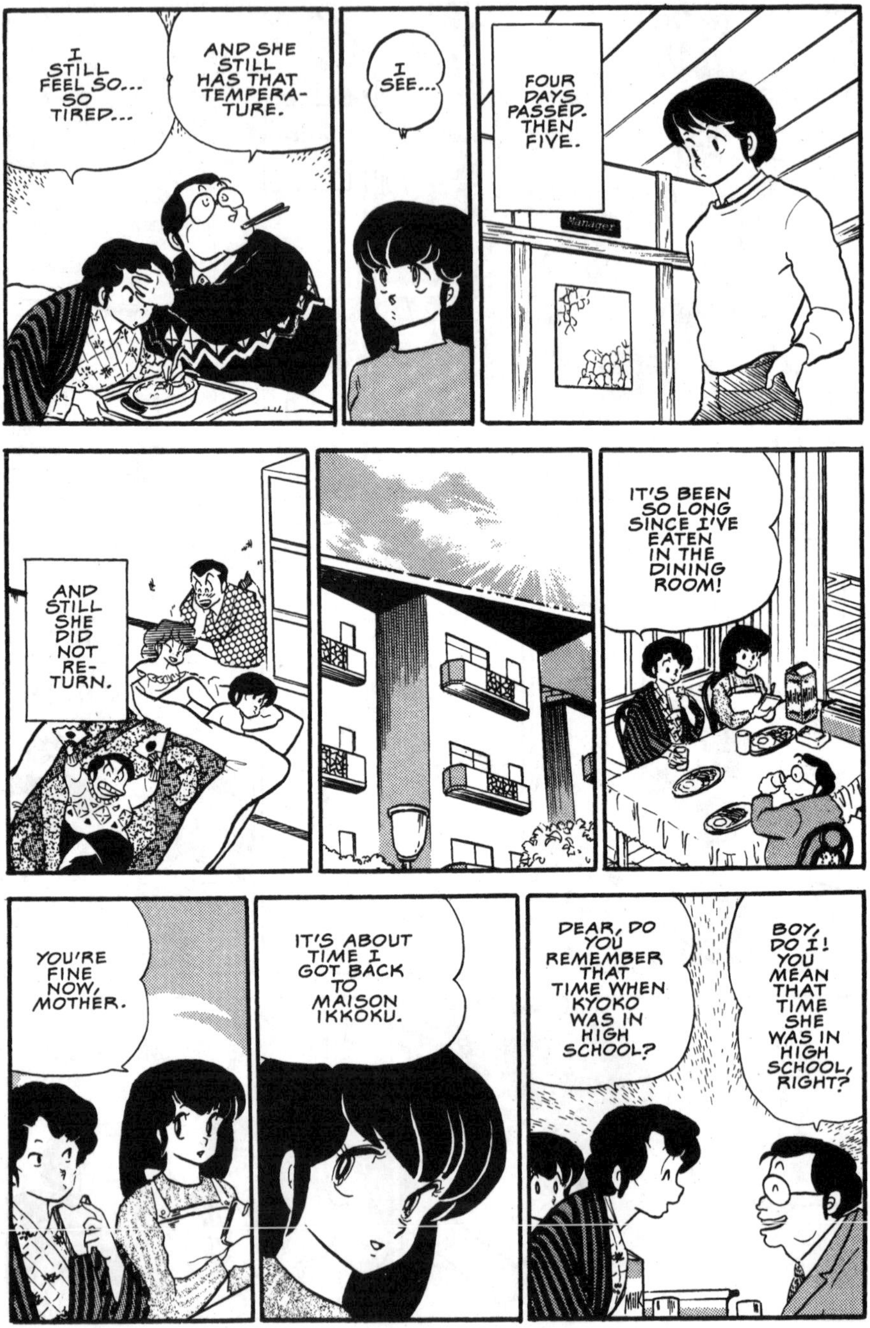
I STILL FEEL SO... SO TIRED...
AND SHE STILL HAS THAT TEMPERATURE.
I SEE...
FOUR DAYS PASSED. THEN FIVE.
Manager
AND STILL SHE DID NOT RETURN.
IT'S BEEN SO LONG SINCE I'VE EATEN IN THE DINING ROOM!
YOU'RE FINE NOW, MOTHER.
IT'S ABOUT TIME I GOT BACK TO MAISON IKKOKU.
DEAR, DO YOU REMEMBER THAT TIME WHEN KYOKO WAS IN HIGH SCHOOL?
BOY, DO I! YOU MEAN THAT TIME SHE WAS IN HIGH SCHOOL, RIGHT?

I REALLY... SHOULDN'T BE AWAY FOR MORE THAN A WEEK...

AND THEN THERE WAS THAT TIME ON VACATION!

YEAH, YEAH, ON VACATION!

YOU KNOW, THESE FLUS CAN RELAPSE PRETTY BADLY.

MOTHER, YOU'RE COMPLETELY OVER IT!

WHAT ARE YOU TALKING ABOUT?! SHE NEEDS AT LEAST TWO OR THREE MORE DAYS OF REST!

GLARE

WHOOPS! LOOKS LIKE IT'S TIME FOR OL' DAD TO GO TO WORK!

HAVE A NICE DAY.

I'LL BE HOME EARLY TODAY.

SATURDAY, YOU KNOW.

DON'T LET HER LEAVE, NO MATTER WHAT.

ONCE SHE GOES BACK TO WORK, WHO KNOWS WHEN SHE'LL VISIT AGAIN!

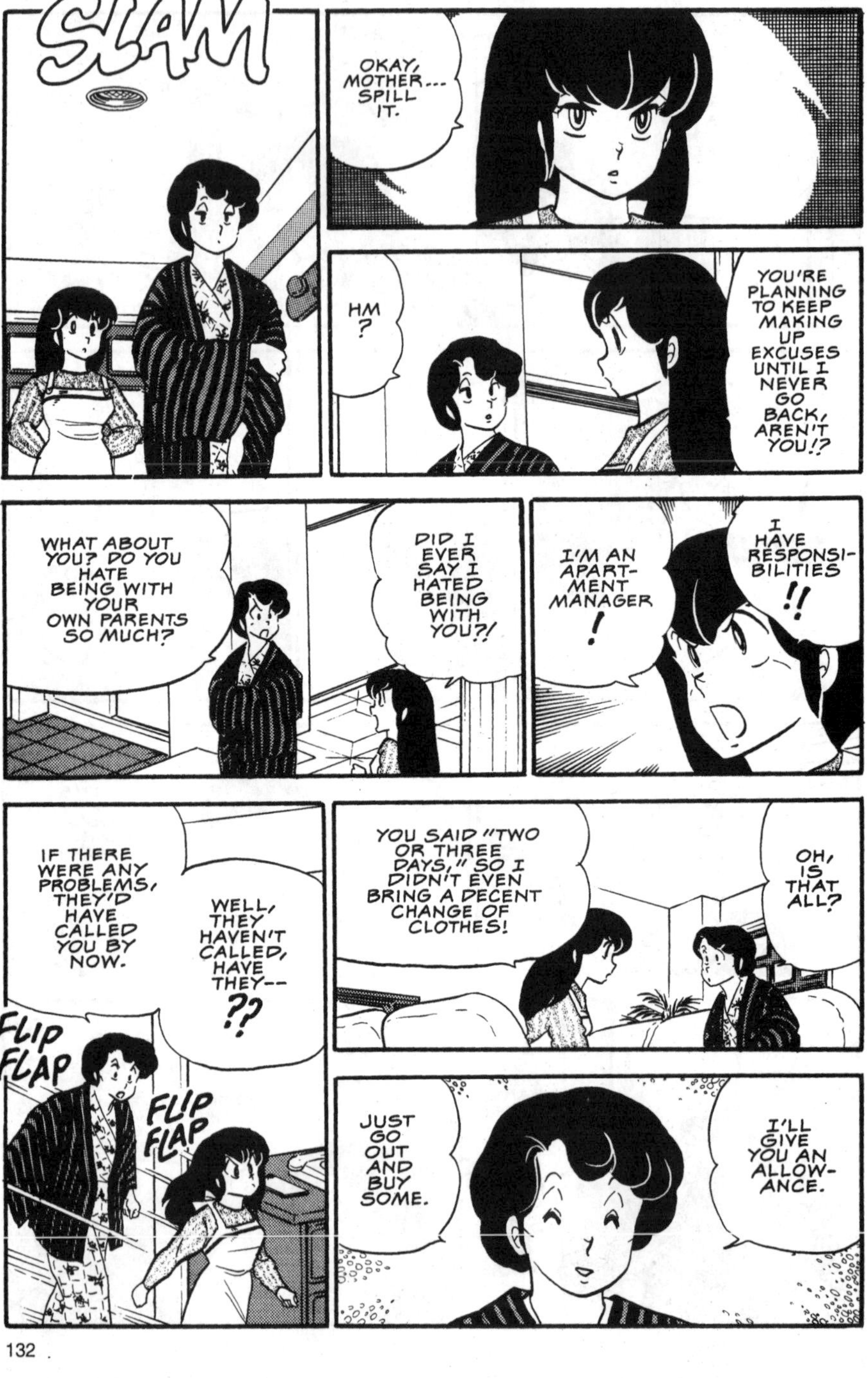
SLAM
OKAY, MOTHER... SPILL IT.
HM?
YOU'RE PLANNING TO KEEP MAKING UP EXCUSES UNTIL I NEVER GO BACK, AREN'T YOU!?
WHAT ABOUT YOU? DO YOU HATE BEING WITH YOUR OWN PARENTS SO MUCH?
DID I EVER SAY I HATED BEING WITH YOU?!
I'M AN APARTMENT MANAGER!
I HAVE RESPONSIBILITIES!!
IF THERE WERE ANY PROBLEMS, THEY'D HAVE CALLED YOU BY NOW.
WELL, THEY HAVEN'T CALLED, HAVE THEY-- ??
FLIP FLAP
FLIP FLAP
YOU SAID "TWO OR THREE DAYS," SO I DIDN'T EVEN BRING A DECENT CHANGE OF CLOTHES!
OH, IS THAT ALL?
JUST GO OUT AND BUY SOME.
I'LL GIVE YOU AN ALLOWANCE.

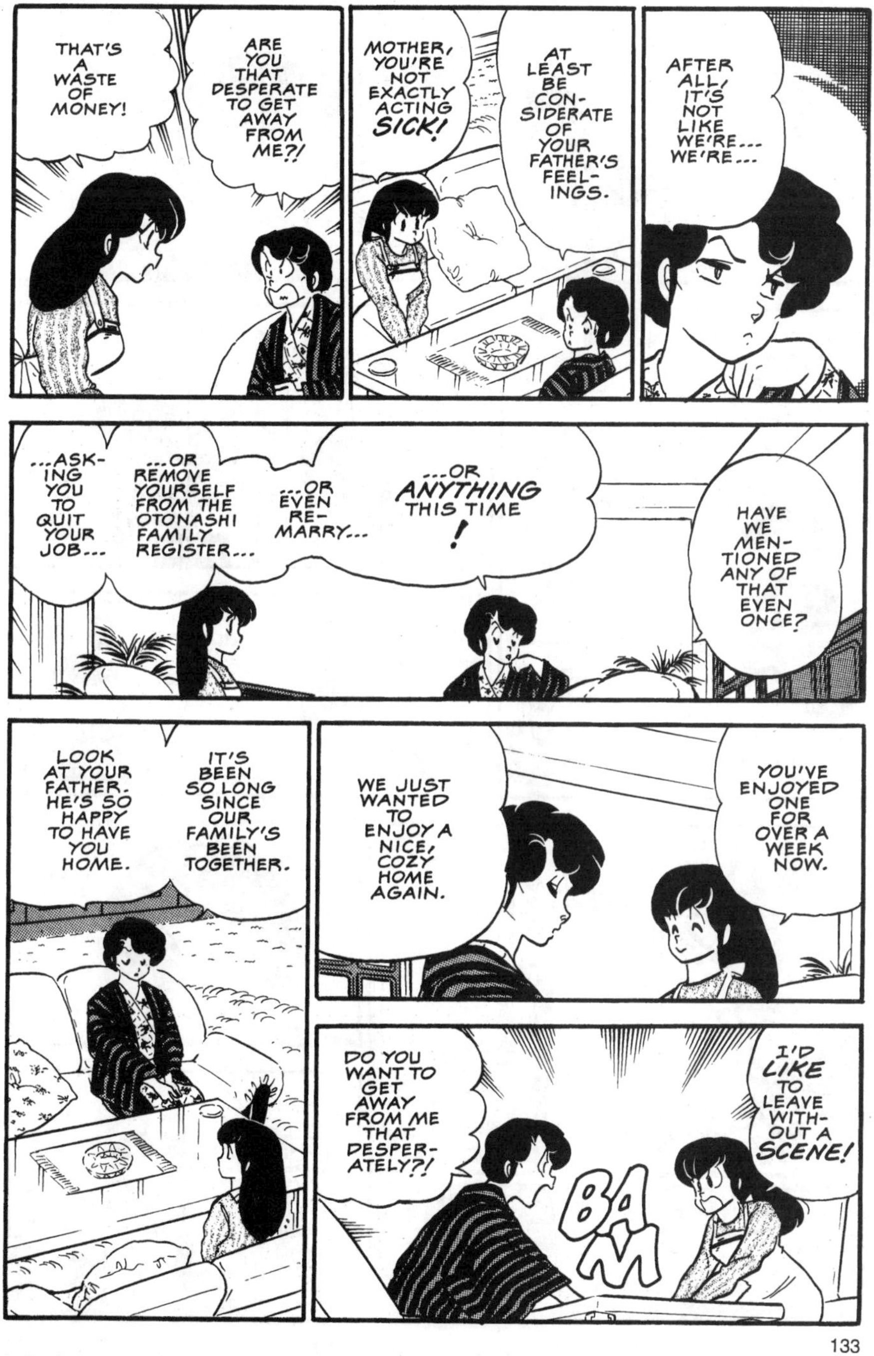
THAT'S A WASTE OF MONEY!
ARE YOU THAT DESPERATE TO GET AWAY FROM ME?!
MOTHER, YOU'RE NOT EXACTLY ACTING SICK!
AT LEAST BE CONSIDERATE OF YOUR FATHER'S FEELINGS.
AFTER ALL, IT'S NOT LIKE WE'RE... WE'RE...
...ASKING YOU TO QUIT YOUR JOB...
...OR REMOVE YOURSELF FROM THE OTONASHI FAMILY REGISTER...
...OR EVEN REMARRY...
...OR ANYTHING THIS TIME!
HAVE WE MENTIONED ANY OF THAT EVEN ONCE?
LOOK AT YOUR FATHER. HE'S SO HAPPY TO HAVE YOU HOME.
IT'S BEEN SO LONG SINCE OUR FAMILY'S BEEN TOGETHER.
WE JUST WANTED TO ENJOY A NICE, COZY HOME AGAIN.
YOU'VE ENJOYED ONE FOR OVER A WEEK NOW.
DO YOU WANT TO GET AWAY FROM ME THAT DESPERATELY?!
BAM
I'D LIKE TO LEAVE WITHOUT A SCENE!

FIRST OF ALL, I CAN'T *SLEEP* WITHOUT MY OWN *PILLOW!*

PILLOW *?!* OH, REALLY?

THEN IF YOU HAD YOUR OWN PILLOW, YOU'D BE FINE, RIGHT?

IT HAS TO BE *THAT* PILLOW. THE ONE IN MY ROOM AT MAISON IKKOKU.

NOW, IF WE'RE FINISHED WITH THIS NON-SENSE...

WHAT ARE YOU DOING?

JUST LEAVE IT TO YOUR MOTHER.

VRR VRR...

BRRRING

HELLO, MAISON IKKOKU.

HUH?

HER PIL-LOW?

SILLY, ISN'T IT? BUT KYOKO IS INSISTING ON IT.

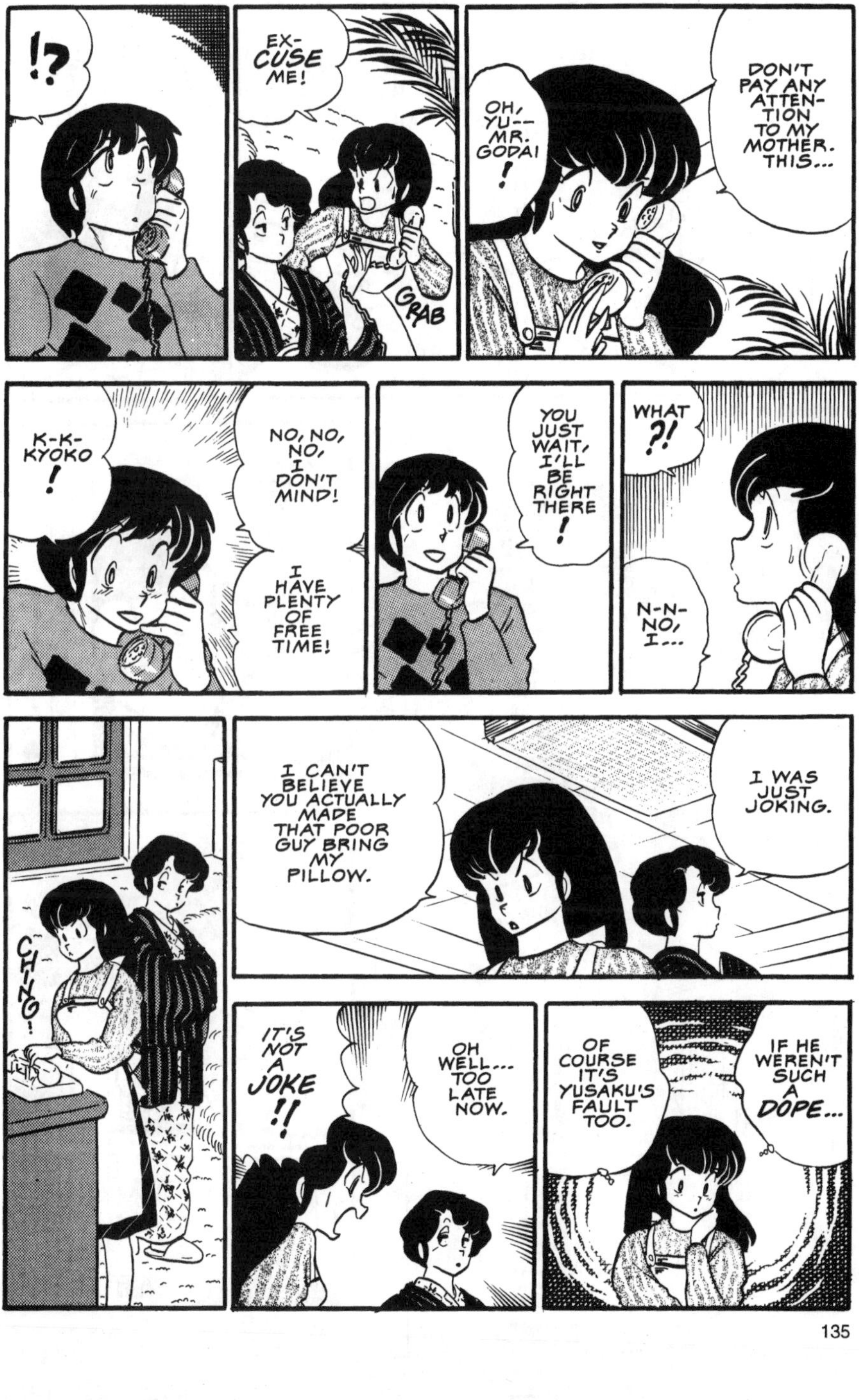
!?
EX-CUSE ME!
GRAB
OH, YU-- MR. GODAI!
DON'T PAY ANY ATTENTION TO MY MOTHER. THIS...
K-K-KYOKO!
NO, NO, NO, I DON'T MIND!
I HAVE PLENTY OF FREE TIME!
YOU JUST WAIT, I'LL BE RIGHT THERE!
WHAT?!
N-N-NO, I...
CHING!
I CAN'T BELIEVE YOU ACTUALLY MADE THAT POOR GUY BRING MY PILLOW.
I WAS JUST JOKING.
IT'S NOT A JOKE!!
OH WELL... TOO LATE NOW.
OF COURSE IT'S YUSAKU'S FAULT TOO.
IF HE WEREN'T SUCH A DOPE...

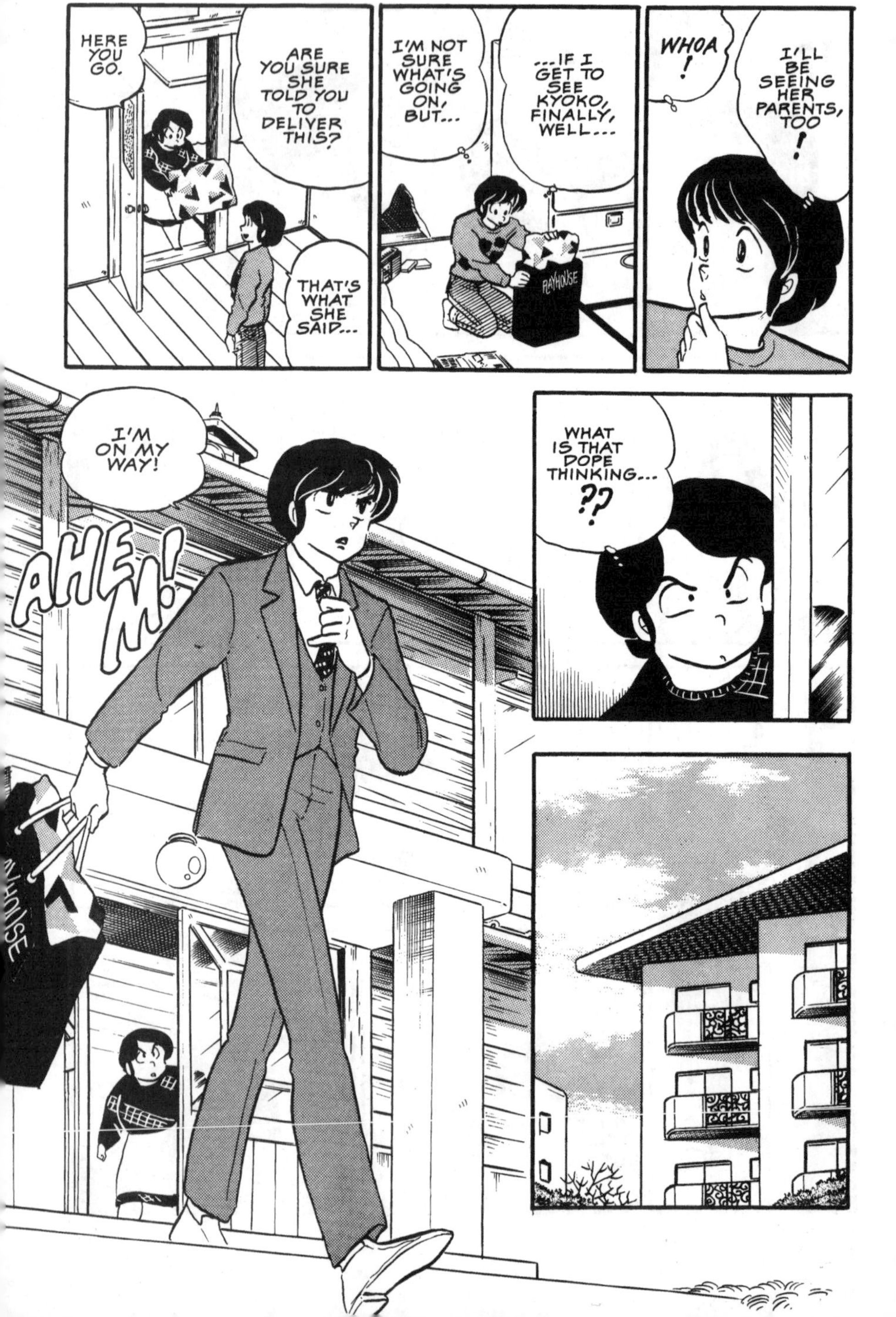
HERE YOU GO.
ARE YOU SURE SHE TOLD YOU TO DELIVER THIS?
THAT'S WHAT SHE SAID...
I'M NOT SURE WHAT'S GOING ON, BUT...
...IF I GET TO SEE KYOKO, FINALLY, WELL...
PLAYHOUSE
WHOA!
I'LL BE SEEING HER PARENTS, TOO!
AHEM!
I'M ON MY WAY!
WHAT IS THAT DOPE THINKING...??

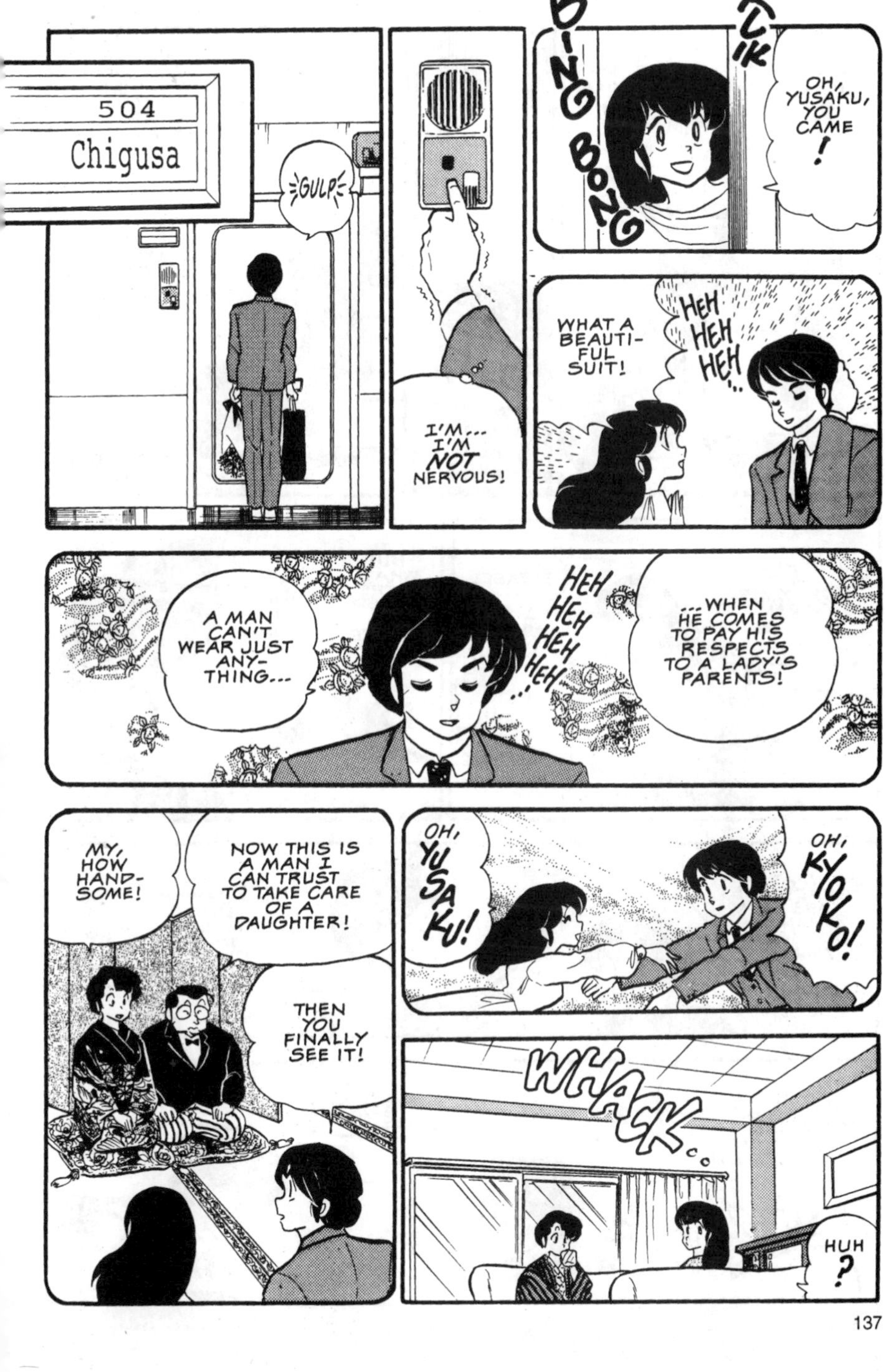
504
Chigusa
GULP
I'M... I'M NOT NERVOUS!
BING BONG
KLIK
OH, YUSAKU, YOU CAME!
WHAT A BEAUTIFUL SUIT!
HEH HEH HEH...
A MAN CAN'T WEAR JUST ANYTHING...
HEH HEH HEH HEH...
...WHEN HE COMES TO PAY HIS RESPECTS TO A LADY'S PARENTS!
MY, HOW HANDSOME!
NOW THIS IS A MAN I CAN TRUST TO TAKE CARE OF A DAUGHTER!
THEN YOU FINALLY SEE IT!
OH, YUSAKU!
OH, KYOKO!
WHACK
HUH?

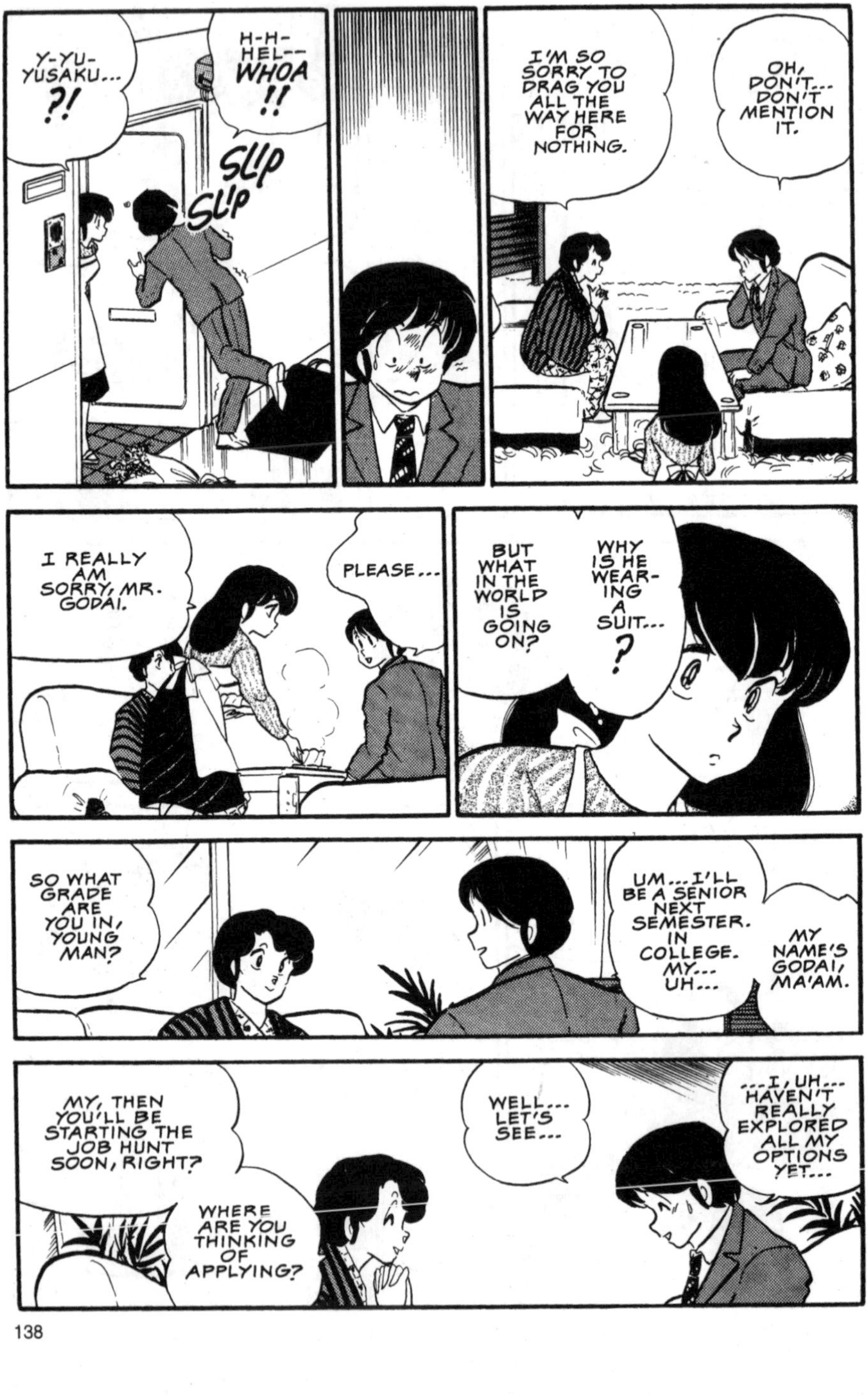
Y-YU-YUSAKU... ?!
H-H-HEL-- WHOA !!
SLIP SLIP
I'M SO SORRY TO DRAG YOU ALL THE WAY HERE FOR NOTHING.
OH, DON'T... DON'T MENTION IT.
I REALLY AM SORRY, MR. GODAI.
PLEASE...
BUT WHAT IN THE WORLD IS GOING ON?
WHY IS HE WEARING A SUIT... ?
SO WHAT GRADE ARE YOU IN, YOUNG MAN?
UM... I'LL BE A SENIOR NEXT SEMESTER. IN COLLEGE. MY... UH...
MY NAME'S GODAI, MA'AM.
MY, THEN YOU'LL BE STARTING THE JOB HUNT SOON, RIGHT?
WHERE ARE YOU THINKING OF APPLYING?
WELL... LET'S SEE...
...I, UH... HAVEN'T REALLY EXPLORED ALL MY OPTIONS YET...

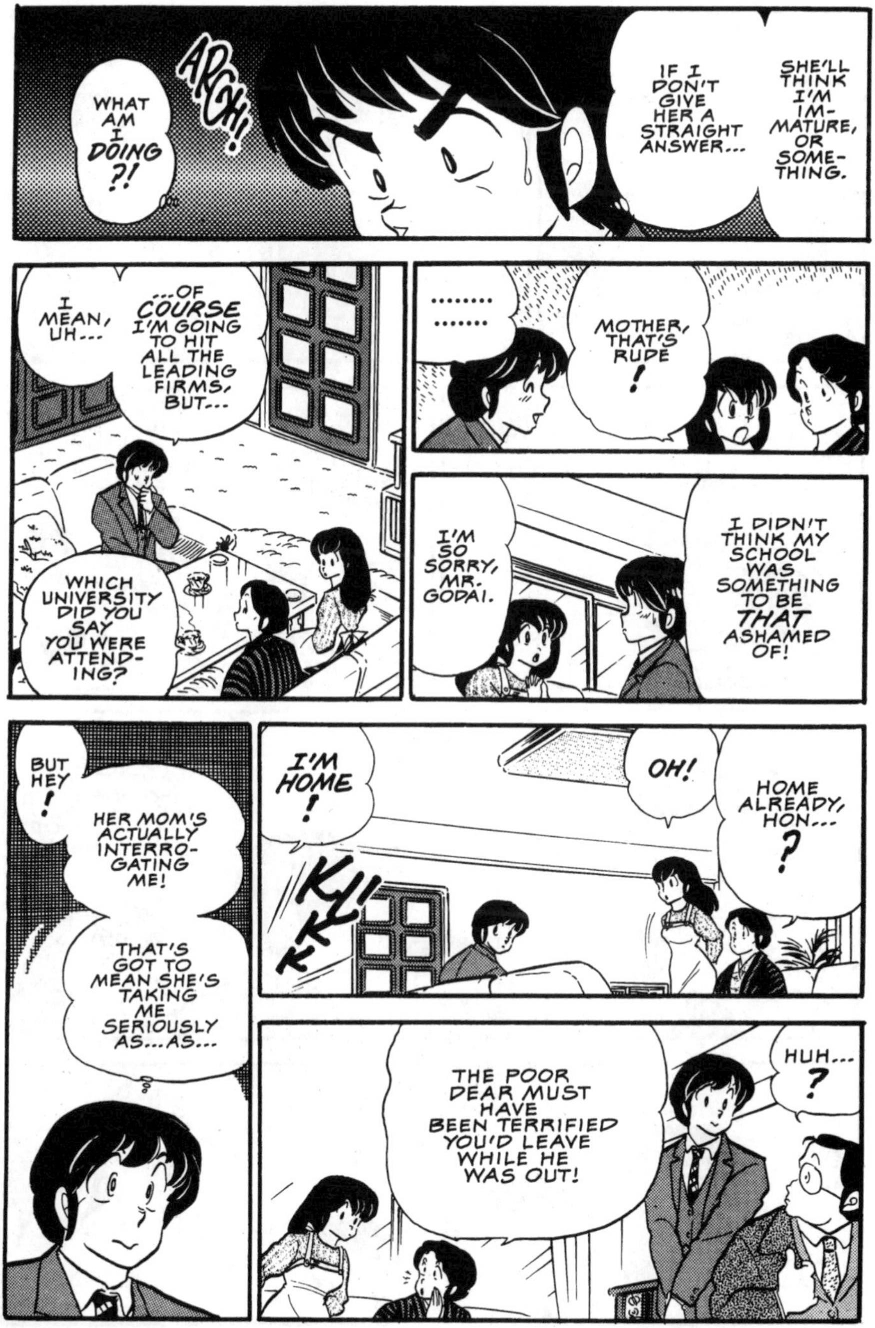
WHAT AM I DOING?!
ARGH!!
IF I DON'T GIVE HER A STRAIGHT ANSWER...
SHE'LL THINK I'M IMMATURE, OR SOMETHING.
I MEAN, UH...
...OF COURSE I'M GOING TO HIT ALL THE LEADING FIRMS, BUT...
WHICH UNIVERSITY DID YOU SAY YOU WERE ATTENDING?
....
....
MOTHER, THAT'S RUDE!
I'M SO SORRY, MR. GODAI.
I DIDN'T THINK MY SCHOOL WAS SOMETHING TO BE THAT ASHAMED OF!
BUT HEY!
HER MOM'S ACTUALLY INTERROGATING ME!
THAT'S GOT TO MEAN SHE'S TAKING ME SERIOUSLY AS...AS...
I'M HOME!
KLIK KLIK
OH!
HOME ALREADY, HON...?
THE POOR DEAR MUST HAVE BEEN TERRIFIED YOU'D LEAVE WHILE HE WAS OUT!
HUH...?

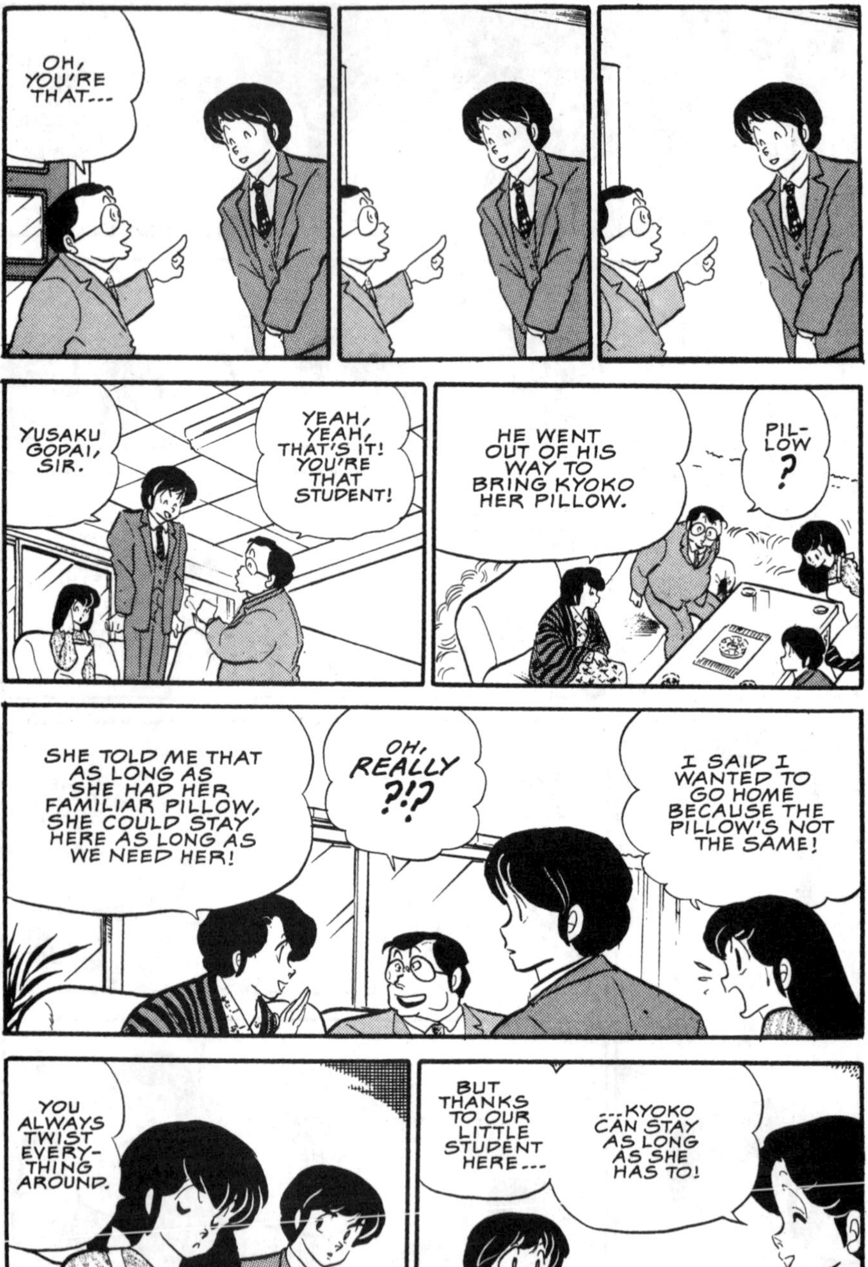
OH, YOU'RE THAT...
YUSAKU GODAI, SIR.
YEAH, YEAH, THAT'S IT! YOU'RE THAT STUDENT!
HE WENT OUT OF HIS WAY TO BRING KYOKO HER PILLOW.
PIL-LOW ?
SHE TOLD ME THAT AS LONG AS SHE HAD HER FAMILIAR PILLOW, SHE COULD STAY HERE AS LONG AS WE NEED HER!
OH, REALLY ?!?
I SAID I WANTED TO GO HOME BECAUSE THE PILLOW'S NOT THE SAME!
YOU ALWAYS TWIST EVERY-THING AROUND.
BUT THANKS TO OUR LITTLE STUDENT HERE...
...KYOKO CAN STAY AS LONG AS SHE HAS TO!

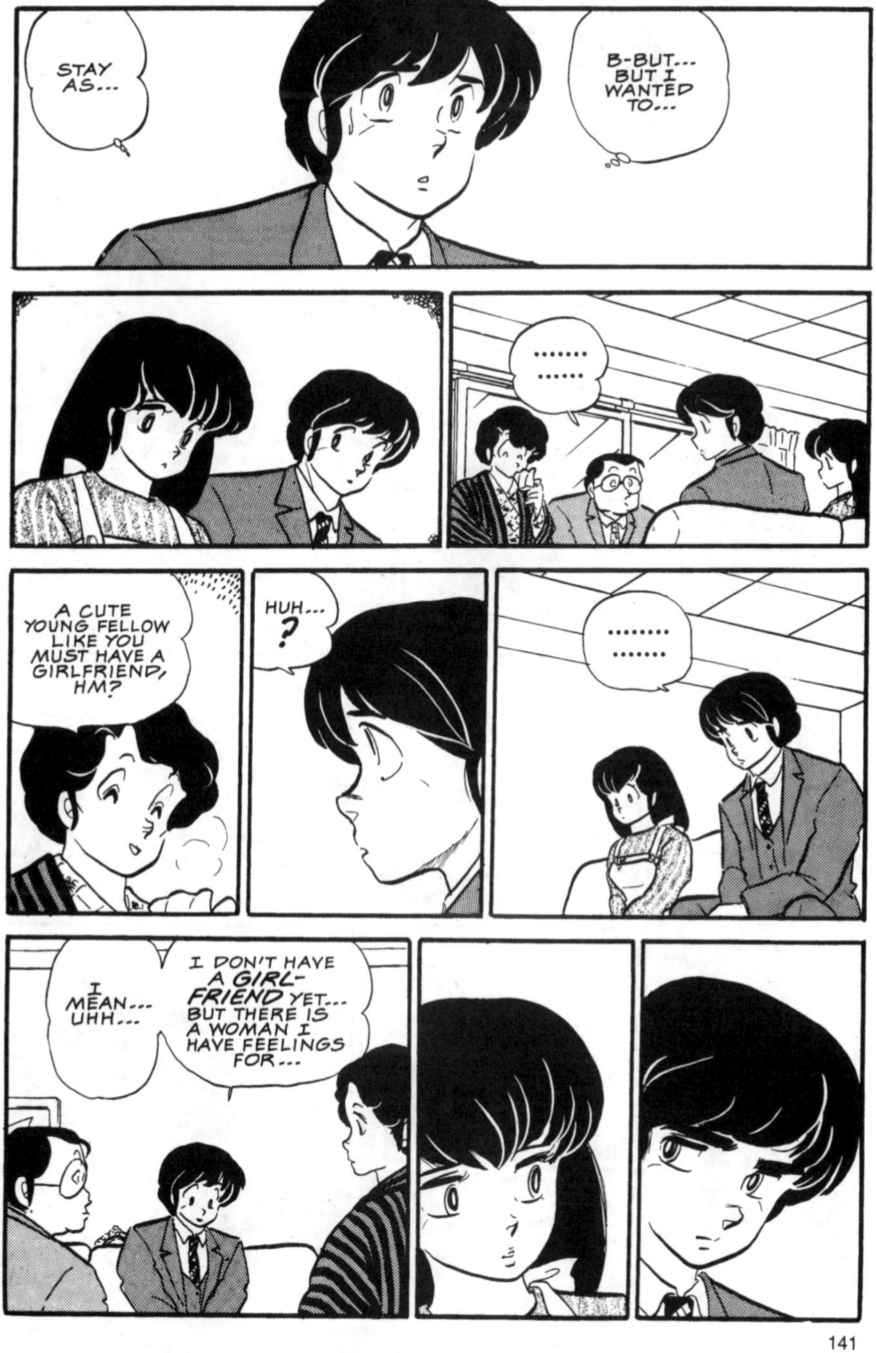
STAY AS...
B-BUT... BUT I WANTED TO...
....
A CUTE YOUNG FELLOW LIKE YOU MUST HAVE A GIRLFRIEND, HM?
HUH...?
....
I MEAN... UHH...
I DON'T HAVE A GIRLFRIEND YET... BUT THERE IS A WOMAN I HAVE FEELINGS FOR...

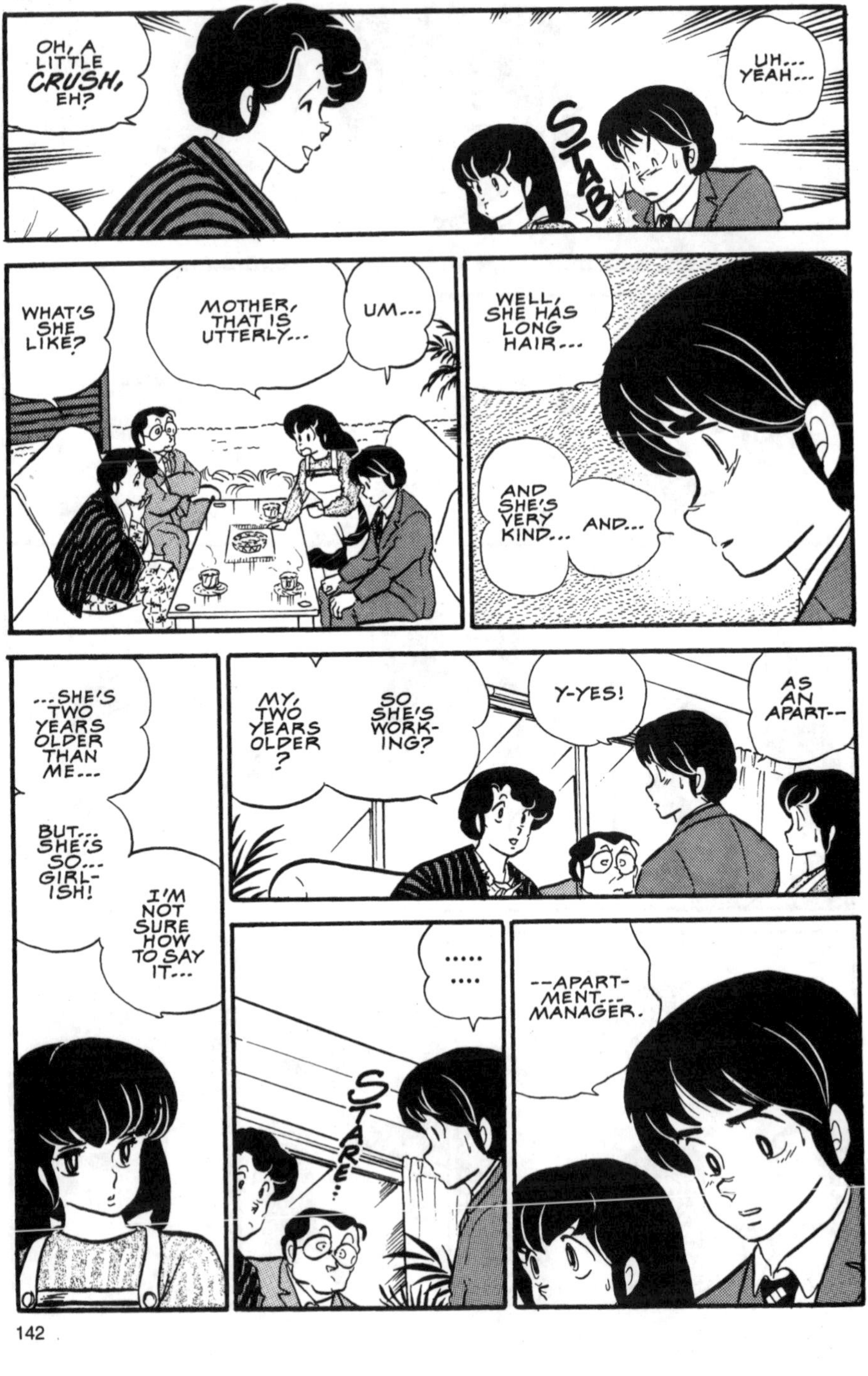
OH, A LITTLE CRUSH, EH?
UH... YEAH...
STAB
WHAT'S SHE LIKE?
MOTHER, THAT IS UTTERLY...
UM...
WELL, SHE HAS LONG HAIR...
AND SHE'S VERY KIND... AND...
...SHE'S TWO YEARS OLDER THAN ME...
BUT... SHE'S SO... GIRL-ISH!
I'M NOT SURE HOW TO SAY IT...
MY, TWO YEARS OLDER?
SO SHE'S WORK-ING?
Y-YES!
AS AN APART--
.....
....
STARE...
--APART-MENT... MANAGER.

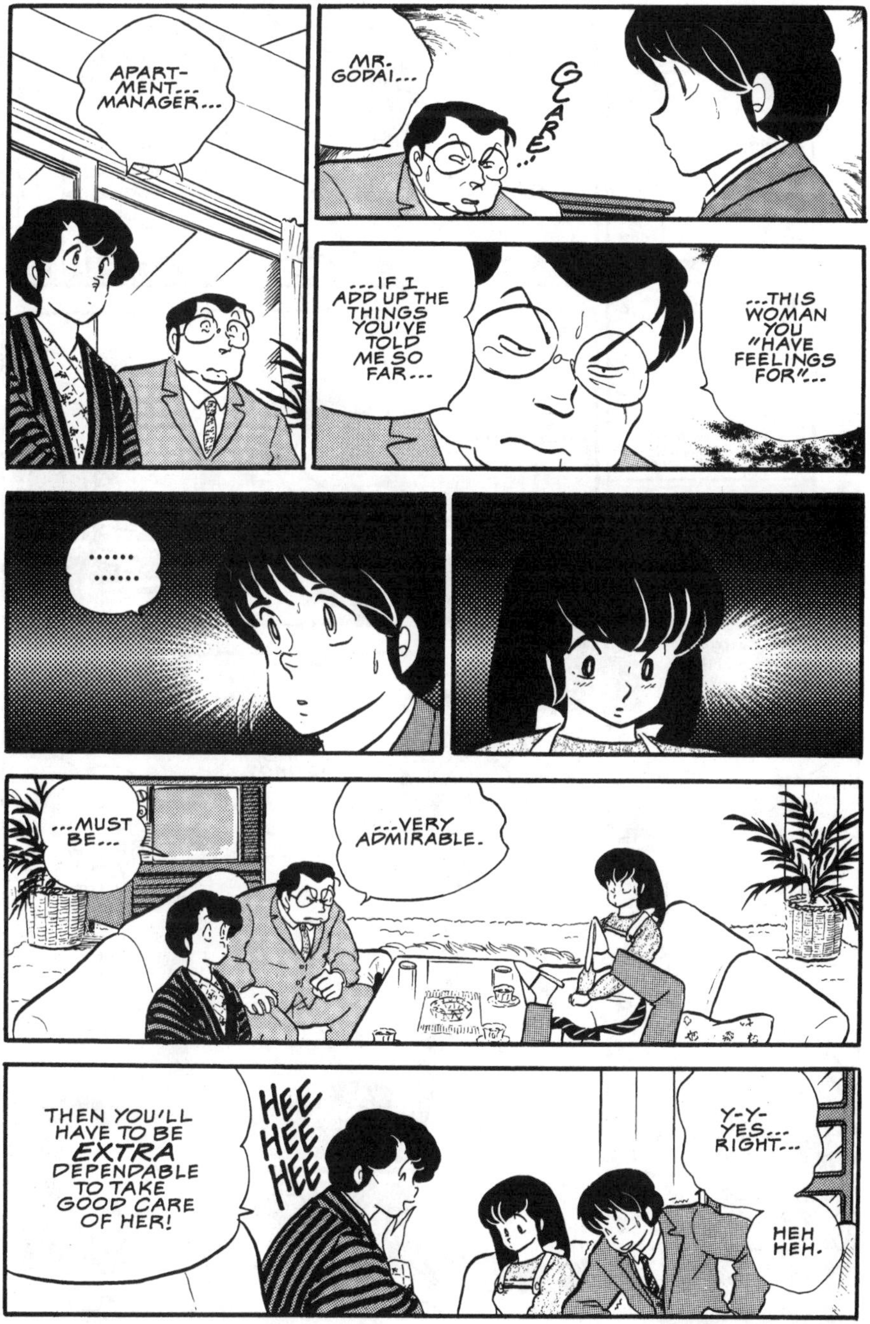
APARTMENT-MENT... MANAGER...
MR. GODAI...
GLARE...
...IF I ADD UP THE THINGS YOU'VE TOLD ME SO FAR...
...THIS WOMAN YOU "HAVE FEELINGS FOR"...
....
...MUST BE...
...VERY ADMIRABLE.
THEN YOU'LL HAVE TO BE EXTRA DEPENDABLE TO TAKE GOOD CARE OF HER!
HEE HEE HEE
Y-Y-YES... RIGHT...
HEH HEH.

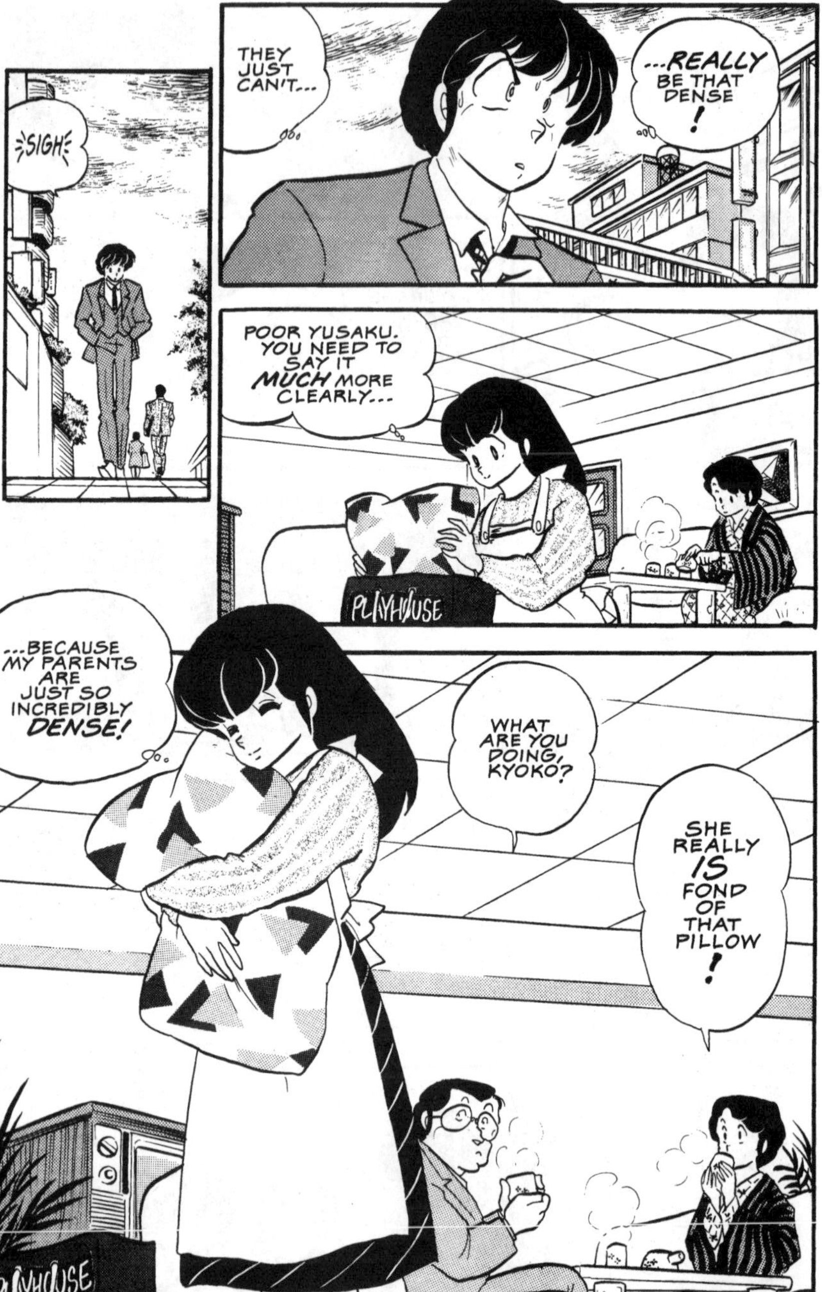

SIGH
THEY JUST CAN'T...
...REALLY BE THAT DENSE!
POOR YUSAKU. YOU NEED TO SAY IT MUCH MORE CLEARLY...
PLAYHOUSE
...BECAUSE MY PARENTS ARE JUST SO INCREDIBLY DENSE!
WHAT ARE YOU DOING, KYOKO?
SHE REALLY IS FOND OF THAT PILLOW!
PLAYHOUSE

PART 7

THE FACE IN THE DARKNESS

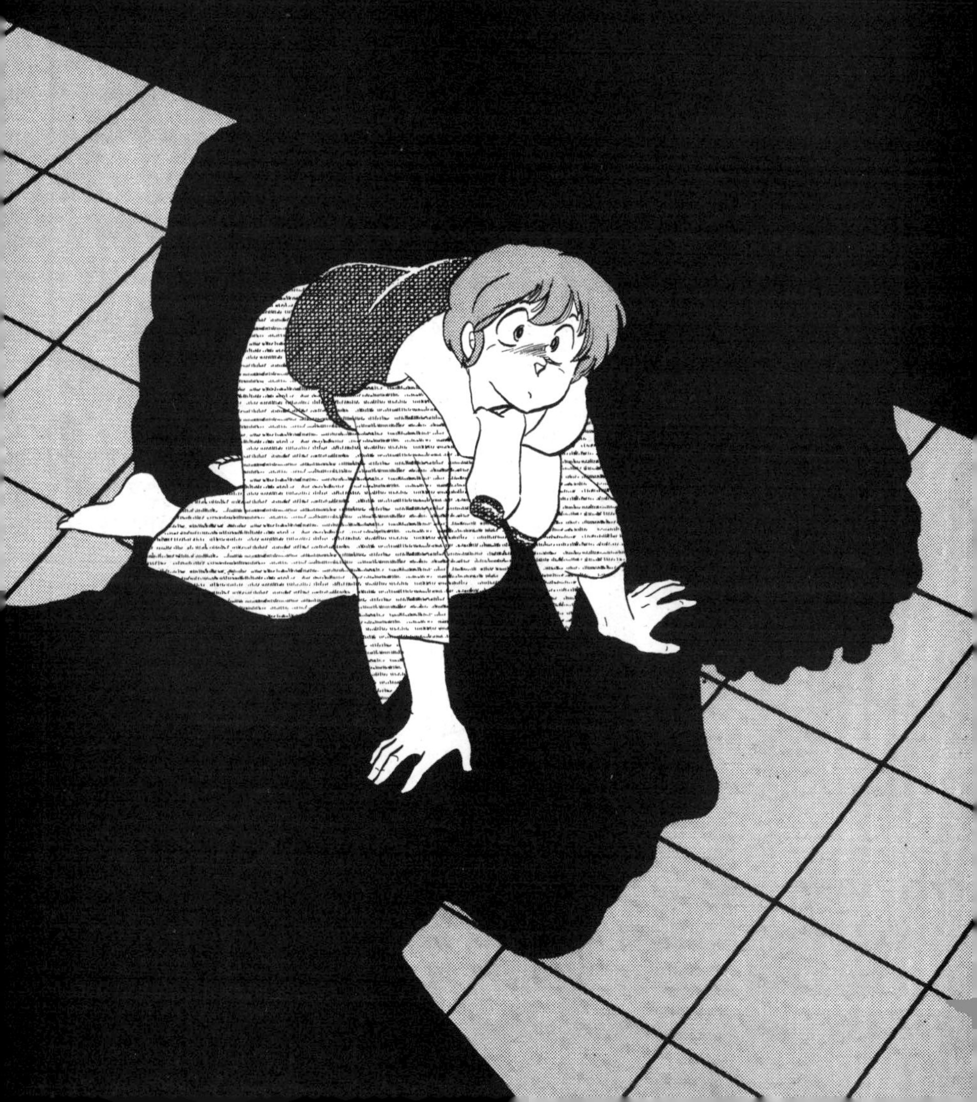

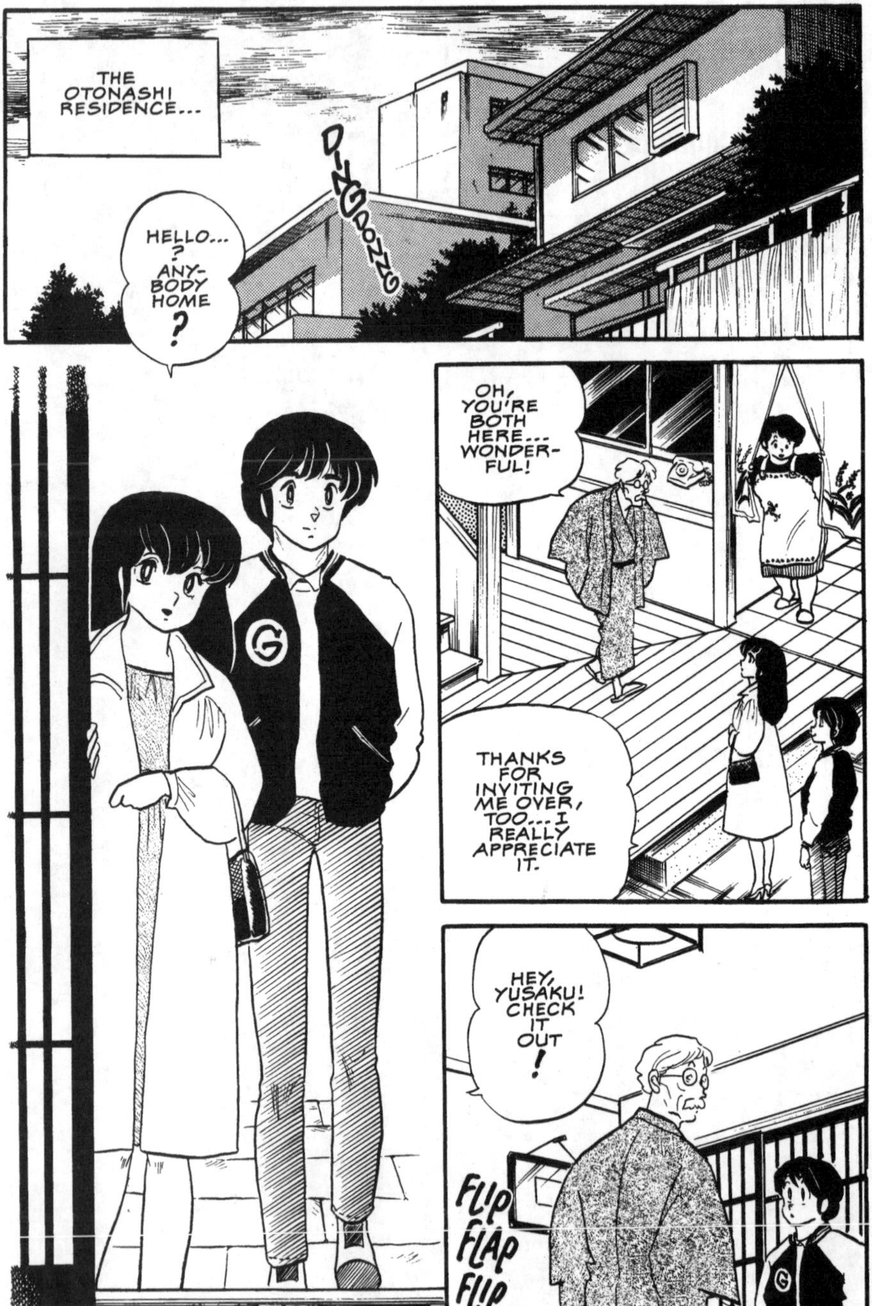
THE OTONASHI RESIDENCE...
DING DONG
HELLO...? ANYBODY HOME?
OH, YOU'RE BOTH HERE... WONDERFUL!
THANKS FOR INVITING ME OVER, TOO... I REALLY APPRECIATE IT.
HEY, YUSAKU! CHECK IT OUT!
FLIP FLAP FLIP

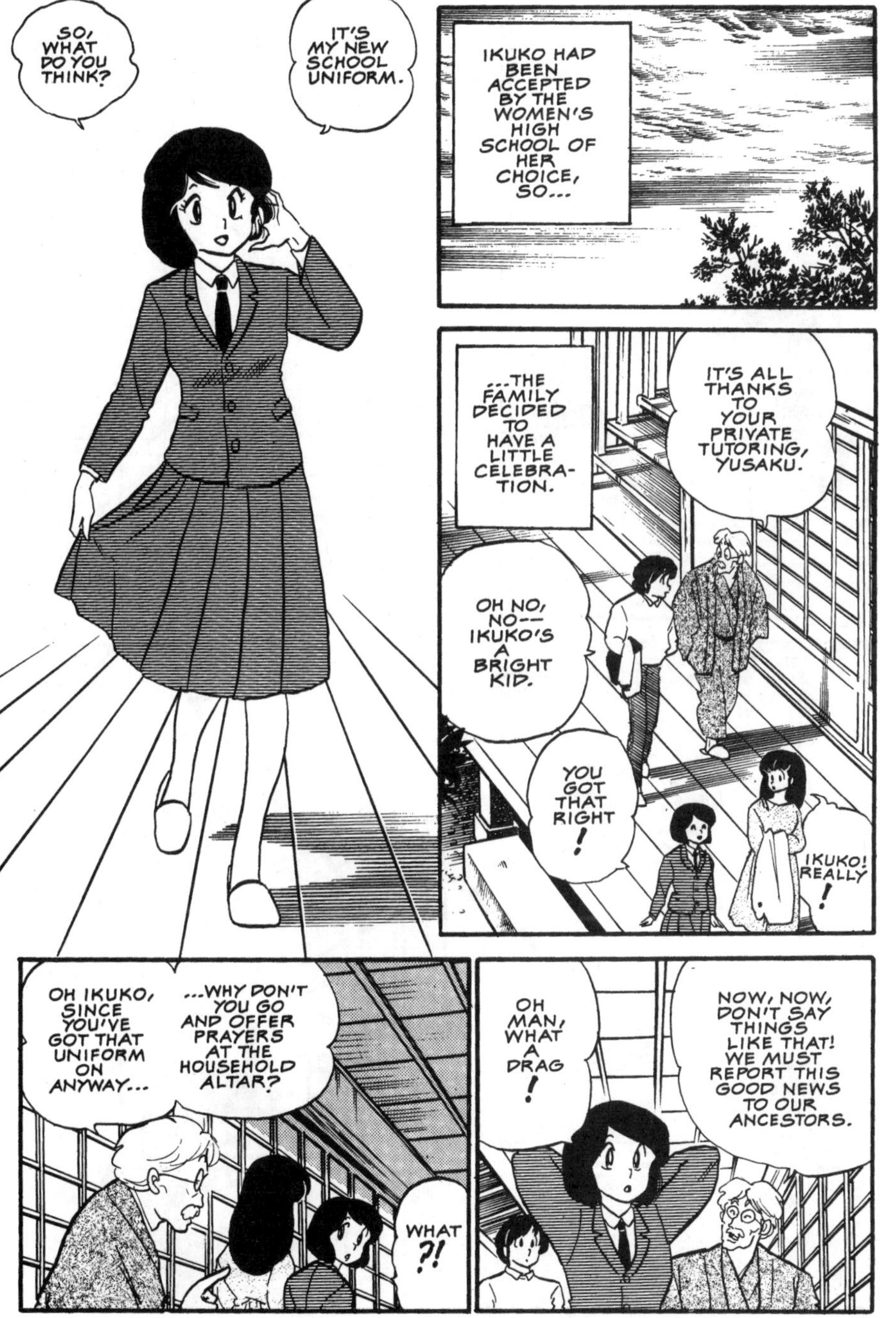
SO, WHAT DO YOU THINK?
IT'S MY NEW SCHOOL UNIFORM.
IKUKO HAD BEEN ACCEPTED BY THE WOMEN'S HIGH SCHOOL OF HER CHOICE, SO...
...THE FAMILY DECIDED TO HAVE A LITTLE CELEBRATION.
IT'S ALL THANKS TO YOUR PRIVATE TUTORING, YUSAKU.
OH NO, NO-- IKUKO'S A BRIGHT KID.
YOU GOT THAT RIGHT!
IKUKO! REALLY!
OH IKUKO, SINCE YOU'VE GOT THAT UNIFORM ON ANYWAY...
...WHY DON'T YOU GO AND OFFER PRAYERS AT THE HOUSEHOLD ALTAR?
WHAT?!
OH MAN, WHAT A DRAG!
NOW, NOW, DON'T SAY THINGS LIKE THAT! WE MUST REPORT THIS GOOD NEWS TO OUR ANCESTORS.

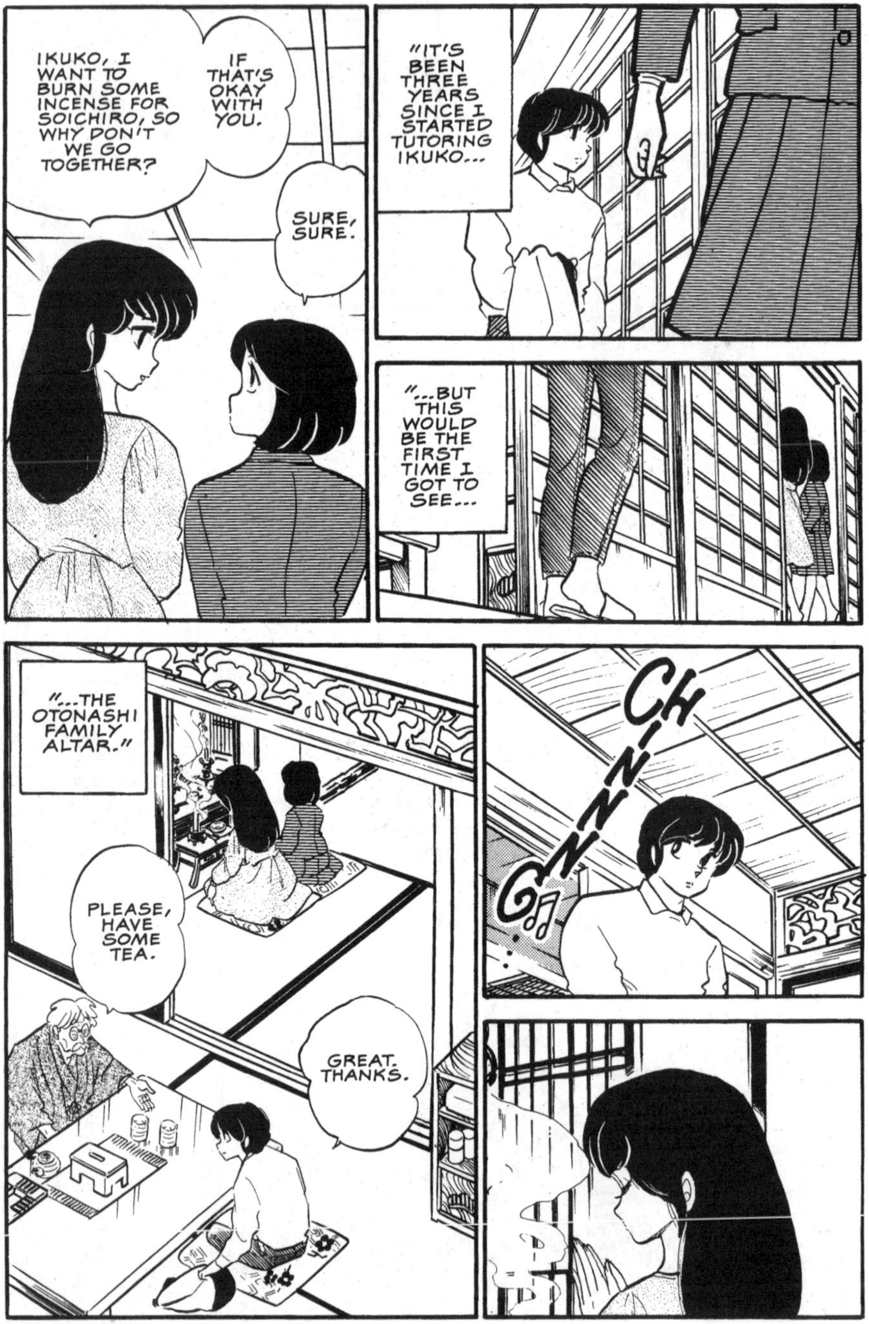

IKUKO, I WANT TO BURN SOME INCENSE FOR SOICHIRO, SO WHY DON'T WE GO TOGETHER?
IF THAT'S OKAY WITH YOU.
SURE, SURE.
"IT'S BEEN THREE YEARS SINCE I STARTED TUTORING IKUKO...
"...BUT THIS WOULD BE THE FIRST TIME I GOT TO SEE...
"...THE OTONASHI FAMILY ALTAR."
PLEASE, HAVE SOME TEA.
GREAT. THANKS.
CHINNNG

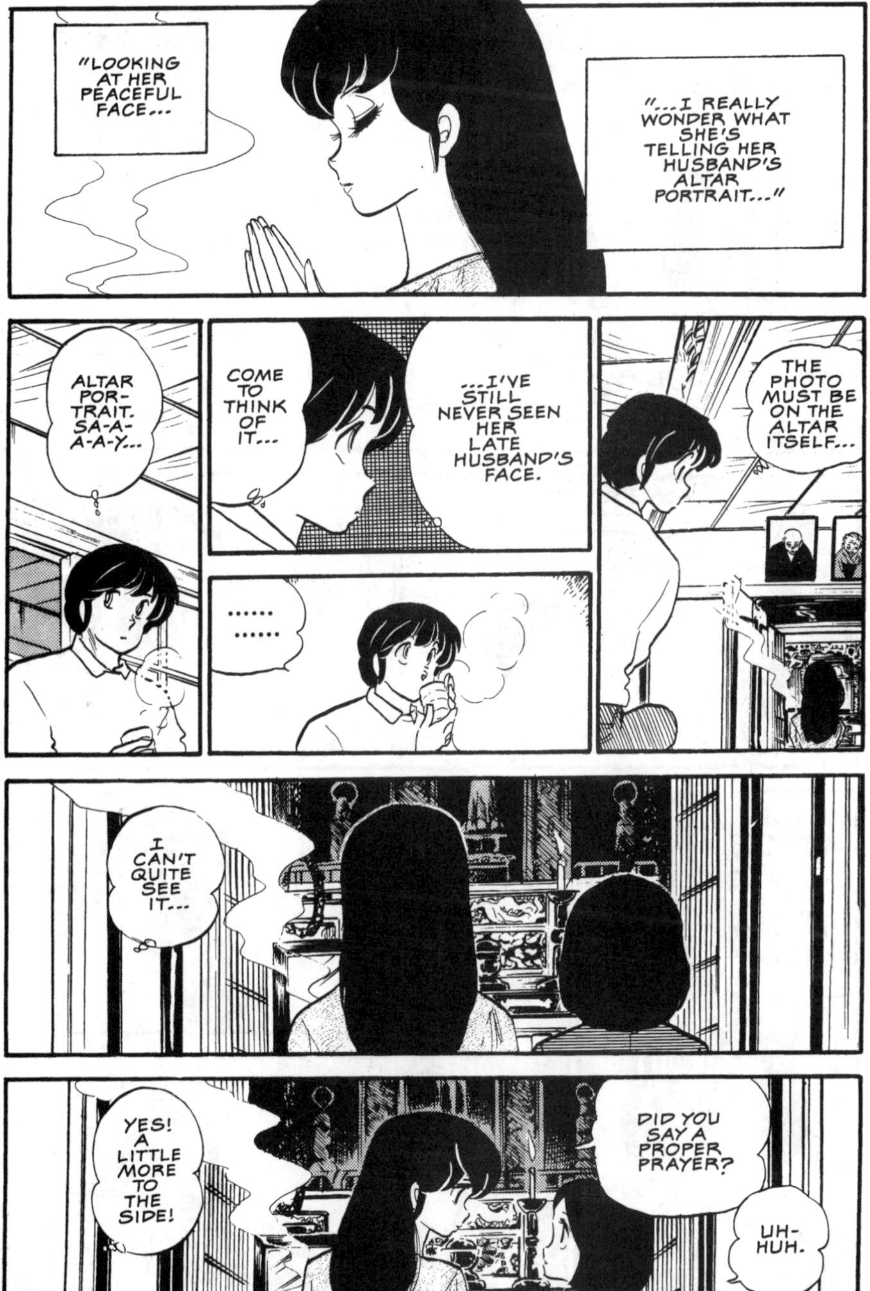
"LOOKING AT HER PEACEFUL FACE...
"...I REALLY WONDER WHAT SHE'S TELLING HER HUSBAND'S ALTAR PORTRAIT..."
ALTAR POR-TRAIT. SA-A-A-A-Y...
COME TO THINK OF IT...
...I'VE STILL NEVER SEEN HER LATE HUSBAND'S FACE.
......
......
THE PHOTO MUST BE ON THE ALTAR ITSELF...
I CAN'T QUITE SEE IT...
YES! A LITTLE MORE TO THE SIDE!
DID YOU SAY A PROPER PRAYER?
UH-HUH.

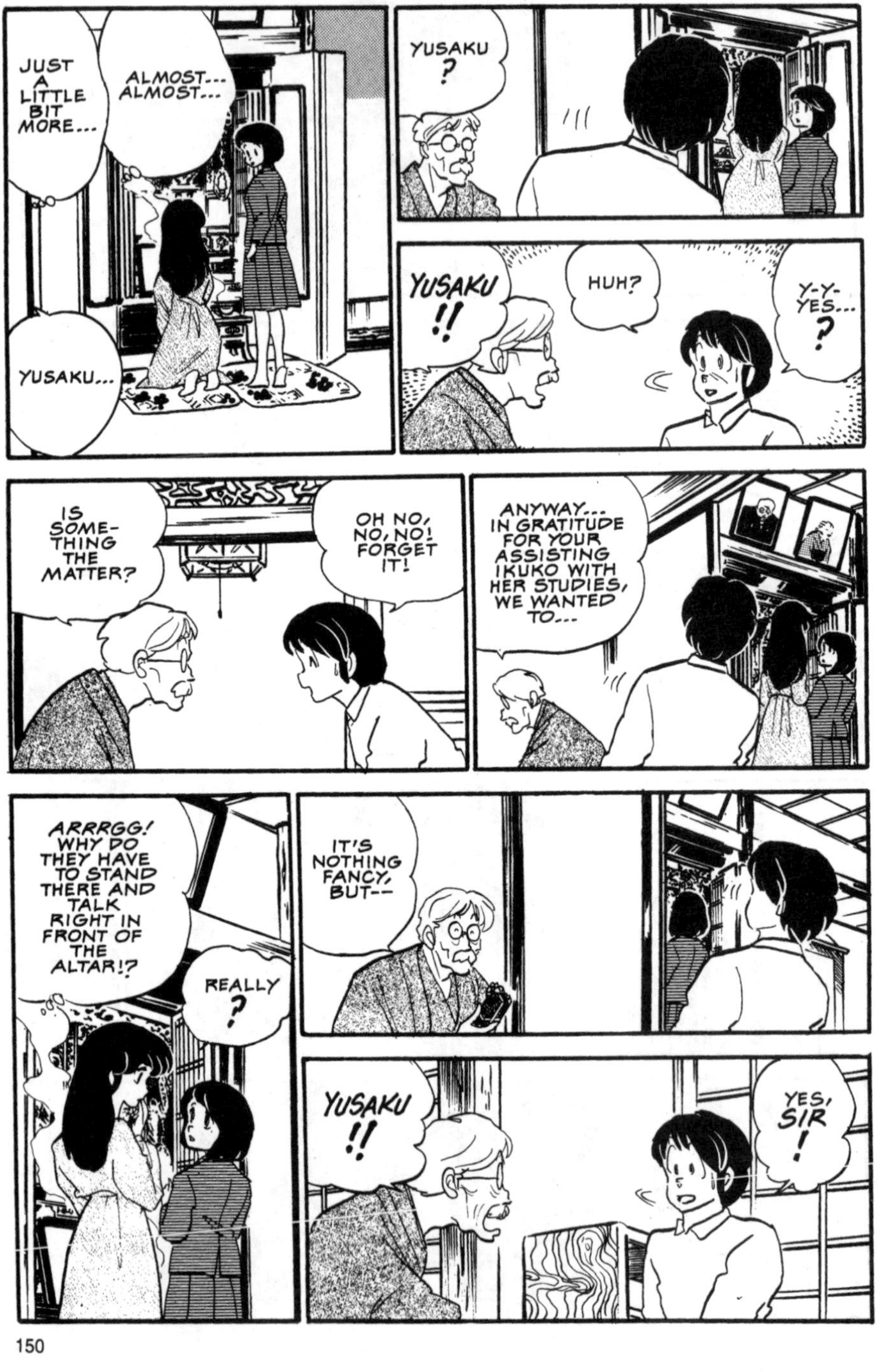
JUST A LITTLE BIT MORE...
ALMOST... ALMOST...
YUSAKU...
YUSAKU ?
YUSAKU !!
HUH?
Y-Y-YES... ?
IS SOMETHING THE MATTER?
OH NO, NO, NO! FORGET IT!
ANYWAY... IN GRATITUDE FOR YOUR ASSISTING IKUKO WITH HER STUDIES, WE WANTED TO...
ARRRGG! WHY DO THEY HAVE TO STAND THERE AND TALK RIGHT IN FRONT OF THE ALTAR!?
REALLY ?
IT'S NOTHING FANCY, BUT--
YUSAKU !!
YES, SIR !

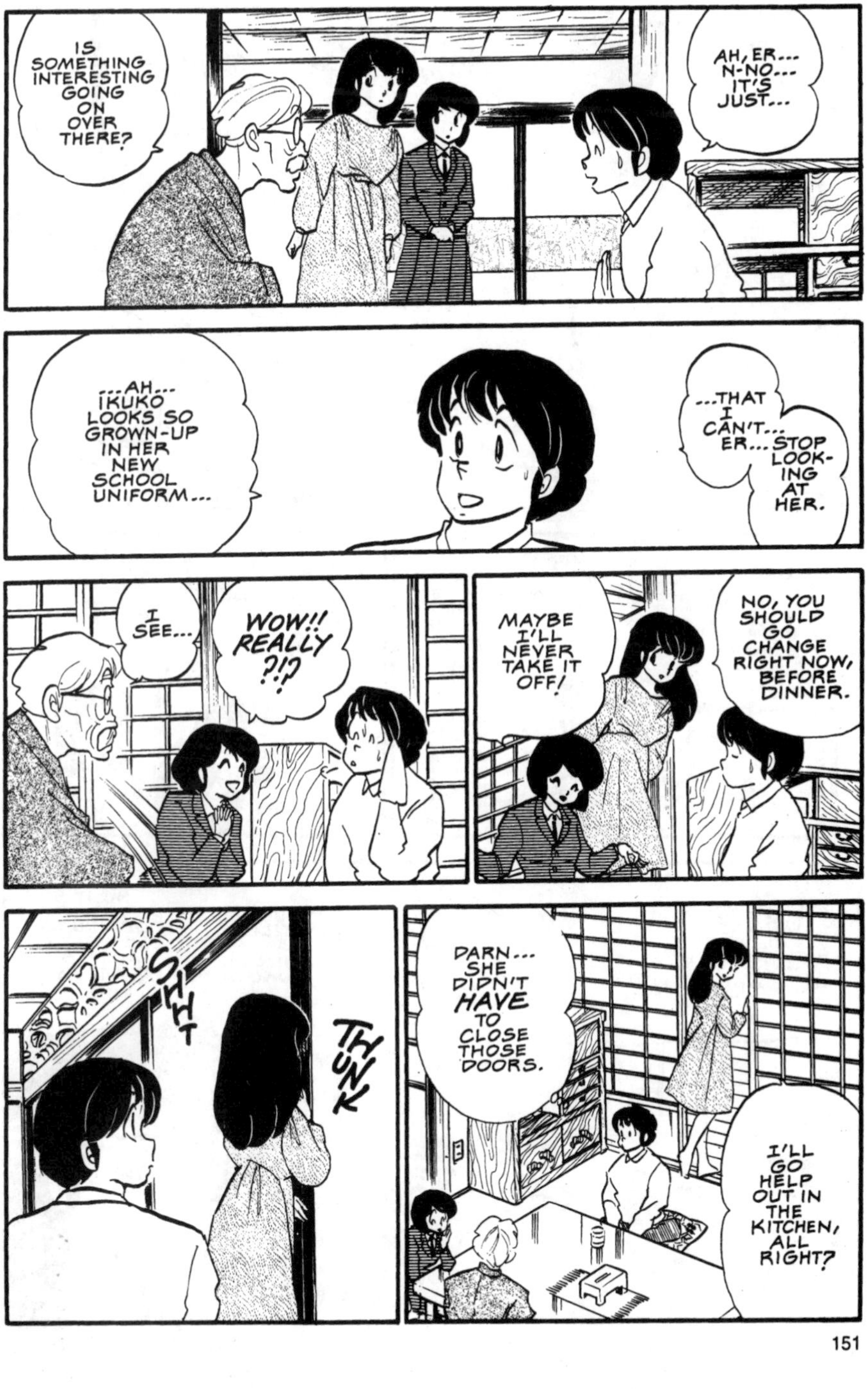
IS SOMETHING INTERESTING GOING ON OVER THERE?
AH, ER... N-NO... IT'S JUST...
...AH... IKUKO LOOKS SO GROWN-UP IN HER NEW SCHOOL UNIFORM...
...THAT I CAN'T... ER... STOP LOOKING AT HER.
I SEE...
WOW!! REALLY ?!?
MAYBE I'LL NEVER TAKE IT OFF!
NO, YOU SHOULD GO CHANGE RIGHT NOW, BEFORE DINNER.
SHHT
THUNK
DARN... SHE DIDN'T HAVE TO CLOSE THOSE DOORS.
I'LL GO HELP OUT IN THE KITCHEN, ALL RIGHT?

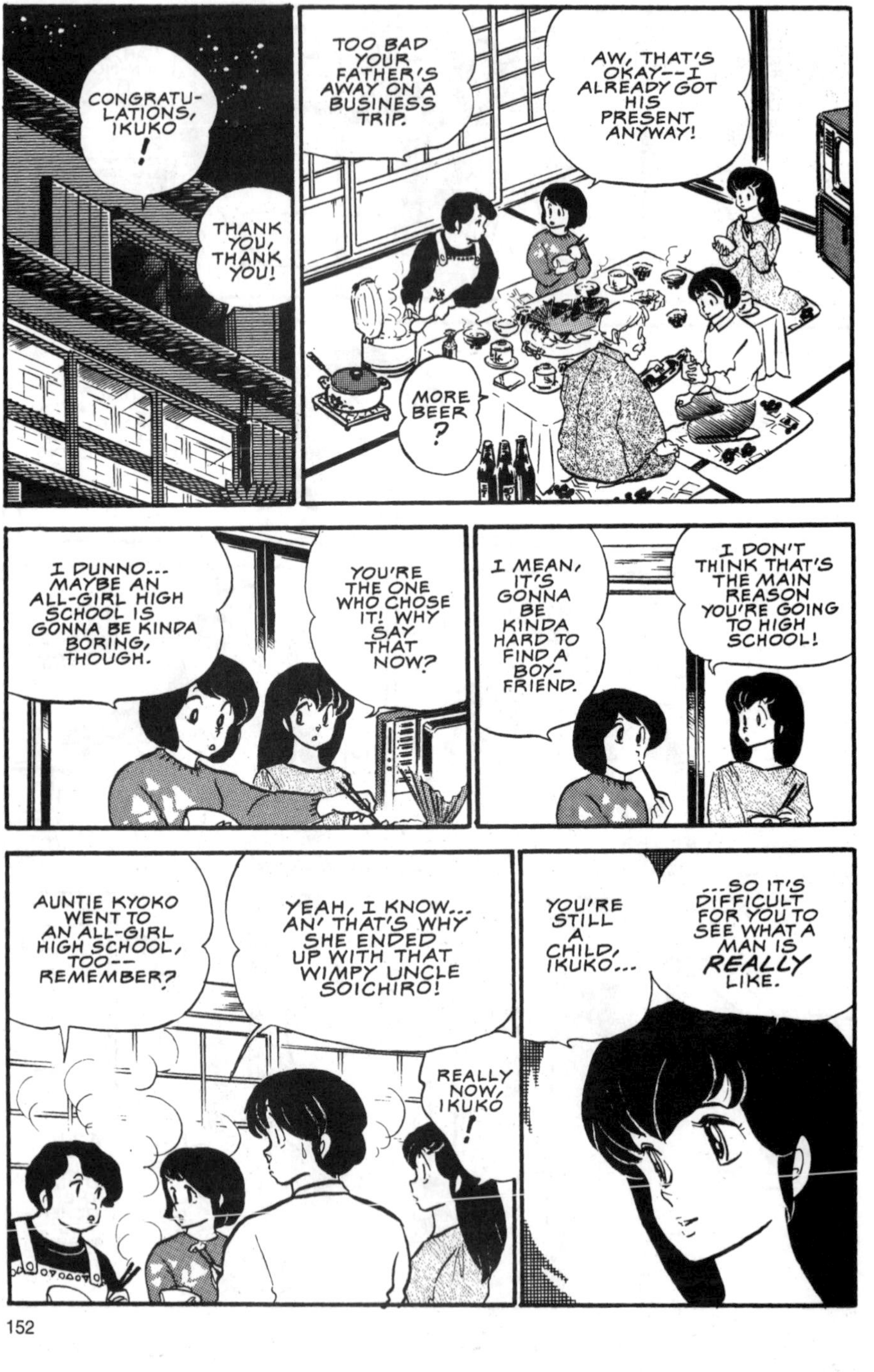

CONGRATULATIONS, IKUKO!
THANK YOU, THANK YOU!
TOO BAD YOUR FATHER'S AWAY ON A BUSINESS TRIP.
AW, THAT'S OKAY--I ALREADY GOT HIS PRESENT ANYWAY!
MORE BEER?
I DUNNO... MAYBE AN ALL-GIRL HIGH SCHOOL IS GONNA BE KINDA BORING, THOUGH.
YOU'RE THE ONE WHO CHOSE IT! WHY SAY THAT NOW?
I MEAN, IT'S GONNA BE KINDA HARD TO FIND A BOY-FRIEND.
I DON'T THINK THAT'S THE MAIN REASON YOU'RE GOING TO HIGH SCHOOL!
AUNTIE KYOKO WENT TO AN ALL-GIRL HIGH SCHOOL, TOO--REMEMBER?
YEAH, I KNOW... AN' THAT'S WHY SHE ENDED UP WITH THAT WIMPY UNCLE SOICHIRO!
REALLY NOW, IKUKO!
YOU'RE STILL A CHILD, IKUKO...
...SO IT'S DIFFICULT FOR YOU TO SEE WHAT A MAN IS REALLY LIKE.

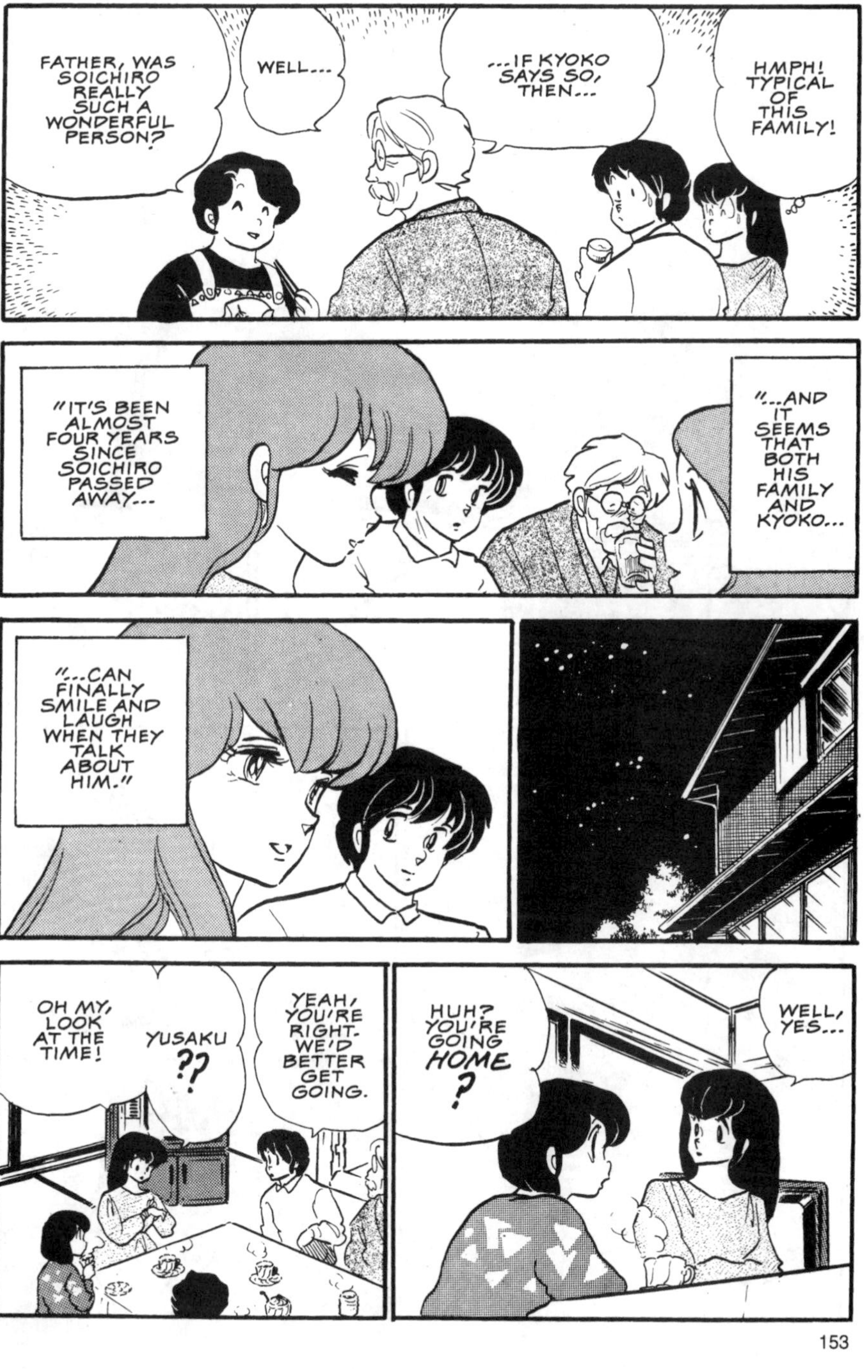
FATHER, WAS SOICHIRO REALLY SUCH A WONDERFUL PERSON?
WELL...
...IF KYOKO SAYS SO, THEN...
HMPH! TYPICAL OF THIS FAMILY!
"IT'S BEEN ALMOST FOUR YEARS SINCE SOICHIRO PASSED AWAY...
"...AND IT SEEMS THAT BOTH HIS FAMILY AND KYOKO...
"...CAN FINALLY SMILE AND LAUGH WHEN THEY TALK ABOUT HIM."
OH MY, LOOK AT THE TIME!
YUSAKU ??
YEAH, YOU'RE RIGHT. WE'D BETTER GET GOING.
HUH? YOU'RE GOING *HOME*?
WELL, YES...

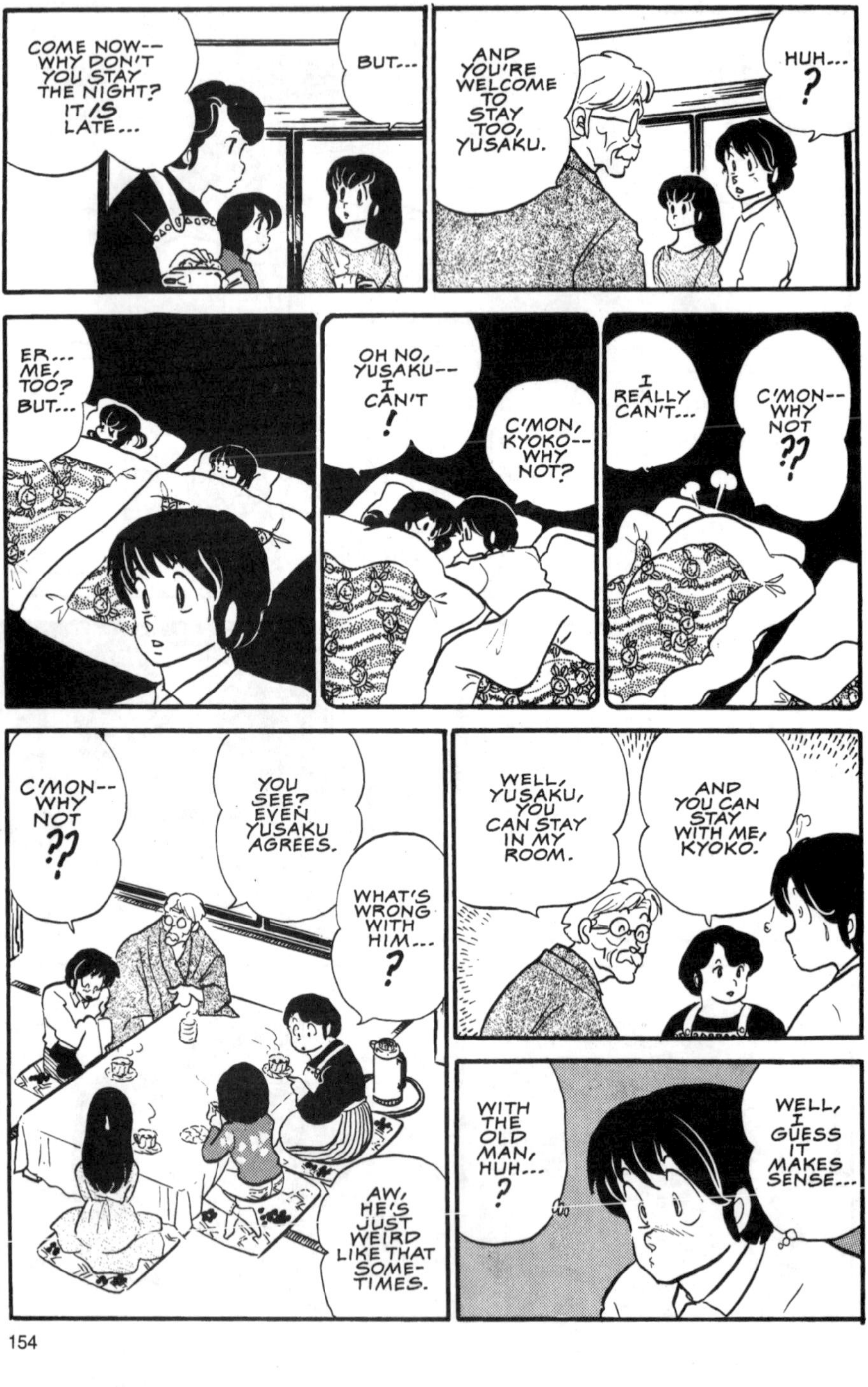
COME NOW-- WHY DON'T YOU STAY THE NIGHT? IT IS LATE...
BUT...
AND YOU'RE WELCOME TO STAY TOO, YUSAKU.
HUH... ?
ER... ME, TOO? BUT...
OH NO, YUSAKU-- I CAN'T !
C'MON, KYOKO-- WHY NOT?
I REALLY CAN'T...
C'MON-- WHY NOT ??
C'MON-- WHY NOT ??
YOU SEE? EVEN YUSAKU AGREES.
WHAT'S WRONG WITH HIM... ?
AW, HE'S JUST WEIRD LIKE THAT SOME-TIMES.
WELL, YUSAKU, YOU CAN STAY IN MY ROOM.
AND YOU CAN STAY WITH ME, KYOKO.
WITH THE OLD MAN, HUH... ?
WELL, I GUESS IT MAKES SENSE...

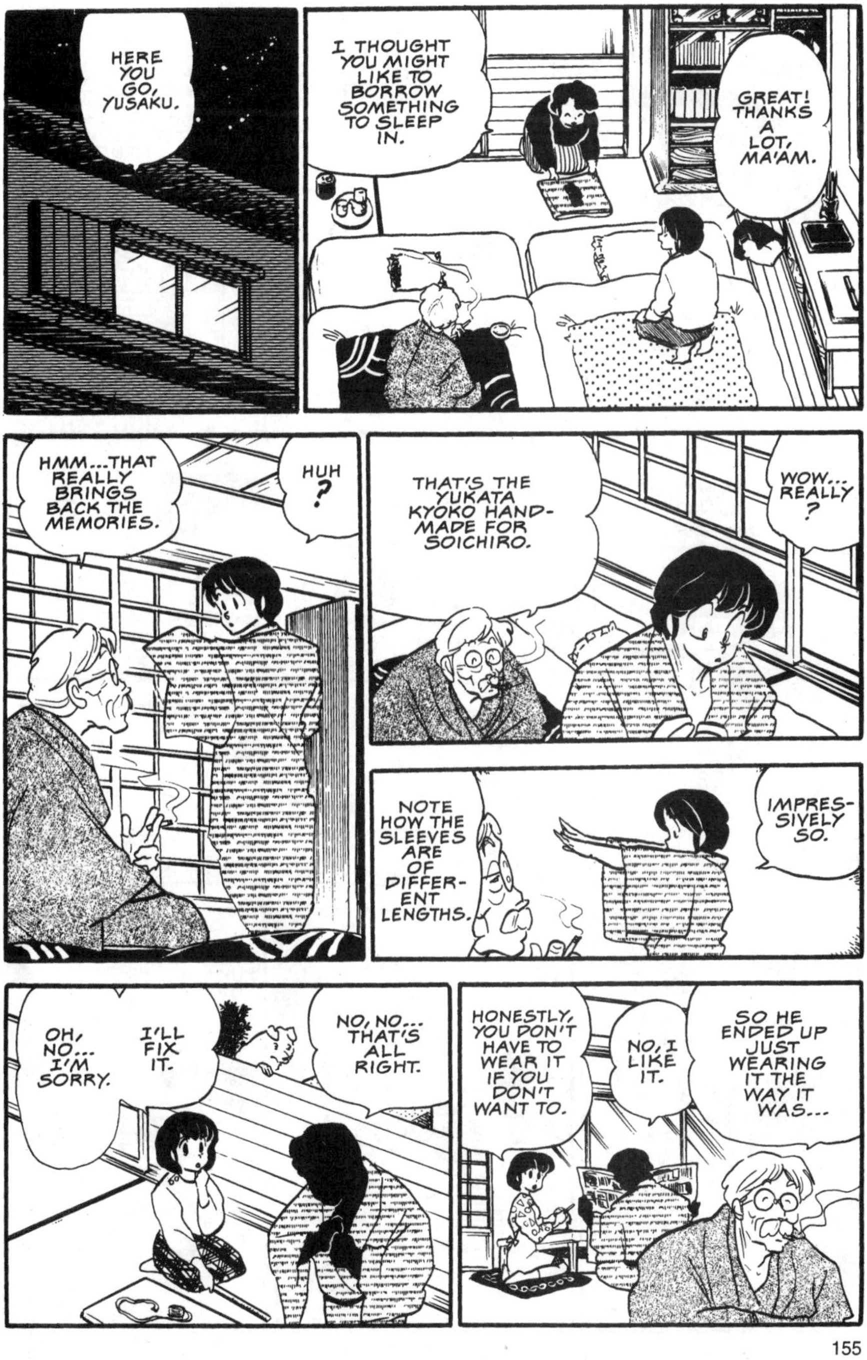
HERE YOU GO, YUSAKU.
I THOUGHT YOU MIGHT LIKE TO BORROW SOMETHING TO SLEEP IN.
GREAT! THANKS A LOT, MA'AM.
HMM...THAT REALLY BRINGS BACK THE MEMORIES.
HUH?
THAT'S THE YUKATA KYOKO HAND-MADE FOR SOICHIRO.
WOW... REALLY?
NOTE HOW THE SLEEVES ARE OF DIFFER-ENT LENGTHS.
IMPRES-SIVELY SO.
OH, NO... I'M SORRY.
I'LL FIX IT.
NO, NO... THAT'S ALL RIGHT.
HONESTLY, YOU DON'T HAVE TO WEAR IT IF YOU DON'T WANT TO.
NO, I LIKE IT.
SO HE ENDED UP JUST WEARING IT THE WAY IT WAS...

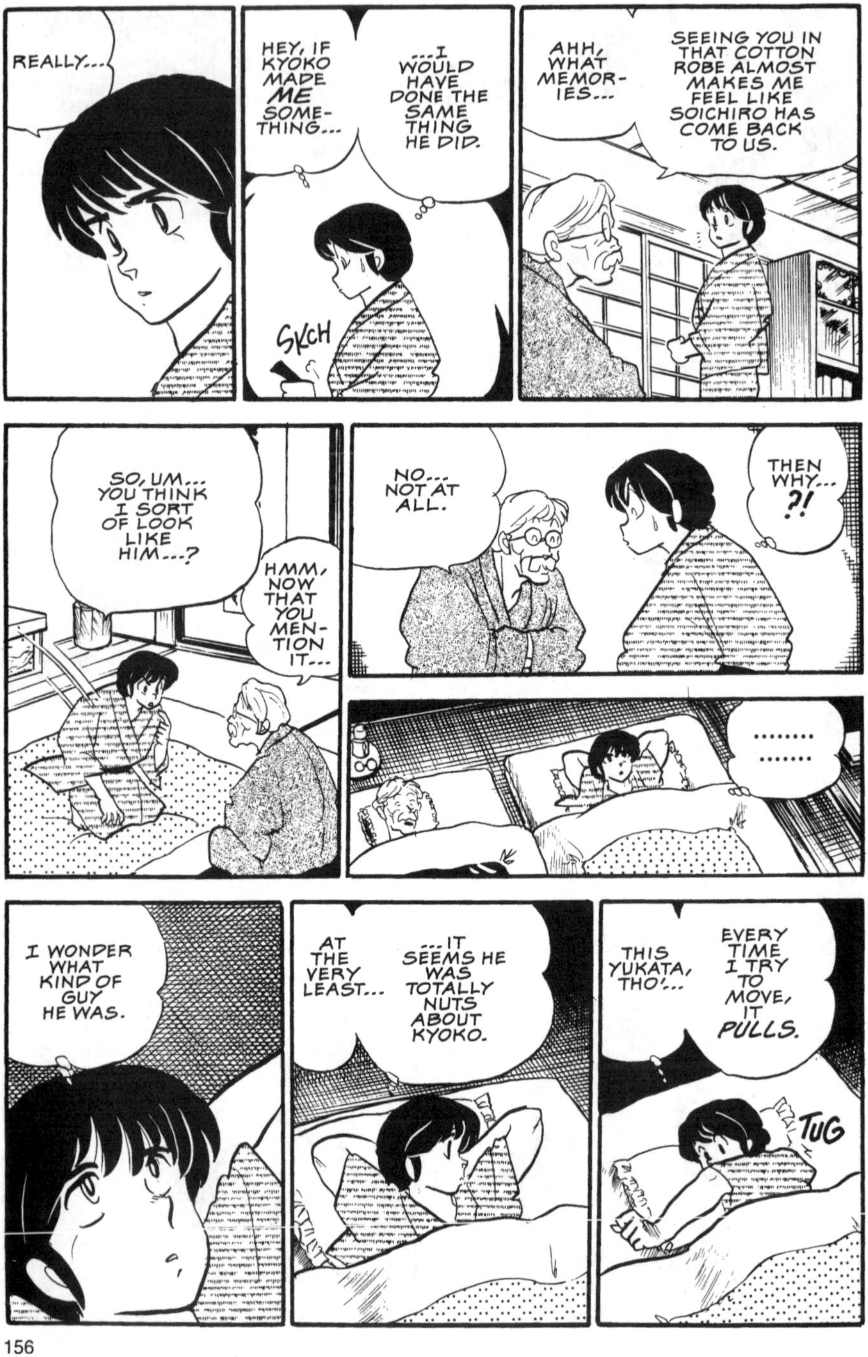
REALLY...
HEY, IF KYOKO MADE ME SOMETHING...
...I WOULD HAVE DONE THE SAME THING HE DID.
SKCH
AHH, WHAT MEMORIES...
SEEING YOU IN THAT COTTON ROBE ALMOST MAKES ME FEEL LIKE SOICHIRO HAS COME BACK TO US.
SO, UM... YOU THINK I SORT OF LOOK LIKE HIM...?
HMM, NOW THAT YOU MENTION IT...
NO... NOT AT ALL.
THEN WHY...?!
....
....
I WONDER WHAT KIND OF GUY HE WAS.
AT THE VERY LEAST...
...IT SEEMS HE WAS TOTALLY NUTS ABOUT KYOKO.
THIS YUKATA, THO'...
EVERY TIME I TRY TO MOVE, IT PULLS.
TUG

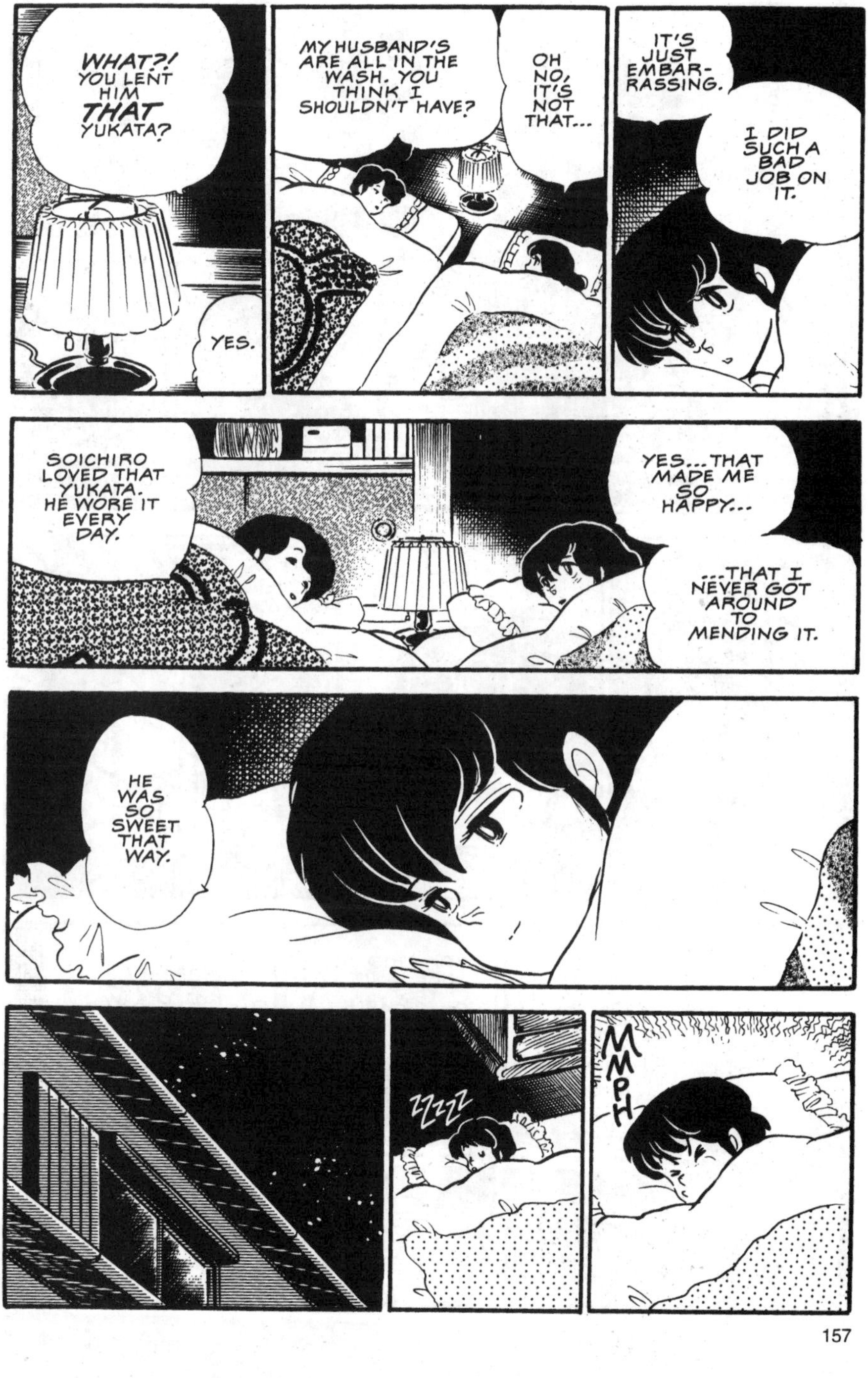
WHAT?! YOU LENT HIM THAT YUKATA?
YES.
MY HUSBAND'S ARE ALL IN THE WASH. YOU THINK I SHOULDN'T HAVE?
OH NO, IT'S NOT THAT...
IT'S JUST EMBARRASSING.
I DID SUCH A BAD JOB ON IT.
SOICHIRO LOVED THAT YUKATA. HE WORE IT EVERY DAY.
YES...THAT MADE ME SO HAPPY...
...THAT I NEVER GOT AROUND TO MENDING IT.
HE WAS SO SWEET THAT WAY.
ZZZZZ
MMPH

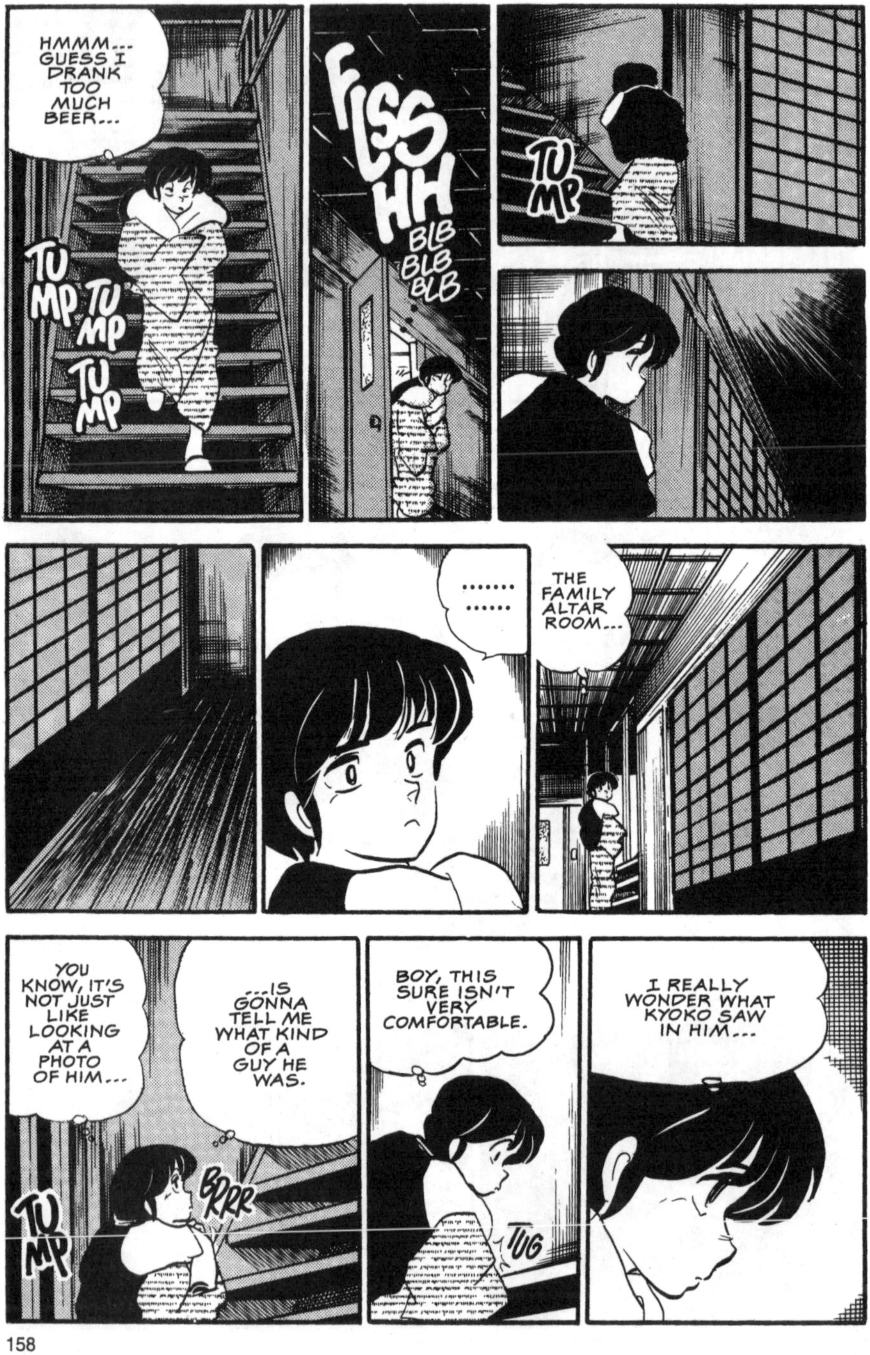
HMMM... GUESS I DRANK TOO MUCH BEER...
TUMP TUMP TUMP
FLSSHH
BLB BLB BLB
TUMP
....
......
THE FAMILY ALTAR ROOM...
YOU KNOW, IT'S NOT JUST LIKE LOOKING AT A PHOTO OF HIM...
...IS GONNA TELL ME WHAT KIND OF A GUY HE WAS.
TUMP
BRRR
BOY, THIS SURE ISN'T VERY COMFORTABLE.
TUG
I REALLY WONDER WHAT KYOKO SAW IN HIM...

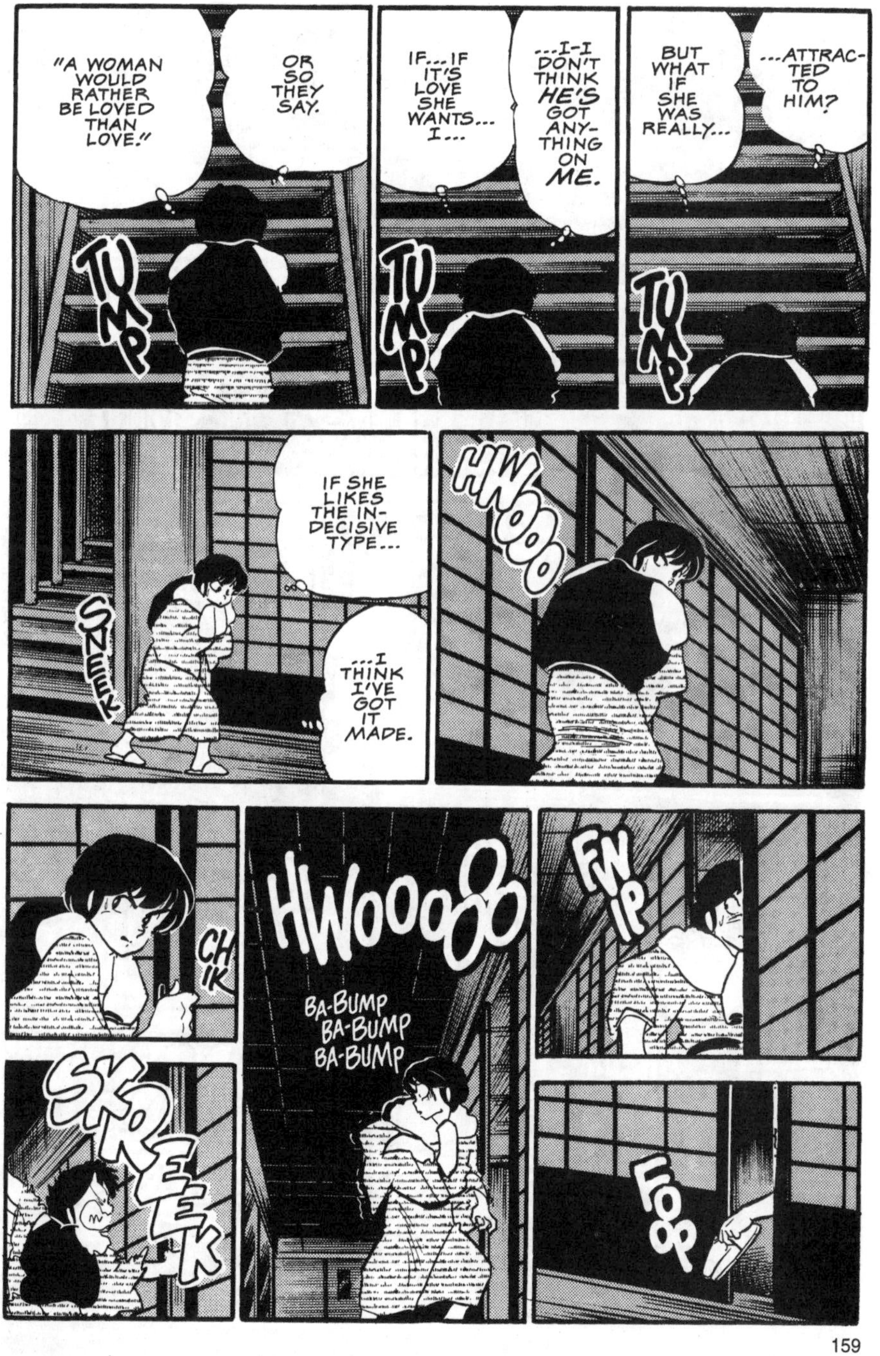
"A WOMAN WOULD RATHER BE LOVED THAN LOVE."
OR SO THEY SAY.
TUMP
IF... IF IT'S LOVE SHE WANTS... I...
...I-I DON'T THINK HE'S GOT ANYTHING ON ME.
TUMP
BUT WHAT IF SHE WAS REALLY...
...ATTRACTED TO HIM?
TUMP
SNEEK
IF SHE LIKES THE INDECISIVE TYPE...
...I THINK I'VE GOT IT MADE.
HWOOO
CHIK
HWOOOOO
BA-BUMP BA-BUMP BA-BUMP
FWIP
SKREEEK
FOOP

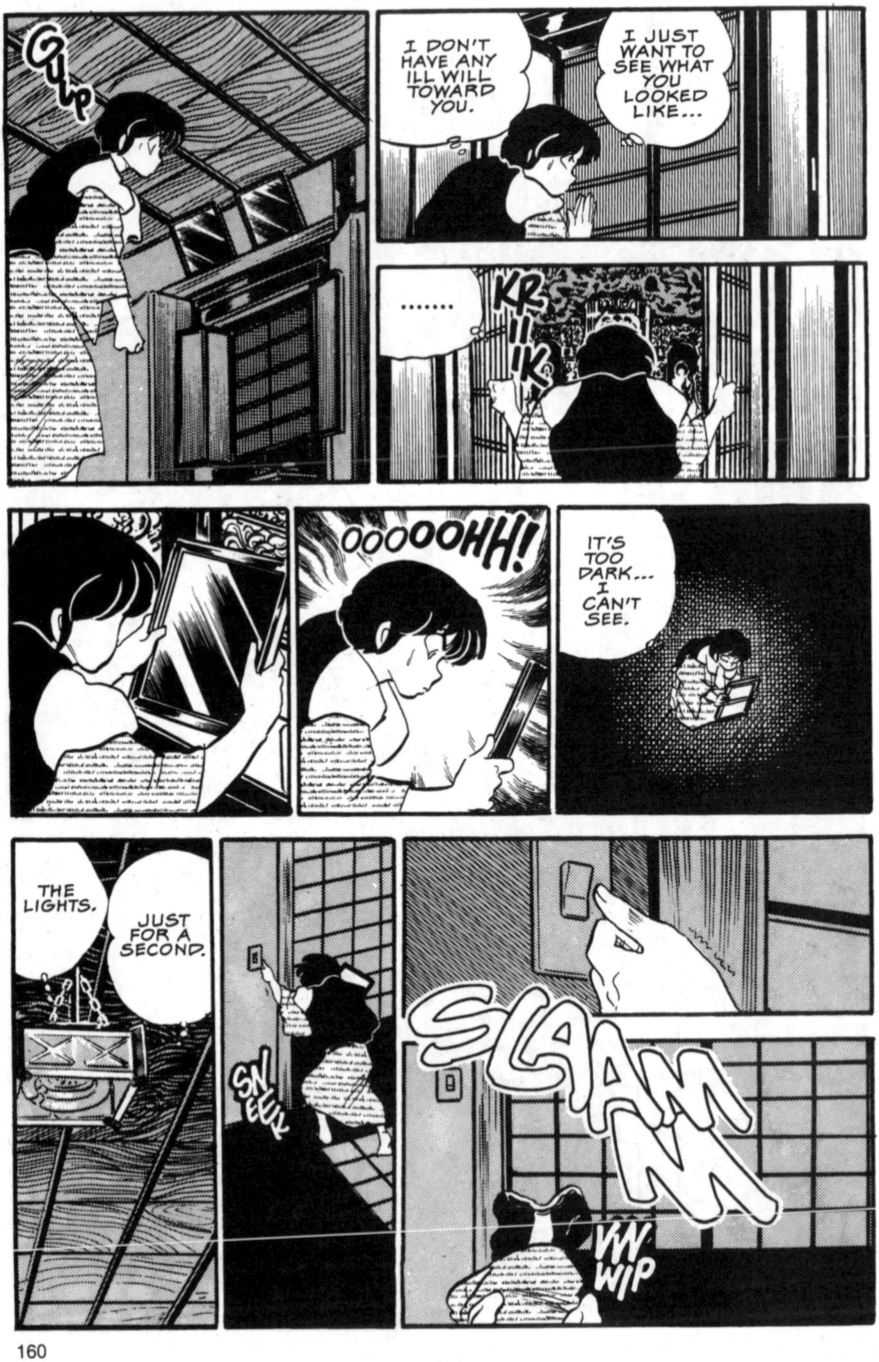
GULP
I DON'T HAVE ANY ILL WILL TOWARD YOU.
I JUST WANT TO SEE WHAT YOU LOOKED LIKE...
....
KRIIK
OOOOOOHH!
IT'S TOO DARK... I CAN'T SEE.
THE LIGHTS.
JUST FOR A SECOND.
SNEEK
SLAAMM
VWWIP

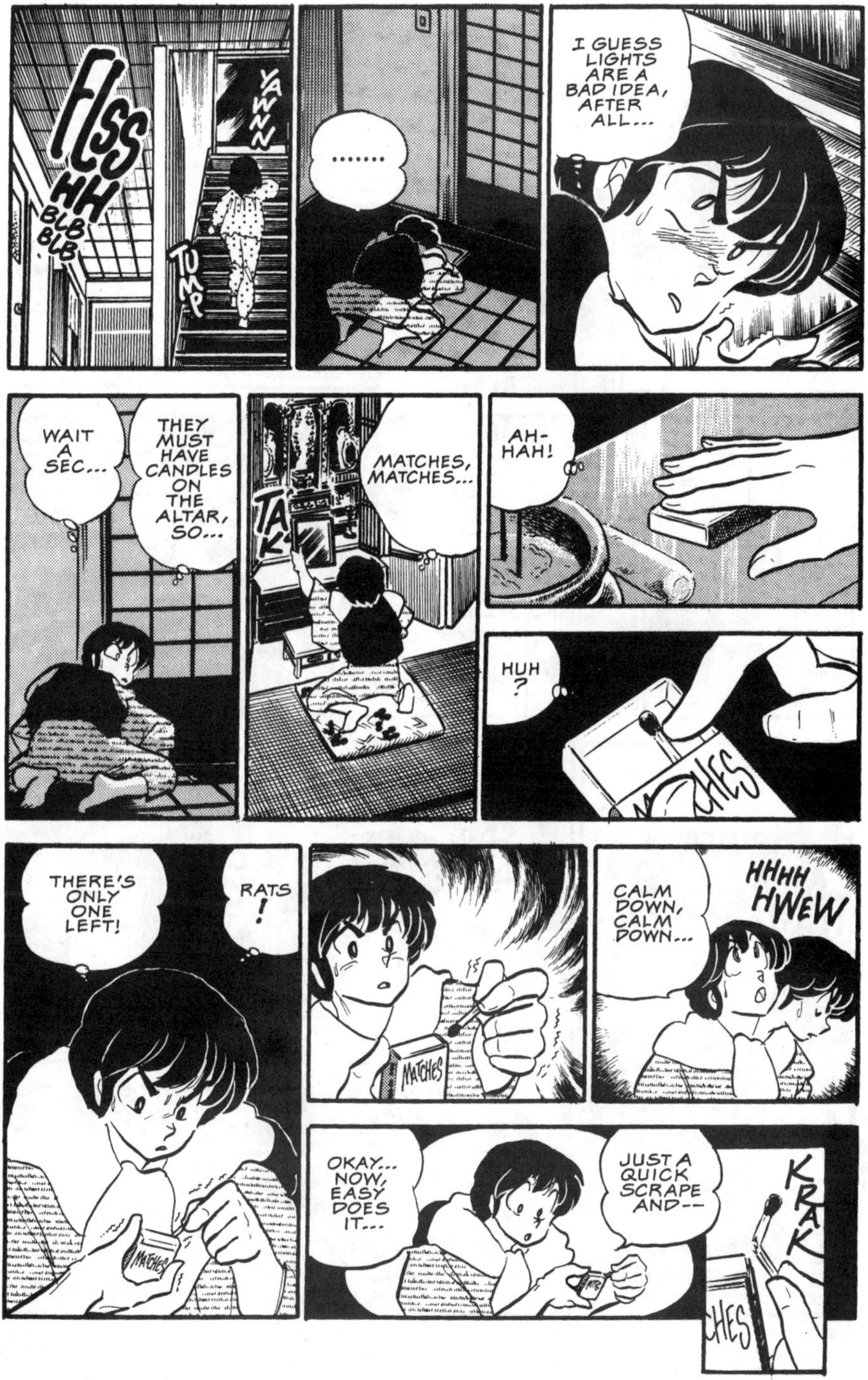
FLSSHH BLB BLB
YAWNN
TUMP
....
I GUESS LIGHTS ARE A BAD IDEA, AFTER ALL...
WAIT A SEC...
THEY MUST HAVE CANDLES ON THE ALTAR, SO...
MATCHES, MATCHES...
TAK
AH-HAH!
HUH?
MATCHES
THERE'S ONLY ONE LEFT!
RATS!
MATCHES
MATCHES
CALM DOWN, CALM DOWN...
HHHH HWEW
OKAY... NOW, EASY DOES IT...
JUST A QUICK SCRAPE AND--
KRAK
CHES

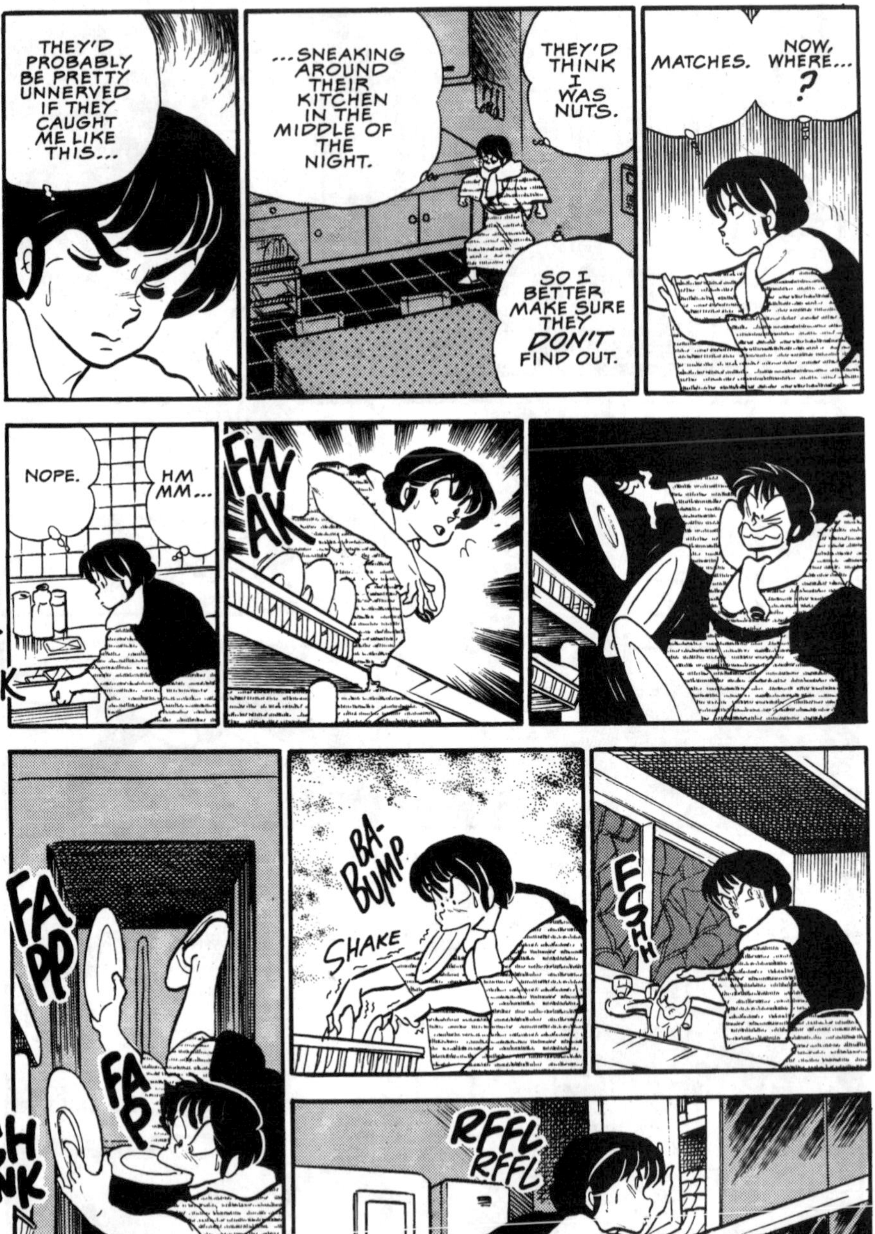
THEY'D PROBABLY BE PRETTY UNNERVED IF THEY CAUGHT ME LIKE THIS...
...SNEAKING AROUND THEIR KITCHEN IN THE MIDDLE OF THE NIGHT.
THEY'D THINK I WAS NUTS.
SO I BETTER MAKE SURE THEY DON'T FIND OUT.
MATCHES.
NOW, WHERE...
?
NOPE.
HMMM...
KTAK
FWAK
FAPP
FAP
CHNK
BA-BUMP
SHAKE
FSHH
RFFL RFFL

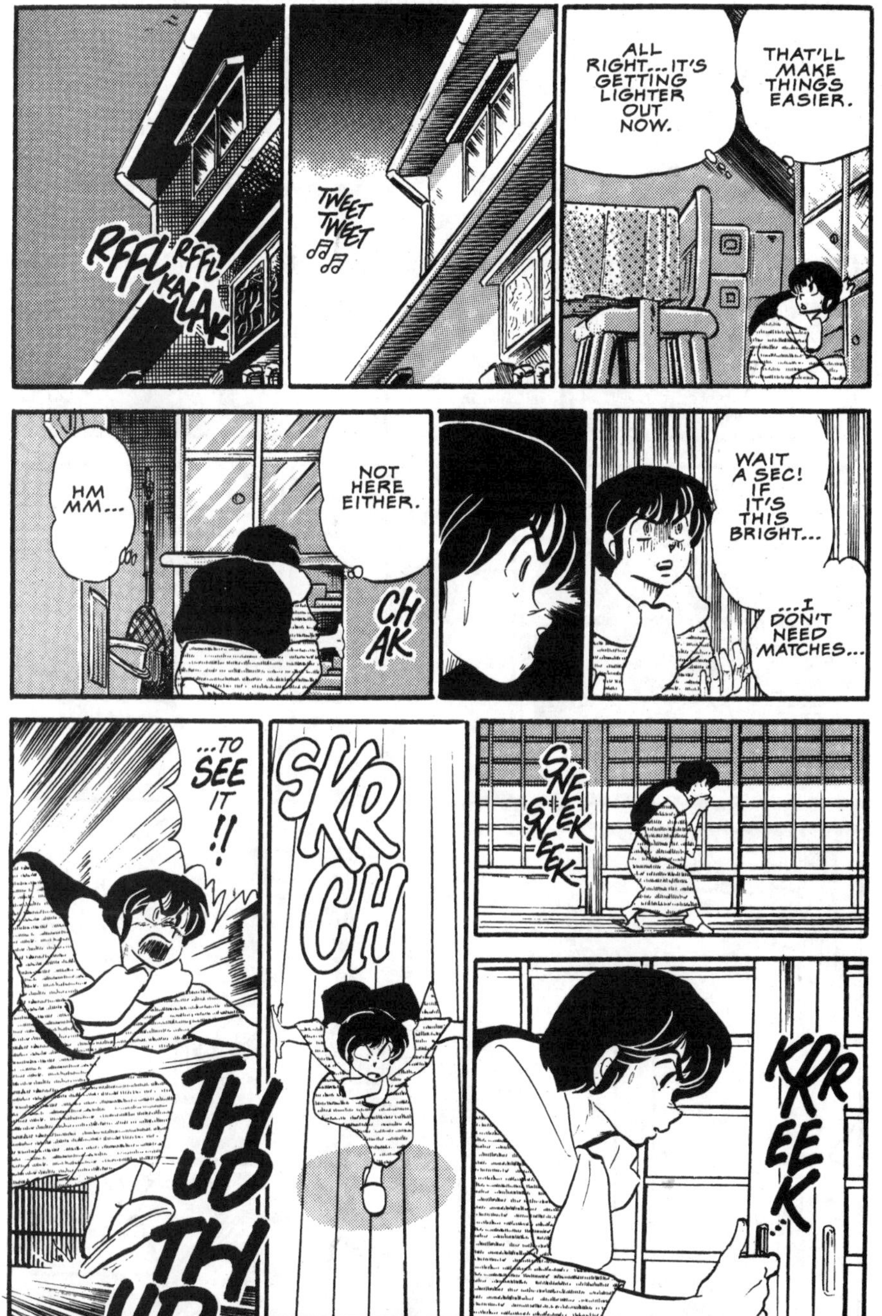
RFFL RFFL KA LAK
TWEET TWEET
ALL RIGHT... IT'S GETTING LIGHTER OUT NOW.
THAT'LL MAKE THINGS EASIER.
HM MM...
NOT HERE EITHER.
CH AK
WAIT A SEC! IF IT'S THIS BRIGHT...
...I DON'T NEED MATCHES...
...TO SEE IT!!
THUD THUD
SKR CH
SNEEK SNEEK SNEEK
KRR EEK

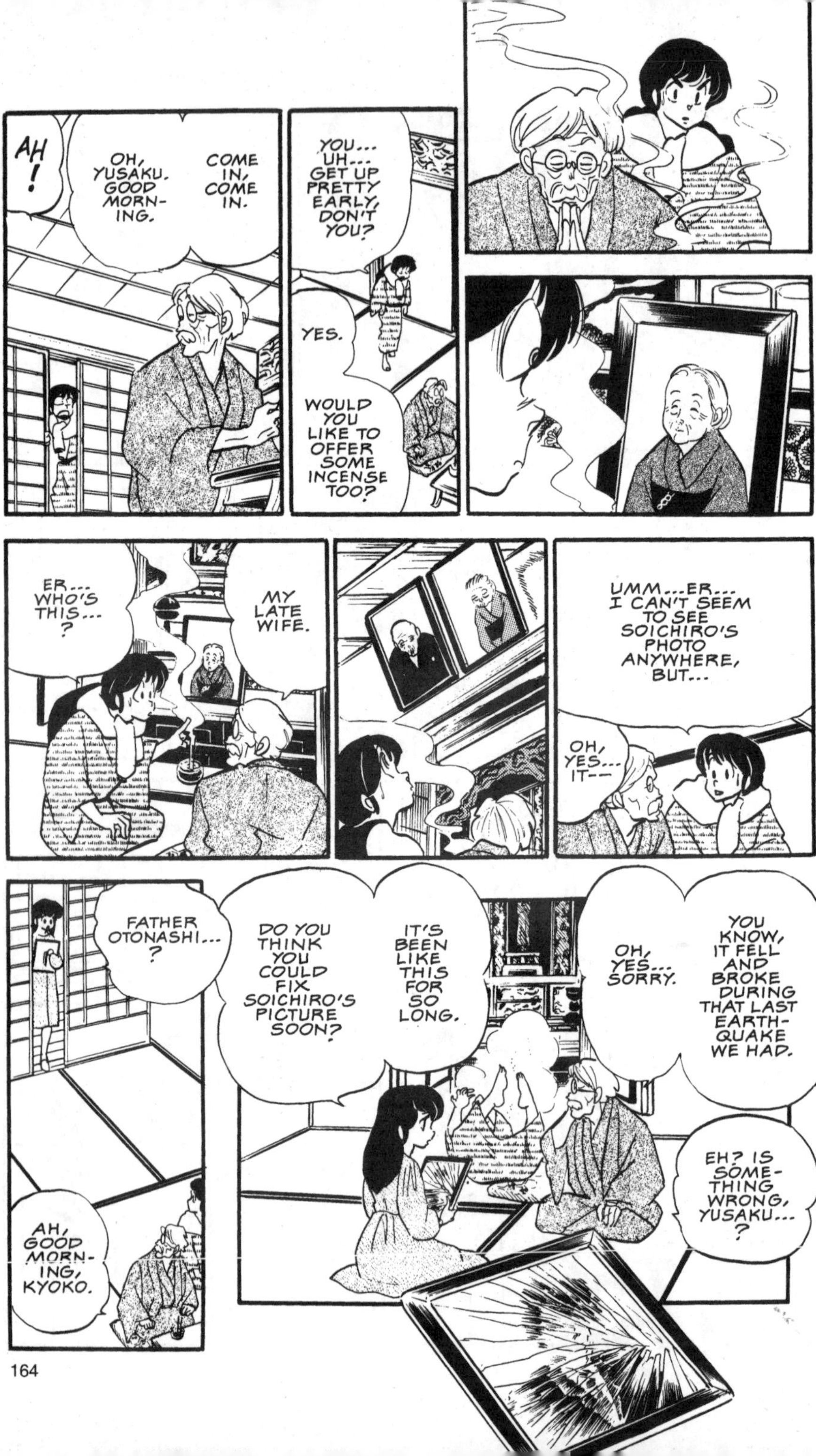
AH!
OH, YUSAKU. GOOD MORNING.
COME IN, COME IN.
YOU... UH... GET UP PRETTY EARLY, DON'T YOU?
YES.
WOULD YOU LIKE TO OFFER SOME INCENSE TOO?
ER... WHO'S THIS...?
MY LATE WIFE.
UMM...ER... I CAN'T SEEM TO SEE SOICHIRO'S PHOTO ANYWHERE, BUT...
OH, YES... IT--
FATHER OTONASHI...?
AH, GOOD MORNING, KYOKO.
DO YOU THINK YOU COULD FIX SOICHIRO'S PICTURE SOON?
IT'S BEEN LIKE THIS FOR SO LONG.
OH, YES... SORRY.
YOU KNOW, IT FELL AND BROKE DURING THAT LAST EARTHQUAKE WE HAD.
EH? IS SOMETHING WRONG, YUSAKU...?

PART 8

A GRAVE MATTER

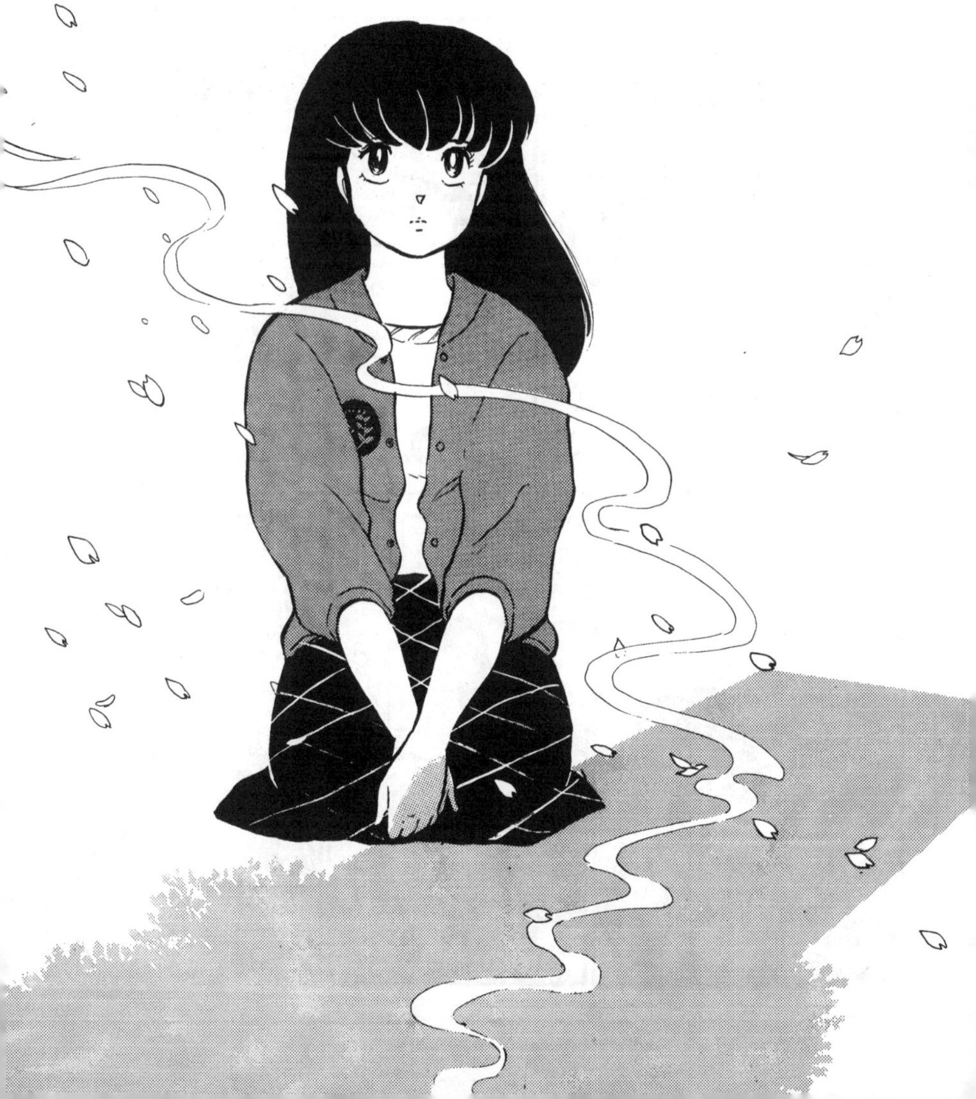

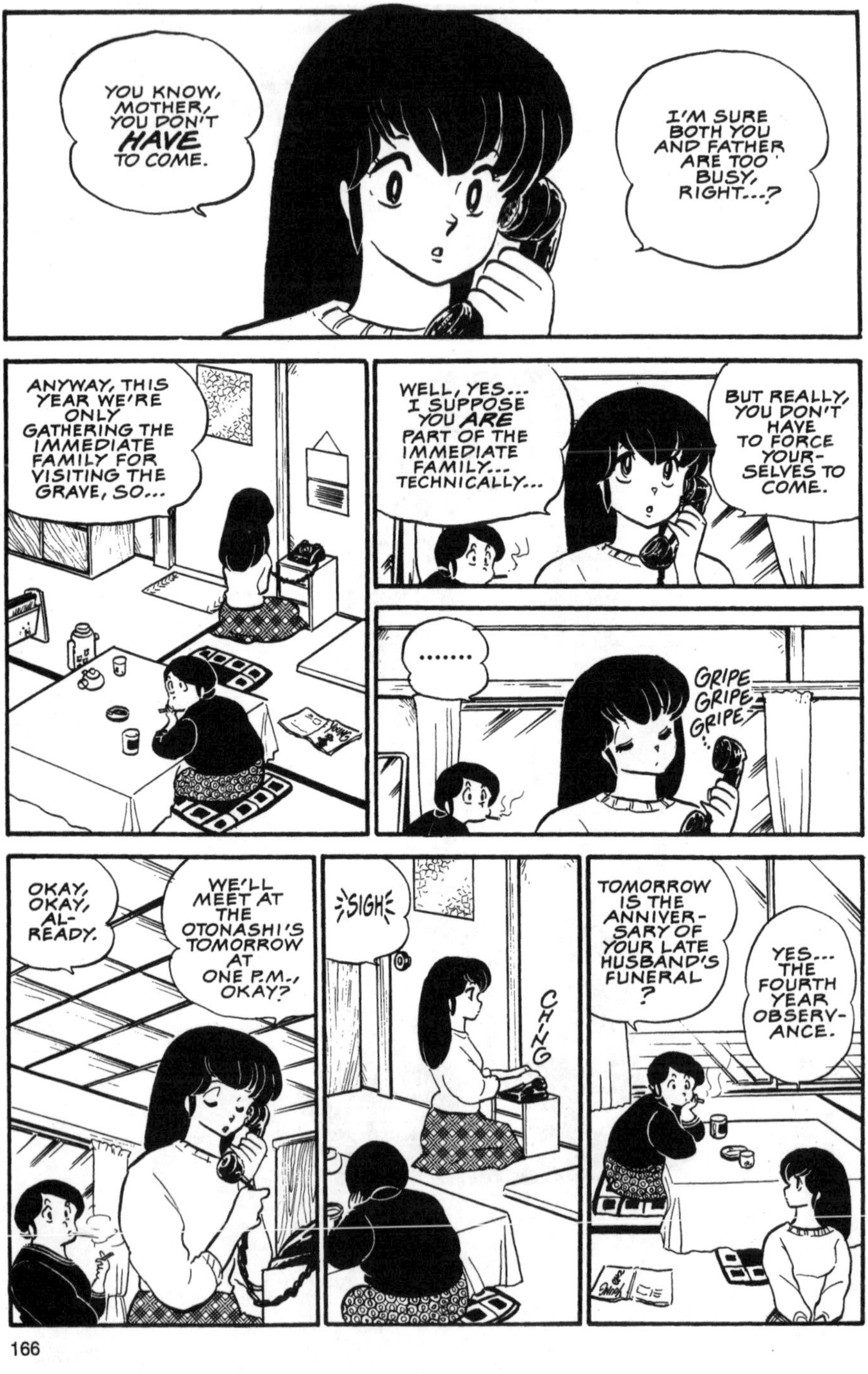
YOU KNOW, MOTHER, YOU DON'T HAVE TO COME.
I'M SURE BOTH YOU AND FATHER ARE TOO BUSY, RIGHT...?
ANYWAY, THIS YEAR WE'RE ONLY GATHERING THE IMMEDIATE FAMILY FOR VISITING THE GRAVE, SO...
WELL, YES... I SUPPOSE YOU ARE PART OF THE IMMEDIATE FAMILY... TECHNICALLY...
BUT REALLY, YOU DON'T HAVE TO FORCE YOUR-SELVES TO COME.
....
GRIPE GRIPE GRIPE
OKAY, OKAY, AL-READY.
WE'LL MEET AT THE OTONASHI'S TOMORROW AT ONE P.M., OKAY?
SIGH
CHING
TOMORROW IS THE ANNIVER-SARY OF YOUR LATE HUSBAND'S FUNERAL?
YES... THE FOURTH YEAR OBSERV-ANCE.

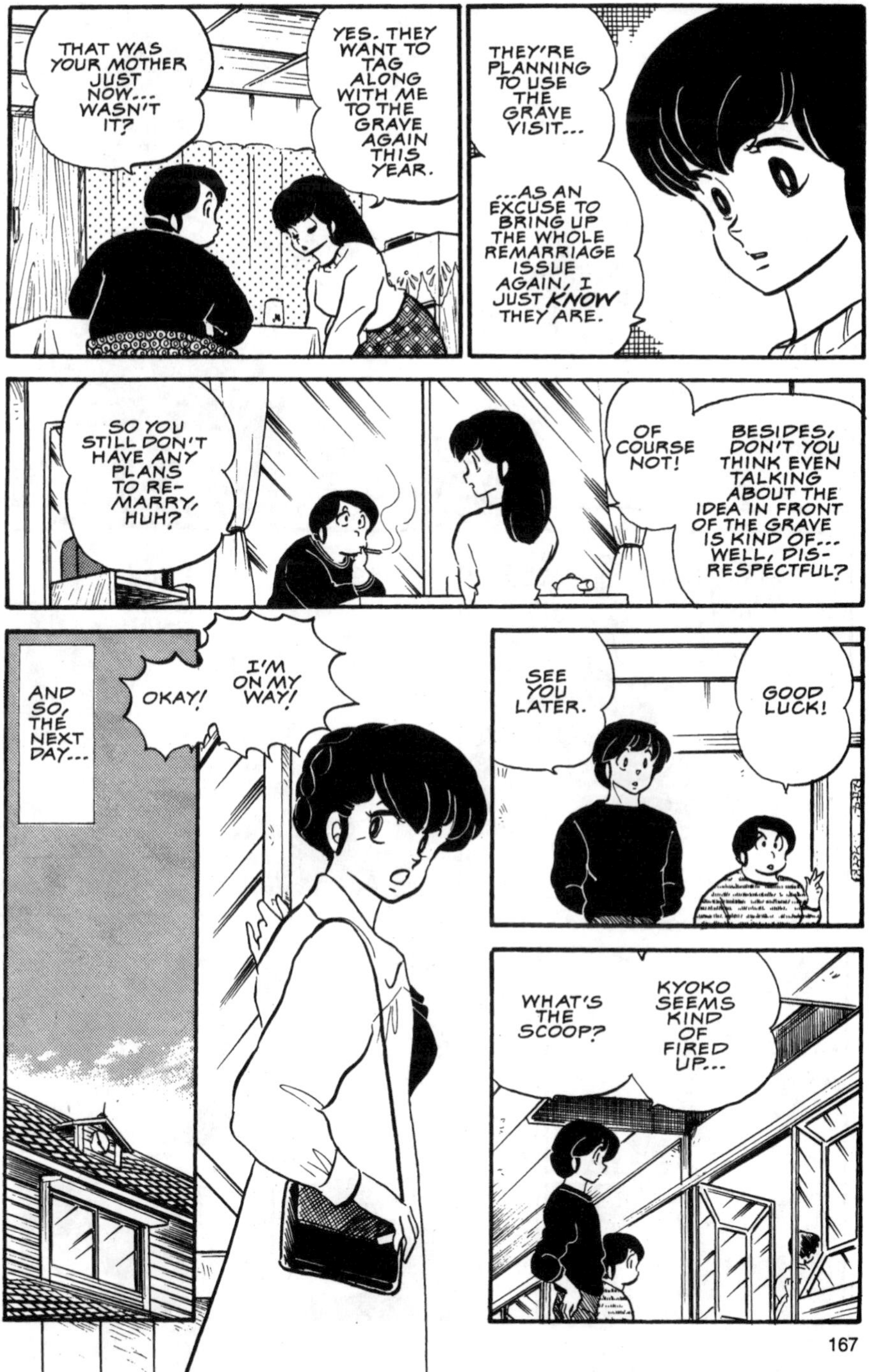
THAT WAS YOUR MOTHER JUST NOW... WASN'T IT?
YES. THEY WANT TO TAG ALONG WITH ME TO THE GRAVE AGAIN THIS YEAR.
THEY'RE PLANNING TO USE THE GRAVE VISIT...
...AS AN EXCUSE TO BRING UP THE WHOLE REMARRIAGE ISSUE AGAIN, I JUST KNOW THEY ARE.
SO YOU STILL DON'T HAVE ANY PLANS TO RE-MARRY, HUH?
OF COURSE NOT!
BESIDES, DON'T YOU THINK EVEN TALKING ABOUT THE IDEA IN FRONT OF THE GRAVE IS KIND OF... WELL, DIS-RESPECTFUL?
AND SO, THE NEXT DAY...
OKAY!
I'M ON MY WAY!
SEE YOU LATER.
GOOD LUCK!
WHAT'S THE SCOOP?
KYOKO SEEMS KIND OF FIRED UP...

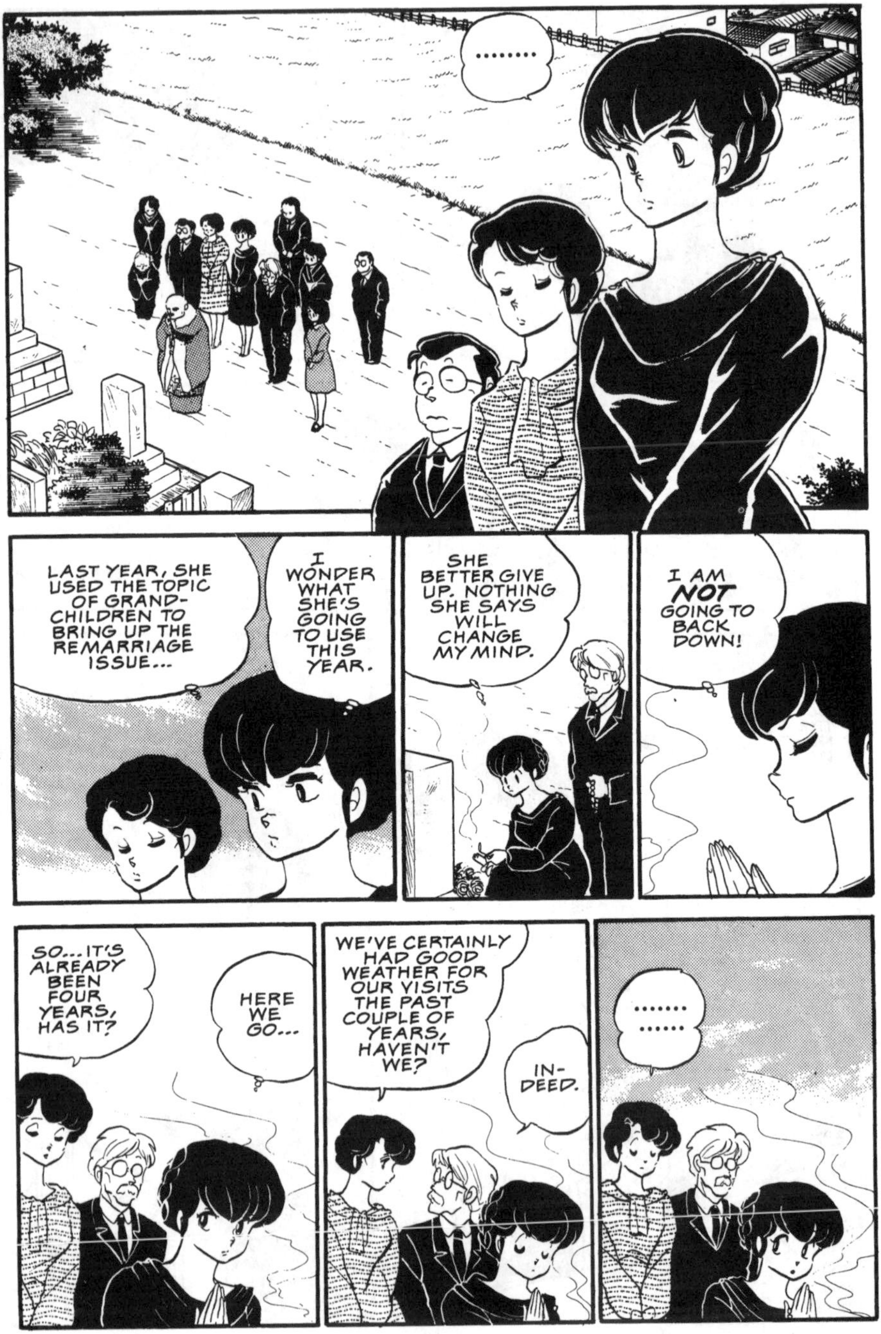
....
LAST YEAR, SHE USED THE TOPIC OF GRAND-CHILDREN TO BRING UP THE REMARRIAGE ISSUE...
I WONDER WHAT SHE'S GOING TO USE THIS YEAR.
SHE BETTER GIVE UP. NOTHING SHE SAYS WILL CHANGE MY MIND.
I AM NOT GOING TO BACK DOWN!
SO... IT'S ALREADY BEEN FOUR YEARS, HAS IT?
HERE WE GO...
WE'VE CERTAINLY HAD GOOD WEATHER FOR OUR VISITS THE PAST COUPLE OF YEARS, HAVEN'T WE?
IN-DEED.
....
....

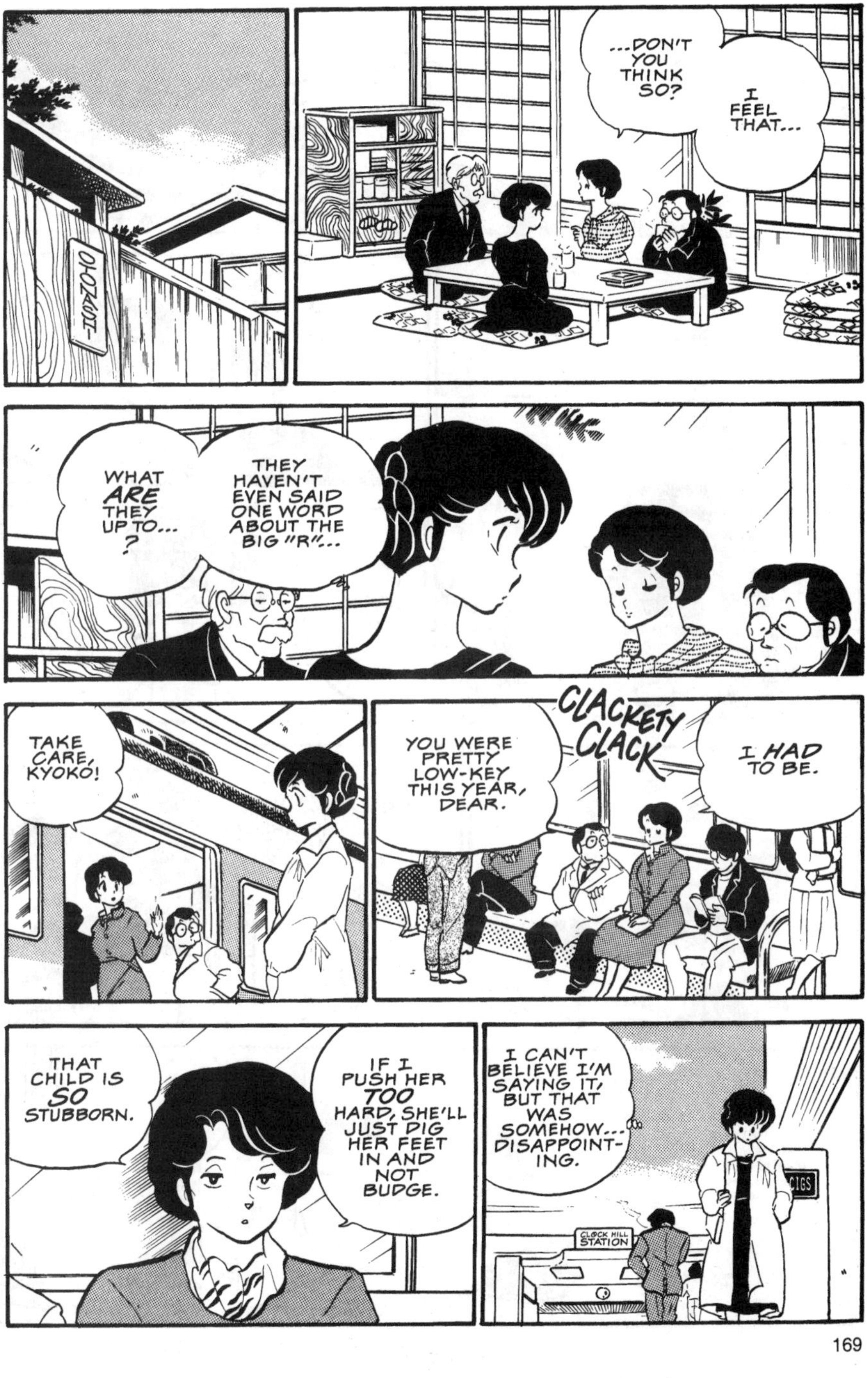
OTONASHI
...DON'T YOU THINK SO?
I FEEL THAT...
WHAT ARE THEY UP TO...?
THEY HAVEN'T EVEN SAID ONE WORD ABOUT THE BIG "R"...
TAKE CARE, KYOKO!
CLACKETY CLACK
YOU WERE PRETTY LOW-KEY THIS YEAR, DEAR.
I HAD TO BE.
THAT CHILD IS SO STUBBORN.
IF I PUSH HER TOO HARD, SHE'LL JUST DIG HER FEET IN AND NOT BUDGE.
I CAN'T BELIEVE I'M SAYING IT, BUT THAT WAS SOMEHOW... DISAPPOINTING.
CLOCK HILL STATION
CIGS

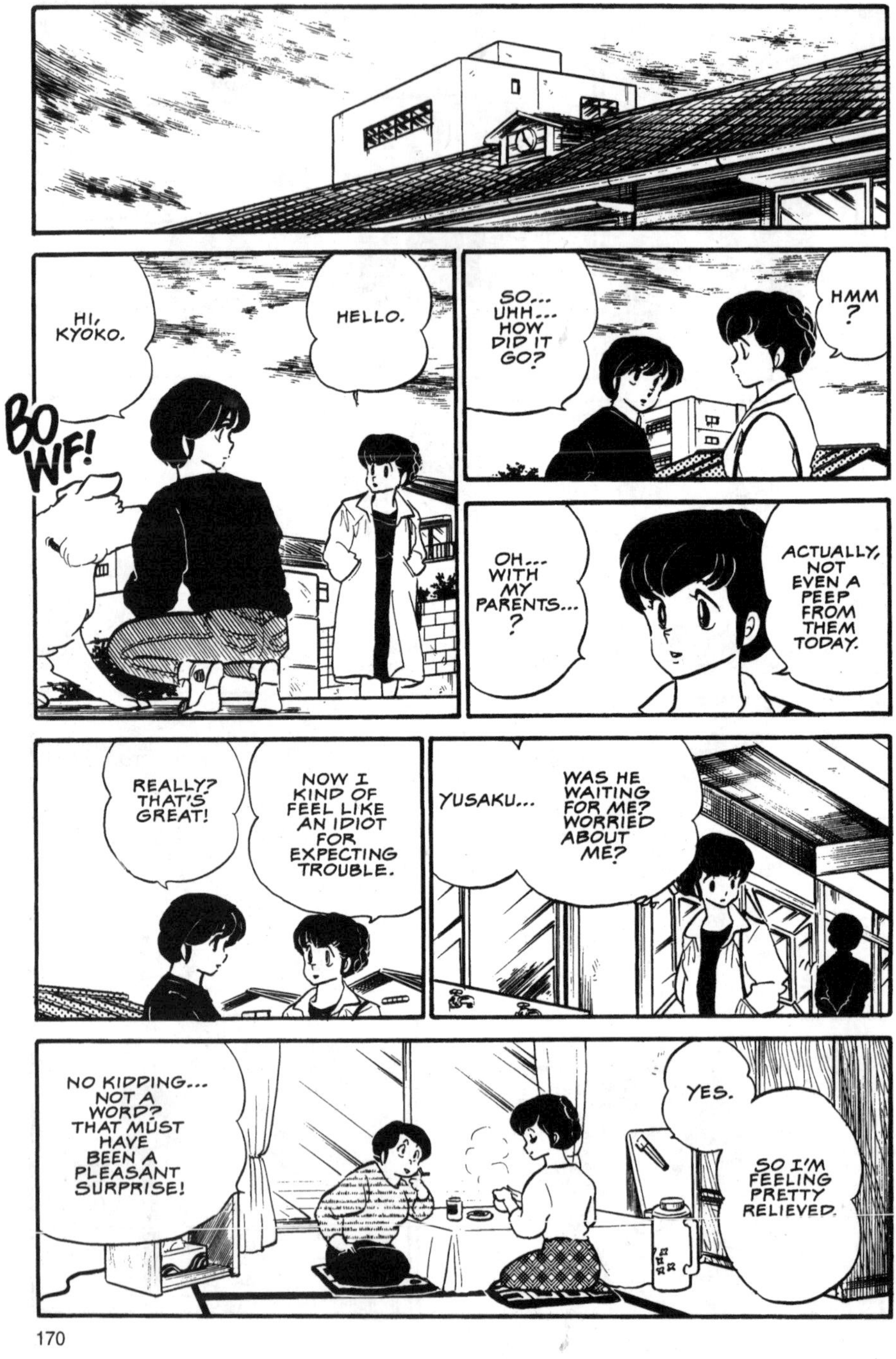
HI, KYOKO.
HELLO.
BOWF!
SO... UHH... HOW DID IT GO?
HMM?
OH... WITH MY PARENTS...?
ACTUALLY, NOT EVEN A PEEP FROM THEM TODAY.
REALLY? THAT'S GREAT!
NOW I KIND OF FEEL LIKE AN IDIOT FOR EXPECTING TROUBLE.
YUSAKU...
WAS HE WAITING FOR ME? WORRIED ABOUT ME?
NO KIDDING... NOT A WORD? THAT MUST HAVE BEEN A PLEASANT SURPRISE!
YES.
SO I'M FEELING PRETTY RELIEVED.

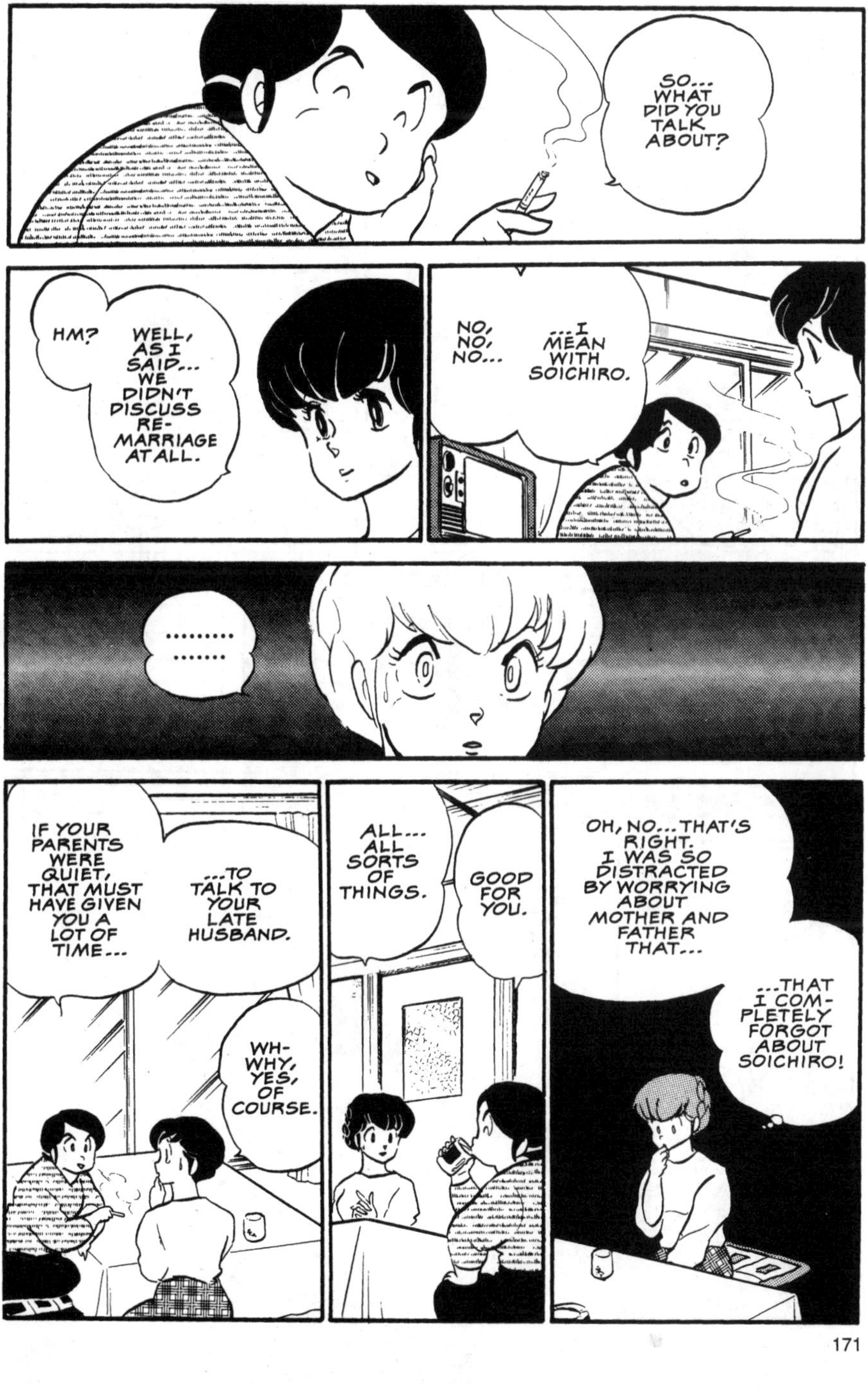
SO... WHAT DID YOU TALK ABOUT?
HM?
WELL, AS I SAID... WE DIDN'T DISCUSS RE-MARRIAGE AT ALL.
NO, NO, NO...
...I MEAN WITH SOICHIRO.
....
....
IF YOUR PARENTS WERE QUIET, THAT MUST HAVE GIVEN YOU A LOT OF TIME...
...TO TALK TO YOUR LATE HUSBAND.
WH-WHY, YES, OF COURSE.
ALL... ALL SORTS OF THINGS.
GOOD FOR YOU.
OH, NO... THAT'S RIGHT. I WAS SO DISTRACTED BY WORRYING ABOUT MOTHER AND FATHER THAT...
...THAT I COMPLETELY FORGOT ABOUT SOICHIRO!

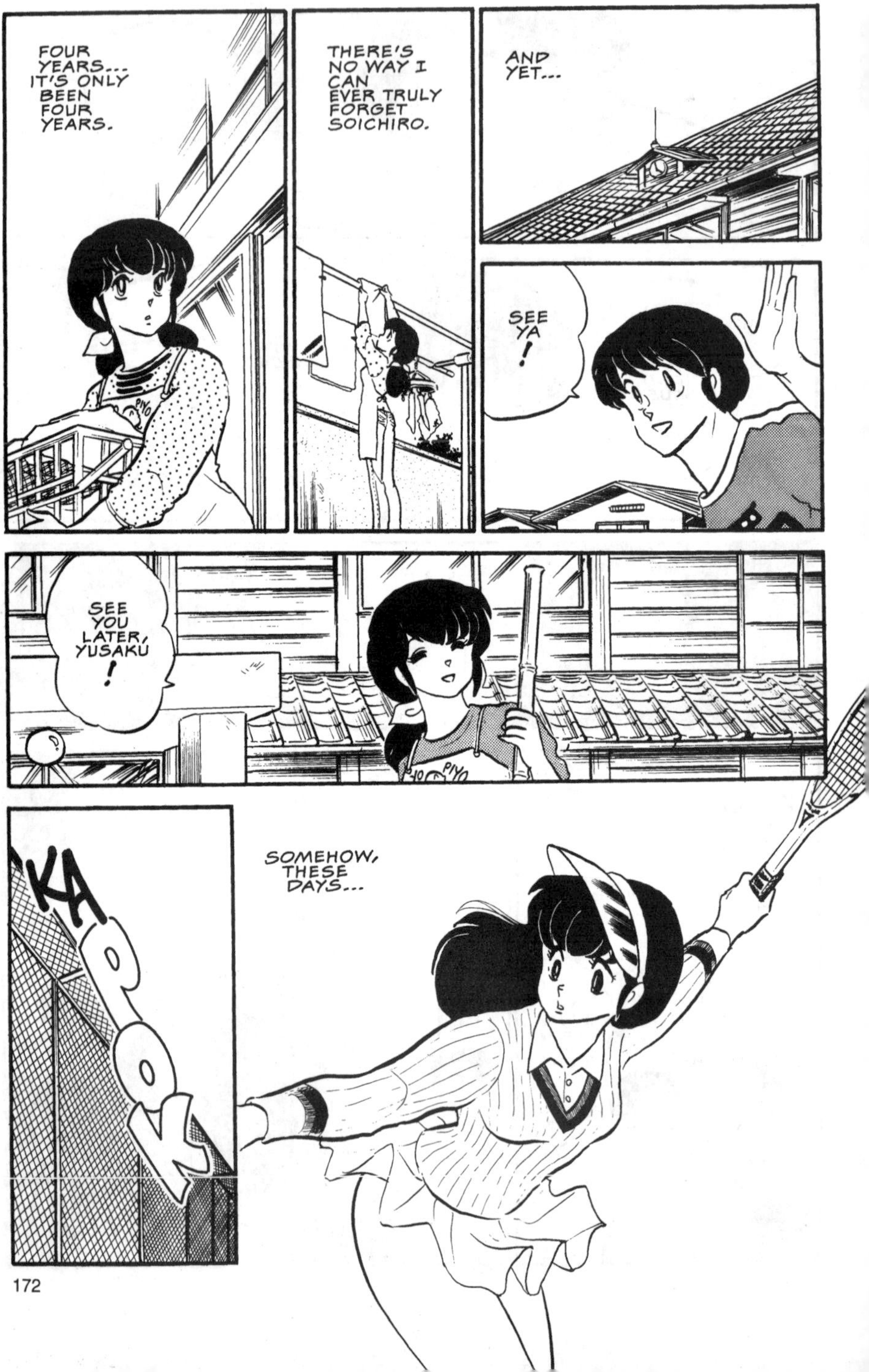
FOUR YEARS... IT'S ONLY BEEN FOUR YEARS.
THERE'S NO WAY I CAN EVER TRULY FORGET SOICHIRO.
AND YET...
SEE YA!
PIYO
SEE YOU LATER, YUSAKU!
PIYO
KA
POK
SOMEHOW, THESE DAYS...

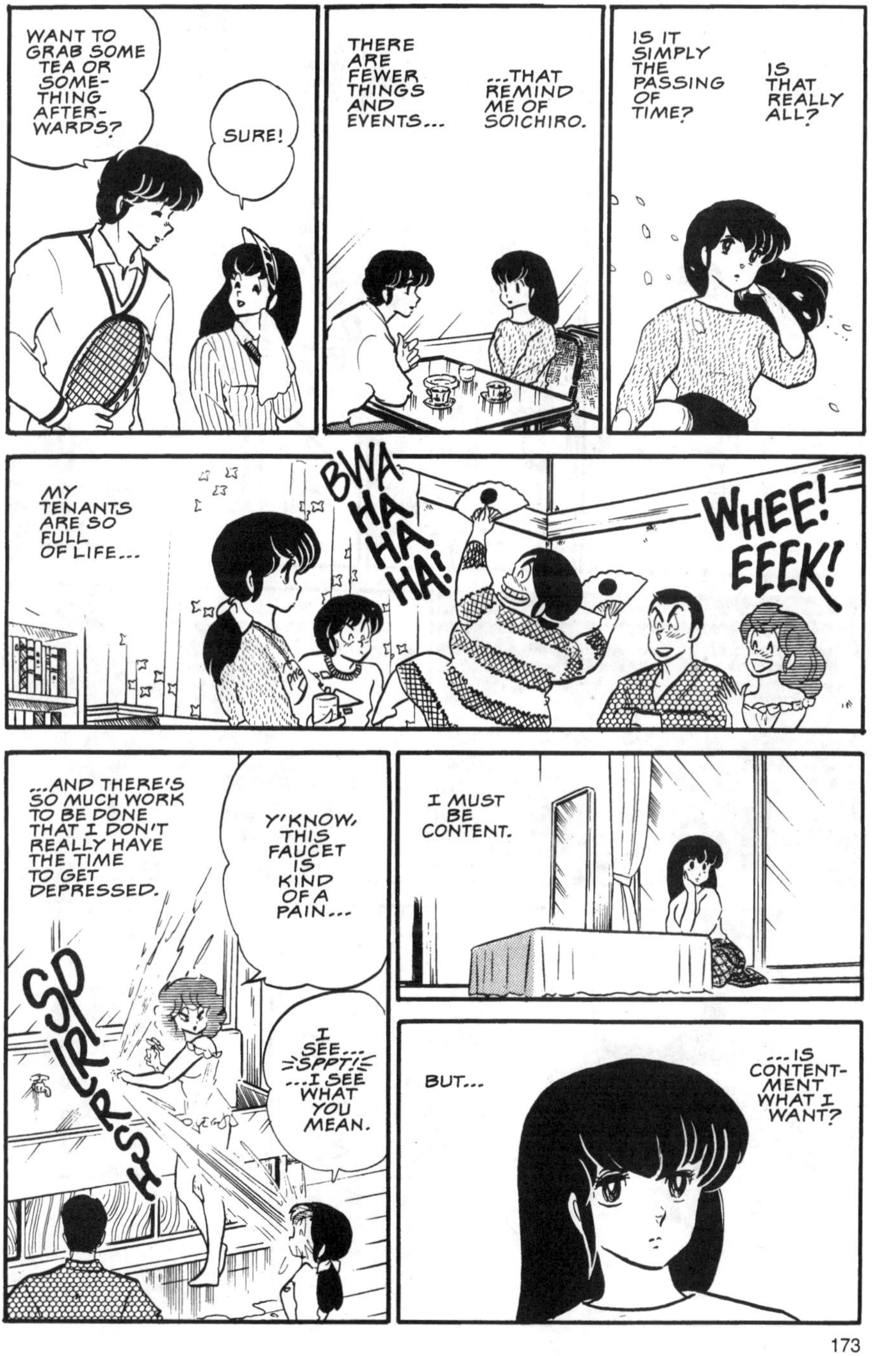
WANT TO GRAB SOME TEA OR SOMETHING AFTERWARDS?
SURE!
THERE ARE FEWER THINGS AND EVENTS...
...THAT REMIND ME OF SOICHIRO.
IS IT SIMPLY THE PASSING OF TIME?
IS THAT REALLY ALL?
MY TENANTS ARE SO FULL OF LIFE...
BWA HA HA HA!
WHEE! EEEK!
...AND THERE'S SO MUCH WORK TO BE DONE THAT I DON'T REALLY HAVE THE TIME TO GET DEPRESSED.
Y'KNOW, THIS FAUCET IS KIND OF A PAIN...
SPRRSH
I SEE... SPPT! ...I SEE WHAT YOU MEAN.
I MUST BE CONTENT.
BUT...
...IS CONTENTMENT WHAT I WANT?

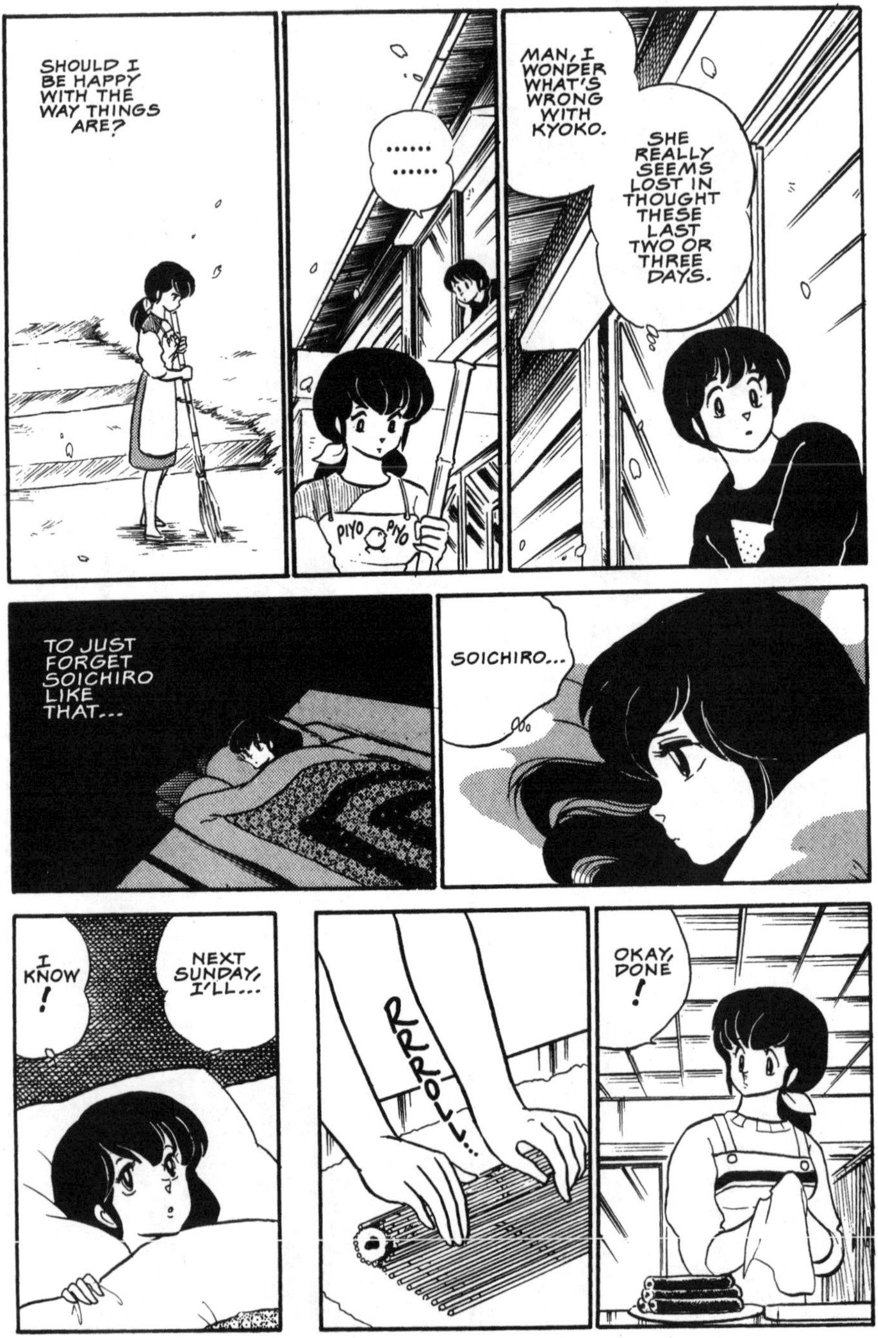
SHOULD I BE HAPPY WITH THE WAY THINGS ARE?
......
......
MAN, I WONDER WHAT'S WRONG WITH KYOKO.
SHE REALLY SEEMS LOST IN THOUGHT THESE LAST TWO OR THREE DAYS.
TO JUST FORGET SOICHIRO LIKE THAT...
SOICHIRO...
I KNOW!
NEXT SUNDAY, I'LL...
RRROLL...
OKAY, DONE!

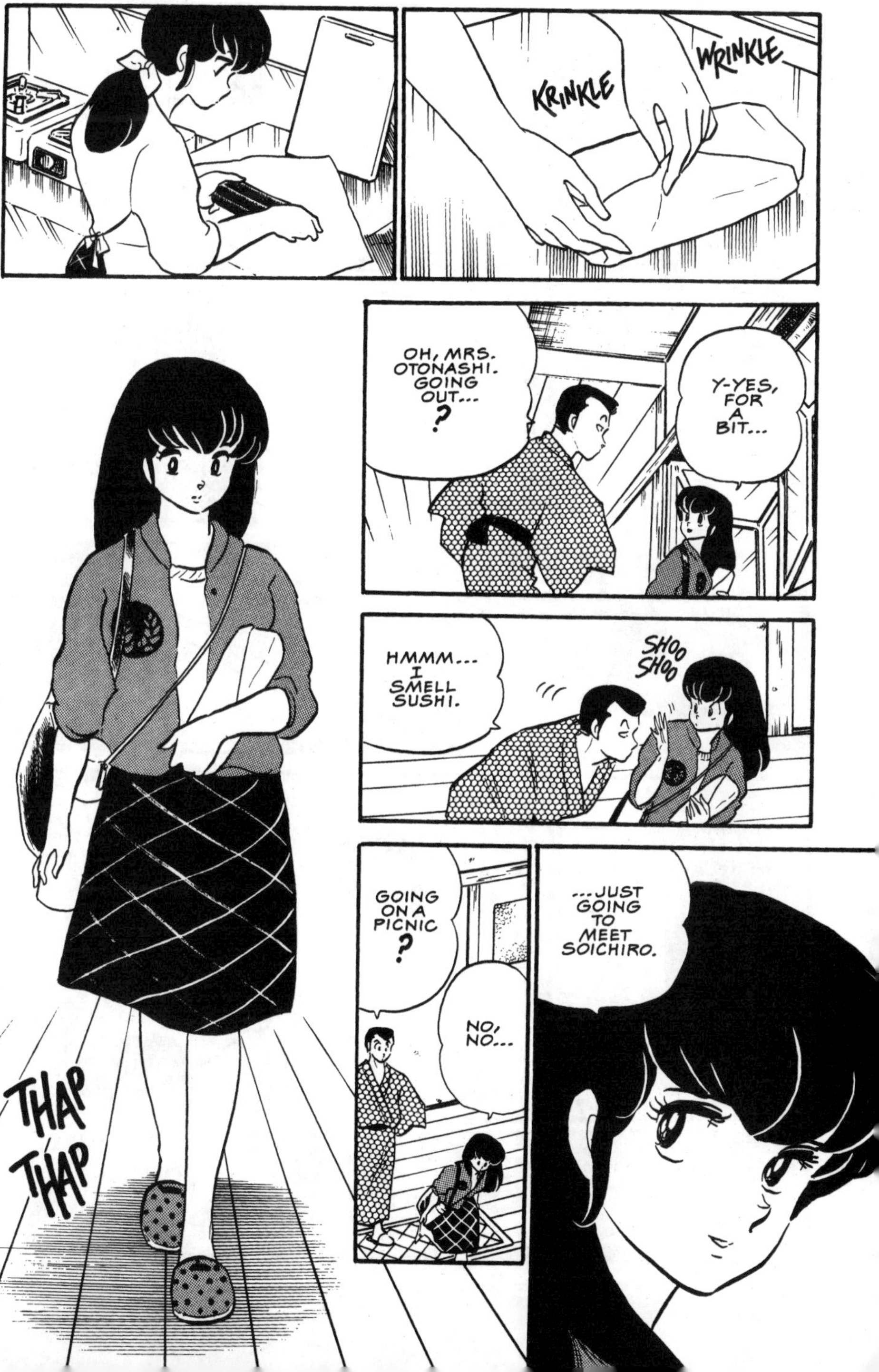
KRINKLE
WRINKLE
THAP THAP
OH, MRS. OTONASHI. GOING OUT...?
Y-YES, FOR A BIT...
HMMM... I SMELL SUSHI.
SHOO SHOO
GOING ON A PICNIC?
NO, NO...
...JUST GOING TO MEET SOICHIRO.

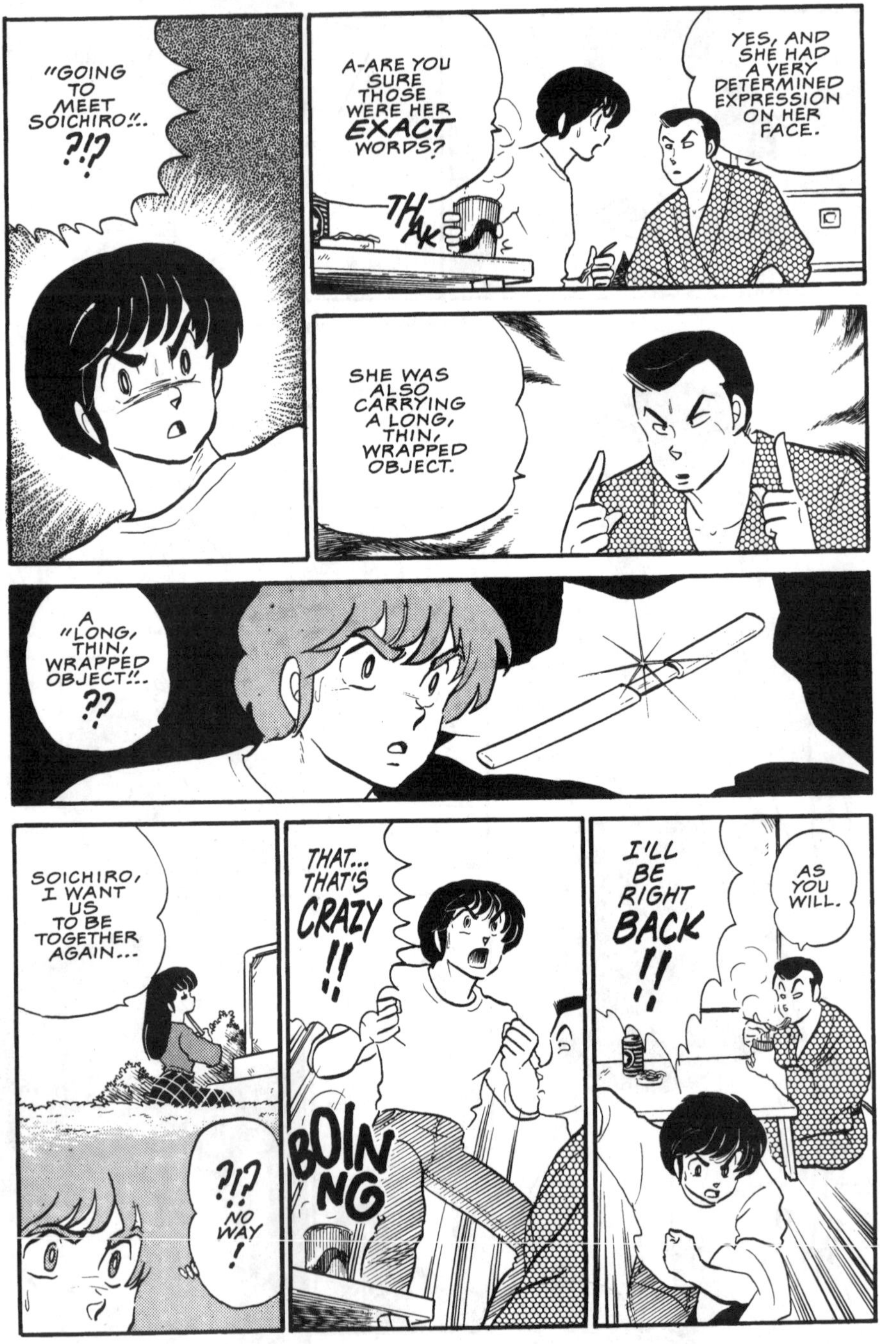

"GOING TO MEET SOICHIRO"... ?!?
A-ARE YOU SURE THOSE WERE HER EXACT WORDS?
THAK
YES, AND SHE HAD A VERY DETERMINED EXPRESSION ON HER FACE.
SHE WAS ALSO CARRYING A LONG, THIN, WRAPPED OBJECT.
A "LONG, THIN, WRAPPED OBJECT"... ??
SOICHIRO, I WANT US TO BE TOGETHER AGAIN...
?!? NO WAY!
THAT... THAT'S CRAZY!!
BOINNG
I'LL BE RIGHT BACK!!
AS YOU WILL.

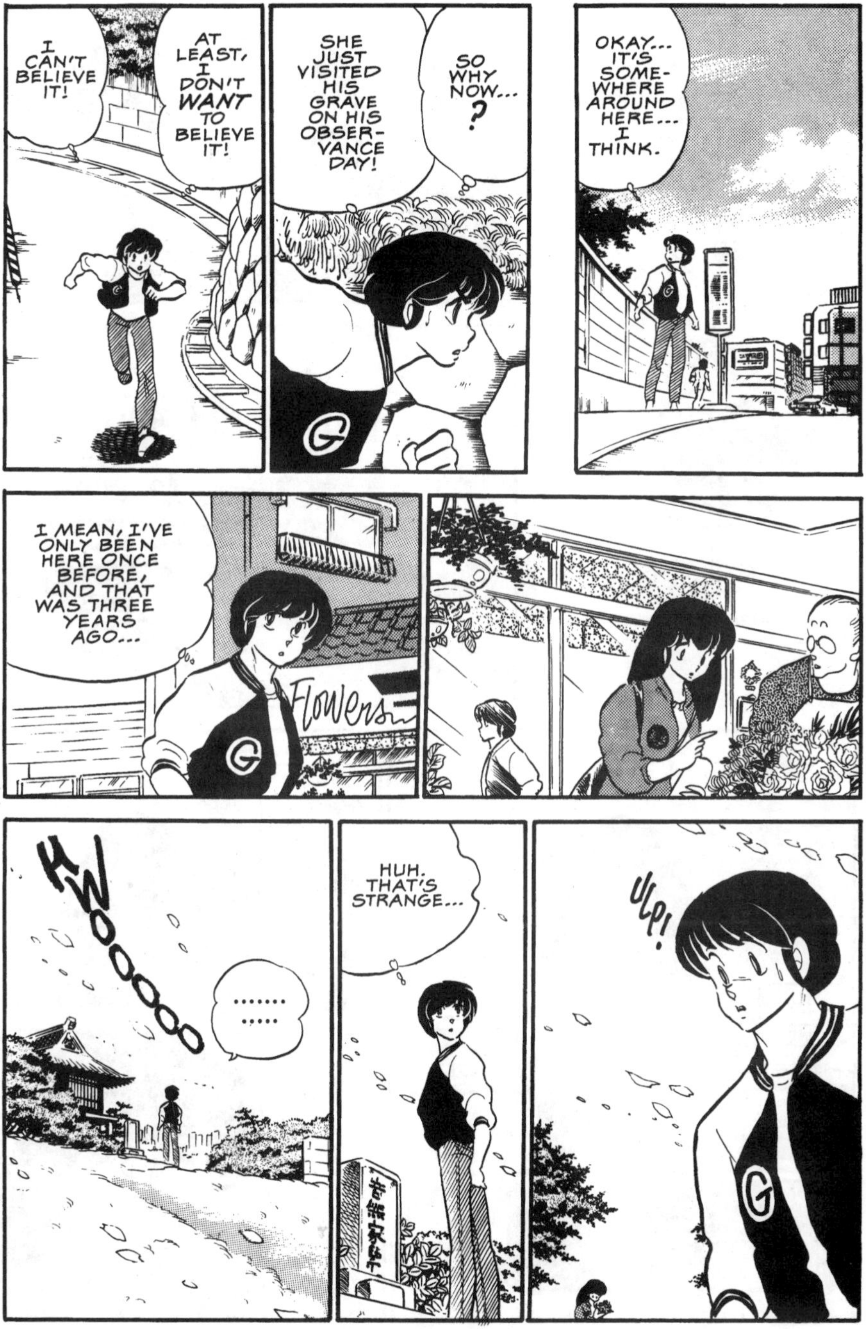
I CAN'T BELIEVE IT!
AT LEAST, I DON'T WANT TO BELIEVE IT!
SHE JUST VISITED HIS GRAVE ON HIS OBSERVANCE DAY!
SO WHY NOW... ?
OKAY... IT'S SOMEWHERE AROUND HERE... I THINK.
I MEAN, I'VE ONLY BEEN HERE ONCE BEFORE, AND THAT WAS THREE YEARS AGO...
Flowers
KWOOOOO
....
HUH. THAT'S STRANGE...
ULP!

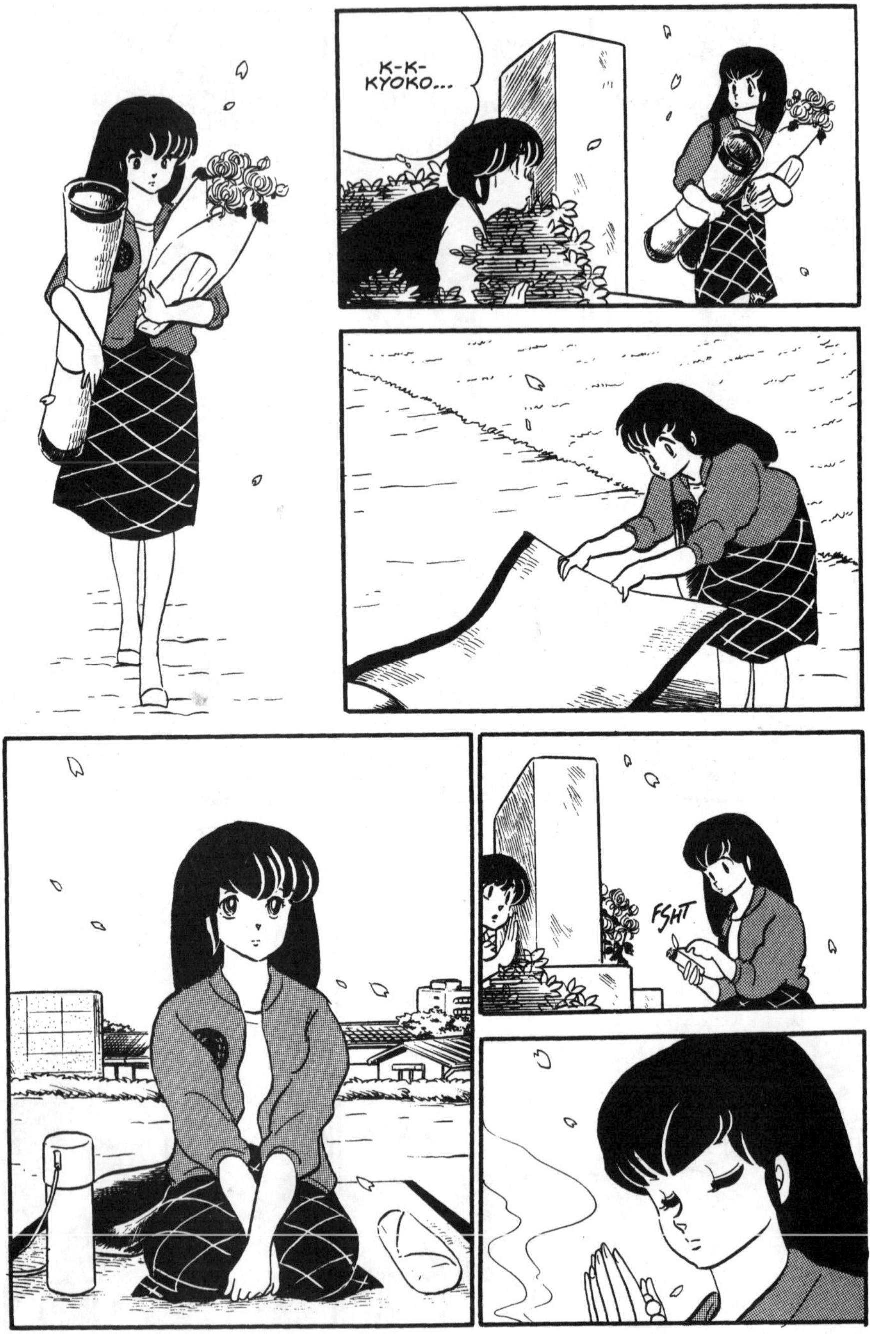
K-K-KYOKO...
FSHT

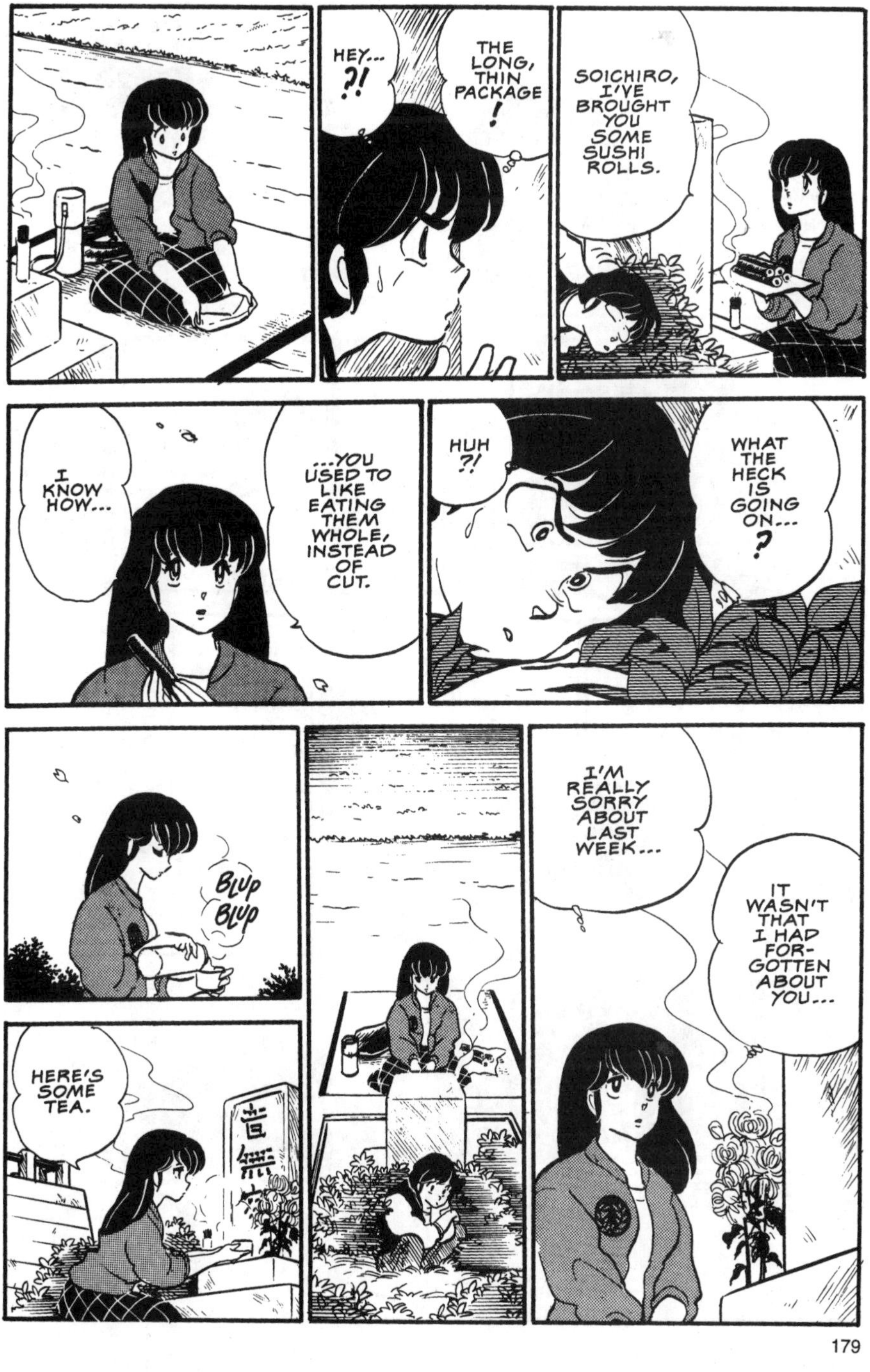
HEY... ?!
THE LONG, THIN PACKAGE!
SOICHIRO, I'VE BROUGHT YOU SOME SUSHI ROLLS.
I KNOW HOW...
...YOU USED TO LIKE EATING THEM WHOLE, INSTEAD OF CUT.
HUH ?!
WHAT THE HECK IS GOING ON...?
BLUP BLUP
HERE'S SOME TEA.
I'M REALLY SORRY ABOUT LAST WEEK...
IT WASN'T THAT I HAD FOR-GOTTEN ABOUT YOU...

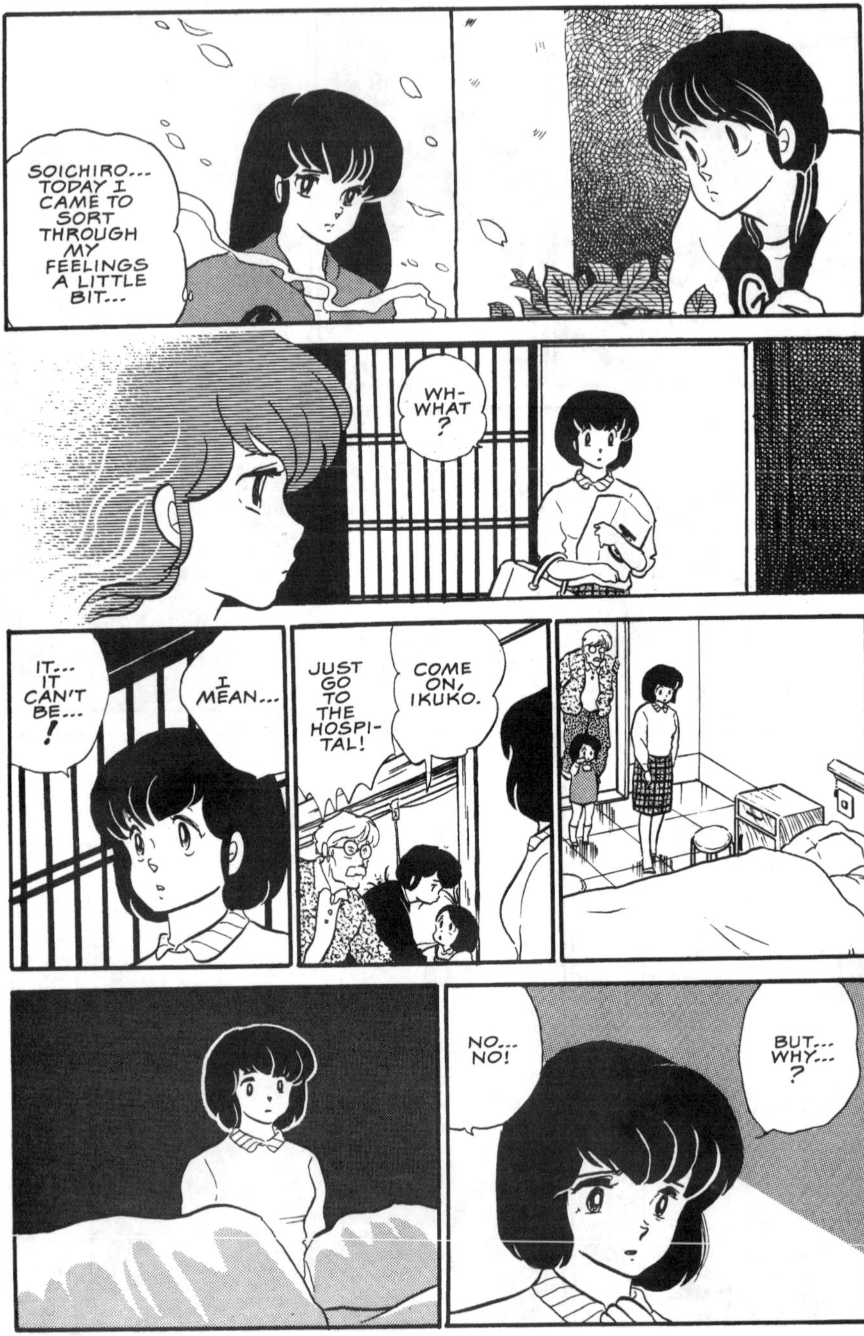

SOICHIRO... TODAY I CAME TO SORT THROUGH MY FEELINGS A LITTLE BIT...
WH-WHAT?
IT... IT CAN'T BE...!
I MEAN...
JUST GO TO THE HOSPITAL!
COME ON, IKUKO.
NO... NO!
BUT... WHY...?

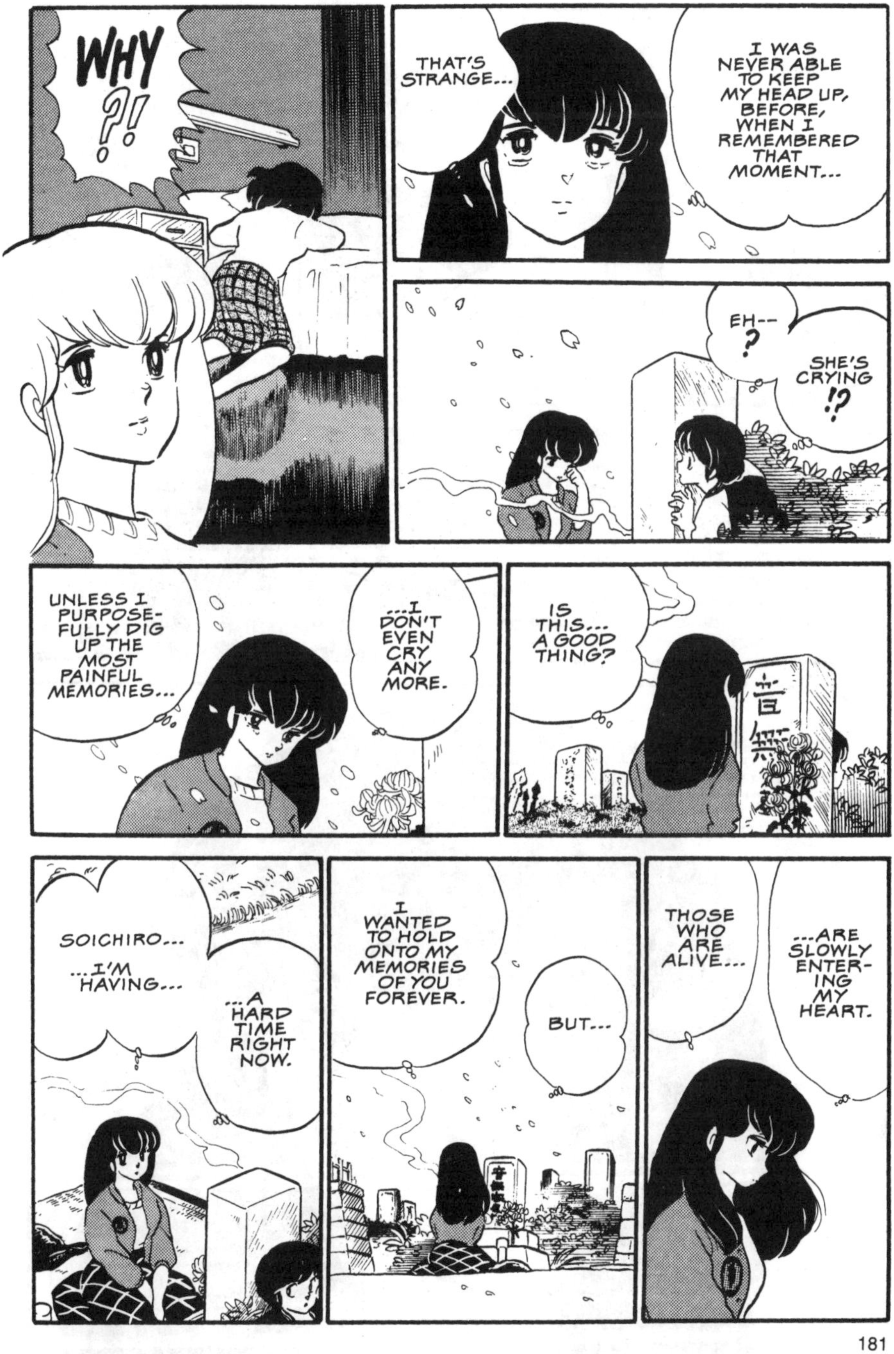
WHY ?!
THAT'S STRANGE...
I WAS NEVER ABLE TO KEEP MY HEAD UP, BEFORE, WHEN I REMEMBERED THAT MOMENT...
EH-- ?
SHE'S CRYING !?
UNLESS I PURPOSE-FULLY DIG UP THE MOST PAINFUL MEMORIES...
...I DON'T EVEN CRY ANY MORE.
IS THIS... A GOOD THING?
SOICHIRO...
...I'M HAVING...
...A HARD TIME RIGHT NOW.
I WANTED TO HOLD ONTO MY MEMORIES OF YOU FOREVER.
BUT...
THOSE WHO ARE ALIVE...
...ARE SLOWLY ENTER-ING MY HEART.

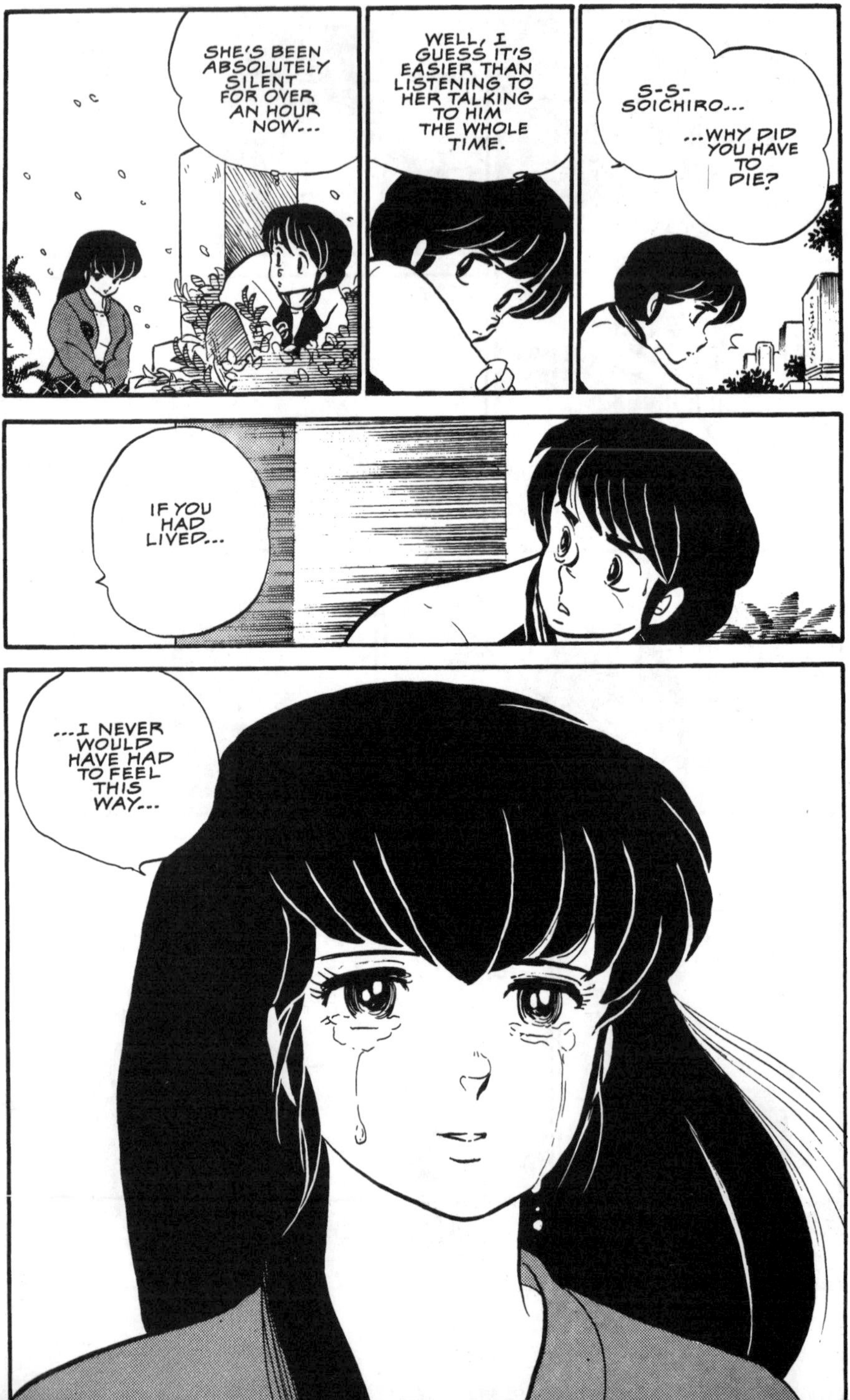
SHE'S BEEN ABSOLUTELY SILENT FOR OVER AN HOUR NOW...
WELL, I GUESS IT'S EASIER THAN LISTENING TO HER TALKING TO HIM THE WHOLE TIME.
S-S-SOICHIRO...
...WHY DID YOU HAVE TO DIE?
IF YOU HAD LIVED...
...I NEVER WOULD HAVE HAD TO FEEL THIS WAY...

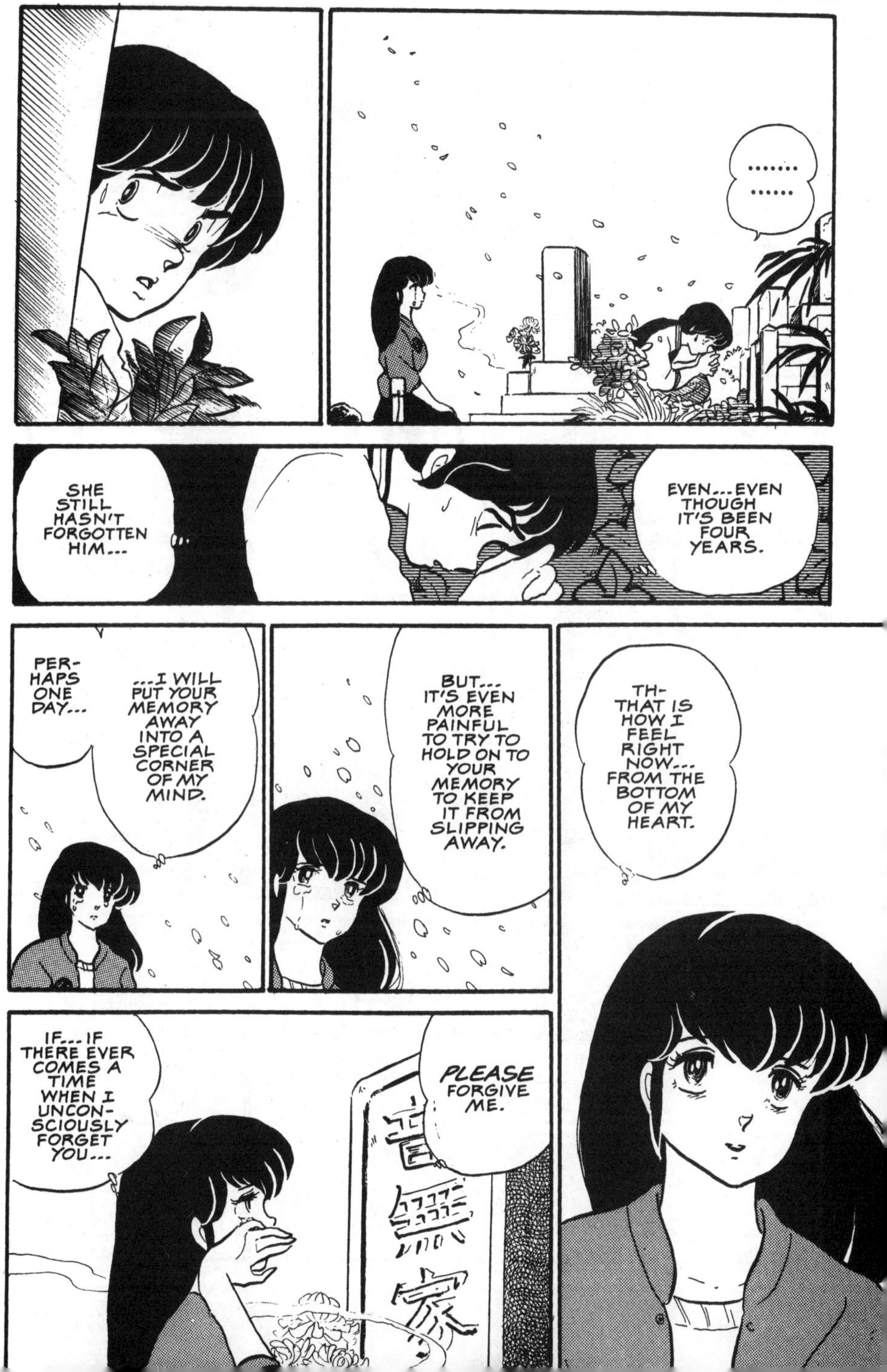
....
....
SHE STILL HASN'T FORGOTTEN HIM...
EVEN... EVEN THOUGH IT'S BEEN FOUR YEARS.
PER-HAPS ONE DAY...
...I WILL PUT YOUR MEMORY AWAY INTO A SPECIAL CORNER OF MY MIND.
BUT... IT'S EVEN MORE PAINFUL TO TRY TO HOLD ON TO YOUR MEMORY TO KEEP IT FROM SLIPPING AWAY.
TH- THAT IS HOW I FEEL RIGHT NOW... FROM THE BOTTOM OF MY HEART.
IF... IF THERE EVER COMES A TIME WHEN I UNCON-SCIOUSLY FORGET YOU...
PLEASE FORGIVE ME.

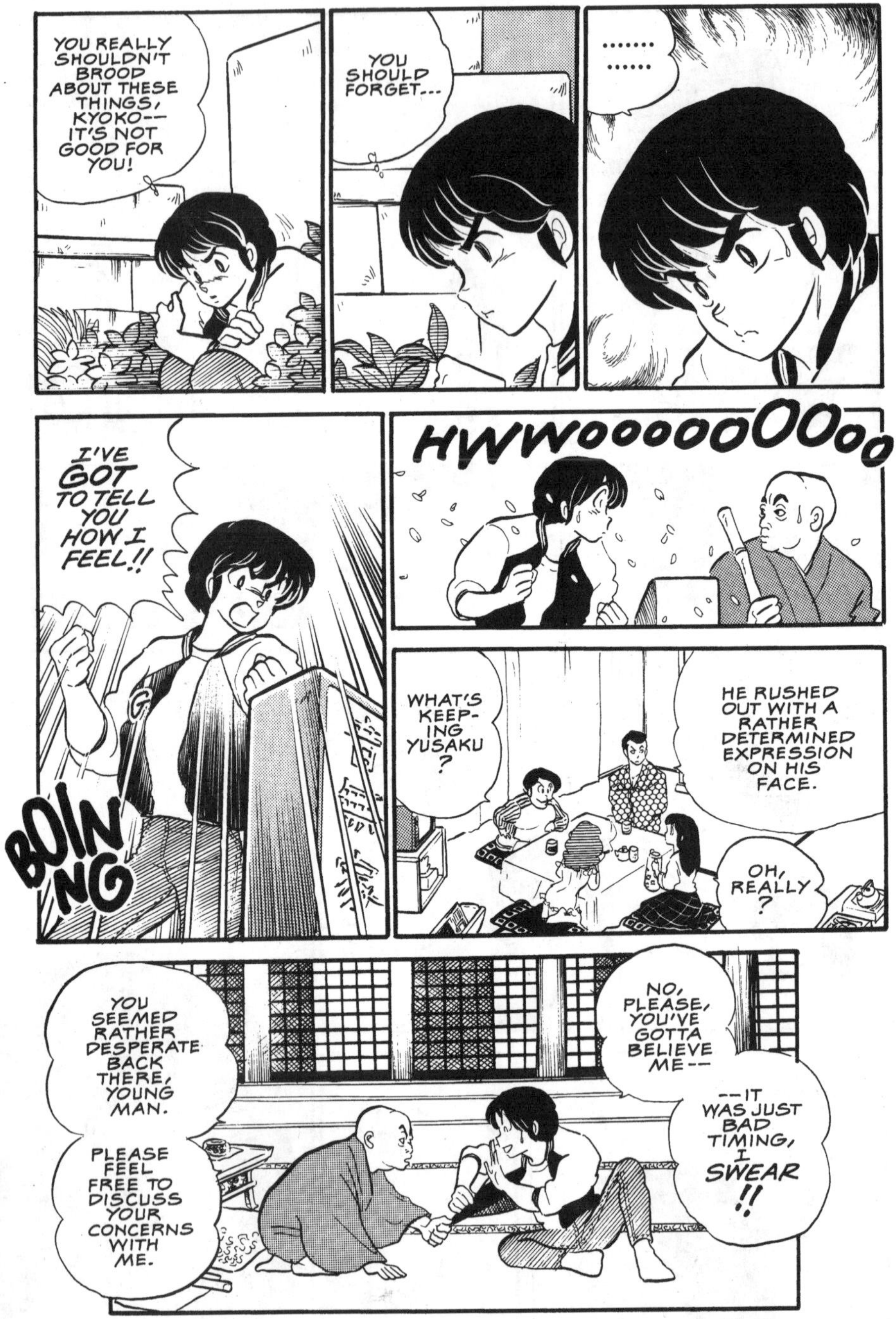
YOU REALLY SHOULDN'T BROOD ABOUT THESE THINGS, KYOKO-- IT'S NOT GOOD FOR YOU!
YOU SHOULD FORGET...
....
......
I'VE GOT TO TELL YOU HOW I FEEL!!
BOING
HWWoooooOOoo
WHAT'S KEEP-ING YUSAKU ?
HE RUSHED OUT WITH A RATHER DETERMINED EXPRESSION ON HIS FACE.
OH, REALLY ?
YOU SEEMED RATHER DESPERATE BACK THERE, YOUNG MAN.
PLEASE FEEL FREE TO DISCUSS YOUR CONCERNS WITH ME.
NO, PLEASE, YOU'VE GOTTA BELIEVE ME --
--IT WAS JUST BAD TIMING, I SWEAR !!

TO BE CONTINUED...